Coming Out
Under Fire

Coming Out Under Fire

The History of Gay Men and Women in World War Two

Allan Bérubé

The Free Press
A Division of Macmillan, Inc.
NEW YORK

The Free Press
A Division of Simon & Schuster
1230 Avenue of the Americas
New York, NY 10020

The Free Press and colophon are trademarks
of Simon & Schuster Inc.

Manufactured in the United States of America

10 9 8 7 6 5 4 3 2 1

Library of Congress Cataloging-In-Publication Data

Berube, Allan.
 Coming out under fire: the history of gay men and women in
World War Two/ Allan Berube.
   p. cm.
   Includes bibliographical references
   ISBN 0-7432-1071-9
   1. United States – Armed Forces – History – World War, 1939-1945.
   2. United States – Armed Forces – Gays – History – 20th Century.
   3. Gays – United States – History – 20th Century. I. Title.
   D769.2.B46 1990
   940.54'0973'08664—dc20   89-25653
                                             CIP

For Brian

Contents

Preface and Acknowledgments

One day in the fall of 1979, I was sitting on my living room floor in the Haight-Ashbury district of San Francisco sorting hundreds of World War II letters into piles by author, date, and place. A neighbor's friend had salvaged these papers and photographs from a dumpster when he had noticed that they included letters written by gay GIs. Having stashed them in his closet for five years, he gave them to me when my neighbor told him how interested I was in gay history.

As I carefully opened each envelope and read the letter inside, I found myself entering the secret world of gay soldiers who served in the Army during World War II. Most of these dozen or so GIs had met at an Army base in Missouri, where they had formed their own clique that met daily in the service club. As they were transferred to separate Army bases, both stateside and overseas, they wrote to one another about what it was like to be gay wherever they were stationed—their romances, the gay bars they visited, and the dilemmas they faced as homosexuals in the military.

Reading those letters ten years ago changed my life. It made me want to know more about both lesbian and gay GIs in World War II, so I set out to uncover and make public their hidden stories. Sponsored by the San Francisco Lesbian and Gay History Project, I put together a slide presentation—"Marching to a Different Drummer"—that was based on my preliminary research. Using it to spread the word about what I was learning, raise funds for my research, and find veterans to interview, I presented the slide show more than one hundred times throughout the

United States and Canada, sponsored by local community groups, churches, veterans' organizations, universities, and informal networks of friends. Working part-time to pay the bills, I spent several years interviewing veterans, combing through newspapers and magazines in libraries, reading war novels, requesting military documents through the Freedom of Information Act, and searching through archives. At the same time, under the auspices of the Capp Street Foundation, I and other members of the History Project established the World War II Project to maintain the oral histories, photographs, letters, military records, and memorabilia that I was accumulating.

What slowly emerged from my research was a story that was more complex and disturbing than I had imagined at the outset, one that directed my attention to the social history of the American soldier and to the role the military has played in changing society. Begun as the story of how gay* Americans had served their country, this book evolved into a history of how the military's mobilization for war made soldiers confront homosexuality in their personal lives and changed the ways that homosexuality fit into American institutions. I realized that the nature of my subject was pulling me from the margins of minority history into the mainstream of American history.

This book is one of the first to grow out of a grass-roots movement that in the late 1970s set out to uncover the history of ordinary lesbians and gay men. My own education as a historian took place over the course of a decade within the study groups of the San Francisco Lesbian and Gay History Project. Made up of academics, community activists, writers, filmmakers, and other interested people, the study groups created a supportive environment for exchanging information, doing research, challenging each other's assumptions and interpretations, introducing new ideas, and developing ways to return our history to our communities. It was the small movement of such community-based historians, many of whom used slide shows to present their work to academic as well as popular audiences, who have been largely responsible for developing a new social history of lesbians and gay men in the United States.

The process of taking my World War II slide show on the road has allowed me to do a kind of work that is rare for historians—to engage in an ongoing public dialogue with the communities whose history I was documenting and to which I belonged. Audience members told me when I was neglecting important experiences, raised ethical and

---

* Here and throughout the book, I use "gay" as gay people used it in the 1940s, to refer to either men or women.

political problems, gave me new research leads, agreed to be interviewed, collected funds to pay for research expenses, or encouraged me to press on. I am indebted to the thousands of people who attended my slide shows and to those who participated in the many public and private discussions that followed. Dozens of organizations also have supported my research by inviting me to present my slide show—from the Metropolitan Community Church in North Hollywood, California, and the North Shore Gay Alliance in Salem, Massachusetts, to the Sociologists' Gay Caucus of the American Sociological Association and the Committee on Lesbian and Gay History of the American Historical Association. Although I cannot acknowledge every individual and organization by name, I could not have completed this book without their interest and support.

More than one hundred gay men and lesbians offered to be interviewed about their experiences during the war, only seventy-one of whom I was able to interview. To protect their privacy, some of their names do not appear in this book. But their letters to me and taped interviews have been preserved in the collection of the World War II Project and their voices inform the history that I have written. The time and effort they have taken to share their personal stories have enabled me to reconstruct the rich social and personal lives of gay GIs during the war, and to see military policies from the points of view of the people they directly affected. (A partial list of the names of interviewees appears in the Note on Sources.)

The research for this book has been truly a cooperative effort. Many people sent me leads, offered me sources from their work, or assisted me in other ways. These include Larry Bush, JoAnn Castillo, George Chauncey, Jr., John Costello, Len Evans, Eric Garber, Jesse Gathering, Bert Hansen, William Hartman, Gregory M. Herek, Bruce Herman, Ross Higgins, Tom Holt, Doug Ischar, John Judge, Jonathan Ned Katz, Gerard Koskovich, Waverly Lowell, Michael Lumpkin, Alan Miller, Daniel Ostrow, Joseph Schuman, Judith Schwarz, Jim Steakley, Peg Stone, Sharon Ullman, Bill Walker, Doug Wichman, and Gary Wotherspoon. I wish to thank Don Lloyd and Marci Bernstein for sending the box of World War II letters my way in 1979; Eric Garber, Joshua Goldfinger, Brian Keith, Lyn Paleo, and Douglas Warner for outlining oral-history interviews; Allan Troxler and Greg Lamb for conducting interviews; Bill Walker for organizing the archives of the World War II Project; Larry Brinkin for giving me his IBM PC and Andy Seal for teaching me how to use it; Linda Gardner, Nancy Shaw, and Holly Wilder for helping me with administrative matters; and the many people who welcomed me into their homes during my research trips or made donations to the World War II Project. *The Advocate, Mother Jones,* and *The Front Page* gave me the first opportunities to publish my preliminary research and ideas.

I conducted most of the library research for this book on the campuses of the University of California at Davis, Berkeley, and San Francisco. At the National Archives in Washington, D.C., and in Suitland, Maryland, Richard Crawford, Richard A. von Doenhoff, Kenneth Heger, Wilbert Mahoney, Fred Pernell, and many other helpful members of the staff guided me through the maze of government records or undertook the painstaking task of photocopying and "sanitizing" names from hundreds of pages of military documents so they could be released for public use. I also wish to thank Janice F. Goldblum, deputy archivist at the National Academy of Sciences in Washington, Jim Kepner at the International Gay and Lesbian Archives in Los Angeles, William Baxter at the American Psychiatric Association Library in Washington, Bill Walker at the archives of the San Francisco Bay Area Gay and Lesbian Historical Society, Rudy Clemen at the archives of the National Headquarters of the American Red Cross in Washington, and the staff at the Washington Navy Yard library for their helpful assistance.

I am deeply indebted to all of the members of the San Francisco Lesbian and Gay History Project who in our study groups engaged in an honest and free flow of ideas and among whom this book was conceived and nurtured. These include JoAnn Castillo, Honey Lee Cottrell, Rob Epstein, Jeffrey Escoffier, Estelle Freedman, Eric Garber, Amber Hollibaugh, Tom Holt, Mike Immel, Ruth Mahaney, Frances Reid, Gayle Rubin, Liz Stevens, Sharon Ullman, Bill Walker, Walt Westman, and Roberta Yusba. I also wish to thank Jean Bergman, William Denebeim, Frances Doughty, Michael Helquist, Carol Vance, and William Woods, for helping me develop my ideas and for staying in touch while I undertook the solitary task of writing a book. My sister Annette Bérubé, my mother Florence Bérubé, and many patient friends gave me vital emotional and practical support when writing took over most aspects of my life.

I have been inspired and influenced by the work of other historians and archivists who have helped to create the new social history of lesbians and gay men in the United States, including George Chauncey, Jr., Madeline Davis, John D'Emilio, Martin Bauml Duberman, Lisa Duggan, Deborah Edel, Estelle Freedman, Jonathan Ned Katz, Elizabeth Lapovsky Kennedy, Michael Lynch, Lawrence R. Murphy, Joan Nestle, Esther Newton, Michael Scherker, and Judith Schwarz. I also have been influenced by the theoretical writings of Jeffrey Weeks, Michel Foucault, and Erving Goffman, as well as by the groundbreaking social history work of Linda Gordon on social workers and their clients in Boston, Allan Brandt on venereal disease policies, Susan Porter Bensen on work culture in department stores, and Roy Rosenzweig, Kathy Peiss, and Christine Stansell on working-class men and women, leisure, and street life.

Among those who read drafts of the manuscript and offered useful criticism, I am particularly indebted to Jeffrey Escoffier for helping me draw out my ideas, develop my narrative, and sharpen my argument chapter by chapter; to John D'Emilio for his undying confidence in me and for helping me identify the main themes of this book; to Estelle Freedman for her companionship during our many work sessions and for encouraging me to place my work in larger contexts; and to CDR Robert Siverling, USN (Ret.) for helping me understand the everyday workings of the military bureaucracy. Joyce Seltzer, senior editor at The Free Press, guided me with wisdom and patience through the difficult processes of structuring the book, drawing out my main points and arguments, and developing a narrative line. I am indebted to Charlotte Sheedy, my literary agent, for believing so strongly in this book from the start.

Finally I want to express my gratitude to Brian Keith, my life partner and best friend from 1983 until his death from AIDS in March 1987. He gave me many things, not the least of which was a stronger commitment to my work. Before he died he asked me to promise him not to let my grief keep me from finishing this book. It hasn't been easy, but with these words, Brian, I keep my promise.

Introduction

"Why We Fight"

When German tanks and bombers invaded Poland in September 1939, the United States was not prepared to enter a war in Europe. Years of isolationism, neutrality acts, military budget and pay cuts, and competition from New Deal social welfare programs had left the peacetime Army and Navy backward, neglected, and unable to fill their ranks with volunteers. The Army (which included the Air Corps) was a small organization that between the wars did not exceed two hundred thousand soldiers and officers; the Navy (which included the Marine Corps) barely reached an active-duty strength of one hundred thousand. In 1939 the U.S. Army still had to rely on surplus weapons and uniforms from World War I, the Navy's Atlantic Fleet was weak (relying on the Royal Navy to defend Atlantic waters), and most airplanes were not fit for combat. Military service itself was an unpopular, low-status occupation. Judges sometimes sentenced young male offenders to Army service as punishment; Army privates received half the pay of men in the Civilian Conservation Corps. Even slight decreases in the high unemployment rates of the late depression hurt Army enlistments.

But in 1940, after Germany's continuing victories in Europe and air bombings of Britain, public opinion—still deeply divided over conscription and any possible declaration of war—slowly turned away from isolationism, allowing the still-neutral United States to start a limited mobilization. President Roosevelt called for the nation to become an "arsenal of democracy" that would provide arms for Britain's war against

Germany. After much national debate, Congress in September 1940 passed the nation's first peacetime conscription act and set the maximum number of draftees called to active duty at nine hundred thousand. Conscripts now began to fill the Army's ranks.[1]

Before the peacetime mobilization of 1940–41, the Selective Service System and the Army and Navy had not concerned themselves with sexual orientation when screening men for military service. But when more than 16 million men between the ages of twenty-one and thirty-five registered for the draft in October 1940, Selective Service officials felt free to set strict qualification standards for military service. With so many men available, the armed forces decided to exclude certain groups of Americans, including women, blacks in the Marines and Army Air Corps, and—following the advice of psychiatrists—homosexuals. The rationale for disqualification was the same for each of these groups. Officials believed that they made poor combat soldiers, their presence in units would threaten morale and discipline, and their integration would turn the military into a testing ground for radical social experimentation rather than a strong fighting force.[2]

Traditionally the military had never officially excluded or discharged homosexuals from its ranks. From the days following the Revolutionary War, the Army and Navy had targeted the act of sodomy (which they defined as anal and sometimes oral sex between men), not homosexual persons, as criminal, as had their British predecessors and the original thirteen colonies. Any soldier or officer convicted of sodomy, whether he was homosexual or not, could be sent to prison.

But in World War II a dramatic change occurred. As psychiatrists increased their authority in the armed forces, they developed new screening procedures to discover and disqualify homosexual men, introducing into military policies and procedures the concept of the homosexual as a personality type unfit for military service and combat—a concept that was to determine military policy for decades after the war. Their success in shifting the military's attention from the sexual act to the individual had far-reaching consequences. It forced military officials to develop an expanding administrative apparatus for managing homosexual personnel that relied on diagnosis, hospitalization, surveillance, interrogation, discharge, administrative appeal, and mass indoctrination.

The bombing of Pearl Harbor in December 1941, however, and the ensuing declaration of war, denied the military the luxury of disqualifying large groups of Americans from the manpower pool. By the end of the war in 1945, the armed forces had enlisted not 900,000 but more than 16 million citizens and residents, 10 million of whom were draftees.

Most soldiers* were unmarried white young men—35 percent of Navy personnel were teenagers—but other groups filled the military's ranks as well. Seven hundred thousand were black (4 percent), 350,000 were Mexican American, 275,000 were women (2 percent each), and 30,000 were Japanese American. In addition, Selective Service drafted 48,000 Puerto Rican, 19,000 American Indian, and 12,000 Chinese American soldiers.[3] No census was taken of the number of gay men and lesbians who entered the military. But if Alfred Kinsey's wartime surveys were accurate and applied as much to the military as to the civilian population, at least 650,000 and as many as 1.6 million male soldiers were homosexual.[4]

Among the American soldiers of World War II who were privately homosexual were many with familiar names. Tyrone Power started as a private in the Marine Corps in 1942, achieved the rank of first lieutenant, was sent to the South Pacific with a Marine Transport Command, and was among the first pilots to fly supplies into Iwo Jima under artillery fire. Rock Hudson enlisted in the Navy after graduating from high school and served as an airplane mechanic in the Philippines. Photographer Minor White served from 1942 to 1945 with the Army Intelligence Corps in the South Pacific, where he was wounded in jungle combat. Novelist and essayist Gore Vidal enlisted in the Army in 1943 after high school, serving as first mate on an Army transport ship in the Aleutians. Novelist John Cheever was drafted in May 1942 and served in the Army Signal Corps making training films. Merle Miller, who later became a biographer of presidents Truman and Johnson, served in the Army as an editor of *Yank,* the enlisted men's magazine, in both the Pacific and Europe. Novelist John Horne Burns entered the Army as a private right after Pearl Harbor and served in North Africa and Italy.[5]

As these and other men went off to war, women filled jobs in heavy industry and other defense work, widely expanding their presence in the paid labor force and increasing their ability to live independently. Although relatively few women entered the military, their inroads into such a traditionally masculine institution symbolized how dramatic were the wartime changes, and led the military to adopt its first policies regarding the screening, discharge, and management of lesbian personnel.

With so many gay Americans entering the military to meet their country's call, their presence and the expanding antihomosexual policies and procedures came into increasing conflict. Military officials, even

*Here and throughout the book I use "soldiers" and "GIs" to mean enlisted personnel and noncommissioned officers, both male and female, in all branches of the armed forces.

as they developed a rationale for why homosexuals could not function in the armed forces, knew that they could not afford to exclude most gay recruits. At the same time, the gay men who were drafted or enlisted, and the lesbians who volunteered, began to realize that the military was prepared to discharge them as undesirables if their homosexuality became known. Since most were eager to do their part for the war effort, their awareness of the military's antihomosexual policies placed them in a double bind.

When Pearl Harbor was bombed, Stuart Loomis and his gay college pals together faced the dilemma of how to serve their country while escaping the military's widening antihomosexual net. That Sunday afternoon, they gathered at a soda fountain in downtown Omaha where they listened to a rebroadcast of President Roosevelt's speech to Congress and argued, over malted milks and peanut butter sandwiches, about what they were going to do. "We were already hearing stories of people who had been caught in gay activities and dishonorably discharged," Loomis recalled, "and we had friends in the service who were telling us 'Don't go in!' " Some of the boys in his crowd sought medical deferments, even though they faced the stigma of being classified 4-F (unacceptable) during the war. Others tried to get deferrable jobs in defense plants. But most, like Loomis himself, didn't want to avoid military service as they responded to their president's call for national unity and heard him declare December 7, 1941, the "day that will live in infamy."

Thousands of patriotic gay men and lesbians faced similar dilemmas as they weighed the sacrifices and opportunities of military service against those of remaining civilians during a national emergency. For many the desire to join their peers in serving their country was too powerful to ignore. Bill DeVeau was inducted when he was a freshman at Boston University in 1943 after Congress passed the Teenage Draft Act. It seemed to him that "everyone in my age group went into the service that year—and you would have been ashamed if you didn't go in." Against the wishes of his family, Vincent Miles dropped out of college in 1943 and in his hometown of Davenport, Iowa, enlisted in the Army, which assigned him along with other black trainees to the 92nd Infantry Division. When Jacquelyn Beyer was an undergraduate at the University of Colorado, she decided to enlist in the Army after a recruiter came to the campus and made the Women's Army Corps sound inviting. Her mother, who raised her to be independent, wouldn't let her enlist until she received her degree, so she went to summer school, took extra courses to finish in three years, and then became a Wac.

Some gay teenagers were so eager to enlist that they signed up before they finished high school. Their motives were varied. In February 1943 seventeen-year-old Tom Reddy was still too young to be drafted, but he quit high school, said good-bye to his family in New Jersey, and joined the Marine Corps. He wanted to "find out about myself all by myself. I knew pretty much that I was gay. I was engaged to marry a girl when I left, and I knew that wasn't exactly what I wanted. I think one of the reasons I enlisted was because everybody told me the Marine Corps was going to make a man out of me." Maxwell Gordon also left home to join the armed forces. His mother had single-handedly raised him and his older brother on an income that was "hand to mouth," and had told them that they had to support themselves as soon as they turned seventeen. Gordon chose the Navy in 1942 because his brother had already enlisted and because "there was a lot of naval activity in Southern California. It just seemed to me a natural thing."

Betty Somers was one of many gay Americans who separated from their partners to enlist. She left college and a "lovely romance" with a woman student to join the Marines because she didn't think she could live with herself unless she joined the fight. "I really wanted to serve my country," she recalled. "I expected to make any kind of sacrifices and I expected to go overseas." Bob Ruffing also left his lover, as well as his job as a high school English teacher on Long Island. Their relationship was breaking up anyway, he recalled, and "I didn't like teaching and suddenly Pearl Harbor happened. I went out immediately and joined the Navy. I started out having good thoughts about World War II because it got me out of this dilemma that I was in." Charles Rowland tried to enlist in Cleveland with his boyfriend, who had heard rumors (which were untrue) that the Marine Corps "had the buddy system and you could stay together forever throughout the service." When the couple went down to enlist, his boyfriend was accepted but Rowland was rejected because of poor vision. "So that ended our affair," he recalled. Late in 1942 Rowland was drafted into the Army.

As these and other young people entered military service, they became part of a massive wartime migration of Americans. Along with the 16 million men who left home to become soldiers were nearly as many civilians—most of them women—who left home to find war work. Black men and women in the South moved north and to the West Coast where defense jobs were plentiful; Japanese Americans were "relocated" from the West Coast to internment camps inland; millions of others moved from small towns and rural areas into the booming port cities and industrial centers. The uprooting of so many Americans during the war disrupted the everyday lives of a generation of young men and women, exposing them to the power of the federal government and the vast expanse of the United States, the great variety of its people, and ways of life they had not imagined.[6]

Once they left the constraints of family life and watchful neighbors, many recruits were surprised to find that military service gave them opportunities to begin a "coming-out" process. The meaning of the phrase "coming out" itself expanded as the war began to change gay life. In the 1930s "to come out" or "to be brought out" had meant to have one's first homosexual experience with another person. But by 1941 gay men and women were using "coming out" to mean that they had found gay friends and the gay life, and were saying that circumstances in their lives, not just their first sexual partner, had brought them out. A person could come out to others part way by "dropping hairpins" to hint that one was "queer" rather than "normal"—the most common words used both by gay people and the general public in the war years. But when one felt safe or daring enough, one could come out all the way by pulling out every last pin and "letting one's hair down," a phrase that by World War II already had migrated into popular slang from gay culture.[7]

During the 1930s and 1940s, young men and women who grew up feeling homosexual desires had little help coming out. They were likely to lead isolated lives, not knowing anyone else like themselves, with no one to talk to about their feelings and often unsure of who or what they were. There were no publicly gay leaders or organizations to act on their behalf, no press to acknowledge their existence or the problems they faced, no discussions of homosexuality on the radio, and only a few tragic novels with characters who were called "sexual inverts." In the cities, gay men and women who had found each other were able to form their own private social circles or to patronize a small number of gay bars and nightclubs. But these were hard to find, often disreputable or illegal, and attracted only a small minority of all people who were gay.

The massive mobilization for World War II relaxed the social constraints of peacetime that had kept gay men and women unaware of themselves and each other, "bringing out" many in the process. Gathered together in military camps, they often came to terms with their sexual desires, fell in love, made friends with other gay people, and began to name and talk about who they were. When they could get away from military bases, they discovered and contributed to the rich gay nightlife— parties, bars, and nightclubs—that flourished in the war-boom cities.

But the military's expanding antihomosexual policies also forced many citizen-soldiers and officers to come out against their will. Draftees were brought out whenever induction examiners publicly rejected them for military service as homosexual, or when they were caught or "declared themselves" to escape harassment and received undesirable discharges. Their self-declarations began to add a political dimension to the previously sexual and social meanings of coming out. Those veterans who fought to upgrade their undesirable discharges for homosexuality began to define their struggle with the government as one for justice and equal rights, ideas that became a prerequisite for a political movement. Twenty years later, lesbian and gay male activists stretched this political meaning even further, so that coming out became a public statement that one was both gay and proud—the cornerstone of a political movement.

As the military's management of homosexuals grew in importance during the war, three groups of personnel—administrators, psychiatrists, and GIs—found themselves engaged in conflicts with one another. The social and political changes that grew out of their confrontations must be examined not so much as the story of how the military victimized homosexuals, but of how a dynamic power relationship developed between gay citizens and their government and how it transformed them both. From draft boards and induction stations to the battlefields of Europe and the Pacific, members of the armed forces lived out daily tensions between the expanding antihomosexual policies, the need for the efficient use of all personnel, and their private sexual lives. In the process gay male and lesbian soldiers discovered that they were fighting two wars: one for America, democracy, and freedom; the other for their own survival as homosexuals within the military organization.

CHAPTER

1

Getting In

Early in 1943 Robert Fleischer, who lived with his family on Manhattan's Upper West Side, went down to the Grand Central Palace induction station for his physical. When he reached the psychiatrist's office at the end of the line, he was scared to death of being found out. This nineteen-year-old draftee wanted desperately to get into the Army to avenge the death of a cousin who had been killed at Pearl Harbor, but he had heard that the Army was rejecting gay men for military service. Carefully planning to hide his homosexuality from Army examiners, Fleischer was surprised when the psychiatrist merely asked him "Do you like girls?" to which he responded with a truthful yes because, he recalled forty years later, "I *liked* girls!" Fleischer wondered why the psychiatrist hadn't figured him out. "My God," he thought, "couldn't he see my curly platinum blond hair that was partly bleached, the walk, maybe the sissy *S* in my voice—all the things that I thought would give me away?" But as he left the induction station, he sighed with relief that he had been found fit to serve in the United States Army.

Fleischer was one of 18 million young men in the United States who were examined at 6,400 draft boards and 108 induction stations during World War II.[1] His encounter with the Army psychiatrist took place because an expanding military screening system increasingly focused on homosexuality. Before the war, the military had had no official procedure for preventing gay men from entering its ranks. But when the war heated up in Europe, psychiatric consultants to the Selective Service System in Washington began to piece together a rationale and initial procedures for excluding homosexuals. As their colleagues at induc-

8

tion stations across the country received directives from headquarters instructing them to disqualify homosexuals, they faced the same dilemma as the psychiatrist at Robert Fleischer's physical exam—whether to reject these young men and women or ignore them and quietly let them slip into the Army. And as word got out that homosexuals were being rejected, gay men and lesbians had to decide whether to hide or declare their homosexuality to the psychiatric examiners posted at the military's gates.

The psychiatric profession's campaign to promote psychiatric screening got off the ground during the summer of 1940 when, in response to the full-scale German air bombing of Britain, Congress authorized expanded defense budgets and passed the conscription act. Prompted by a growing sense of urgency, and pursuing their agenda of showing how psychiatry could contribute to the war effort, leading American psychiatrists set out to persuade the Selective Service System to give psychiatric as well as physical examinations to selectees.

Two of the most influential psychiatrists in the campaign for "Selective Service psychiatry" were Harry Stack Sullivan and Winfred Overholser. Sullivan, a forty-eight-year-old practicing psychiatrist who described himself as a "slight, bespectacled mild-looking bachelor with thinning hair and mustache," lived in Bethesda, Maryland, with his devoted male companion. By the 1930s Sullivan had broken off from traditional psychoanalysis to create a theory and practice of "interpersonal psychiatry" that profoundly influenced modern American psychiatry. As president of the William Alanson White Psychiatric Foundation and coeditor of the journal *Psychiatry,* Sullivan's aim was to apply the principles of psychiatry to society as a whole. His wartime accomplishment in this area was to design and implement what journalist Alfred Deutsch called a "magnificent plan for psychiatric screening of draftees." [2] Overholser, also forty-eight, but a married man with children, used his positions as superintendent of Saint Elizabeths Hospital in Washington and chairman of the National Research Council's Committee on Neuropsychiatry to help Sullivan implement his plan. [3] Together with Harry A. Steckel, chairman of the American Psychiatric Association's Military Mobilization Committee, of which Sullivan and Overholser were members, these men developed the military's wartime program for psychiatric screening. [4] Amid the confusion and uncertainty in Washington during the peacetime mobilization, it took only these few men with vision, an agenda, and dedication to bring about rapid and far-reaching policy changes.

In May 1940, as soon as President Roosevelt asked Congress to expand the armed forces, Sullivan and his colleagues at the White Foundation went to work drawing up their screening plan. At the same time Overholser, at the request of the Federal Board of Hospitalization, wrote a memorandum that convinced Roosevelt and his Selective Service advisers of the need for such screening. In late October, following the first draft registration day, Sullivan, Overholser, and Steckel met at National Headquarters in Washington with Selective Service Director Clarence Dykstra and representatives of the War Department to draw up a final version of Sullivan's proposal. They called for the appointment of over thirty thousand local board examiners who would conduct psychiatric interviews no shorter than fifteen minutes, the establishment of over six hundred Medical Advisory Boards with one psychiatrist on each to review problem cases, a second psychiatric interview at Army induction stations, and an extensive program to educate all examiners in the basic principles of psychiatry. Within a few weeks the Army adjutant general and the director of Selective Service issued directives to all Army corps areas and draft boards launching this new program. A month later, Sullivan was appointed as psychiatric consultant to SSS Director Dykstra, who was friendly with psychiatrists and fully supported Sullivan's plan. Thus began what was called the "honeymoon period" in the marriage of psychiatry and the Selective Service.

Psychiatrists used economic arguments to convince War Department and Selective Service representatives of the necessity of psychiatric screening. The federal government, they argued, had spent over one billion dollars caring for the psychiatric casualties of World War I, who—by the beginning of World War II—still occupied more than half of all Veterans Administration hospital beds.[5] Screening could reduce these costs by weeding out potential psychiatric casualties before they became military responsibilities. But these psychiatrists also promoted screening to enhance the prestige, influence, and legitimacy of their profession, which other physicians had for decades dismissed as the "Cinderella" of the medical specialties. Military screening offered psychiatrists the opportunity to introduce tens of thousands of physicians and draft board members to the value and basic principles of psychiatry.

These early efforts to establish a screening program to determine the mental health of potential soldiers carved out the territory on which others would build an antihomosexual barrier and the rationale for using it. Ironically, both Sullivan and Overholser, as well as some of their colleagues, shared what they called "enlightened" views on how the military should handle its homosexual personnel. Harry Stack Sullivan himself was homosexual but kept this part of his life private. Professionally, he believed that sexuality played a minimal role in causing mental

disorders and that adult homosexuals should be accepted and left alone—
a controversial position that made him a dissident among psychoanalysts
in the United States.[6] Winfred Overholser, from his position on the
National Research Council, crusaded more actively against the military's
traditional system of sending homosexuals to prison. Whenever he could,
he tried to shift, as he wrote to a colleague, "the hard-boiled attitude
of some of these worthies" toward one of accepting homosexuality as
a problem to be handled by psychiatrists, not prison guards. Overholser
believed that military officials, as well as the public, did not think ration-
ally about homosexuality because the subject was "so overlaid with
emotional coloring that the processes of reason are often obscured." [7]
Although both of these men believed that some "overt" or "confirmed"
homosexuals should be excluded from the armed forces for their own
good and for the good of the military, they and many of their colleagues
cautioned that these rejectees should not be punished, discriminated
against, or morally condemned.

Sullivan's initial plan for psychiatric screening, consistent with
his own psychiatric theory, included no references to homosexuality.[8]
But his belief in the relative unimportance of "sexual aberrations" in
determining mental illnesses was undermined as his plan passed through
Washington bureaucratic channels. To each revision of Sullivan's initial
plan, other psychiatrists added fragments of the more-dominant psychiatric
theory that homosexuality was a mental disorder that should disqualify
a man for military service. Throughout the war, whenever psychiatrists
tried to reform the military's policies on homosexuals, their proposals
were subjected to this same process of compromise and modification.
Memoranda were reviewed by committees and circulated among officials
who attached "indorsements" stating their own opinions, objections,
and suggestions for revisions. The most activist psychiatrists were frustrated by the red tape that passed their proposals through this military
chain of command, placing final decisions in the hands of a few high-
ranking officials, many of whom harbored prejudices against both psychiatry and homosexuality. This bureaucratic process itself, by expanding
the volume of directives, memoranda, and revisions, helped build the
momentum of the military's wartime preoccupation with homosexuality.

The first directive to grow out of Sullivan's initial plan for psychiatric
screening, Medical Circular No. 1, was issued by the Selective Service
on November 7, 1940, to more than 30,000 volunteer physicians at
local draft boards.[9] Sullivan called this circular "a child's guide to psychiatric diagnosis" because its purpose was to explain psychiatry to community physicians who had had no training in psychiatry and who were

likely to doubt its scientific merit or clinical value.[10] Circular No. 1 explained in lay terms five psychiatric "categories of handicap"—expanded to eight in later revisions—and concluded with a list of miscellaneous "deviations" examining physicians should watch for. Homosexuality was not mentioned in this first screening circular.

By May 1941, however, after the Army Surgeon General's Office had issued its own screening circular to induction station examiners and Selective Service revised Circular No. 1 to bring the two directives into line, both screening directives for the first time included "homosexual proclivities" in their lists of disqualifying "deviations." The Army circular also listed "many homosexual persons" among those to be rejected because of "psychopathic personality disorders," whereas the Selective Service circular instructed draft board doctors to refer all suspected homosexual cases to the regional Medical Advisory Board psychiatrists for closer examination.[11] In January the Navy had issued its own directive inaugurating a procedure for eliminating the "neuropsychiatrically unfit." [12] It had declared unfit those individuals "whose sexual behavior is such that it would endanger or disturb the morale of the military unit"—a new Navy screening category that as yet only implicitly disqualified homosexuals.

Thus, by mid-1941, several months before the United States declared war, the administrative apparatus for screening out homosexuals at three examination points—the Selective Service System, the Army, and the Navy—was already in place and backed by Director of Selective Service Clarence Dykstra, the surgeons general of the Army and Navy, and their respective psychiatric consultants.

Sullivan, Overholser, Steckel, and other psychiatrists who developed the new screening guidelines began their project by modifying the military's more rudimentary World War I qualification standards to reflect the changes in psychiatric theory that had developed in the 1920s and 1930s. The mental-disorder categories in World War I had been based on the brain-disease model of insanity—the dominant psychiatric theory in the United States in the first two decades of the twentieth century. The brain-disease model classified various mental and "moral" (emotional) abnormalities—among which homosexuality was included—as symptoms of brain lesions and neurological disorders caused by heredity, trauma, or bad habits such as masturbation, drunkenness, and drug addiction. Most physicians considered neurology to be the most scientific approach to mental disease, and it was for this reason that the primary focus of military screening for mental defects during World War I was on intelligence and the nervous system rather than on personality disorders. If any homosexuals were rejected as such in World War I, it was because they had physiological disorders or had prison or insane asylum records as "sex perverts," not because they had homosexual personalities or tendencies.

In the early twentieth century, there still was no professional consensus on the causes, description, treatment, and nomenclature for homosexual conditions. But most psychiatrists believed in the brain-disease model and developed surgical or physical-therapy procedures to treat homosexual patients.[13] During the second and third decades of this century, however, a minority of psychiatrists in the United States moved beyond the mere description and categorization of symptoms and began to relate them to one another as progressive stages in the development of mental disease. The marginal but growing interest during these years in Freud's psychoanalytic theories, which described homosexuality more as a psychosexual than a constitutional condition, was only part of the American profession's increasing attention to the personality behind the symptoms. This new approach took into account a patient's unique life situation, integrating biological and personality factors, and led psychiatrists to try to diagnose severe disorders in their early stages in an effort to prevent mental disease. Sullivan, Overholser, and their colleagues who developed the military's World War II policies were schooled in this psychoanalytic approach to mental illness. By the late 1930s psychoanalytic theory and techniques had dominated American psychiatry and had spawned dissidents who, like Sullivan, developed their own schools of thought.

Immediately after World War I, those psychiatrists who believed that they could identify men with less grossly observable personality disorders, screen them out of the military, and prevent psychiatric casualties in combat succeeded in changing Army regulations. In 1921 the Army issued expanded psychiatric screening standards that remained in effect until the eve of World War II.[14] The framers of these interwar standards drew on the theories of personality development to construct their list of psychiatric disorders, but the military regulations encased these new psychiatric concepts in the theory and language of degeneration, which ranked human beings into hierarchical categories based on characteristics that were considered inferior or "degenerate" by virtue of their deviation from a generally white, middle-class, and native-born norm.

The framers of the Army's interwar physical standards listed feminine characteristics among the "stigmata of degeneration" that made a man unfit for military service.[15] Males with a "degenerate physique," the regulation explained, "may present the general body conformation of the opposite sex, with sloping narrow shoulders, broad hips, excessive pectoral and pubic adipose [fat] deposits, with lack of masculine hirsute [hair] and muscular markings.'' A young man with a ''scant and downy beard'' or a ''female figure'' was also to be closely observed for evidence of ''internal glandular disturbances.'' In addition to these ''anatomical'' stigmata of degeneration, the interwar standards listed ''sexual perversion''—a broad category that included oral and anal sex between men— as one of many ''functional'' stigmata of degeneration. The Army standards also listed ''sexual psychopathy'' as one of many ''constitutional'' psychopathic states—biologically based psychiatric conditions that, through heredity, bad habits, or injury, caused a person to lose the ability to adjust to civilized society. With these 1921 standards, the Army established its first written guidelines for excluding men who displayed feminine bodily characteristics or who were sexual ''perverts'' or ''psychopaths.''

During the two decades between the wars, however, without pressure from the psychiatric profession and with a shortage of volunteers, psychiatric screening standards existed only on paper and were rarely implemented.[16] In their 1940–1941 revisions of the interwar standards, Sullivan and the other framers of the psychiatric screening plan for World War II dropped such outdated biological categories as ''anatomical and functional stigmata of degeneration.'' But throughout World War II, both the Army and Navy continued to describe homosexuality as a ''constitutional psychopathic state'' and to diagnose homosexual men and women as ''sexual psychopaths.''

After Selective Service issued Medical Circular No. 1 to draft board physicians, Harry Stack Sullivan began the second phase of his screening plan—to teach the nation's psychiatrists how to put into practice the new guidelines for mass psychiatric screening. In December 1940 Sullivan, Overholser, and Steckel were appointed as a three-man advisory committee to the Selective Service to plan and direct a series of regional two-day seminars that took place from January to July 1941.[17] At the same time, the Navy Surgeon General's Office, Bellevue Hospital in New York, and the Menninger Clinic in Topeka, Kansas, also held seminars on military psychiatric screening for their personnel.[18] Lecturers advised psychiatrists to teach others in the medical profession what they had learned at the seminars. Many of the lectures were published throughout 1941 in psychiatric and medical journals, educating an even wider audience of professionals.

The psychiatrists who conducted these seminars greatly expanded their profession's discussion of how the rejection of homosexuals could improve the military's preparedness for war. Seminar lecturers described gay men exclusively within the context of mental illness, referring to them as clinical cases rather than as members of a social group. Replacing the jargon of degeneracy with the jargon of psychoanalysis, they used the term *homosexual,* which had originated within the psychiatric profession, and spoke of latency, tendencies, proclivities, and personality types. They discussed homosexuality not as a distinct phenomenon but as an aspect of three personality disorders: psychopaths who were sexual perverts, paranoid personalities who suffered from homosexual panic, and schizoid personalities who displayed homosexual symptoms.[19]

Throughout the seminars, lecturers began to piece together a psychiatric rationale for rejecting gay men as mentally disordered personalities. The reason for excluding them as psychopaths was that, like other men in this "wastebasket" category, they were considered to be irresponsible troublemakers who were unable to control their desires or learn from their mistakes and thus threatened the other men.[20] The reason for excluding them as schizoid and paranoid personalities was that, while many of these men could be competent and well adjusted in civilian jobs, they were considered to be too introverted to adjust to the regimentation, lack of privacy and gregariousness of modern military life and were expected to become the target of other men's hostilities.[21] In short, sexual psychopaths were described as sexual deviants—they disruptively acted out their homosexual desires—while schizoid and paranoid personalities were described as gender deviants—they were too effete, too much the "sissy," to become good soldiers. Lecturers based these descriptions on small clinical samples of deeply troubled patients and ignored the majority of gay men who never sought psychiatric treatment and had adapted to their sexuality. Nor did they take into account the resilient young effeminate men who had learned how to defend themselves growing up on city streets, playgrounds, farms, and in factories during the years of the depression. By placing the discussion of homosexuality and effeminacy within these categories of psychiatric disorders, the seminars did much to consolidate and promote the notion that homosexuality itself was a form of mental illness that made a person unfit for military service.

Seminar lecturers attacked the popular belief that military service could "make a man" out of "mama's boys," sissies, and homosexuals. For years, judges who had ordered juvenile offenders to join the Army as an alternative to serving time in prison had helped to give the Army this reform school reputation. "Literally thousands of families today," Dr. Leo H. Bartemeier told a Chicago seminar audience in May 1941, "are hoping that the discipline and the regularity of army experience will snap their sons out of their shyness and their day dreaming and put 'some real stuff' into them. Many physicians seem to share the same notion." [22] Citing lessons learned from World War I, lecturers predicted that such men, if allowed into the military, would only become psychiatric casualties, fill up hospital beds, and further burden the taxpayer. Only psychiatry, not military service, could help them. They had no place in a military organization that was looking for the best of the nation's young men.

It was easier for these lecturers to put together a rationale for rejecting homosexuals than to teach their audience of psychiatrists exactly how to detect selectees who had successfully hidden their homosexuality from families, friends, teachers, employers, and even their wives. Most seminar lecturers had had no personal experience with the stresses of military life. [23] To distinguish from other selectees those men who they believed were the most susceptible to emotional breakdowns, including men with homosexual tendencies, lecturers tried to develop interview techniques designed to detect the slightest "signs and clues" that would reveal hidden personality traits and tendencies. [24] Examining psychiatrists had only a few minutes at best to interview each registrant. Under such circumstances, they had to use stereotypes, hunches, and guesses rather than procedures with any scientific basis.

With few real examples from their practice to draw on, lecturers made up hypothetical interviews and presented crude interview techniques as if they were precision tools for detecting the slightest signs of "latent" homosexuality or worries about being queer or unmanly—characteristics that could be identified in most young men. One proposed technique was to force the selectee to expose himself physically to the examiner. If the boy or young man was not already naked, psychiatrist Dexter Means Bullard told a Washington seminar audience, "it is advisable to have the candidate strip and to make a brief physical examination, since so much more can be seen under these circumstances." What could be seen was whether the naked selectee felt self-conscious about his hair, scalp, shape of his head, eyes, nose, ears, mouth, pimples, or other parts of his body. [25] A selectee's discomfort with his body or his having been teased for being physically different—hardly unusual in a young male—were some of the "slight signs" that might suggest homosexual tendencies and other disqualifying defects. Bullard's suggestion that the selectee be kept undressed throughout the interview reflected a common belief among examiners that physical nakedness could reveal the "naked truth" about the hidden aspects of a man's personality.

A selectee's curiosity or embarrassment about masturbation or other sexual matters was also interpreted as indicating a potential for homosexual problems. Such a man, psychiatrist Douglas A. Thom told a Boston seminar audience, may ask the examiner, "Has masturbation affected my brain? Has it made me impotent? Can people tell? Is it true that masturbation makes one crazy? Why do I get embarrassed with women? What attracts me to men, especially when I have been drinking? Why have I been approached by so many 'fairies'? Do they think I am one? Perhaps I am and do not know it. I get queer impulses at times toward men which frighten me. People look at me suspiciously, and sometimes I think they make remarks about my appearance. I know I am not a 'he man.' " [26]

Another problem, Dexter Means Bullard explained during the Washington seminar, was how to get a response from the more sophisticated and educated men, "who maintain the aloof detachment of unconcern or what appears to be a gentlemanly reserve" but whose manner had led "the local examining physician to suspect queerness or difference." Such men, he believed, could be prone to homosexual problems or panic in the service. When interviewing them, "a frank statement of fact may elicit the desired information. 'You have been referred to me because the doctor who gave you the physical examination did not quite know what to make of you. What did you think of that examination?' 'Well, it was all right—' 'But what?' 'Well, I didn't see the reason for all of it.' 'What did he examine that you did not think necessary?' 'Oh, I just didn't like his manner.' 'Go on.' 'Oh, I don't know. I don't like people feeling my privates or anus.' He will probably not say anus. 'Tell me about it.' 'Well, that's just none of his business. I didn't like the way he looked at me.' A direct question—'How did he look at you'—will probably receive the answer, 'I don't know,' or 'I just didn't like it.' An indirect question—'What did you think of him'— may elicit 'Oh, nothing.' 'Surely you thought something?' 'Well, to tell you the truth he looked at me kind of funny. You know. . . .' At this point," Bullard concluded, "I believe the inquiry may well be dropped. There is enough revealed for us to be sure of future homosexual difficulties." [27]

Boys or men who seemed to be effeminate, sensitive, or immature, according to some of the lecturers, were as important to detect as those who were self-conscious, embarrassed, or reserved. These males, according to Bullard, were the "modestly unobtrusive, quiet and gently mannered chaps and certain others of rather youthful appearance with sensitive features and an air of refinement, sometimes with slightly effeminate mannerisms or gestures. How will life in the training camp effect [sic] them? How will they like the idea of a common shower, of having no privacy? . . . Are they disgusted by dirty stories whose point is strongly oral or anal? Do they experience discomfort when sexual matters are vulgarly referred to? Do they seem to feel that all women are sacred? Have they failed to break away from the early attachment to the mother and to find a substitute? Fear of impotence might be serious and its actuality a profoundly disturbing problem. One may feel that these babies need to be toughened,'' Bullard concluded, ''but service life makes more immediate demands on everyone concerned than it offers opportunities for hurrying these preadolescents on to a well developed maturity.'' [28] This and other seminar lectures were variations on the same theme— careful psychiatric screening could detect males with the potential for homosexual difficulties that made them unfit for military service. Excluding them before induction would better prepare the armed forces to fight a war.

With standardized screening guidelines in place and the final seminar completed in July, Sullivan had accomplished the first two phases of his screening plan. But the next phase—to organize similar nationwide psychiatric seminars for the thirty thousand volunteer local board physicians—was never implemented. State Selective Service directors believed that local board physicians were too hostile toward psychiatry to attend meetings on the subject and that an angry public suspected that the already high rate of psychiatric rejections meant that the military was pampering sissies and rewarding complainers.[29] It was at this point that the expansion of the Selective Service System's psychiatric educational program reached a limit. For the rest of the war, national headquarters used only printed directives, including guidelines for identifying homosexual registrants, to instruct local draft boards how to screen men for military service.

The honeymoon between psychiatry and the Selective Service during the first half of 1941 was short lived. It was over by year's end when a new Selective Service director, Major General Lewis B. Hershey, clashed with Harry Stack Sullivan, the psychiatric consultant he inherited, over the importance of psychiatric screening. Unlike his predecessor Clarence Dykstra, Hershey was hostile to psychiatry and represented to Sullivan the kind of hard-line military official who thought that the psychiatrically unfit were whiners who needed to be toughened up. Under Hershey's direction, the Selective Service eliminated psychiatric examinations at local boards—over much protest from the psychiatric profession—

handing the job over to examiners at Army induction stations. Sullivan's bitter resignation in November signaled the beginning of a serious rift between the psychiatric profession and the Selective Service System. Hershey waited more than a year to replace Sullivan with another psychiatric consultant, while Overholser and his fellow psychiatric consultants to the government shifted their attention away from the Selective Service to the screening programs of the Army and Navy.[30]

When war was declared in December 1941, the nation suddenly faced the challenge of raising an army of many millions of men and women instead of the one-million-man force for which the Selective Service had planned since the fall of 1940. Under pressure to streamline induction procedures and now carrying the burden of psychiatric screening, the Army lowered its entrance standards to accept more men, allowing local examiners to ignore the minor defects of examinees, such as mild stuttering, marginal intelligence, and minor paralysis, that would not interfere with military duties.[31]

But at the same time, clarifications of previously vague psychiatric screening procedures suggested a tightening of antihomosexual screening standards. Throughout 1941 Overholser and his colleagues on the National Research Council committee had studied the psychiatric sections of the Army's mobilization regulations to prepare for the revisions that would follow such a declaration of war. They incorporated these expanded psychiatric sections into the early-1942 revisions of army mobilization regulations, including a new paragraph, written by NRC committee member Lawrence Kubie, entitled "Sexual Perversions," which established the Army's antihomosexual screening procedures for the rest of the war.[32]

The 1942 regulation for the first time defined both the homosexual and the "normal" person, listed telltale signs of homosexuality and clarified procedures for rejecting gay draftees. "Persons habitually or occasionally engaged in homosexual or other perverse sexual practices" were "unsuitable for military service" as was any man with "a record as a pervert." The regulation further defined sexual deviance by describing the sexually "normal" man as one who had a "conventional attitude toward sexual problems." It listed three possible signs for identifying male homosexuals, all of them based on gender deviance: "feminine bodily characteristics," "effeminacy in dress and manner," and a "patulous [expanded] rectum." All three of these markers linked homosexuality with effeminacy or sexually "passive" anal intercourse and ignored gay men who were masculine or "active" in anal intercourse.

The regulation's attention to the mannerisms and gestures of effeminate men was new, previous regulations having focused only on female physiology in male recruits. The rationale behind rejecting "physically normal yet effeminate and 'sissy' " men was that, in the words of one psychiatrist, they would become "subject to ridicule and 'joshing' which will harm the general morale and will incapacitate the individuals for Army duty." [33] In February 1942 a study of screening at the Boston Induction Station recommended that "even the man who, without homosexuality, is so effeminate in appearance and mannerisms that he is inevitably destined to be the butt of all the jokes in the company, should be excluded." [34] By 1943 a group of doctors had developed the Cornell Selectee Index, a paper-and-pencil test designed to streamline psychiatric examinations, which used "occupational choice" questions to screen out effeminate selectees. Men who checked off interior decorator, dancer, and window dresser were considered to have difficulty with their "acceptance of the male pattern." [35] A Cooperative School Report Form that draft boards sent to a selectee's high school to get the "impressions of teachers" also asked about the student's effeminacy.[36] Army examiners were instructed to regard all effeminate recruits as potential homosexuals and to refer them to a psychiatrist for more careful examination.

The 1942 Army regulation also introduced a procedure for handling the man who voluntarily "admits or claims homosexuality." By mid-1941 self-declared gay men already had made up the majority of those rejected for homosexuality by the Selective Service in New York City.[37] Examiners feared that heterosexual men also would claim to be homosexual to avoid military service. The 1942 Army standards addressed this problem by requiring examiners to send the self-declared gay selectee back to his local draft board for a "social investigation" into his background to determine whether he was truly homosexual or just a malingerer. Following their own logic, Army and Navy psychiatrists coined the convoluted term *reverse malingerer* to define as a medical problem those patriotic gay men who did not voluntarily declare themselves but instead "slipped through" induction stations in order to serve in the military.[38]

Fearing that masses of young men would now claim to be homosexual to escape the draft, hard-line military officials argued for the necessity of maintaining a widespread revulsion toward homosexuality both inside and outside the military to deter potential malingerers. At the same time, some psychiatrists took an opposing point of view, expressing their concern that selectees rejected for homosexuality would experience harassment or discrimination. When an Army rejectee was sent back home, his draft board members and staff were given copies of his physical examination record, which they treated with only limited confidentiality. Employers could discover his homosexuality because, under the 1940

Selective Service Act, they had a right to ask for a man's draft record as a condition of employment. The psychiatric diagnoses written on draft records were explicit, often humiliating, and seemed punitive. Harry Stack Sullivan, who was particularly sensitive to sexual stigmas, complained that a rejectee could discover in his file that he had been diagnosed as a "sexual psychopath." When his former employer would ask to see his record before hiring him back, Sullivan added, "much pointless embarrassment, misunderstanding, and aggravation of handicap resulted." [39]

In practice the screening of selectees and enlistees for military service forcibly engaged psychiatric examiners and the nation's young men in intense face-to-face confrontations. During the interviews, both examiners and examinees responded to each other with lies and deceptions, tricks and traps, hunches and second guesses, to either discover, hide, or declare the "truth" of the examinee's sexuality. These encounters were repeated thousands of times over at draft boards, induction centers, and Navy training stations across the country as thousands of examiners tried to sort examinees into various psychiatric categories while meeting manpower needs. Never had the government cast its antihomosexual net so wide.

Newspaper and magazine editors did not shy away from publishing articles that announced the military's new efforts to screen out homosexuals. "We question [the selectee] about his sexual habits," wrote a physician in the *Saturday Evening Post,* "and, in general, about his relationship with the opposite sex. If there is reason to suspect it, we try to find out whether the selectee is homosexual, a common enough aberration, but one which the Army has found it necessary to exclude from its ranks." "The [Navy] psychiatrists," wrote a reporter in a full-page story in the *Washington Sunday Star,* "will be on the lookout for any number of mental illnesses or deficiencies that would make the recruit a misfit." This reporter listed homosexuals among the people the Navy wanted to "weed out." Similarly, a 1942 article in *Time* magazine reported that the question "How do you get along with girls?" was one of many that the "eagle-eyed specialist" routinely "machine-gunned" at the selectee during the induction physical.[40] Such press coverage further disseminated to the public the notion that homosexuals were unfit for military service because they were mentally ill. Military unfitness was one of the few contexts in which the popular media discussed homosexuality at all during the war.

Often embarrassed by the subject, people further spread the word in jokes about selectees whom examiners mistook for homosexual because they didn't "like girls." "A young man who had just been drafted," went a joke reported by a *San Francisco Chronicle* columnist in 1943, "was being examined at Grand Central Palace. The psychiatrist's assistant asked the routine question: 'Do you go out with the girls?' The draftee shook his head and answered firmly: 'No.' The assistant called the psychiatrist, who repeated the question. Again the draftee answered firmly: 'No.' 'Why don't you go out with girls?' the doctor asked. 'Because,' said the draftee, 'my wife won't let me.' " [41]

In the hands of military examiners, the precision tools for detecting hidden homosexuality that were discussed in the Selective Service seminars became blunt instruments. Millions of teenage boys and young men were asked point-blank if they liked or dated girls, if they were homosexual or had had homosexual experiences or feelings, or if they masturbated with or had sex with other men or boys. This was the first time most of these young men, regardless of their sexuality, had had to account for their homosexual practices or tendencies to anyone, let alone the federal government. The vast majority simply answered that they liked girls and that they were not homosexual—answers they were sure that the examiners wanted to hear and that would make them appear to be normal. Asking and answering the homosexual question became a new military ritual that forced each selectee to make a public statement about his sexuality and to wonder privately if he might be queer.

Self-identified gay men, however, had the most to risk in deciding how to answer the homosexual question. Some faced this dilemma alone, but others talked and argued with their friends about what to do. Stuart Loomis, who served as an Army psychologist, recalled that even early in the war, the question "was pretty general knowledge" among his circle of gay friends in Omaha, Nebraska. "That was our big debate at the time," he explained. "You had to decide, were you going to try to go in and cover and take your chances or were you going to declare yourself and stay out?"

Many selectees who led privately homosexual lives, including some with familiar names, avoided having to answer the homosexual question because they were exempt from military service for other reasons. A Quaker and a conscientious objector, black civil rights activist Bayard Rustin spent twenty-eight months in federal prison as a noncooperator with the Selective Service System. Christopher Isherwood in 1942 registered as a conscientious objector in Philadelphia, but he passed the draftable age before he could be inducted into alternative service. In May 1942, Montgomery Clift tried to join the Army, but was classified 4-F because he suffered from chronic dysentery. Liberace was drafted but disqualified because of a childhood back injury. Because James Baldwin was the eldest son of a father who was ill, he was exempt from the draft, but he worked as a civilian for the Army in Belle Mead, New Jersey. Attorney Roy Cohn—who in the 1950s helped Senator Joseph McCarthy purge suspected communists and homosexuals from federal jobs—pulled political strings to evade the wartime draft by repeatedly being nominated and rejected for West Point, stalling his induction until the draft act expired in October 1946.[42]

Gay veterans who were not exempt from military service clearly remember how and why they answered no when examiners asked them if they were homosexual. Most did not want to be rejected for military service or stigmatized as queer in their hometowns. Lying to pass as heterosexual, even to "the discerning psychiatrist for a period of five or ten minutes," as one gay man wrote shortly after the war, came easily to men who "had been successfully practicing concealment from families, employers, friends, and others for many years."[43] "How did I know to lie?" recalled Vince Carelli, who as a seventeen-year-old in June 1945 joined the Navy in Cleveland, Ohio. "Cunning. I didn't want to have the social stigma of saying I declared myself to be a homosexual and I'm not going to go into the service. At that time it seemed to be a terribly important thing to have a good service record. We were sold on that idea." Charles Rowland, who at twenty-five was drafted in Phoenix, Arizona, recalled that he "knew an awful lot of gay people but nobody, with one exception, ever considered not serving. We were not about to be deprived the privilege of serving our country in a time of great national emergency by virtue of some stupid regulation about being gay." "All you have to do is to tell them you're queer, and you're out," explains a gay character in Christopher Isherwood's World War II novel *The World in the Evening*. "I couldn't do that, though. Because what they're claiming is that us queers are unfit for their beautiful pure Army and Navy—when they ought to be glad to have us."[44]

Gay selectees who said no sometimes believed that they were telling the truth. Some did not yet think of themselves as gay. In early 1942, right after Pearl Harbor was bombed, twenty-year-old Woodie Wilson enlisted in the Air Force at an induction station outside Harrisburg, Pennsylvania, where, he recalled, "I was asked the big question 'Are you a homosexual?' And I certainly said no and didn't believe I was." Others could truthfully say no because they had not yet had any sexual experiences or, like Robert Fleischer, were asked only if they "liked girls.'' Still others had never heard the clinical term *homosexual* before and guessed that it didn't apply to them. "Going into the service the word 'homosexual' was used,'' recalled Raymond Mailloux, who in July 1943 was drafted into the Army in Fall River, Massachusetts, at the age of eighteen. "And like everyone else, of course, I said no. Because I truly did not know what 'homosexual' meant. We didn't call it that. We called it more or less being 'queer' or 'fruit.' And it wasn't even till later that I knew it pertained to women also.''

Occasionally, rather than lie, a gay man directly confronted an examiner who questioned him about his homosexuality. When Lester Ellis, a Hollywood actor who was examined after Selective Service started drafting older men, completed and passed his physical examination, he recalled, "I was sent upstairs to see the psychiatrist. He sat behind a big desk, talking on the phone. As I waited I saw he had a big piece of paper in front of him and glancing down I saw listed alphabetically many names of friends and colleagues of mine in the motion picture industry whom I knew to be homosexual. When he got off the phone, he said 'We have heard about men like you.' I said, '*We* have heard about men like *you*, so don't start.' He said, 'Do you want to be in the Armed Forces?' I said, 'As far as I am concerned, I am already in.' So he signed the paper and let me go.'' [45]

Not all examiners were heterosexual. Those who were gay could make it easier for gay men to get into the service. Twenty-eight-year-old Bob Ruffing, a high school English teacher, joined the Navy right after Pearl Harbor was bombed and was examined at a Navy recruiting station on Long Island. At the end of his physical, Ruffing recalled, he "walked into this office and here was this man who was a screaming belle—lots of gold braid, but he was a queen if ever I saw one! And he asked me the standard questions, ending up with, 'Did you ever have any homosexual experiences?' Well, I looked him right in the eye and I said, 'No!' And he looked right back and said, 'That's good!' The two of us lying through our teeth.''

Many examiners neglected to ask the question at all, or asked it in a perfunctory way, because it embarrassed them or because they wanted to protect the young man from being stigmatized or had to meet their region's manpower quotas. When Maxwell Gordon, a teenager who knew he was gay, enlisted in the Navy in the middle of 1942 and was examined in downtown Los Angeles, he saw a psychiatrist "for maybe eight or ten seconds.'' The examiner asked him " 'Do you like girls?' and I said, 'I can take them or leave them.' '' But the examiner never pursued this ambiguous answer because, Gordon explained, "there were hundreds, hundreds of people. Nineteen forty-two was just, if you were warm, they would take you."

By beginning to instruct examiners to reject homosexual selectees, the military inadvertently granted to gay men the new and powerful option of escaping compulsory service by declaring their homosexuality. Critics complained that psychiatric screening only encouraged these and other men to claim that they were mentally ill. "There is a definite danger," the *Christian Century* editorialized in 1944, "in teaching a person to evade responsibility by considering his personality weaknesses a 'disease' over which he has no control." [46] Psychiatrists found themselves defending self-declared homosexuals as honest men who admitted that they were mentally ill, while military officials, war boosters, and even gay contemporaries could portray them as slackers trying to shirk their military duty.

Gay men debated with their friends about whether to declare themselves and how to do it, often relying on each other to rally around a selectee once he had decided to declare himself. Donna Smith remembered dressing up her nineteen-year-old gay pal in makeup and scarves and then accompanying him to the induction station in Los Angeles, where he succeeded in being rejected within a matter of minutes. But men who chose to declare themselves also could face the anger of their gay friends. Ernest Cole, a gay man who enlisted in the Navy in 1940, recalled that his friend who declared himself to his draft board "got out of it," but Cole "didn't respect him. I thought this guy was a traitor, in a sense." Answering yes to the homosexual question could cause a man to lose the respect of his gay friends as well as that of his family and his hometown community.

Men who had no doubts that they were gay discovered that examiners did not always understand or believe them when they tried to declare themselves. In 1942 twenty-five-year-old Donald Vining wrote in his diary a detailed description of the problems he faced when he tried to tell his induction examiner that he was homosexual. Vining was a conscientious objector but he decided to declare himself as homosexual because his family could not afford the $35 per month maintenance fee for doing alternative service in a work camp. He first talked over his decision with his more experienced gay friend George, who had been examined several weeks before Vining. "I know now," Vining wrote in his diary, "that it's very unlikely that I'll have to go in the Army. I know what questions are asked by the psychiatrists and I have only to answer truthfully to get turned down flat."

Three weeks later, the "momentous day" took place when Vining was bused from his home in Bordentown, New Jersey, to Camden for his induction physical. Stripped to his "shorts, shoes and socks," Vining first had his physical examination, then "finally [the] neuro-psychological, which was what I had been waiting for." During the interview, he wrote, "the psychiatrist I got proved very nice but I feared for one panicky moment that my goose was cooked." The psychiatrist had merely asked him " 'Do you get along with women all right?' and I couldn't see that as a good opening at all, it being so meaningless. I hesitated and stammered, hunting for an opening, and then finally said 'Well, I don't know. I don't associate with them much.' That got things on the right path and he was marvelously tolerant, taking the whole thing easily and calmly, without shock and without condescension."

To protect this selectee from being stigmatized as homosexual, the psychiatrist wrote on the medical record, according to Vining, the ambiguous clinical phrase "sui generistic 'H' overt." The Army classification officers, however, were not satisfied with this diagnosis. They "couldn't figure it out," Vining wrote, "so sent me back with a note [which said] 'Lt. Stern, English, please.' He came right back to the classification officers with me and quite a discussion buzzed." The psychiatrist and the Army officers argued about diagnostic categories for homosexuals and whether homosexuality alone could disqualify a selectee. The psychiatrist warned the Army officers that "if they passed me and I got into trouble, they would too. After Stern left the lieutenant said the diagnosis should be written out obviously and it was put down as 'homosexualism—overt' which is a bald way to have it go back to the Bordentown [draft] board." Vining worried about how the stigma of such an explicit diagnosis would affect him back home, despite the fact that his mother knew he was gay. "I don't give a hoot for my own part," he wrote. "It's only the effect on Mother, who's really known about town." [47]

While Vining decided early on that he would declare himself, twenty-eight-year-old Raymond Myers was not so sure what he should do. Myers, a schoolteacher who lived in Chicago, knew that he was gay. When he was called up for an examination in 1942, expecting to be asked about homosexuality, he did not declare himself, partly because it might affect his teaching job. But at a second examination Myers changed his mind, not because he wanted to stay out of the military but because he was afraid that in the service he would be exposed and punished. Like Vining, Myers found the psychiatrist at the draft board to be tolerant and helpful. "When I first went in for the interview with him, I said, 'If you looked at my record, you know I am a schoolteacher. What I have to tell you would be very bad for me if it ever got out.' He questioned me at great length, probably to find out that I wasn't fooling or trying to pull something off just to get out of being drafted." The psychiatrist satisfied himself that Myers was not malingering and told him not to worry about the confidentiality of his diagnosis. "We will word it in such a way," he told Myers, "that if these records were dug up a thousand years from now, there would be no way of their pinning homosexuality onto you." Myers was rejected for military service, but his homosexuality did not appear on his draft records.

The conflict between their responsibilities both to protect patient confidentiality and to screen homosexuals from military service placed physicians in a difficult ethical position.[48] Some examiners worried that by performing their duty they would ruin lives. "Many [homosexuals] have probably passed me on my Induction Centre work," wrote a concerned Laguna Beach psychiatrist to the Army in Washington on behalf of his gay selectees. "Of course we throw them out when we find them, but it should not be regarded as a crime and the matter should be very closely kept, as when eliminated, they have hard times getting a job." [49] Other physicians who were concerned that gay draftees would be harassed in the military tried to help them get psychiatric exemptions for homosexuality, even though such a rejection threatened to expose and stigmatize a man as queer. In 1942 one prominent doctor wrote a letter for an employee to take to the induction center stating that he was homosexual. But the letter was "disregarded and the colored lad in question inducted. I should view it as a tragedy," he wrote to his colleague Winfred Overholser, "if, through no fault of his own, he were to wind up in Federal prison" for homosexual offenses.[50]

While some physicians felt morally obligated to protect gay selectees from discrimination and harassment, others felt equally obligated to report their gay patients to military authorities to protect the morals of the nation's young soldiers. In October 1941 a Chicago physician wrote to Washington to report the name and whereabouts of one of his patients who had confided during treatment that he was homosexual. His patient had just been drafted, had gone undetected by induction examiners, and was stationed at a training camp in California. "I realize that it is extremely unethical for me," the physician admitted, "to have revealed the name of a patient, and therefore I must unfortunately (and with regret and apologies) make this letter anonymous." The physician was worried that gay inductees would "contaminate our fine boys," including his two sons in the service. In response, the Surgeon General's Office tracked down the gay draftee and had him reexamined for discharge as homosexual.[51]

Although physical and psychiatric screening was initially directed toward male selectees, the military also began to screen women as soon as they were allowed to enter the armed forces. World War II was the first time that American women could officially serve in the Army other than as nurses. In World War I the Navy had been the first branch of the military to enlist women who were not nurses, assigning 10,000 women to positions as "yeomen" or, in the slang of the day, "yeomanettes"—women who did typing and office work. But by the middle of World War II, each branch of the service had established women's divisions. The largest women's branch, the Women's Auxiliary Army Corps (which became the Women's Army Corps in the summer of 1943), accepted 140,000 women, the Navy WAVES 100,000, the Women Marines 23,000, and the Coast Guard SPARS 13,000.[52]

Because of women's marginal status in the military before World War II, neither the Army nor the Navy had developed policies and procedures concerning lesbians. The men's branches, by contrast, had built their World War II antihomosexual policies on the foundation of a criminal justice system that for more than a century had prosecuted men for sodomy. Criminal law generally ignored lesbian sexual acts, and women were rarely prosecuted in court for engaging in sex with other women. Not only in the law but in most areas of American life lesbians were ignored either as nonexistent or as less significant than gay men. At first, reflecting this history of invisibility, psychiatrists and military officials issued no policies or procedures for screening out lesbians. Only gradually did they define what they perceived to be a lesbian problem, waiting until the end of the war to issue directives specifically aimed at excluding lesbians from the armed forces.

Ironically, the double standard toward the screening of women and men, combined with their history of invisibility, enabled lesbians to enter the military undetected. Phillis Abry left a secure job as a lab technician for R.C.A. in Princeton, New Jersey, to join the WAAC because she "wanted to be with all those women." Helen Harder quit her welding job at the North Carolina Shipyard in Wilmington to join the Women's Army Air Corps because she wanted to be with her girlfriend and had always dreamed of being a pilot. Women who had heard that the military was screening draftees and volunteers for homosexuality prepared themselves for how they would answer the question during their physical examinations. "I remember being very nervous about them asking me if I had any homosexual feelings or attitudes," Abry recalled. "I just smiled and was sweet and feminine!"

In reality Abry and most other female applicants were never asked the homosexual question. The Army, Navy, and Marine Corps did not initially develop any screening procedures for women and instead relied on existing procedures for examining men. But regulations that advised examiners to look for "effeminacy in dress and manner" and a "patulous rectum," or for such psychiatric disorders as "mama's boys," were meaningless when applied to women.[53] Overworked examiners had neither the time nor the inclination to adapt existing procedures to the needs of women. Many female volunteers did not receive a basic gynecological examination, and until 1945 most women were accepted into the Army, according to its chief psychiatric consultant, William Menninger, "without even a semblance of a psychiatric exam" that might have detected lesbians.[54]

The pressure to meet unfilled personnel quotas also kept recruiting officers and examiners from prying into the sexual lives of female volunteers. Recruiting officers had to lure women from their homes, from better-paid defense industry jobs, and from other branches of the military to meet their monthly quotas. Recruiters for the WAAC and (later) WAC failed to ask questions that might disqualify women, waived examinations at faraway induction stations because the long trip might discourage applicants, and pressured Army examiners to overlook minor defects. Whenever women were examined, the more aggressive techniques that physicians used on captive male draftees—such as interviewing a naked selectee about his sex life—were not used because they threatened to scare away rather than attract female volunteers.[55] During the exams, female masculinity, unlike male effeminacy, was not considered to be a disqualifying defect, reflecting the military's need for women who could perform traditionally male work. "It should be noted," a group of Marine Corps examiners at Camp LeJeune advised their colleagues, "that women showing a masculine manner may be perfectly normal sexually and excellent military material." [56] Although none of the military branches compiled statistics on the number of lesbians rejected for military service, it is likely that throughout most of the war, examiners rejected few if any female applicants for homosexuality or masculinity.

From 1942 to late 1944, Women's Army Corps Director Colonel Oveta Culp Hobby and other WAC officials, in an effort both to fight the double standard in physical examinations and win public respect for the Corps, pressured the Army to conduct more thorough screening of female applicants. At the same time several controversies arose regarding screening that focused directly on lesbian Wacs, eroding their invisibility and laying the groundwork for antilesbian policies. In November and December 1942, WAAC personnel officers and Colonel Hobby's office issued a report that listed forty-eight women, including three lesbians, who had been accepted into the Corps even though they had been known in their home communities as having "very bad traits and habits." In response, the adjutant general issued a confidential letter to all commands ordering recruiters to look into "the applicant's local reputation" and to consider nine categories of "undesirable habits and traits of character," one of which was "homosexual tendencies," when interviewing applicants.[57]

During the same months, a study of why women signed up to become Waacs revealed that some applicants had enlisted out of masculine or lesbian motives. Lt. Col. Vance Sailor, chief of the Appointment and Induction Branch of the Adjutant General's Office, hired a private research firm to conduct the study using forms collected in Chicago WAAC recruiting stations. Most applicants had indicated that they chose the WAAC out of patriotism, but many of these women also gave qualifying statements. Reasons for applying that suggested masculine or lesbian motives included "loves a uniform and what it stands for," "always wanted to be a boy and join Army," seeks "companionship of girls with similar patriotic desire," wants "opportunity to mix with other girls," and wants to "make friends and work with other women."[58] Possibly in response to this study's findings, an officer in the WAAC director's office the same month revised the recruiter's interview sheet and asked the director of personnel to put it into practice. She proposed that recruiting officers try to "get under the patriotic motive" by asking the applicant four standard questions about why she wanted to join the WAAC, one of which was, Is it to be with other girls? She wanted recruiters to word this question in such a way that they would "catch questionable women"—that is, lesbians.[59]

But these proposals for stricter screening still conflicted with the personnel shortage during the rapid early expansion of the WAAC. Throughout 1943 WAAC/WAC quotas went up while applications went down due to competition from industry and the other military branches. In an attempt to meet the quotas, the adjutant general, Maj. Gen. James A. Ulio, against Colonel Hobby's objections and contradicting his earlier letter to WAAC recruiters, actually lowered the physical and psychiatric standards for women applicants. An angry Director Hobby protested up the chain of command to Chief of Staff General George C. Marshall that despite shortages, acceptability standards should be raised and clarified, not lowered. In May 1943, finally responding to Hobby's pressure, the surgeon general appointed Maj. Margaret D. Craighill, former dean of the Women's Medical College of Pennsylvania, as his first Consultant for Women's Health and Welfare, an appointment that Colonel Hobby called "our first ray of hope." Major Craighill's assigned task was to bring about specific uniform standards for the examination of all women applicants.[60]

Throughout the summer of 1943, Major Craighill toured induction centers to determine why WAAC screening had been so lax. While she was on tour, the Women's Army Corps was established as part of the Army, a change that entitled Wacs to receive Army benefits. The conversion bolstered Colonel Hobby's campaign for stricter standards by increasing the War Department's interest in rejecting unfit applicants before they required hospitalization at government expense. By the end of September 1943, Major Craighill finally convinced the War Department to order gynecological and psychiatric examinations of every applicant and to publish standards of acceptance and disqualification that were specifically formulated for women.[61] But despite these official changes on paper, Army examiners, still under pressure to fill quotas, in practice continued to conduct only cursory screening of applicants.[62]

In 1944, while the offices of the WAC director and the surgeon general continued to press for tighter screening, a scandal broke out at the WAC Training Center at Fort Oglethorpe, Georgia—one of the two operating at the time.[63] In May 1944 the mother of a twenty-year-old Wac private at Fort Oglethorpe discovered some love letters from a Wac sergeant to her daughter. Shocked, she immediately wrote to Washington, charging that the Women's Army Corps was "full of homosexuals and sex maniacs" and threatening that "unless this vice is cleaned out I am going to reveal that scandal to the world." The War Department responded to her charges by dispatching from the Inspector General's Office in Atlanta to Fort Oglethorpe an investigative team, led by Lt. Col. Birge Holt and Capt. Ruby E. Herman, to conduct what became more than a month of secret hearings on the presence of lesbians in the Women's Army Corps.[64]

WAC officers at Fort Oglethorpe told Colonel Holt and Captain Herman that little or no screening for homosexuality had been conducted, and that lesbians had entered the WAC in greater numbers since early 1943, when the adjutant general had ordered looser screening standards to meet unfilled quotas.[65] The commander of the military police detachment at Fort Oglethorpe, Capt. Dorothea Wilson, who had previously served as a recruiting officer, testified, "They are still coming in, if you may judge by appearances." [66] The post commander, Col. Howard Clark, stressed the need for identifying lesbians before they entered the WAC by more carefully checking each applicant's background, but he admitted that identifying lesbians was not an easy task. "These women don't wear armbands," he explained, "they are not branded on the forehead, they all look alike, the decent women and the bad ones, you can't tell them apart, until you catch them in the overt act." [67] In their secret report to the inspector general, Colonel Holt and Captain Herman recommended tighter screening to detect lesbians.[68]

By August 1944, despite unfilled quotas, the inspector general's investigative team, Colonel Hobby, William Menninger, Major Craighill, and others finally convinced the War Department to take seriously their recommendations for more stringent psychiatric screening of applicants. Out of their campaign to eliminate the Army's double standard for examining women, these officials, ironically, laid the groundwork for the Army's first explicit instructions for excluding lesbians.

In October 1944 General Marshall released antilesbian instructions as part of a medical technical bulletin (TB MED 100) entitled "WAC Recruiting Station Neuropsychiatric Examination." This directive told medical examiners how to conduct uniform psychiatric screening of applicants and explicitly established homosexuality as a category of disqualification from the Women's Army Corps. It designated the examining psychiatrist as the officer who must "be on guard against the homosexual who may see in the WAC an opportunity to indulge her sexual perversity. Homosexuals are quickly detected and cause no end of difficulty," the directive warned. "Without exception, they should be excluded at the time of examination." Despite this firm policy of exclusion, the directive still included no guidelines for identifying lesbian applicants, and there was little time to implement it. "Most of the WAC recruiting was over," noted Major Craighill, before this "partially adequate program was adopted." [69]

In early 1945, when Pat Bond went down to the Blackhawk Hotel in Davenport, Iowa, to enlist in the WAC, she discovered that lesbians were still being accepted even after the October 1944 directive had been issued. The recruiting officer, Bond recalled, "looked sort of like all my old gym teachers in drag. Stockings, little earrings, her hair slicked back and very daintily done so you couldn't tell she was a dyke, but *I* knew!" Bond explained that many "butch" lesbians she knew applied for the WAC "wearing men's clothes—wearing argyle socks and pin-striped suits and the hair cut just like a man's with sideburns shaved over the ears—the whole bit." Despite these women's masculine appearance, the examiners "let them in like that—much to the credit of the army psychiatrists. They would say, 'Have you ever been in love with a woman?' You would say, 'Of *course* not!' sitting there in your pinstriped suit.'' [70]

The antihomosexual wall that psychiatrists began to build around the military during World War II, although full of holes, was a new feature on the American sexual landscape. Posted at the gates were the psychiatric examiners, many of them looking for hidden homosexuals while trying to meet military quotas and not ruin rejectees' lives. To help examiners distinguish gay men from other inductees, psychiatrists wrote into military regulations lists of stereotyped signs that characterized gay men as visibly different from the rest of the population. At the same time, officials in the women's branches, to deal with their personnel shortages, downplayed the importance of the lesbian stereotype, challenging the popular notion that masculine women were lesbians. [71] So many gay men were able to hide their homosexuality from examiners, while so many examiners were trying to find ways to let them in, that by the end of the war, after examining nearly 18 million men, the military had officially rejected only 4,000 to 5,000 as homosexual. [72]

The new screening directives and procedures, however, though ineffective in excluding the vast majority of gay men, introduced to the military the idea that homosexuals were unfit to serve in the armed forces because they were mentally ill. The military's more traditional means of handling homosexuality, which operated within its criminal justice system, was to define the sex act as the problem, for which the offender was tried and punished. The idea that homosexuals were mentally ill, on the other hand, defined the person, even when there was no sexual act, as disruptive of morale and unfit to serve. As psychiatrists wrote this idea into military regulations and directives, the belief that gay men and lesbians constituted a class of people who must be excluded from the armed forces became an important part of military policy. Ironically, this policy shift occurred at a critical time when the armed forces desperately needed to recruit every available man and woman to serve in the nation's defense.

CHAPTER
2

Fitting In

Shortly after Pearl Harbor was bombed, Winfred Overholser realized that, despite psychiatric screening, the demands of war would force the military to accept and integrate most gay selectees. "I have an idea," he wrote, "that the Army will take the 'boys' . . . in, unless they are extremely persistent offenders. Apparently the Army is likely to relax somewhat its attitude toward these cases, although I speak entirely off the record in this matter." [1] Throughout the war, Overholser and other psychiatrists, as well as a few military officials, privately acknowledged that gay men had become vital members of the armed forces. "We certainly cannot go so far out on a limb," confided an Army psychiatrist to another medical officer in 1944, "as to say that, generally speaking, homosexuals have no place in the Army." [2] Some of the "most efficient and admirable women" in the Women's Army Corps, added Brig. Gen. William Menninger after the war, were lesbian. [3]

So many gay male and lesbian recruits entered the services that officials could neither discharge them all nor ignore them. Neither could recruits ignore the homosexual tensions they faced in the gender-segregated training centers. To adapt to these conditions, trainees, psychiatrists and classification officers, beginning in basic training and continuing through training for more specialized duties, each found ways to manage homosexuality within the military environment and to integrate gay men and women into military life.

New recruits—most of them teenagers or in their early twenties and removed from their families, friends, and neighbors for the first time—were forced to adapt every part of their lives to the demands of military discipline and culture. Millions of men—at the rate of fourteen thousand a day in the summer of 1942—poured into more than 250 training centers across the country.[4] Robert Fleischer was shipped from Manhattan to Fort Dix, New Jersey, and then on to Camp Hulen, Texas, where he completed his basic training. The WAAC shipped Phillis Abry from New Jersey to the First WAAC Training Center at Fort Des Moines, Iowa. Several hundred thousand other women arrived at the WAC Training Center at Fort Oglethorpe, Georgia; the Women Marines Training Station at Camp LeJeune, North Carolina; the WAVES Naval Training Station at Hunter College in New York City; and at other women's training centers. From the moment these young men and women stepped off the bus, they began six to eighteen weeks of rigorous indoctrination, drill, and physical exercise that would transform them from civilians into disciplined soldiers.

Military discipline was the backbone of basic training. A disciplined work force—from the WAC clerk-typist to top brass in Washington—enabled the rapidly growing military organization to operate more efficiently as a hierarchical, bureaucratic machine during this time of national crisis. Instructors taught both male and female trainees to obey orders instantly, to place the interests of their units above their own, to contribute to the morale of their outfits, and to be patriotic, courageous, loyal and proud. Trainees learned how the military was organized, how orders went through the chain of command and how to comply with the rules and "privileges" of military courtesy. Before World War II the military never had subjected women to these rigors of basic training. But although women still were not allowed to fight in combat or to take combat courses, Army and Navy indoctrination during the war set out for the first time to transform each female trainee into "a physically fit, psychologically well-adjusted, well-disciplined soldier."[5]

Discipline also had another purpose—it prepared the male soldier for combat. Most of the basic training courses for men were in combat preparedness because the military considered each man a potential combat fighter. Training in combat discipline was intended to help the infantryman overcome his resistance to killing and his fear of dying so that he would keep fighting when his life was in danger. Stereotyped as "a man's job and a man's job alone,"[6] the ability to fight in combat defined what being a woman or an effeminate man was not. Arguments for excluding gay men from the military and women from combat were based on the same set of negative gender stereotypes—gay men and all women were supposed to be soft, unaggressive, defenseless, and physically weak. But despite the hardship and hypermasculine mystique of combat training, most healthy, able-bodied young men of average intelligence and strength—including those who were homosexual and even effeminate—could and did pass the test. "The heaviest thing I'd ever lifted was a fork to my mouth," quipped Bill Thompson, who as a young gay recruit went through boot camp at the San Diego Naval Training Station. "Getting out there and marching and running and pushups and holding rifles out and don't make a sound and finally the rifles become very, very heavy—I just kept thinking, 'I'm not going to make it' and some of them didn't. But I made it." Heterosexuality was not a functional prerequisite for making it through basic training.[7]

To prepare male recruits for the extreme psychological demands of combat, officers during basic training stripped away each man's civilian identity, placed him under great physical and emotional stress, and—with drill and repetition, rewards and punishments—trained him to act like a soldier and initiated him into military life. During the first few hours after his arrival at the training center, he was bombarded with assaults on his individuality. Officers administered an oath subjecting him to military law, cut his hair, issued him a uniform, gave him a serial number and rank, assigned him to a training unit and barracks, and scheduled every minute of his time. He began a strict regimen of mass calisthenics, close-order drill, inspections, roll calls, and marching to make him practice obeying orders on reflex and to make him experience himself as an important but replaceable unit in the military machine. Mass drills and company punishment for individual infractions forced the recruit to identify his personal well-being with that of his peers. These exercises in group discipline were intended to prepare a unit for situations in which each man's life depended on the teamwork and support of his fellows.[8]

The extreme demands of basic training disrupted the sexual patterns that each male recruit had developed as a civilian and forced him to reorganize them around his military experience. Segregation from wife and other women, total lack of privacy, and little free time immersed the trainee in an all-male military culture that was theoretically heterosexual but rife with homosexual tensions. Every day he saw other men's naked bodies and had no privacy when he showered, used the toilet, or even masturbated. He was lonely and needed new friends, but he had to work out what kinds of affection and intimacy were appropriate in a world without women. The intensity of such an all-male world could force trainees to come to terms with their sexual desires toward men. "You just suddenly are surrounded day and night," recalled Ben Small, who at eighteen enlisted in the Army Air Corps, "by men in shower rooms and barracks without any clothes on and you suddenly realize, 'My God! *This* is what I am. How do I cope?' " Each recruit had to find ways to handle his desires and frustrations while taking care not to talk seriously about homosexual worries for fear of being branded as queer.

To cope with sexual anxieties during basic training, male recruits pieced together their own sexual culture. They posted pinups of women, told sex stories, and used sexual slang to adapt to what Menninger called "a very abnormal life and living arrangement." [9] Sex jokes heterosexualized everyday activities and brought into the open the recruit's private discomfort with the homosexual milieu of military life. GI slang served similar purposes. *Cocksucker* became a favorite putdown among GIs during the war. When a GI was reprimanded by superiors, he was said to have "had his ass reamed." To "tangle assholes" meant to argue or fight; "asshole buddies" were close pals. Recruits playfully called each other "sweetheart." [10]

Much of the male sexual culture of basic training revolved around joking and teasing. Officers knew that humor was a "catharsis and saving grace" that could "function as a safety valve" for a recruit's pent-up feelings. [11] Wartime observers of trainees found "continual joking about homosexual practices" in the barracks. [12] Joking defused secret fears through laughter, and it reassured the men that their uncomfortable feelings were common rather than queer. In some barracks joking became ritualized as "homosexual buffoonery," a spontaneous game in which recruits took turns pretending to be the company queer. An Army psychologist described how the men "kiddingly" played this striptease game with each other when they were getting undressed. "One soldier," he observed, "returning from the shower room in the nude, will be greeted with cat-calls, salacious whistling, and comments like, 'Hey Joe, you shouldn't go around like that—you don't know what that does to me.' Joe will respond by wriggling his hips in feminine fashion after coyly draping a towel around himself. Some of the men will join in the buffoonery by playing the role of the appreciative spectator: 'Ain't he hot stuff though!'; 'C'mon, take it off.' Others act the part of active solicitors for sexual favors: 'How much do you want for sleeping with me tonight?'; 'Come into my bed and I'll give you the time of your life.' " The Army psychologist described this buffoonery as a "definite behavior pattern" among "clinically 'normal' persons" that defended them against the homosexual anxieties stimulated by barracks life. [13]

In such a strange and lonely environment, trainees immediately looked to each other for companionship, pairing up as buddies or forming small cliques in each company. "It is rare to see a soldier or sailor alone," commented two sociologists who studied wartime training-camp life.[14] Each new trainee's primary relationship was with his buddy. He often chose his buddy arbitrarily: He was a bunkmate, came from the same state, or merely stood next to him in line. At first the "unfamiliar situation" and "the need felt for someone to share the discomforts and perplexities of the new life were sufficient for the buddy relationship." But as training progressed, men based these relationships more on shared interests and identities and developed stronger bonds with one another. "Covering up for, defense of, and devotion to one's buddy [were] expected," the two observers explained. Buddies openly expressed for each other "sentiments that would be considered maudlin under other circumstances." [15] The 1922 song "My Buddy," which expressed this tender sentimentality, was revived beginning in 1940 and became one of the most popular songs of World War II, with recordings by Bing Crosby, Frank Sinatra, Sammy Kaye, and others.[16]

William Menninger and other psychiatrists recognized the erotic undertones of these buddy relationships, calling them substitutes for female companionship and a form of "disguised and sublimated homosexuality." [17] But the fact that these companionships were so common and so public could alleviate a man's private fear that his devotion to his buddy might be queer. The lack of privacy during basic training also protected these relationships from suspicion by preventing them from becoming overtly sexual. But despite their public nature, these relationships could allow buddies in stolen moments to talk over personal problems. "I told him things I nevr [sic] told no one before," explains a GI in a poem about basic training by World War II veteran Lincoln Kirstein. "He told me stuff I never heard talked out loud at all." [18] Buddies who in these private moments discovered that they both were gay could give each other unexpected moral support through the hard times of military training.

Trainees found sexual as well as social ways to cope with the homosexual tensions during basic training. They usually didn't experiment sexually with other men until they learned how to bend the rules or until they found themselves paired up in secluded situations. Until then, afraid that their friendships could be "contaminated by erotic feelings" or that their homosexual desires would be found out, they might not touch each other at all. "During the first months in the Army," reported a veteran after the war, "there appears to be a rigid avoidance, in general, of any kind of overt demonstration of friendship which might connote homosexual tendencies'' such as ''overt caressing or any other form of actual bodily contact.'' [19] Trainees who knew they were gay especially were careful not to become too physical with other soldiers. ''You know that you don't dare make any moves,'' explained Jim Warren, who entered the Army in 1941 at age twenty-two, ''especially when you first get into the infantry. So nothing happened in the military until after our thirteen weeks basic training.''

But as men progressed through basic, they found themselves, often unexpectedly, in intimate situations with each other. These included the two-man pup tents during bivouacs, the sleeping accommodations on Pullman train cars during troop movements and the hotel and private home accommodations in towns during overnight passes. In each of these situations, pairs of men could be in bed together with no direct supervision. While the shower rooms and barracks were the public places where homosexual tensions were acted out socially, tents, train berths, and hotel rooms were some of the private places where trainees could act sexually despite or even in response to the military's homosexual taboos.

Toward the end of Army basic training, the recruits spent from three days to two weeks in bivouac, where they put into practice what they had learned in their courses. Often sleeping together in two-man pup tents instead of in barracks, pairs of trainees had rare opportunities to be physically affectionate with each other in private. Raymond Mailloux, who at eighteen was one of the youngest and smallest men in his company, remembered that on bivouac in Louisiana he had many opportunities to sleep in tents on cold nights with older, often married men who nicknamed him ''Junior.'' One veteran of World War I, Mailloux recalled, ''told me that the way to stay warm was to sleep together. I slept with him a few times. He would be right behind me. And to keep warm, he had showed me, I would put my hands between my legs and he'd put his hands between my legs to keep his hands warm. But it was never any groping. Sometimes I would definitely spread my legs to make sure that he could get in there.'' Such private physical intimacy easily could lead to sex. When Robert Fleischer went on bivouac at Camp Hulen, Texas, he recalled, he ''slept in sleeping bags or on the sand, and every once in a while a furtive hand would be on my knee or I'd find somebody unbuttoning my fly.''

Recruits faced similar situations when they were transferred on trains from one camp to another and placed in Pullman cars where they slept ''two in a lower berth, one in an upper.'' [20] Some recruits anticipated these sleeping arrangements with excitement, others with confusion and dread. William Menninger described his own encounter with a man who was nervous about sharing a berth, a problem that "confronted thousands of our soldiers." While Menninger sat in the men's smoking room, eight GIs got on the train. "When the conductor took my Pullman reservation," he recalled, "one of the GI's overheard me say 'lower No. 2.' He hesitatingly came to me as soon as the conductor had left to tell me that he had No. 2. He was greatly assured when he learned that there were two bunks in section No. 2." [21] Saul, a gay man who had decided to remain celibate during his military service, faced his only sexual temptation on a Pullman car. "We were on a troop train with two men in a berth," he explained. "One night a married man threw his arm and leg over me. I was awakened, but I kept my passions under control." [22] Bob Thompson's first sexual experience in the Navy was on a troop train from San Diego to Madison, Wisconsin. "At the end of some of the cars," he recalled, "there were little compartments that would sleep maybe four. I think four of us had the same idea when we got on the train. We just rushed for one of those compartments and all of us were gay. So it was something at night when we closed that door."

Sleeping accommodations off base gave men more privacy for longer periods of time than did pup tents or lower berths. When buddies went into town on overnight passes, they could arrange to share a bed together without any trouble. Because hotel rooms were scarce in military boom-towns, it wasn't unusual for two men to sleep in the same bed. [23] The United Service Organizations (USO) centers also placed servicemen in private homes for the night. Toward the end of their basic training, Robert Fleischer and some of his company mates at Camp Hulen, Texas, "got more friendly and when we could get weekend passes we went away together. There were families in the surrounding communities who would put up GIs to make them feel at home. And you would share bedrooms." It usually wasn't until the recruit could leave his camp on overnight passes that he risked planning sexual liaisons with other men. "You had to be smart enough not to fool around in your own barracks shower or your own barracks," explained Ben Small, who served in the Air Force during the war, "because it would just spread like wildfire. You'd go into town for sex, mainly."

While trainees used these intimate situations to make sex possible, they also found ways to make sex with other men permissible. Recruits generally had sex cautiously and secretly without talking about it with each other or even admitting it to themselves. Silence protected men from exposure and helped them to deny—even to themselves—that they had had sex with a man. Each of Jim Warren's sexual encounters at Fort McClellan, Alabama, was "a mutual situation, it wasn't one-sided," but there was an understanding that "you just don't talk." At night, Raymond Mailloux recalled, the older GIs "held me in their arms, I slept with them. They weren't cruel the next day, but they just would ignore me." Men could feel even more protected from exposure if their sexual partners were from another company, another branch of the service, an allied country's force or civilians they never would see again.[24]

Not all trainees who approached other men for sex were gay. Heterosexual recruits who had had the most sexual experience with women or who felt strong sex drives could initiate sex without being afraid that they were queer, especially if their partner was gay and played the "passive" sexual role. Teenage recruits who were just fooling around with each other, especially if they had been drinking, found themselves unexpectedly becoming sexual. Some older soldiers with more sexual experience in the military taught younger men how to have sex without getting caught. On the other hand, recruits who knew they were gay before entering the service were sometimes the most reluctant to have sex. "I was afraid very often to partake," Robert Fleischer recalled, "because I felt then I would really expose myself and be in terrible trouble as far as everyday life [was] concerned." Gay men who had decided to remain celibate so as not to be caught were sometimes better prepared to resist sexual temptations than were men who didn't think of themselves as homosexual.

Gay trainees, however, if they hadn't decided to be celibate, were more likely to be interested in pursuing sex with men than were other trainees. Gradually they learned how to navigate their way through the sexual maze of military life. Some tried to find other gay men, watching for coded signals—dropped hints, double entendres, and especially eye contact—that could identify who else was gay. "I found that it was quite easy to have sex in the Army," explained Robert Fleischer. "It was very furtive at first, because even the gay ones were afraid to expose themselves because they didn't know if you were going to turn them in or not turn them in. And after a while you knew who was [gay], who wasn't, who [was] to be trusted, who not. There seemed to be available and interested men all through my basic training."

Some servicemen convinced themselves that casual sex with men was not queer if it was just between buddies. To play along with this game, a gay trainee, ironically, could pass as a horny heterosexual. "You start talking," explained Jim Warren, "and you don't say 'I'm straight' or anything, but you say, 'Gee, it sure gets lonely around here without girls.' And [he answers], 'Yes, it sure does.' 'Even to the point of walking around with a hard-on' [you reply]. [He] says 'Yes, I know what you mean.' The next thing you know, [he's] going to the movies with you and it becomes a little twosome. And then later you decide to take a walk somewhere and [say] 'Let's sit down' and from there your hand [is] resting or his hand resting [on your leg], then you're in business. Once that starts, and you realize that he's gone as far as you've gone, he can't say anything and you can't say anything. It's a very cagey game you play." Gay men also could offer to service other men sexually, allowing their partners to retain their self-image as masculine and heterosexual, while themselves risking exposure as the company queer.[25]

Women in basic training conducted their sexual lives differently than did men. Most young women had been raised to be nurturing and romantic and to focus more on relationships than on casual sex. Removed from men's company, they were more likely than men to pair up casually into physically affectionate couples. "Emotional demonstrativeness," explained the WAC's official historian Mattie Treadwell, "was an acceptable trait among women, who thought nothing of kissing or embracing female friends or walking arm-in-arm with them." [26] Such openly affectionate behavior among men would have looked queer to other male soldiers. During the investigation into lesbian activity at Fort Oglethorpe, Georgia, a private testified that "casual embraces" were common at the training center and that she often saw women "go up and put their hand on someone's shoulder." Another sergeant said she sometimes saw two or three women "piled up in one bed" when other women were around. The assistant chief of military police commented that she often saw women in couples in the post exchanges, on the streets in the daytime and "walking along the highways at night." [27] "Everybody was going with someone," recalled Pat Bond, who went through basic training at Fort Oglethorpe, "or had a crush on somebody or was getting ready to go with somebody." Betty Somers recalled that at Women Marines boot camp at Cherry Point, North Carolina, she never saw "any particular reaction" to "women being affectionate with each other."

A female trainee might find herself falling in love with her special friend or even attracted by another woman's attentions.[28] Sarah Davis, a Wave whose nickname was "Sammi," had her first serious love affair with a woman when another Wave she adored made the first move. "I was sitting in the barracks in Florida, and this one woman that I admired greatly—she was a little older than I, a beautiful body, very articulate and a lot of fun. We were sitting next to each other on the couch with our feet propped up on the table and she started stroking my leg and I thought, 'Wow! What's all of this!' I was instantly enchanted with this woman and had a lot of sexual attraction toward her. Eventually we got in bed together.'' The affectionate milieu of barracks life made it difficult for trainees to tell exactly when such close friendships became "strange" or "queer." Wacs at Fort Oglethorpe testified that they drew the line when two women were always with each other, went behind closed doors together, "smoked off the same cigarette," kissed long kisses or called each other "darling, sweetheart." [29]

Relationships in which one partner appeared to be masculine and therefore was perceived to be sexually motivated especially could raise the suspicions of other women. Working-class lesbian slang, which many enlisted and noncom Wacs learned to use during the war, called the masculine partner the "dyke," the "lesbian," the "butch" or—among black servicewomen—the "dagger." The feminine partner was the butch's "lady," "girl," or "girlfriend." Variations of the butch/girlfriend relationship were the norm in working-class lesbian bars and appeared in the women's military branches as well, even between women who did not identify as lesbian and were not sexual with each other. [30] "There is always one who acts, walks, and pays attention to the other, the same as a devoted male," reported the assistant chief of the military police at Fort Oglethorpe, "one waiting on the other; for instance, a girl spills a little bit of water on her skirt, and the other is patting her knees, and so forth; lighting her cigarette," she added. "Just acting like a man." [31]

Female soldiers and officers had several explanations for why women formed butch/girlfriend relationships in basic training. Some butch women believed that feminine women put them in the men's role because there were no men around. [32] Betty Somers explained that some of the heterosexual Women Marines at Camp LeJeune "began to turn to me and other women who perhaps were what you would consider the more butch. And I did notice that towards the end of boot camp, women that I had not even done anything to entice, had begun to hang around more. And even on some of our walks to grab your arm and squeeze you and call you their 'date.' " At Fort Oglethorpe, a butch WAC sergeant testified that trainees who had hero-worship crushes on their sergeants initiated these relationships and let their emotions run away with them. [33] Several "girlfriends," on the other hand, testified that they had enjoyed the attentions of the butch women who had approached them. The WAC psychiatrist at Fort Oglethorpe explained that it was natural for trainees without men to slide into a "hero worship affectionate engagement" with stronger women.[34] The lesbian butch and her girlfriend, and the student with a crush on her teacher, both served as models for the more visible lesbian couples in the military. The sisterly relationships between feminine women, even if they were erotic, stood out less conspicuously as "queer."

Some women in these couples managed to find places to court, neck, and make love both on and off the base. Enlisted women and noncoms, because they did not have the privacy, income, or other privileges of women who were commissioned officers, found privacy in semipublic places in ways similar to those of working-class lesbian civilians. At Fort Oglethorpe, couples stole moments of indoor privacy in hallways, empty barracks, latrines, supply rooms, and orderly rooms. They slept together in rooms for noncommissioned officers where there were two beds. Two women were caught necking in a car at the post parking lot at night and couples were frequently seen going into the woods together after dark but before bed check. During the first weeks of basic training all women were restricted to their base, but after a few weeks, when they could get passes, butch women propositioned potential girlfriends by asking them to go into town for dinner and an overnight stay at a hotel. On Christmas Eve in 1943, when all the hotel rooms were filled in nearby Chattanooga, a butch/girlfriend couple from Fort Oglethorpe who wanted to spend the night together "went to the USO, and they gave us this address where they rented rooms to Wacs." [35]

Throughout the war, Army and Navy officials struggled with how to manage the homosexual behavior, tensions, and relationships among trainees that seemed to increase as the military population expanded. "As you know," wrote Captain Forrest M. Harrison from the Navy Surgeon General's Office to Winfred Overholser in August 1942, "the problem of the homosexual in the Naval Service and what to do with him is ever before us. . . . It seems likely," Harrison predicted, "that under these circumstances homosexuality may become more widespread .in the service as the war progresses." [36]

Military officials developed several approaches toward managing the homosexuality of their personnel. When challenged from the outside, particularly by concerned parents or clergy, their public stance was to condemn behavior considered to be immoral in the wider culture, including profanity, drunkenness, erotic pictures, extramarital sex, lesbianism, homosexuality, and prostitution. Within the organization, however, military officials took a more understanding approach toward the male soldier's "immoral" heterosexual behavior but continued to condemn homosexuality. Officers had traditionally warned servicemen, during mandatory periodic readings of the Articles of War and the Articles for the Government of the Navy, that sodomy was a serious criminal offense that would be punished with long prison terms and dishonorable discharge.[37] During World War II the procedures for screening and discharge were supposed to supplement these criminal sanctions by excluding homosexuals from military service.

But neither the new exclusionary measures nor the laws against sodomy could eliminate homosexuality from military life or even keep it under control. Periodic warnings against committing acts of sodomy sometimes made matters worse by increasing the trainee's interest in homosexuality. When William Johnson first arrived at Tuskegee Air Field in Alabama—a racially segregated aviation school for black men—he and the other trainees were read the Articles of War. "We were warned about punks," he recalled. "These were the so-called homosexuals. My eyes were wide open because I didn't know [about them], and I was looking for them. I didn't see them around, but I was told that they were around."

During the war, psychiatrists proposed a third approach for managing homosexuality that focused more on environmental conditions than on the homosexual person or the criminal sex act. Drawing on the practical experience of military officers as well as on psychoanalytic concepts, they described the military's living arrangements as "unnatural" and therefore likely to provoke "unnatural" responses in both male and female soldiers. William Menninger, Winfred Overholser, and other psychiatric consultants to the military defined barracks life as an object of scientific study, described it as a matrix of sexual anxieties, and offered solutions to individual conflicts that required the skills of professional therapists. They generally assumed that most men and women had latent homosexual or bisexual tendencies that could surface in same-sex environments; that normal sex drives, if suppressed, would be channeled into abnormal outlets if not sublimated into other activities; that sexual anxieties, if not dealt with directly, could lead to neuroses and psychoses; and that an individual's extreme hostility toward homosexuals was an overreaction to his or her own repressed but unconscious homosexual interests. They reinterpreted barracks life in terms of "socio-sexual frustration," "reactions to sexual deprivation," and "erotic tendencies." [38]

William Menninger went so far as to characterize the entire wartime army, in a "technical, psychiatric sense," as "fundamentally a homosexual society." The Army's success, he believed, "depended on the ability of men to get along with, live with, and work with other men, and to accept the almost total exclusion of women from their lives." To do this "certain adjustments were required of the 'normal' " trainee in the form of both physical and psychological substitutes for marital heterosexuality. When women were not available, "many men discovered satisfaction in a physical interest in other men, which often surprised them." [39] Two medical officers stationed at Fort Benjamin Harrison, Indiana, similarly noted that the "prevailing masculine milieu" of Army life led many trainees to engage in masturbation and homosexuality and provoked "conflicts and anxieties about homosexuality." [40] Another observer believed that the military was actually "producing homosexuals by blocking normal sex activities." [41] These doctors, as well as some nonmedical officers, believed that homosexual anxiety, relationships, and behavior were occupational hazards of military life rather than problems caused by homosexuals. [42]

The Women's Army Corps, more than any of the men's branches, officially dealt with homosexuality as an environmental problem. A lecture to WAC officer candidates on homosexuality, prepared by the Surgeon General's Office and revised by WAC officials, pointed to the "conditions of group living unnatural to the majority of mature women" more than to the "overt, active homosexual" as the cause of lesbian behavior in the Corps. Officers were told that "every person is born with a bisexual nature" and that "every woman possesses some traits that are usually regarded as masculine." When "a large number of people of the same sex are in constant association," these "recessive traits become more evident." Any Wac could "gravitate" toward homosexual practices "because of her new close association with women and the lack of male companionship which she had known in civilian life. The universal desire for affection may have impelled her, when deprived of family, friends, and home contacts, to turn to homosexual relationship [sic] as a means of satisfying this feeling." [43]

With this psychological redefinition of barracks life, military psychiatrists proposed new measures for managing the homosexuality of trainees, including educational lectures, guidance, supervision, and reassignment of personnel, with criminal prosecution and discharge to be used only as last resorts against the most overt, disruptive, and unreformable homosexuals.

During the war, officials began to develop educational materials to train officers how to manage homosexuality among enlisted personnel. In August 1943 the post chaplain at Fort Bliss, Texas, sent a proposal to Army Chief of Chaplains Major General William R. Arnold outlining how chaplains might respond to soldiers seeking help with homosexual problems. Army and Navy training courses for doctors who would serve as psychiatrists included brief sections on how the military handled sexual psychopaths. Many military psychiatrists had attended the Selective Service seminars where they had heard lecturers discuss homosexuality in the military. And beginning in May 1943, WAAC/WAC officer candidates received lectures on homosexuality in their sex hygiene training courses.[44] It seemed a logical next step to prepare "mental health" or "sex hygiene" lectures on homosexuality for trainees as well.

In 1944 WAC officers who favored extending such lectures to trainees expressed their views to members of the investigative team at Fort Oglethorpe, who also heard strong objections from other officers. Their secret testimony outlined both sides of a debate that continued for many years inside the Army and Navy. The policy on trainee lectures in effect at Fort Oglethorpe in 1944 had strictly prohibited "any instruction or even any reference to the subject of homosexuality."[45] Even a trainee's question about homosexuality was "turned off in class" and handled privately by the instructor, who would refer her to a doctor for a "sick call" appointment.[46]

Both the resident counselor of the training center, Jane Witmer McKaskle—a social worker—and the post commander, Col. Howard Clark—a regular army officer—opposed the ban on discussing homosexuality with trainees. They argued that a frank discussion would help the trainee control her own impulses and identify the lesbians around her. "These are grown women, supposedly," McKaskle testified. "Most of them have heard at least dirty jokes about it; they hear the firemen and the men over in the Service Club say, 'What are you going to do with that bunch of "queers" over in such and such a company?'. You may be enlightening a lot of people who wouldn't be enlightened," she added, "but on the other hand, they may be 20 or over, and it may be time they got enlightened."[47] Colonel Clark concurred. "I would treat the matter," he testified, "exactly as we treat, for example, venereal disease. We have finally dragged the general subject of venereal disease into the open to fight it in the open rather than burrowing under the ground. I think that a dignified but detailed course of instruction in lesbianism could have nicely been incorporated in the general instruction to the WAC."[48]

But the highest-ranking Wacs at the training center, Col. Elizabeth C. Strayhorn and Capt. Eleanor F. Roberts, countered that open discussion would make trainees too curious about homosexuality and suspicious of ordinary friendships without preventing lesbians from engaging in covert sexual activity. They believed that enforced ignorance and strict silence on the subject were the best prophylactics for homosexual behavior. The Women's Army Corps had barely survived a nationwide slander campaign, and officers were cautious about doing anything that would make the public associate the WAC with homosexuality.[49] In its final report, the inspector general's investigative team concluded that trainee lectures could serve as one of several "preventive measures designed to better guard against the inception and practice of such acts."[50] Despite these recommendations the controversy over such lectures was not resolved.[51] For most of the war military psychiatrists were not authorized to lecture trainees on how to cope with homosexuality. Lt. Col. Patrick Madigan, the Army's chief psychiatrist, maintained that such lectures were not necessary because the average male soldier already felt a "natural repugnance" toward homosexuals and "readily recognize[d] such a type" without having to be taught.[52]

Psychiatrists, however, were able to give recruits standardized lectures on "mental hygiene" and "personal adjustment" that were designed to help them cope with the many emotional problems of military life. Trainees could only infer that such advice also applied to their problems with homosexuality. Medical officers reassured male recruits that their strange emotions and frustrations during basic training were caused by abnormal living conditions and did not mean that they personally had gone soft, crazy, or impotent. "Every one of us has the same problem!" they were told. Lecturers encouraged male recruits to joke and gripe in order to "let off steam"; to be tough, "*take* it," and "develop *guts*"; to push "gloomy and blue" thoughts "forcibly into the background" of their minds; to take part in exhausting physical exercise so that they were "too dog-tired to think"; and to rely on each other for support. But if a personal problem became too serious for a trainee to handle by himself, lecturers told him not to "brood over it" but to confide in an officer. "Go to your company commander, to your chaplain, to any medical officer or to the post psychiatrist. . . . You will find then that if you take these things that you're secretly sore about and drag them up to the surface by talking about them to somebody they will disappear."[53] A lecture to WAC officers similarly emphasized that a WAC trainee "finding herself disturbed by any sex problem with which she is unable to cope" should seek help from her officers.[54] The GI version of this message was "Go tell it to the chaplain!"—a cynically polite way to tell a complaining buddy to shut up.[55] Medical lecturers who thus advised trainees to discuss their emotional problems with an officer may have inadvertently encouraged some of them to "come out." The few gay trainees who couldn't handle the sexual tensions or ridicule in basic training did heed this advice and took their troubles to the chaplain and psychiatrist.[56]

Some civilian psychiatrists and psychologists went outside military channels to give male trainees more direct advice on how to handle their homosexual troubles. In 1943 a committee of the National Research Council joined the publishers of the *Infantry Journal* and Penguin Books to release a twenty-five-cent paperback entitled *Psychology for the Fighting Man,* which in part served this purpose. The popular handbook included a disclaimer that its authors' views did not represent those of the Army or Navy. It reassured the trainee who was troubled by his homosexual feelings that "other men are confronted with just about the same problem as he is, and that, while they may never find an escape from them, most men manage to endure them and do not allow them to impair their efficiency seriously." It was normal for men who had their first sexual experiences with men while in the Army to react in different ways. Some may be "only mildly disturbed" by what they have done, others "will suffer from mental conflict." They may feel ashamed, guilty, inferior to the other men, and afraid that they "will become a confirmed homosexual and become unable to enjoy normal sexual intercourse" when they get back home. A man in this situation may also "feel afraid of being found out and punished by dishonorable discharge and a long sentence."

The handbook's authors tried to reassure the soldier who was upset about his homosexual feelings that as long as he was "seriously worried and dissatisfied with himself, the chances are that he may be all right again when he returns to normal conditions of life." But, they warned, he "should put up a strong fight with himself to control his homosexual impulses and find some other outlet for his sex drive as soon as he can," such as athletics, dancing, band concerts, mass singing, and religion. The "only real permanent relief" for this and other sex problems in the military was for the soldier to put "his whole heart into the business of training for war and destroying the enemy," to speed the victory, and to return home.[57] The fighting man thus could rest assured that worries about homosexuality were a manageable part of many soldiers' lives.

Officials in the Women's Army Corps also strongly advocated guidance for homosexual problems. The leadership in the women's branches based their procedures for managing personnel more on educational than military traditions. High-ranking officers in the women's branches had been recruited from women's colleges for their administrative expertise and to reassure parents that their daughters were safely in the hands of experienced women.[58] Their *in loco parentis* approach emphasized guidance, counseling, supervision and, as a last resort, expulsion, more than courts-martial and prison sentences.[59] They were inclined to manage couplings between women soldiers and between women officers within these college traditions. Training instructors told each WAC officer candidate that it was her duty to win the confidence of women engaged in lesbian relationships so that they and the officer in charge could solve any problems by bringing them "out into the light, admitted, and laid open for discussion." [60]

In addition to offering personal guidance, WAC officers were instructed to make environmental adjustments to prevent trainees from forming homosexual relationships. To combat loneliness and boredom, commanding officers were told to give trainees "opportunities of wholesome and natural companionship with men" and to keep them busy with a "well-filled, active, and interesting life." To make living conditions more "unfavorable to the development of homosexuality," they were told to maximize supervision and minimize privacy. "Barrack life on the whole reduces the opportunity for such indulgence" because women were rarely left alone, while housing women in small groups or in pairs, especially in "hotel rooms with fewer occupants," only encouraged homosexual relationships. To keep curiosity under control, officers were told to "minimize as much as possible any talk regarding homosexuality" since it "may prove to be conducive to the very curiosity which may serve as a cause." If an officer suspected that two women had become lovers, she could discreetly shift the rooms of many women or transfer them to different assignments so that the couple was split up without being specifically targeted.[61]

An extraordinary aspect of WAC policy was that it specifically advised officers to try to mold the lesbian desires of Wacs into qualities that made better soldiers. Such advice grew out of psychiatrists' attempts to apply their concepts of transference and sublimation to the interpersonal dynamics of military life. Trainees who had "potential homosexual tendencies" could be "deterred from active participation" in sexual relations by encouraging them to sublimate their desires into a " 'hero-worship' type of reaction." Lesbian tendencies, WAC officers were told, if rechanneled into admiration for a woman officer, could sometimes motivate a trainee to become an exemplary soldier. An officer, "by the strength of her influence," could "bring out in the woman who had previously exhibited homosexual tendencies a definite type of leadership which can then be guided into normal fields of expression, making her a valued member of the corps." [62] This advice stood in stark contrast to the military's official position that homosexuals threatened morale and discipline, and was the most radical aspect of the newly emerging therapeutic approach toward managing homosexuality in the military environment.

The proponents of this approach also redefined as a psychological problem a soldier's intolerance toward homosexuals. Many military psychiatrists believed that extreme antihomosexual hostility had its origins in repressed homosexual desires, that it was unhealthy and disruptive, and that it was controllable through education and counseling. "One can suspect," wrote Menninger about this problem, "that those who denounce adult homosexual individuals with feelings of great hostility may very possibly be overreacting to their own unconscious wishes in that direction." [63] This position portrayed male and female soldiers who tolerated "well-adjusted" homosexuals as emotionally secure themselves and indirectly challenged officers who believed that hostility toward homosexuals was a desirable trait of character for the soldier.

The handbook *Psychology for the Fighting Man* included one of the strongest wartime statements promoting tolerance toward gay GIs. Its authors informed the "fighting man" that, despite Selective Service screening, some homosexuals had been admitted into the Army and had become good soldiers. These men had "no feelings of inferiority or shame" or "mental conflict" over their homosexuality, and "readily apply their interest and energy to the tasks of army life. If they are content with quietly seeking the satisfaction of their sexual needs with others of their own kind, their perversion may continue to go unnoticed and they may even become excellent soldiers." The authors drew the line of intolerance not around these men, but more narrowly around the soldier "who forces his attentions upon normal men." [64] This precise definition of the problem-homosexual enabled some mental health professionals to support the military's antihomosexual policies in principle while promoting the integration of most gay soldiers, so long as sufficient guidance and supervision were available and the other men were taught how to accept their gay peers.

Trainees usually learned on their own how to put up with one another's differences in order to get through the rigors of basic training. They did hear pleas for tolerance not only from psychiatrists but from the war propaganda they were exposed to every day. Political speeches, editorials, war posters, Hollywood films, and other public media called for unity and portrayed American soldiers as defending the ideals of democracy, equality, and freedom against the totalitarian Axis enemies.

Newspapers published soldiers' stories about how they had learned in the "melting pot" of the barracks that tolerance was the great lesson of the war. It was "essential to democracy," wrote an Army major in the *New York Times*. "It is the realization of our dependence upon every man in the team, whether we like him or not. . . . In the armed forces [the average man] has for daily companions all the characters of life's drama."[65] But inspired more by necessity than idealism, male trainees responded to the demands of basic training by developing their own pragmatic ethic of tolerance: "I won't bother you if you don't bother me."

Trainees could extend this live-and-let-live attitude even to their gay company-mates. Some gay GIs certainly were harassed and abused by their fellow soldiers, but the more common experience of gay GIs was of uneasy acceptance unless they aggressively pursued uninterested men.[66] "It was the first time I really was away from my family at home," recalled Robert Fleischer of his first days as a teenage recruit at Fort Dix. "I was both frightened and lonely, and all these guys looked like they were going to sock you right in the face. But of course they weren't—they were feeling the same emotions I was feeling." Fleischer and many other gay veterans recall that they "got more flak" for being New Yorkers, Southerners, Jews, or blacks than for being gay. Cartoonist Bill Mauldin's amoralistic attitude toward drinking and sex in the Army infantry reflected the same hard-boiled tolerance that many soldiers could feel toward gay GIs. It "is not a question of should or shouldn't in the Army," Mauldin wrote in 1945. "It's here to stay and it seems to us here that the best way to handle it is to understand and recognize it, and to arrange things so those who have appetites can satisfy them with a minimum of trouble for everybody."[67] The culture of basic training, with its emphasis on team work and group solidarity, discouraged troublemakers from spreading rumors that could send a fellow GI to prison and reflect badly on every other man and officer in his company.[68] This constraint on making trouble created a tense atmosphere in the barracks in which soldiers put up with each other so long as everyone played by the rules.

Male trainees tried to make peace in the barracks by creating places for themselves and others who were different. Nearly everyone could represent a particular "type," be tagged with a nickname and assigned a particular social role.[69] Common types included Sad Sack, Junior, Goldbricker, Joker, Egghead, and Dumb Cluck. Nicknames attached to feminine roles included Softie, Sister, and, more affectionately, Pinup Girl.[70] "I was very, very much aware that I was unathletic," recalled

Hank Vilas. "I remember once in grenade practice it fell on my toe. So I kind of reacted to that by being the company mascot. The only thing I could do was laugh about it, which I did, and I was reasonably well-liked." [71] The men also invented rituals for making stubborn nonconformists fit in, such as scrubbing down with a heavy brush the man who never took a shower. The game of "homosexual buffoonery" was another ritual in which men in an outfit identified particular homosexual roles and set their own rules for who would fit in. If both gay and effeminate men played the game—found their places and stayed there or carefully bent the rules—they had a good chance of getting along with the other men.

Gay soldiers invented their own double-duty roles which they played not only to fit in socially but also to create sexual opportunities for themselves. "I consider myself quite an actor," wrote Jerry Watson, who served as an infantryman, to a gay friend in 1944. "I have not two personalities, but many. I can act the young, friendly, palsy walsy kid . . . who would not object to perverse advances made by my buddies . . . , or I can be the quiet, thoughtful individual, with . . . closed mouth (sometimes very necessary) with sad, or mysterious eyes, and sometimes with a twinkle, or the scholar, interested in nothing but the consuming of book material and the like, or the flippant ageless fairy, tho with some dignity and reserve. Then again, I can be the sportsman, who usually commits himself to perversity if the conditions warrant, or the young man who seems to be like the others in his crowd, drinking jammily, and ending up the party with more liquer [*sic*] at someone's country retreat. Well, they all center around the great nucleus of pleasure." [72] These roles—the kid, the introvert, the bookworm, the fairy, the good sport, and the party drunk—were built around effeminate or affectionate qualities and could both suggest and mask the player's sexual interest as well as protect potential sexual partners from perceiving themselves as queer.

Many effeminate GIs were surprised to discover that they, too, could find a place for themselves in military life. Feminine styles in male barracks were rich and varied. The most extreme effeminate stereotype was the recruit who assumed the lisping speech and mincing or swishy mannerisms of a "fairy"—soldiers called these men "pantywaists," "sissies," or "a bit lacy." [73] A recruit who was more mildly effeminate could be bookish, artistic, spoiled, delicate, a "mama's boy," fastidious, unathletic, devoutly religious, sentimental, or merely a "soft-handed white collar worker from New York City." [74] Even the most extremely effeminate man could be accepted affectionately if he played an asexual role. Vaudeville and Hollywood had developed a variety of characters in comic effeminate roles, played by such well-loved actors as Bert Lahr, Grady Sutton, Edward Everett Horton, and Franklin Pangborn. These "professional sissies" were delightful and lovable comedians whose wit and charm won the hearts of other characters as well as their audiences.[75] In the barracks, and particularly during soldier variety shows, men with the most extreme effeminate qualities—especially if they were witty and funny—could be similarly valued as company comedians, clowns, screwballs, and entertainers.

Less extremely effeminate men could be accepted in roles such as the company egghead, poet, artist, or mascot. When soldiers put out their own newsletters, "soft-handed" men with typing skills became an asset. All soldiers were forced to perform some traditionally feminine jobs including housekeeping, sewing, kitchen duty, and other work that gay men were expected to be good at.[76] As a result, officers could interpret some effeminate behavior as exemplary for a soldier. "After inspecting his enlisted men's quarters," noted an Army NCO, "an officer praised an extremely effeminate G.I. who took delight in the meticulous arrangement of his belongings as 'the best damned soldier in the outfit.' "[77] The more an effeminate trainee integrated himself into the group in useful ways, the easier it was for the other men to like him and to ignore any evidence that he might be queer. Effeminate men could be "uneasily tolerated," in the words of gay World War II veteran John Horne Burns, "so long as they made the gesture of masculinity."[78]

To fit in, many men figured out ways to change their behavior and appearance. Some merely put a check on any telltale signs. When Maynard Smith was assigned as personal secretary to the recruiting service district commander in downtown Columbus, Ohio, a gay man he was billeted with came up to him one day and said, "You're gay, aren't you?" "I looked around quickly—just absolutely shocked!" Smith recalled. "How do you know?" Smith insisted. "It's the way you behave," was the reply, "and the way you move your hands and the way you lift your eyes to heaven periodically." "Well," Smith concluded, "thank you. I won't do that again." Others decided to learn how to be more masculine. Two weeks into boot camp, Tony Isaac was being called a sissy and a fruit. At first not knowing what to do, he finally "picked the roughest, toughest guy . . . and started copying everything he did. I even held my cigarette the same way. When he spit, I spit."[79]

When effeminate gay men could not or would not pass as masculine, the other recruits might either ostracize and taunt them from the first day of basic training or tolerate them and sometimes even enjoy their presence. Jerry Watson, a twenty-eight-year-old gay soldier stationed at an Army base in Arizona, in 1943 wrote to a gay civilian friend about how he and his "swishy" buddy were treated in their company. "She does the bump on the street corners," Watson wrote, "powders her ass and applies perfume in her barracks—and tells anyone who makes comment to kiss her ass—throws her ass around in the taverns, and rolls her eyes and gestures like mad. ['She'] and I are both called 'girls' and 'dear' in our Company," Watson added, "and appear to get along splendidly with everyone." [80] By contrast, William Johnson recalled that in the barracks at Tuskegee Army Air Field the "punks" were "constantly looked upon askance" by the other men. Howard Taylor, who considered himself "effeminate in gestures and speech" and "attracted to men," also was rejected by his fellow trainees in basic training in Texas, where he "was immediately sized up as a fairy." The other men, he wrote in 1944, "can make life one miserable hell with their jibes and taunts and petty persecutions." When Taylor was transferred to a camp in Missouri and became mail clerk, the others nicknamed him "the little mother of the males" and made him the object of their flirtations. "Because I'm mail clerk," he wrote, "they come around me, cooing and winking their large innocent eyes, flexing their muscles, and smiling those tantalizing brilliant smiles." Taylor was both insulted and intrigued by the other men's ambivalent attentions. [81]

To protect themselves from ridicule or ostracism, gay trainees could band together into little cliques that, when the other men caught on, could also be labeled with nicknames. Ben Small recalled that in his Army Air Corps company, gay trainees "kind of migrated to other gays in the barracks, and sometimes it would be referred to as the 'fruit corner' or the 'fruit salad' or something like that." But the men assigned these nicknames with good humor and not "with much violent intent," Small explained. In some barracks gay cliques coexisted with other cliques such as the intellectual or college crowd, the literary clique, the news addicts, the sports fans, the farm boys, and the men from the same region or city. [82] Cliques gave lonely trainees a chance to belong to their own group of like-minded friends—a home away from home.

In the women's branches the social role most visibly identified as lesbian was that of the butch. Wacs recognized butches by their masculine appearance; butches, in turn, displayed particular masculine traits to declare themselves to other women. At Fort Oglethorpe, according to one WAC private, a "mannish haircut" was "considered the thing to do if you were out to attract another girl." [83] Butches presented themselves "by the manner of wearing the clothing, by posture, by stride, by seeking 'to date' other girls such as a man would, and when with other girls pay all the bills and be solicitous and otherwise conduct themselves as normally as a man would with a woman.'' [84] Wacs also identified the butches among them by the way they walked, talked, smoked their cigarettes, drank out of beer bottles, and jealously guarded their girlfriends.[85] Before the WAAC became part of the Army in July 1943, women were not yet required to wear uniforms at all times, so that butch Waacs were able to wear civilian men's clothes off-base and even pass as men.[86] As an important part of lesbian culture, however, the butch role could isolate a woman from those who didn't want to associate with lesbians and could identify her as lesbian to the authorities.

Butch women occupied a higher social status in basic training than did effeminate men, although each could be stigmatized as sexually queer. Effeminate men were not powerless, but they generally were teased, tolerated, or protected by the other men. Butches were more likely to take charge, to be the protectors, teachers, and even leaders and NCOs of a unit. Sissies could be taunted and made to feel incompetent in a military environment; butches could be the objects of hero worship and were expected to know how to function well in a man's world. The day that Pat Bond arrived at Fort Oglethorpe for her basic training in 1945, she noticed that the butches felt right at home. "We went in the mess hall," she recalled, "and there were all these dykes sitting around with their feet up on the table in fatigues with Li'l Abner boots saying [in a deep voice] 'Hey Henry, pass the salt!' " The gay cliques in women's units were often organized around butches and their girlfriends.[87]

Despite the efforts of government propagandists to portray women soldiers as completely feminine, the women's branches developed a masculine milieu that helped butches fit in. "For some reason the army attracts gay women," Pat Bond recalled. "Then I thought it was because of the uniform. We wore what amounted to a men's uniform except we wore a skirt. We wore a tie, and we wore the Eisenhower jacket. And your hair had to be off your collar—it had to be that short." Military uniforms actually could make feminine women seem out of place. "There comes a time," commented two naval officers, "when every woman likes to be appealing and 'devastating,' but it is a little difficult to achieve in a man's shirt and tie and a two-piece suit!" [88] The nicknames women soldiers gave each other often were tomboyish or outright dykeish— Tommie, Junior, Brat, Spike, Slugger, Detail, Mike, and Butch.[89] WAVES trainees at Hunter College even nicknamed Capt. Mildred McAfee the "Old Man," after the traditional Navy nickname for the ship's captain, or just "Miss Mac," while Wacs nicknamed their sergeants "Simon Legree." [90] WAVES trainees were rated as "apprentice seamen" and could achieve ratings such as radioman, yeoman, mailman, and laundryman.[91] Popular jokes and cartoons played on the theme that women soldiers were masculine. "The C.O. of the Waves at Smith College," went one joke in *Stars and Stripes*, "is allowing the gals to drink while off duty . . . provided 'they drink like gentlemen.' " [92] Butch women could find a place for themselves in this masculine milieu where they were at least tolerated and at most revered by other women. The limits of tolerance toward butch women were tested not so much by their masculinity as by their real or alleged sexual activities with other women, especially when antilesbian rumors were in the air.

At the same time that men and women struggled to fit in to the social world of basic training, classification officers had to find places for them in the military organization. When officers believed that a male or female trainee was gay, they could try to make them fit in by channeling them into particular duties, associating jobs with people whose personalities, interests, skills, and mannerisms fit popular notions of what it meant to be queer. People assigned to these jobs usually crossed traditional gender boundaries—women who did masculine work and men who did feminine work. Ironically, the informal process of segregating gay men and women into "gay" duties—a process that included both assignment and self-selection—not only integrated them as homosexuals more deeply into the military organization but also helped them to develop their own work cultures as gay soldiers and officers.

During World War II, medical officers began to generalize about what special talents they believed gay male soldiers possessed and what job classifications typically included them. "In the military," wrote two Navy doctors who studied gay patients on their psychiatric ward, "we find homosexuals in the capacities of hospital corpsmen, yeomen and chaplain's assistants" and in civilian life "in such occupations as beautician, music teacher, actor, bookkeeper, etc." [93] Lt. Col. Lewis Loeser, who supervised a study of 270 homosexual patients at the 36th Station Hospital in England, similarly concluded that these men had "considerable talent in stenographic, musical, clerical and special service [entertainment] activities." Homosexual officers and enlisted men, he believed, were also "lacking in temperament and skills necessary to the combat soldier." [94] Military duties such as clerks, yeomen, court stenographers, pharmacist's mates, medics, hospital corpsmen, chaplain's assistants, chauffeurs, Special Services personnel, female impersonators, and "camoufleurs" (those who designed camouflage) were generally believed to include a disproportionately large number of gay men. These jobs were noncombative and either traditionally done by women, artistically self-expressive, or involved personal service to other men.

Effeminate gay men, butch lesbians, and others assigned to cross-gendered jobs did not represent the majority of gay male and lesbian GIs—they were merely the most visible. Heterosexual personnel certainly served in these capacities while gay personnel served in a wide range of other duties. Gay men served as chaplains, construction engineers, radiomen, tank drivers, transport airmen, air navigators, cannoneers, pilots, airplane engine mechanics, psychologists, doctors, assistant adjutants, and recruiters. Many also served in combat on land and at sea. A 1945 study of 183 homosexual servicemen concluded that these men's jobs "varied a good deal, covering many phases of wartime activity from that of gunnery officer aboard a destroyer, or air combat intelligence work, to labor relations work in factories making munitions. Some individuals were in the most active part of the fighting fronts, several did their whole service in the United States." [95] Similarly, lesbian personnel served in the traditionally feminine jobs to which most military women were assigned.

Classification officers were supposed to base all job assignments on personnel needs. Male trainees had experience in eight thousand civilian jobs yet had to be assigned to only eight hundred job classifications in the military, the most important of which was combat soldier. Classification officers only secondarily took into account each recruit's civilian work experience, scores on standardized aptitude tests, personality traits or interests.[96] Yet "deliberately or not," classification officers did develop makeshift procedures for differentiating homosexuals and selecting them for particular duties.[97] Recruits whose interests, skills, and mannerisms reflected popular gay stereotypes—men who were male secretaries or nurses and women with short haircuts who wore slacks and drove trucks—were prime candidates for assignment to those duties associated with homosexuals. Gay men and lesbians could sometimes select these assignments for themselves by appearing to be gay or, when possible, by signing up for training courses in these jobs, hoping to be more comfortably surrounded by sympathetic rather than hostile coworkers. In this way the military's job classification process, despite its inefficiency in matching civilian experience with military duties, reproduced and institutionalized popular notions of homosexual work.

Some of the service duties considered appropriate for gay male GIs were those into which black male soldiers were channeled as well.

To release white soldiers for combat, the Army and Navy assigned black men to two areas of noncombat work: heavy labor duties such as those in construction, engineer, ordnance, and truck maintenance units, and service duties such as being cooks and bakers, hospital and mess attendants, and supply and office clerks.[98] The stereotypically feminine domestic and service duties were the jobs into which classification officers sometimes channeled black GIs who seemed to be gay or effeminate.

Because the United States military services had always been male domains, the women's branches themselves, especially the more masculine WAC and Women Marines, gained reputations as havens for lesbians. Women who enlisted in the military faced a public perception that they might be "dykes." Government propaganda addressed these stereotypes only indirectly by emphasizing the feminine heterosexuality of female soldiers. But officers in the women's branches more directly tried to control behavior that the public could perceive to be lesbian. In 1943 the handbook for Waacs at Fort Des Moines warned that "dancing together in public places in uniform" and wearing "mannish haircuts" were both "taboo." Betty Somers reported that during Women Marines basic training in 1944 at Camp LeJeune, her commanding officer ordered her to change her masculine-looking upsweep hairdo to a permanent to "make sure our hair was feminine." After basic, however, especially when women were assigned to specialized duties, these initial antimasculine restrictions could be relaxed. "We got sideburns shaved over the ears, my dear," recalled Pat Bond. "We really carried on!"[99]

Because female soldiers were a novelty in the United States, the press, psychiatrists, and other observers monitored their work performance, often commenting on the masculinity or femininity of their jobs. In 1945 a group of Marine Corps medical officers described the most feminine assignments in the Women Marines as "clerks, secretaries, storekeepers, salespersons, bookkeepers and receptionists" and the most masculine assignments as "plumbers, welders, mechanics, carpenters, parachute riggers, truck drivers, chauffeurs, guards, radio operators, electricians, plane dispatchers [and] signalmen."[100] Despite the popular belief that women soldiers were masculine, only a minority of women in the military actually were allowed to serve in these traditionally masculine jobs.[101] Black Wacs generally found themselves excluded from technical and clerical work and assigned instead to kitchen, housekeeping, and laundry duties.

Military jobs that were popularly tagged as lesbian included the unmarried career officer, the tough sergeant, and the physical training instructor—especially those assigned to permanent training cadres. With no history of women officers to draw on, administrators who selected the first WAAC officers looked for the same qualities, including strong voices and an aggressive manner, that made good male officers.[102] But when some WAAC officers, using male drill instructors as their models, became known for their rough language and hostile attitudes toward trainees, Colonel Hobby tried to intervene. "It seems to me lately," she told a group of WAC officers in December 1943, "that I have seen too many women officers who are hard. The last thing we want to accomplish is to masculinize a great group of women." [103] Tough drill instructors, physical training instructors—women who had been civilian gym teachers—and WAC sergeants also were often tagged as lesbian because of their masculine roles. *Yank* described a WAAC first sergeant stationed in North Africa as "a former physical ed instructor" who "clips her hair short and wears pants." [104] "My commanding officer was Minnie the gym teacher," recalled Pat Bond. "She had a man's haircut, the whole thing. In fact when she'd check the barracks at night, the women would scream—they thought a man was loose." [105]

But the women who were thought most likely to be lesbian were the motor vehicle operators and mechanics—the truck drivers and grease monkeys. Motor transport school was the most popular specialist course in training centers and was one of the few "masculine" duties open to black women.[106] At Fort Des Moines, WAC motor corps trainees learned maintenance, repairs, lubrication, convoy operation, vehicle recovery, and blackout driving.[107] They had the highest morale, while those in the traditionally feminine cooks' courses had the lowest. The motor vehicle operators' course, explained a psychiatrist at Fort Des Moines, "is a masculine type of occupation and probably goes furthest in fulfilling the needs of those women who enlist in the army through a strong motivation of masculine identification." [108] Women drivers had excellent safety records and were eager to operate heavy trucks and even army tanks.[109] At Fort Sill, Oklahoma, a male sergeant put a WAAC driver on a ten-ton truck to "take some of the ego out of her." "Well," he told a *Yank* correspondent, "she took that man-killer out on our torture course, as we call the driving range, and shoved it around like a baby carriage." [110] The commanding officer of a motor transport company at Fort Oglethorpe testified that the women in her group were frequently accused of being lesbian "because they wear coveralls." [111] Their "masculine uniforms, appearance, and mannerisms," explained the psychiatrist at Fort Des Moines, encouraged the further "development of marked masculine traits," all of which led to "unwarranted criticism of the women drivers." [112]

Such a powerful stereotype drew even more lesbians to the motor vehicle groups and helped to socialize them as butches. Betty Somers was impressed by the number of lesbians assigned to the motor vehicle unit on the Marine Corps base at Cherry Point, North Carolina—women she described as "butchy-acting and smoking with the cupped hand and drinking the beer from the bottle and short haircuts." The resident counselor at the Fort Oglethorpe Training Center observed that women tended to become more butch after their assignment to the motor corps. One such Wac who had been accused of being the "aggressor" in a relationship with another Wac had "cut her hair short" on entering the motor transport company. The counselor advised this "boyish-appearing girl" to let her hair grow long and not to "lie down on the bed with anyone." [113]

One of the most common military duties that could label a man as gay was that of the male secretary, typist, or stenographer. As the rapidly expanding bureaucracy of the "paper" Army and Navy demanded greater numbers of both male and female clerical workers, these jobs became essential to the war effort. By 1944, 35 percent of Army personnel were assigned to clerical duties. Military officials had lobbied Congress to establish women's branches so that women could take over these duties, but because women made up only 2 percent of the armed forces, the need for male clerical workers remained great. [114] Men who did office work were called "clerks" in the Army and "yeomen" in the Navy. Clerks had low status in the military bureaucracy, but they could be promoted to positions as section heads in which they supervised whole office staffs. They were well aware that they were doing "women's work," especially when they saw women replacing other male clerks to free them for combat. Soldier slang gave these men feminine nicknames such as Cluck (connoting a hen), Dolly Dancer (a soldier on office duty who especially catered to officers), Gertrude, and, of course, "yeomanette." [115]

Gay male recruits who had been civilian typists and secretaries quickly learned how much the military needed their skills. Officers even bent the rules to put these men to work immediately. When Charles Rowland, who was drafted in late 1942, was still standing in line with other naked men at the induction station in Phoenix, a noncom asked if any of them typed and Rowland replied that he was a fast typist. "They pulled me out of the line," he recalled. "There was this desperate need, because the Army ran on typewriters and mimeograph machines in those days. So before I even had basic training, I was given a job as a typist."

Another "gay" job was that of the chaplain's assistants. These enlisted men, in the words of one former chaplain's assistant, were "gentlemen's gentlemen"—clerks with musical training who aided the chaplain and helped to maintain the morale and welfare of the men. Writing letters home, listening to other men's troubles, organizing soldier shows, setting up for church services, directing the choir, and playing the organ were some of their duties.[116] The civilian counterparts to this job were the church organist, the choir director and the music teacher. "You name one, you got 'em all," recalled Chuck Tarrance, who served as an Army chaplain on Angel Island in San Francisco. "It's the stereotype, but I think a very true stereotype. Out of all the chaplain's assistants I knew, I can't think of one that I don't think now is gay." Chaplains, however, were not similarly labeled. Those not Catholic were usually married and the moral teachings of their faiths were traditionally antihomosexual.

Civilian male nurses who served as hospital corpsmen and pharmacist's mates also were thought to be gay. The Army and Navy used these men in specialized areas such as venereal disease, genitourinary and psychiatric nursing as well as on battleships and other combat situations where women were excluded. But because the nursing profession had been traditionally female, "men nurses," as they preferred to be called, were often stigmatized as sissies who were attracted to women's work. As a civilian vocation for men, nursing had low status and little prestige. In addition, nursing involved the physical care of men and had sexual overtones for both male and female nurses. The *Stars and Stripes* ran a news story about a pharmacist's mate who was "yoo-hooed" by the other men and gay male nurses and pharmacist's mates appeared as stereotyped characters in war novels after the war.[117]

The Army and Navy each had differing policies toward the male nurses in their ranks. The Navy, ignoring the popular belief that these men were queer, allowed them to enlist as nurses and gave them the same commissioned rank and pay as women in the Nurse Corps. The Navy actively recruited male nurses in the pages of the *American Journal of Nursing* and at nursing conventions. "Your sphere of service with the armed forces is of major importance," an officer from the Navy Bureau of Medicine and Surgery told a 1942 forum of male nurses in New York City.[118] The Navy's wartime policy, in fact, chipped away at the negative stereotype of male nurses and helped to raise their status in civilian life after the war. By contrast, Army policy strongly reinforced the popular stigma against these men. The Army assigned male nurses to duties other than nursing or placed them at the bottom of a two-tier nursing system based on gender. Unlike nurses who were women, male nurses were not commissioned and could not even date their female colleagues because of differences in rank.

Male trainees had mixed feelings toward the "gay" duties available to them in the military. Those who didn't want to be identified as queer could try to avoid them. When in 1942 novelist John Cheever was stationed at Camp Gordon, Georgia, he was offered a promotion to corporal as a chaplain's assistant but turned it down because, he wrote to his wife, "the captain offered it to me with a leer." [119] Other trainees wondered if their assignment to these jobs meant that their officers suspected that they were gay. "I have no question in my mind," recalled Martin Stow, who served in an infantry rifle company in Louisiana, "that somebody along the way said, 'Stow is probably gay. What are we going to do with him? Thank God he has all the qualifications to be a chaplain's assistant.' " Still other trainees deliberately pursued these jobs because they already had the skills or wanted to work in the company of other gay men. Frank Jacober applied for the chaplain's assistant position because he had studied music in school and had played piano in a gay bar before entering the Army. Male nurses were the most organized as a group in actively seeking out such military assignments. By 1940 more than eight thousand civilian men had graduated from nursing schools as registered nurses. "Men nurses expect to assume their part of the country's defense with the rest of the men," wrote a male RN shortly after the attack on Pearl Harbor. Responding to their country's need for their professional skills, some even tried to enlist in the Army or Navy Nurse Corps but were rejected because Congress had restricted these services to women. [120]

Trainees who were assigned to these stereotyped duties, whether or not they were gay, often developed styles and attitudes on the job that were associated with homosexuals. David Schneider, a young soldier who went on to become an eminent anthropologist of American culture, was a keen participant observer of GI work culture. Among Army office clerks, he wrote after the war, "there is no special imperative toward masculine behavior as there is with the line soldier." The clerical soldier was more concerned with preserving his status in the office with his eye on promotion. Clerks expressed their aggression toward those who got undeserved promotions not with physical fights but by using more "circumscribed, circuitous modes": the "disarming smile," the double-entendre joke, the "fantastic, ritual exchange of carefully camouflaged knife thrusts." The "a-sexual character" of Army clerk culture, moreover, carried with it "threats of homosexuality" that left clerks vulnerable to stigmatization by men in more masculine duties. They responded to this stigma by deriving power not from physical aggression but from the bureaucracy itself, authoritatively quoting the "minutae and esoterica" of military regulations to put those who needed their services in their place.[121] These defensive postures reinforced the stereotype of gay male office clerks as bitchy, patronizing, and pompous when dealing with the public.

Gay soldiers in training for such duties could develop a camaraderie with each other that they often couldn't find in basic training or in other specialized jobs. After completing boot camp, Maxwell Gordon was assigned to yeoman school at the San Diego Naval Training Station. "Here's all these interesting people from all over the United States," he recalled. "There were some teachers and some clerks and office workers. For the most part they were rather 'sensitive' boys. . . . I thought, 'Oh, these are more my kind of people. You know, we can communicate.' " All the student yeomen were assigned to the same company and barracks. "It was simply accepted," Gordon continued, "that there were certain people who paired off. . . . We became very chummy, quite close, very fraternal, very protective of each other." On the job this camaraderie could become more covert unless all the men were gay. Because Charles Rowland and most of the other clerks assigned to the induction station at Fort Snelling, Minnesota, were gay, they dubbed their office the "Seduction Station." But when others were around, Rowland recalled, the gay clerks related to each other "pretty carefully." When a new gay man was assigned to the office, "you'd recognize each other by a glance, maybe a smile and then that was it. You had established the fact that you knew each other and you knew what you knew."

The nature of these duties allowed effeminate gay men to express themselves in ways that would have seemed out of place in other lines of work. Twenty-two-year-old "S.R.C.," a gay chaplain's assistant with an "effeminacy of bearing, speech and mannerisms," was, according to a Navy psychiatrist's report, "a sincere, conscientious worker" who had maintained "an excellent record" and was "well-adjusted to military life." Despite his effeminacy, "S.R.C." had "acquired the respect of all who came in contact with him. In addition, he taught music to members of officers' families on the military base, and was highly regarded as to his character and musical ability." [122] Effeminate servicemen who had indispensable skills, higher rank, or friends at the top had the freedom to be the most outrageous on the job. "I remember the mimeograph operator," Charles Rowland recalled. "he was a kind of queen. He was in complete charge of the mimeograph operation for this whole [induction station] complex. And he was a swishy bitch, but got away with it because of his rank and because of his position." "G.B.G.," a black Army private who was obviously effeminate and wore makeup and perfume off base, was never harassed in his various duties as hospital ward attendant, assistant clerk in an engineer outfit, and supply clerk in a quartermaster battalion.[123]

Although stereotyped work could offer gay soldiers a degree of safety from harassment and promised them the company of others like themselves, it also could broadcast to hostile men that one might be gay. Maxwell Gordon recalled that at the San Diego Naval Training Station he and the other yeoman trainees "would march in formation to school, and of course being yeomen there was a little whistling and so forth. The other companies, they would pass remarks about us being sissy or something because yeomen had a reputation." Men in these jobs sometimes tried to protect themselves from public ridicule by sticking together or becoming indispensable.

Male nurses in the Army went even further and as a group organized to overturn the Army's discriminatory policies against them, frequently portraying themselves as a minority group fighting for equal rights. They protested as individuals and through their professional organizations to Congress, President Roosevelt, Eleanor Roosevelt, and the surgeons general. They asked to be admitted to the Nurse Corps and, when drafted, to be awarded the "rank and pay equal to that awarded our women co-workers" and to be assigned to duties as nurses. They received support from the major nurses' and medical associations, public health officials and members of Congress. In 1943 a bill was introduced in Congress to give male nurses temporary commissioned status in the Army for the duration of the war, but was defeated in the Senate. In their letters of protest, some nurses tried to defend their profession by rejecting the stereotype that they were sissies or queers. "Men nurses are not what they used to be," wrote the administrator of a school for male nurses, "but highly trained Professional Men of good Character." [124] "It isn't a sissy job," wrote another nurse serving as a corporal in Iran. "There are many of us men in the army who have taken this training and are proud of it. . . . Why can't we be given equal rank with our present nurses?" [125] Despite these protests, the Army did not change its policy toward male nurses because, the deputy surgeon general claimed, male nurses, if commissioned, could not "without incongruity" do the menial nursing tasks that women were used to doing "by reason of their sex." [126]

Military authorities, fearing public accusations that they condoned or tolerated homosexuality, resisted any public acknowledgment that the armed forces relied on gay personnel or that GIs had anything but "loathing and utter contempt" for their gay peers.[127] Nevertheless, the gay men and women who passed through the military's gates during the war discovered, sometimes to their surprise, that they did have a place in the military. Most may have fit in by passing as heterosexual, but even those who didn't pass found ways to become part of both barracks life and the military organization. They learned how to play the games that enabled them to coexist with other trainees, and they figured out their own ways to cope with the homosexual tensions that everyone faced during basic and specialized training.

At the same time, psychiatrists offered military officials new ways to manage the homosexual dynamics of military life without eliminating homosexuals—through education, guidance, and supervision. Classification officers under pressure to use all available personnel assigned some gay men and lesbians to stereotyped duties where they were tolerated, relied on, and even enjoyed. This unofficial patchwork system for integrating gay male and lesbian trainees, fueled by their desire to contribute to the war effort and fit in, evolved during the war because it served more than threatened military efficiency.

CHAPTER
3

GI Drag
A Gay Refuge

In May 1943, toward the end of his basic training at Camp Hulen, Texas, where he was attached to the 473rd Antiaircraft Artillery (Automatic Weapons) Battalion, Robert Fleischer tried to persuade his commanding officer to approve an all-soldier variety show. "A lot of the guys from the theater world in New York were in the outfit," Fleischer recalled, "and we decided to write our own musical comedy. You had to get permission to do it, and the colonel decided we could. So we titled our show, *The Colonel Wants a Show.*" Fleischer's civilian experience as a fashion designer in Manhattan came in handy at Camp Hulen. "There wasn't a woman in the show," he explained. "We made all our own costumes and sets." Some of the fellows decided to do female impersonation routines, and Fleischer became the star. "I had never been in drag in my life before, but I was Carmen Miranda incarnate! They called me 'Carmelita Ack-Ack,' because the artillery sounds like *ack-ack*. We were a smash! The place fell apart. I was doing sambas in this really outlandish costume of red, yellow, and green beads and some fabric and I had fruit piled on my head. That must have happened in every camp in America!"

From Broadway to Guadalcanal, on the backs of trucks, makeshift platforms, and elegant theater stages, American GIs did put on all-male shows for each other that almost always featured female impersonation routines. Generally overshadowed in histories of the war by coverage of the USO shows and their more famous stars, these shows produced by and for soldiers were as vital to the war effort, incidentally providing gay male GIs with a temporary refuge where they could let their hair down to entertain their fellows. Like Robert Fleischer, gay servicemen signed up as actors and helped shape the military's zany, topsy-turvy world of outrageous drag costumes and witty repartee. They sometimes integrated their gay culture into military life through these shows, bringing it onto center stage in disguise. Military officials used soldier shows and drag routines for their own purposes—to boost soldier morale by allowing soldiers without women to entertain each other and affirm their heterosexuality. Once they had established their masculinity by becoming soldiers, men in these shows could enjoy the benefits of the same wartime relaxation of rigid gender roles that had allowed women to enter both industry and the military.

Soldiers who performed in drag, however, were not totally protected from insinuations that they might be queer. The popular belief that civilian female impersonators were effeminate homosexuals threatened to stigmatize these performers as well and worried their superiors. At a time when the military was beginning to identify and discharge homosexual personnel, officials did not want the public to think that, by sponsoring drag routines, they condoned effeminacy or homosexuality. From their side, gay GIs who performed in drag did not want to be exposed and thrown out of the service in disgrace. Because female impersonation seemed so vital to the war effort, however, soldier-entertainers and military officials, with the help of the press, found ways to use drag entertainment for the duration while walking a fine line between its homosexual and heterosexual meanings.

The impulse to put on shows and perform in dresses generally came from the men themselves—soldiers without women, as well as gay men, had long traditions of spontaneously dressing up in women's clothes.[1] But during World War II, military officials, pressured by GIs, their own morale personnel, and leaders in the civilian theater world to sponsor an organized soldier show campaign, found themselves not only tolerating makeshift drag but officially promoting female impersonation as well. In 1941 representatives from the National Theatre Conference persuaded Brigadier General Frederick Osborn, chief of the Army Special Services Branch, to set up a pilot soldier show program that would supplement the United Service Organizations (USO) camp shows.[2] Special Services was responsible for maintaining soldier morale and supervising recreation, entertainment, welfare, education, and athletics. Top Army administrators resisted at first, but by March 1942, after several trial shows, they finally conceded that soldier theatricals could be ''a necessity, not a frill'' and ''a useful form of discipline for the military mind.'' [3] The Army set up a school at Fort Meade, Maryland, to teach Special Services officers and theater specialists how to assist commanding officers in soldier entertainment. [4] The Navy, through its Welfare and Recreation Section, also sponsored sailor and Marine Corps shows, but these were fewer in number and less formally organized than in the Army. [5]

Given the green light from Washington early in 1942, Special Services personnel, with the cooperation of the American Red Cross and the USO, began to reproduce within the military a version of the civilian theater world. Special Services officers surveyed military records in search of soldiers with show business experience and held ''amateur nights,'' scouting for new talent. They also looked for various ''types'' in the barracks who could become performers, including soldiers who could play women's roles. The ''barracks jokester, the inveterate clown . . . has a special value for a soldier audience,'' noted a writer in *Theatre Arts* magazine. ''The astute director will recognize him as one of the several types that turn up with uncanny regularity in any cross section of enlisted men.'' [6] Special Services officers organized local soldier show workshops both stateside and overseas to train men in scriptwriting, costume and set design, stage managing, directing, ''the application of makeup for G.I. girls,'' and other theatrical skills. [7]

''Blueprint Specials'' were soldier show handbooks published and distributed by Army Special Services Headquarters that contained soldier show scripts, music, and lyrics; stage directions; and designs for sets and costumes, including dress patterns for drag routines. The Blueprint Special for the show *Hi, Yank!* had more than eight pages of dress patterns and illustrations for soldier drag, including instructions for making a ''G.I. showgirl'' gown out of a salvaged blanket and for making the bodice for a ballet tutu out of a GI ''T shirt dyed pink.'' It also mapped out the choreography for a dance sequence for male ballerinas in tutus. These patterns and instructions, explained the authors of one Blueprint Special, were among ''the basic ingredients for a homemade entertainment cake that GI Joes can bake for themselves.'' [8]

The most-famous Special Services theatrical production of World War II was Irving Berlin's all-soldier show, *This Is the Army*. It opened in 1942 on the Fourth of July to a standing-room-only crowd at the Broadway Theatre in New York City in an effort to raise money for the Army Emergency Relief Fund. An instant hit, the show soon became a Warner Brothers film starring Ronald Reagan and George Murphy; its songs—including ''I Left My Heart at the Stage Door Canteen'' and ''This Is the Army, Mr. Jones''—reached the hit parade, and its cast toured the United States, Europe, North Africa, and the Pacific. *This Is the Army* did much to promote the wartime image of Army and Navy drag performers as normal, masculine, combat-ready soldiers. It was "a golden opportunity," in the words of its soldier-director Ezra Stone, "to break down the strong national prejudice in civilian minds against using soldiers for soldier morale." [9]

This Is the Army became the prototypical World War II soldier show and established the three basic wartime styles of GI drag. These were the comic routines, chorus lines or "pony ballets" of husky men in dresses playing for laughs; the skilled "female" dancers or singers; and the illusionists or caricaturists, who did artistic and convincing impersonations of female stars. At least one of these styles played a central role in nearly every musical number in *TITA*, as the show was affectionately nicknamed by its cast and crew. A tenor in uniform sang longingly to "Eileen"—a man in a low-cut dress, makeup, wig, sheer stockings, and casual shoes. In deep, husky voices the burly men in "Ladies of the Chorus"—wearing identical blond wigs and Victorian dresses that displayed their hairy chests—burlesqued dainty women. Men in satin turbans, gowns, and shoulder-length gloves danced a Russian ballet. A zoot-suited black Harlemite teamed up with a black partner in a wig and low-cut dress to perform in a show-stopping tap-dance routine. "Hostesses" clad in short satin dresses, headbows, and slippers served soldiers breakfast in bed and read them bedtime stories before tucking them in at night. In the "Stage Door Canteen" sequence a chorus of hostesses in striped dresses, wigs, and Army boots danced and sang while other soldiers in drag impersonated female stars of the stage and screen.

Reviewers assessed each of *TITA*'s drag routines by its entertainment value, the performers' talents, and their patriotism, protecting the performers from any insinuations that they might be effeminate or homosexual. Reviewers generally agreed that the comic chorus lines—what *Newsweek* called the "traditional ensemble of husky, hairy-legged soldiers strategically padded as ladies of the chorus"—were the lowest form of female impersonation in *TITA*, because they required no skill and were single-joke acts. By contrast, the show's more refined "female" dancers—ironically, the most feminine—received accolades from the press for their dancing skills. The illusionists—whom the *Newsweek* reviewer called "satiric impersonat[or]s of the theater's royalty"—were as popular among the critics as the skilled dancers. The Stage Door Canteen in New York City, observed the *New York Post,* "is used as a background for a series of impersonations of Broadway's celebrities, some of them startlingly effective. Private Alan Manson's portrait of Jane Cowl acting as a stern House Mother while the Army boys flirt with the hostesses catches some of Miss Cowl's most fetching poses, while Private Tilestone Perry presents Lynn Fontanne in one of her most Valentina moods. . . . Private Julie Oshins has apparently studied Gypsy Rose Lee's strip-tease technique carefully. He is charmingly literary about it. . . .''

The reviewers' enthusiastic praise for the drag routines in *This Is the Army,* even for the striptease numbers, masked an underlying uneasiness, not directly discussed, about the homosexual implications of so many young men impersonating women and dancing with, embracing, and singing love songs to other men. Some reviewers responded to this uneasiness by playing along with the gag, celebrating the beauty and sex appeal of the ''women'' on the stage. The reviewer in *Variety* was pleased to discover that not all of the ''dames'' were ''pulchritudinous''— ''some of 'em shaped up as pretty good mice.'' The *Collier's* reporter called the ''gentlemen in gowns'' the ''most beautiful dames on Broadway'' and complained, in a tongue-in-cheek aside, about ''terrifying'' rumors that ''a dame must be dragged in'' for the film version. Other reviewers agreed that the men made good replacements for women, but they also expressed their relief at discovering that the drag routines were not upsetting. It ''has everything except girls,'' concluded a reviewer for the *New York Herald Tribune,* ''and the terrible truth is that you don't miss them.''

The female impersonation performances in *TITA* and other soldier shows as well as on civilian stages were open to a wide range of interpretations by both performers and audiences. On the surface, men in drag played only with the rigidity of gender roles. Spectators willingly pretended that these soldiers in drag were ''women,'' laughing at the clowns who made fun of the situation and standing in awe at the magic performed by the illusionists who appeared to be real women. Male reviewers and GIs in the audience comfortably talked about the sex appeal of the beautiful ''women'' on stage because they also liked looking at women in real life. When there was a joke, it was one-dimensional about gender—big husky men looked silly when they put on women's clothes. The explicit jokes, the magical illusion, the sex appeal, and the boy-girl couples could all seem familiar and reassuring to an audience, especially of men, for whom rigid gender roles and heterosexuality organized everyday life.

But a gay spectator or actor—including those in the cast of *This Is the Army* [10]—could read these same drag performances for their more implicit homosexual meanings. He could enjoy seeing—or being—

the real man in the dress kissing, dancing with, or singing love songs to other men and then enjoy the subsequent wealth of usually unintended double entendres, transforming every aspect of the performance into a homosexual subplot. When he knew there were other gay men in the cast or audience, with a wink or a knowing glance he could share his secret enjoyment with them, expanding his solitary appreciation into a group experience. In this way drag performances, wherever they were held, inadvertently opened up a social space in which gay men expanded their own secret culture. The joke was on the unaware members of the audience—a subplot about homosexuality was being created right before their eyes and they didn't even know it.

The potential for these two levels of meaning created tensions in nearly every drag performance—uneasiness among audiences that something was not right, and fear among gay performers that their ironic and covert innuendos would accidentally be exposed. What gay men called "camp" was in fact their own often risky exploration of these tensions. When drag performances served useful social purposes, as the soldier shows did during the war, then the sponsors and reviewers addressed the audience's uneasiness with reassurances that the performers were normal men and that the drag was just a show, being careful not to raise the specter of homosexuality by referring to it directly. But whenever drag performances became explicitly homosexual and undermined the audience's heterosexual assumptions—when performers impersonated queers or seemed queer themselves—then spectators sometimes became offended and hostile, reviewers attacked the show directly as obscene, authorities closed the show and arrested the actors, and, in the military, discharged the soldier-performers as homosexuals. Gay men's campy use of drag in public entertainment was fun when covert but dangerous when their private joke was exposed for all to see. As a result, gay men usually dressed up in drag only in the privacy of their homes or in the bars and nightclubs outside the margins of respectable entertainment.

By World War II, the once-respected profession of female impersonation had fallen into disrepute. During what has been called the "golden age" of female impersonation in the United States during the first two decades of the twentieth century, female impersonation had been a form of family entertainment that was ostensibly about women and men, not deviant sexuality. Men in minstrel shows and male comedians in vaudeville had used comic female impersonation routines as part of their repertoires, some men building careers performing exclusively in women's clothes.[11] A few female impersonators had crossed over from minstrel shows and vaudeville to the legitimate stage and the silent screen.[12] The most famous of these had been Julian Eltinge, who impersonated women not with comic burlesque but with grace, elegance, and taste. Eltinge had performed in Broadway shows created for him and as women in Hollywood films. He wrote beauty advice columns and published his own beauty magazine, performed in films to raise money for Liberty Bonds, and had a Broadway theater named after him.[13]

During the mid-1920s, however, the golden age of female impersonation on the stage came to an end when vaudeville, after the first talkies appeared in 1927, suffered a dramatic decline.[14] Out-of-work female impersonators flocked to Hollywood looking for off-screen jobs in sound pictures as makeup men and costume designers or found work elsewhere as fashion designers, milliners, dressmakers, and hairdressers.[15] Female impersonators who remained on the dwindling vaudeville circuit developed a bawdier style and were sometimes called "pansy" impersonators. These men not only used sexual double entendre but also explicitly caricatured effeminate homosexuals. "Female impersonation is no longer confined to the delicate, sly satire of a Julian Eltinge," wrote a commentator in 1928. "The stage is full of chorus men, with all the symptoms of homosexuality worn on the sleeve. . . . The vaudeville comedians are . . . invading more and more the regions of the pathologically effeminate." [16]

By the 1930s female impersonation had gone underground in the cities, where drag acts became a form of risqué adult entertainment about both gender and sexuality that was regulated by police and state liquor authorities. After the repeal of prohibition, some female impersonators from the golden age joined a younger generation of drag performers in the new and more intimate night clubs and "queer joints" that were licensed to serve liquor.[17] Many of these establishments, like Finocchio's in San Francisco and Club Richman in New York, employed young men as "chorus girls" and catered to a mixed gay and tourist crowd that was drawn to these sophisticated and particularly gay forms of urban entertainment. Their performers' drag routines often alluded to the slang, clothing, gestures, and intonation that the more outrageous gay men were developing as their own style on the streets, in restaurants and taverns, and at private parties. These artists also impersonated stars of the stage and silver screen, such as Mae West, Marlene Dietrich, Greta Garbo, and Jean Harlow, and imitated the lavish production numbers that had been featured in the Ziegfeld Follies and Hollywood musicals.

At the same time large, formal drag balls became popular from the late 1920s into the 1930s and 1940s, bringing female impersonation by gay men out of the intimacy of nightclubs and into the streets and auditoriums of the cities. These events usually took place on Hallowe'en and New Year's Eve—holidays when the police refrained from arresting people garbed in the clothing of the other sex—and attracted hundreds of participants, thousands of spectators, and much attention from the press. Moving drag into the public arena, these gay events—where men wore extravagant women's clothes and women came dressed as men—took place at the Coliseum Annex in Chicago; the Rockland Palace, Savoy Ballroom, and Manhattan Casino in Harlem; Webster Hall in Greenwich Village; and at large halls in other cities.[18] Pansy drag shows in nightclubs and gala drag balls publicly linked the artistic styles of female impersonation even more closely with homosexuality.

Responding in the 1920s and 1930s to this slow but visible expansion of urban gay nightlife and to the increasingly explicit portrayal of sexuality in commercial entertainment, moral crusaders and church and temperance groups promoted a wide array of antivice laws and other measures, including those that banned homosexual content from the stages of nightclubs and the vaudeville and legitimate theaters. By 1933 Hollywood had established a Motion Picture Production Code to "clean up" the movies as well. The code prohibited the portrayal of "sexual perversion or any inference of it," so that what little drag appeared in motion pictures had to be stripped of any homosexual implications. To crack down on the growing number of nightclubs that catered to the "pansy trade," some cities passed laws that prohibited entertainers from wearing the attire of the other gender in liquor establishments, hoping to discourage acts that might attract gay patrons.[19] Conditions had changed so dramatically that, in the early 1930s, the great Julian Eltinge, attempting to make a comeback at a Los Angeles nightclub, was prohibited from wearing his elegant gowns.[20] The female impersonation profession, noted *Variety* in an obituary for "the last of the major female impersonators," Francis Renault, "has fallen into disrepute and [is] confined mainly to a few cafes located in various cities. It's no longer a type of entertainment that could be viewed by the family trade, but is confined mainly to curiosity seekers."[21]

In 1942, when military officials began to promote soldier theatricals, public relations officers and members of the press worked together to protect GI drag performers from being stigmatized by the popular image of civilian female impersonators as immoral, effeminate, or homosexual. One promotional strategy they used was to portray the new shows as a revival of the soldier show campaign that the military had undertaken in 1918–19, during and after World War I. In their search for a model of respectability, they looked back to this war that had taken place during the golden age of female impersonation, trying to ignore the "pansy" impersonators who performed in the nightclubs and queer bars or at the drag balls of the 1930s and 1940s.

The World War I campaign to entertain soldiers with their own shows, including female impersonations, was indeed a respectable precedent. It had been part of a broader Progressive Era reform movement to protect soldiers from liquor, gambling, prostitution, and venereal disease by organizing programs of wholesome and uplifting recreation in their camps. Military and welfare agency officials had actively encouraged female impersonation in the soldier shows for moral purposes—to keep the men from leaving the camps and to prevent them from mingling with female actresses and other women. Under the auspices of the Commission on Training Camp Activities (CTCA), the Young Men's Christian Association aided military officers in recruiting men from the ranks who had had experience in the theatrical profession and who could perform and train other men to perform in their own company shows.[22]

In this highly organized soldier show campaign—the first in the military's history—many soldiers impersonated not only women but also the greatest female impersonators; comparing a soldier or sailor to Julian Eltinge was the highest compliment.[23] The Army even used Bert Savoy, another of the most respected impersonators in vaudeville, to train soldiers to perform their roles.[24] The most popular soldier show during World War I was Sergeant Irving Berlin's *Yip, Yip, Yaphank* presented by 350 men from Camp Upton, Long Island, who borrowed ideas from vaudeville and the Ziegfeld Follies to provide many situations for dressing in women's clothes. The *New York Times* proclaimed that the show heralded "a new era in musical military affairs."[25] In 1918 and 1919 dozens of other soldier and sailor shows that featured female impersonations followed *Yip, Yip, Yaphank* on Broadway, the vaudeville circuits, in town halls near training camps, and in liberty theaters in Army camps.[26] Female impersonation roles were so popular among the soldiers and sailors in the United States that, according to *Variety,* when the Great Lakes Naval Station issued a wartime call for "aspirants for the wig and skirts" for a sailor show, 125 enlisted men applied for the female roles.[27]

Soldier shows and female impersonation followed American troops overseas to France. But only after the Armistice in November 1918, when 3 million men formed the Army of Occupation in France and Germany, did the requests for soldier shows become what the YMCA called "an irresistible demand." To combat homesickness, boredom, and vice, as well as social tensions between American troops and the French population, the War Department, with the aid of the YMCA, launched a European soldier show campaign that combined the zeal of the moral reform movement with a mobilization of talent only the military could provide. "There [was] nothing in the military history of the world," observed the YMCA report on the campaign, "to compare with the soldier actor mobilization" that followed the Armistice in Europe.[28]

By the middle of the next year, the soldier show mobilization had proved an overwhelming success. During March 1919, recalled soldier show producers James Evans (a civilian) and Capt. Gardner Harding, "36,118 men were costumed for 4,000 productions, divided into 134 units that played in 281 theatres. These costumes ranged all the way from policemen's uniforms to debutantes' ball gowns." To outfit these troupes, actors and actresses in the United States donated trunks full of costumes, including dresses and gowns. "The Army was proud of the A.E.F. 'chorus girls,' " the producers noted, "and every regiment was sure it had the greatest boy-girl in the world."[29] A few critics had objected to this wartime craze for chorus "girls" and the "softening influences" of such frivolous pastimes. But YMCA officials and entertainment officers argued that soldier shows actually protected morals and boosted morale. The YMCA also defended the shows because they promoted "acquaintance and friendship," bringing the men closer to their fellows, an argument that would not have been so convincing had homosexuality been suspected.[30] These arguments won over most critics. The backing of Generals Pershing, March, and Wood also had ensured broad support for the soldier show campaign.[31]

Two decades later, Army public relations materials for *This Is the Army* referred to this earlier campaign to justify the revival of soldier shows and female impersonation for the fighting men of World War II. " 'This Is the Army' . . . follows in the footsteps of its predecessor 'Yip, Yip, Yaphank,' " explained the *TITA* souvenir program prepared by both Army Emergency Relief and Special Services. "The seed that was sown by Irving Berlin . . . in 1918, began to bear fruit with the flood of soldiers pouring into Reception Centers all over the nation. . . . The actors in 'This Is the Army' are carrying on the tradition of the World-War actors . . . the same blood flows in their veins."[32] Using Irving Berlin's pair of Army musicals as a bridge to span the two wars, military publicists identified and promoted a soldier show tradition that was respectable enough to embrace soldier drag routines even in World War II. They presented this tradition to the public wrapped in metaphors—sowing seeds, father-son inheritance, military bloodlines—that evoked heterosexuality, masculinity, patriotism, and family generations rather than "moral degeneracy," effeminacy, or homosexuality.

The press, doing its part, established the war's basic propaganda rules for defending all soldier drag routines as wholesome, patriotic, and masculine. Reviewers of *This Is the Army* praised the "smart good taste," the "spirit of generous good will," and the patriotism of the performers. Reviews were full of superlatives—the *New York Times* called the show "as American as hot dogs or the Bill of Rights"; *Life* called it "a total victory"; the *San Francisco Chronicle* called it the "best soldier show of all time." These early raves set a tone of respect that, for the rest of the war, ran through most press coverage of soldier shows and their drag routines.[33]

To win over a public skeptical of men who seemed to be playing while American boys were already dying in combat, the show's script, as well as Army and press publicity, reassured the public that the cast of *This Is the Army* was ready and eager for combat. In the show's opening chorus, the entire cast sang that, although they wore greasepaint and powder, they were still brave soldiers worthy of representing the U.S. Army. The *TITA* souvenir program featured a photo page of soldiers, training with rifles and bayonets, titled "Soldiers Acting, not Acting Soldiers." Superimposed over lists of each actor's weapons qualifications were photographs of some of the show's female impersonators, with the heading "Ready on the firing line." "On a stage or a battlefield," the program notes explained, "they'll play their parts with equal courage." Soldier entertainment was "of secondary importance only to carrying a gun itself."

Taking their cue from this Army publicity and the show's lyrics, reporters and theater critics did their part to portray the *TITA* actors as fighting men. They highlighted the rigorous discipline the soldiers underwent each day and reassured readers that the men would rather be in combat. *Newsweek* reported that all the soldiers in the show had been "irritated by jeers of 'pretty soft!' from the lay men in the barracks" and they wanted "the world to know that the battle of Broadway is no phony war." A reporter for *Collier's*, after interviewing one of the leading female impersonators in the show, observed that he "isn't too excited about his success. . . . 'I wanna fight . . . not too long, understand. . . . But I wanna fight.' " The myth that every soldier in *TITA* would get his chance to fight was kept alive in the press. When Sheilah Graham interviewed Irving Berlin before the London opening of the show, he explained that after a tour of England and North Africa, the show would disband and "the boys will do the job for which they joined the Army—fighting." [34] Each time *TITA* was shown in movie theaters across the country, real audiences saw the soldier-actors on the screen march off to combat at the end of the film. This was Hollywood's propaganda fantasy. Some of the cast did apply for transfer to combat units, but the War Department did not allow all of these men to leave the show. Most members of the cast went along on its worldwide tour or were assigned to other Special Services units, especially in the Army Air Forces, where they worked in motion pictures, soldier shows, theatrical training, and camouflage education. [35]

This Is the Army was immensely popular and inspired imitations among American and Allied forces around the world. Its initial four-week engagement at the Broadway Theatre in Manhattan was so well-received that the Army extended its run to three months. From October 1942 to August 1943, the show toured the United States, playing in virtually every major city. In Washington the cast put on a special performance for President Roosevelt, who called it the greatest show ever presented in the National Theater. One reporter noted that the president particularly enjoyed the soldier who impersonated Gypsy Rose Lee in her strip routine. [36] The next day Roosevelt told a press conference that "he was glad that it was being made into a motion picture so that members of the armed forces all over the world and all the American people would be able to see it." The cast's reception at the White House the same evening, noted director Ezra Stone, "constituted the highest recognition for the work we believed in." [37]

In November 1943, after a thirteen-month tour of the United States, 165 members of the *TITA* cast found themselves loaded onto a troop ship headed for a tour of Britain. On November 10 the show opened at London's Palladium, then performed before the royal family at a special matinee. During the show's tour of U.S. Army bases in Britain, General Eisenhower decided that all the theaters of war should see it. The cast subsequently toured Allied bases in Algeria, Italy, Egypt, and Iran, then sailed to the Pacific and performed in Australia, New Guinea, the Philippines, the Mariana and Caroline Islands, Saipan, Okinawa, and Hawaii, closing their last performance in Honolulu on October 22, 1945. In all *This Is the Army* traveled 70,000 miles to play one thousand performances before 2.5 million GIs. After the last performance, the cast returned to New York to be discharged. General George C. Marshall decorated Irving Berlin with the Medal for Merit for "extraordinary service to the United States Army in building and maintaining morale among soldiers and civilians." The show's world-wide tour and the honors it received, in the words of its director Ezra Stone, had transformed soldier theatricals from "hodge-podge entertainment" to "planned programs," had "continued to gather prestige for soldier-actors," and had chipped away at "the tendency of some civilians and some higher Army officers to stigmatize our work." [38]

For the rest of the war, male GIs wrote and produced soldier shows for each other wherever American troops were stationed. These were particularly important in basic-training camps, in remote areas where no local civilian entertainment was available, and later in occupied enemy countries where fraternization with the local population was forbidden. Soldiers structured their drag routines in these shows around the three types of female impersonations that were featured in *This Is the Army*, the most popular of which were the pony ballets and chorus lines. In a dream sequence in the Army show *Hi, Yank!*, Sad Sack watches "a basketball ballet with husky GIs in yellow curls and pink skirts as the graceful ballerinas." The 1943 production of *Sad Sacks* at Fort Dix Air Base Theater included "sixty soldiers, attired as 'pin-up' girls." The *Black Cat Revue* at Camp Beale, California, featured an "armored chorus" made up of "four beauties" from the 13th Armored Division. In 1944, when Gypsy Rose Lee appeared at Bergstrom Field near Austin, Texas, she was backed by a local "chorus of GI 'beauties,' " which *Yank* dubbed "Gypsy's 'Girls.' " Overseas, a Greenland GI revue called *Arctic Hotfoot* included soldiers in a "South of the Border" chorus line. The *Yard Birds* Army show in Algiers, according to the *New York Times*, took in "the usual dogface ballet." Other shows included soldiers doing their versions of famous female actresses, movie stars, dancers, singers, and strippers.[39] In their all-male shows, many GIs also found themselves impersonating Wacs. The show *Stars and Gripes*, presented by men at Fort Hamilton, included a comedy skit in which four soldiers played Wacs trying to squeeze into girdles. In the Fort McArthur production of *Hey Rookie*, a chorus line of soldiers in WAC drag sang "With a Gun on His Shoulder or a Girl on His Arm, You Can Tell He's A Yankee Doodle Dandy." [40]

Because the armed forces were racially segregated, black soldiers had to put on their own shows with their own female impersonators. A month after *TITA* opened on Broadway, plans were developed to produce a similar but all-black soldier show entitled *Uncle Sambo*. In Germany the men of the 3966th Quartermaster Truck Company produced their own musical, called *Jumping with Jodie*, which included an all-black nightclub number with several men in drag. Although the cast of *This Is the Army* was racially integrated, the black performers were segregated into a Harlem dance number, so that even the dancing couples with one drag partner were never interracial. Race segregation also encouraged white soldiers to put on blackface minstrel routines. The all-white minstrel number "Mandy" in *TITA* featured men impersonating black women who flirted and danced with men impersonating black men, so that even in blackface the taboo on interracial couples was not broken. Only toward the end of the war, in racially integrated units or military hospitals, did some soldier show numbers include both white and black female impersonators.[41]

The argument that female impersonation was necessary because no women were available grew weaker as women entered the armed forces in a fuller capacity beginning in 1942. Women not only developed their own soldier shows but expressed a desire, with much support from their male comrades, to act the female roles in joint male-and-female productions. Because the Navy had more-uniform policies toward male and female personnel than the Army, although it sponsored fewer and less-organized theatricals, women in the WAVES did perform in Navy shows with men and toured in all-female musical shows.[42]

At first women in the Army tried to do the same thing. In June 1943 members of the WAAC produced two all-female traveling musical comedy shows that were designed to tour the country as *TITA* had done. One show, *WAAC Caravan,* was sponsored by the Second Service Command in New York City. On June 16 its all-Waac troupe left Manhattan for a six-week tour of New York, New Jersey, and Maryland, where each performance was to include a WAAC lieutenant making a recruiting speech, giving the show a practical mission.[43] The same month, Waacs at the 2nd Training Center at Daytona Beach, Florida, put on an all-female musical comedy called *On the Double.* The show was so successful that other military posts in the area requested a tour. The cast and crew of *On the Double* asked the Army to assign them to a touring detachment on a full-time basis, as had been done with the men in *TITA.*

But women's shows in the Army generated controversy rather than celebration in WAAC headquarters. Their performances and the public's response provoked Director Hobby to develop restrictive measures designed to protect the WAAC's public image, throwing the Army's double standard toward its female personnel into sharp relief. Reviewers in Florida newspapers had made leering comments about the WAAC performers in *On the Double,* calling the show "the Amazon's answer" to *This Is the Army* and warning male readers to "Hold your hats, fellows—there's a strip-tease act so good the MP's have to break it up.'' Concerned that the Waacs' show had become sexually titillating to men, Colonel Hobby denied the women's request to go on tour, and ordered a memo issued to all service commands prohibiting Wacs from "singing and dancing in connection with any presentation put on for the public on behalf of recruiting.'' [44]

In July, Colonel Hobby had the War Department issue an even more restrictive WAAC show policy that remained in effect for the rest of the war. It allowed Waacs ''to appear only in those shows performed at home stations for soldiers and their families, which did not take them off their jobs and for which no admission was charged except to defray costs.'' Hobby argued that such protection was necessary because women had worked too hard for acceptance as equals in the military to jeopardize their reputation by singing and dancing onstage, particularly with men or in touring shows. Men could perform in musical comedies, even in women's clothes, because they were prepared for combat. But women in the service, who were barred from combat, could not afford to appear so frivolous.[45] The Army did, however, allow Wacs to perform backstage duties. Women in WAC detachments at various bases served as seamstresses for the shows, designing and fitting tutus, dresses, gowns, and accessories for the men who impersonated women.[46] As a result, the War Department Bureau of Public Relations treated the public to a strange series of photographs of Wacs and other women making up male GIs to look like women.[47]

With the multiplication of all-male soldier shows overseas during and after 1943, producers sometimes tried to replace female impersonators with Wacs, increasing pressure on the Women's Army Corps to loosen its restrictions on WAC performers. On Christmas Eve in 1943, the Army in Algiers opened *Swing, Sister Wac, Swing,* which, noted a *New York Times* correspondent, had a ''large contingent'' of fifteen Wacs who had ''already become known as 'Wactresses.' '' The show was produced with the approval of the commanding officer of the Algiers Central District, Mediterranean Base Command, and supplied by the Red Cross with costumes and props. The ''Wactresses' '' debut received wide publicity in stateside newspapers, where reporters once again portrayed Wacs as sexually titillating entertainers. ''The interest all over Algiers,'' observed the *New York Times* correspondent, ''naturally centers in the fifteen girls in the cast. . . . There is a harem scene in which a dozen of the loveliest Wacs in North Africa sport gauzy pantaloons and bare midriffs.'' In January 1944 the successful show prepared to tour North Africa, Sicily, and mainland Italy. But in February the War Department canceled the tour plans. WAC officials in Algiers had received a flood of complaints from home protesting the harem scene. The War Department, citing Colonel Hobby's circular prohibiting Wac participation in theatrical performances, closed the show.[48]

Commanding officers in remote areas occasionally did allow a Wac to perform in a local show, but the official policy against Wac participation in soldier revues remained in effect for most of the war. Male soldiers who wanted to include heterosexual romance or sex appeal in their shows had to rely on those of their buddies who could best impersonate women. Any male impersonations that women soldiers may have performed in their all-female shows were neither mentioned nor pictured by the press, which was more interested in women who took on men's roles and wore men's clothes in their real wartime jobs.

Despite the publicity campaign to make GI female impersonators appear to be "normal" men, the creation of a military theatrical world with such an embarrassment of riches in drag not only lured gay men into soldier shows but reflected their presence in military show production from the start. Long before the war, the civilian theater world had offered many gay men a haven where they could work as hairdressers, makeup artists, set and costume designers, chorus boys, hair and wig stylists, female impersonators, dancers, and actors.[49] In soldier and sailor shows, these roles were similarly stereotyped as gay. Whether they were masculine or feminine in appearance, outrageous or discreet, gay men found that their interests, styles, and tastes helped shape the military's wartime theater world.

Gay servicemen who performed in drag demonstrated a particular form of bravery. They chose to risk visibility when hiding would have been safer, chose to "act" on a public platform when passively accepting their isolation might have protected them better from detection. Gay GIs who performed in drag acted on many levels at once: They boosted soldier morale, played with gender roles, secretly entertained each other with coded signals, met kindred spirits, and created opportunities to be physically affectionate with other men, all the while pressing against the boundaries that would keep their routines safely heterosexual.

As they did in other stereotyped jobs in the military, gay men, depending on their own fears and desires, could either seek out or avoid the role of female impersonator. Jim Kuzell, who went to boot camp at the San Diego Naval Training Station, helped put together a variety show that "had a lot of drag in it." But he himself wouldn't appear in drag because, he explained, "I felt . . . it would be showing off that I'm gay." Gay GIs who did want to perform in drag, however, could volunteer or, if they had the necessary skills and experience, could be assigned to Special Services units. Some auditioned for roles when they saw notices posted on bulletin boards asking for volunteers to donate their rare free time. Privates Norman Sansom and Woodie Wilson met each other at an audition for *Private Maxie Reporting* at Hunter Field, Georgia. "What we actually auditioned for was the men's chorus," Sansom explained, "but [the producers] found out that the show needed some humor," so these gay performers put together a comedy routine in drag. Other gay GIs put on makeshift shows, were "discovered," and found theatrical careers for themselves in the military. While Tom Reddy was being shipped overseas to the South Pacific, he and some of his buddies put together a variety show they called the *South Pacific Follies*. As a civilian Reddy had played in summer stock. "The only thing we didn't have on board ship," he recalled, "was any women. So that's where my skinny, frail, non-Marine-Corps-type body came in very handy. I became it." By the time the ship reached Noumea, New Caledonia, Reddy was part of an eighteen-man Marine Corps touring show company called the *SoPac Follies.*

Soldiers found ingenious ways to get the dresses and women's shoes, wigs, and makeup they needed for their drag routines. Civilian women near bases in the United States sometimes lent their assistance despite shortages due to rationing. When soldiers at Fort Wayne put on their show, *On the Beam,* the property man—or "wardrobe lady," as he was called in the base newsletter—"came in for a lot of ribbing from clerks in a local store while buying lipsticks and stuff . . . but ended up by talking the girls out of some precious bobby pins they had cached away for themselves!" [50] In Georgia, Privates Wilson, Sansom, and an MP friend obtained their dresses at a downtown Savannah dress shop. According to Sansom, they told the woman who owned the shop "that we were doing this show and could she contribute some dresses that might not be selling. She was absolutely blown out of her mind to see three soldiers walk in and ask for dresses! But at that time everybody was so anxious to do something for the war effort. She was very cooperative and took us into the dressing room. We tried on a lot of gowns! Let me tell you, there was a show going on in that shop with all the customers milling around because, if you can imagine, here was a six-foot-six MP and the two of us, trying on dresses! And she didn't just loan them to us, she *gave* them to us. We in turn told her that we would give her complimentary tickets to the show."

Family members also pitched in. "I wrote to one of my sisters in New York," Robert Fleischer recalled, "to go to the five-and-dime and send me some stuff. The wooden beads, the plumes—she sent me all kinds of cheap fabric.'' After Tom Reddy's mother read an article in the Marine Corps *Leatherneck* magazine about his drag routines in the South Pacific, she sent him a "quick V-Mail letter stating she couldn't have been prouder and was there anything I needed. So I promptly sent back and said, 'Yes, I could use some decent lipstick.' She made a great thing about sending it, and I told her she didn't have to be careful. Just ship it as fast as possible, nobody was going to question it.'' Because these shows were officially heterosexual, soldiers who obtained dresses and makeup were doing a job that amused more than threatened the other men.

In more remote areas overseas, the USO and the Red Cross provided soldiers with dresses and costume materials. ''I was doing a version of a camp show in our spare time,'' recalled Ben Small, who as a gay Army Air Corpsman was stationed at an atoll near New Guinea, ''a little drag number in a parachute. It was just a matter of getting guys together who liked to entertain and putting on a show for the different outfits on the island. I had the effrontery to write to the USO in San Francisco saying, 'Do you have any funny costumes?' Usually it took two months for something to arrive, [but] a couple of weeks later I got called in [to the office] and they said, 'How come you get special air mail delivery?' I said, 'I don't even know what it is' and they said, 'Open it up!' Well, it was dresses. Gold lamé. You have never seen such a collection of shit in your life! Nobody was upset; they just said, 'What the hell is this?' And I said, 'We wanted to do a show and we needed some costumes.' Well, here's everybody in the office from the lieutenant on down trying on dresses! Everybody suddenly becomes a drag queen! That's how we got costumes for the show.''

During World War II, the USO and the Red Cross took over the same task of supplying GIs with dresses that the YMCA had performed during World War I. In Noumea after Tom Reddy's debut drag performance in the marine show *SoPac Follies*, his captain ordered him downtown to the Red Cross headquarters. ''I went down with a couple of other guys,'' he recalled. ''Those two girls at the Red Cross were the greatest. The first thing they said to me was, 'Now, what do you need to make this act go?' I said, 'Well, a red chiffon dress would be sensational!' She said, 'We'll get you one.' They got me stockings and garters and all sorts of fun things. They were great about supplying anything they could within reason. Now to get this kind of equipment for the Marine Corps, you didn't go through Marine Corps channels and say,

'I need four dresses in a size 16.' So somebody did it for you. And it was the Red Cross.'' [51]

On transport ships and isolated bases where welfare agencies were far away, GIs improvised their drag ensembles from whatever materials were at hand, sometimes guided by the costume instructions in the Army's Blueprint Special handbooks. At sea and in the South Pacific, semaphore flags, rope, mops, coconut shells, leaves, and fruit were favorite raw materials.[52] "The semaphore flags were our skirts," recalled Frank Jacober, a gay chaplain's assistant who organized soldier shows in his infantry unit in the Philippines and New Guinea. "We took them and sewed them together. You've got all those colors, you know, it's very pretty! You'd shape them and you'd leave the ends fringing around. We'd take coconut shells and tie them together and they'd become our breasts. And then take those GI mops and put them on our heads.'' When Tom Reddy first put together his drag aboard the troop ship headed toward New Caledonia, he learned how to boil down hemp rope and dry it in the sun to reshape it into ''a stunning blond pageboy wig. Makeup was no big deal. White rice powder and some lipstick and a black pencil made you. Because after all, if you were playing in front of two thousand marines, you're not exactly playing Radio City.'' This homespun style of World War II drag was memorialized in the role of Honey-Bun taken by Luther Billis in the stage and screen productions of the 1949 musical *South Pacific.*[53]

When their materials were assembled, GI female impersonators drew on vaudeville, burlesque, the movies, and nightclub acts to create their drag personas and comedy routines. Impersonations of Carmen Miranda, the Andrews Sisters, Gypsy Rose Lee, and Mae West were standard fare in most soldier and sailor shows, often done in a comic burlesque style. Gay men, however, could transform these common routines into their own works of folk art, embellishing them with accessories, campy asides, double entendres, gestures and tones of voice that created parallel gay meanings for their acts. "It was the way I kept my sanity,'' explained Frank Jacober, "by being able to get into a kind of female role, to express my feminine side a little bit. The only way we got away with it was in drag. When we were doing those shows, and we were dressed up in those crazy costumes, then you could get away with venting your feelings, getting another side of you to kind of have fun with.''

The most daring and skillful GI drag performers were like magicians. They played tricks with gender, becoming masters of the art of illusion with a sense of humor. They created beautiful attractive women out of men, affirming the heterosexuality of their audiences, then played with the implications, covertly challenging the heterosexual norm by becoming men dressed as women hugging, kissing, and singing love songs to other men. Such daring was an important component of "camping"—a style and a self-awareness that many gay GIs brought to their drag routines. Long before the war, gay men had developed "camping" as one of many strategies to survive in a society that questioned their status as men, stereotyped them as effeminate, and harassed them for their sexuality.

Camping could be a flamboyant and public announcement—through gestures, cosmetics, clothing, shrieks, and swishes—that one was a "flaming queen." Or it could be a weapon—the vicious put-down used to attack pretentious closeted "queens" and moralistic heterosexuals and cut them down to size. Camping could be a way to interpret the world from a gay male point of view, playing with ironies in the realms of gender and sexuality; or a commentary on the dominant moral order by elevating the artificial, decorative, sexual, and effeminate to the noble, elegant, tasteful, and divine; or a secret, coded language that bonded gay men together into a culture uniquely their own. Camp slang appropriated common words and enriched them with secret sexual meanings, transforming everyday words such as *gay, temperamental, interesting, brilliant, belle, girl,* and *auntie* into synonyms for gay men. In the language of camp, public toilets were *tea-rooms,* a flaming queen was a *mother superior,* a gay man in jail was a *sister in distress,* a policeman was *Alice Blue Gown,* and sailors were *seafood.* To be well-acquainted with camping was "to know the words and music" that accompanied gay life.[54]

Gay men could use camp as a form of self-defense. It could simultaneously distance them from the humiliation they endured as sexual outcasts while creating an alternative moral order and culture in which gay men were in control. It was a paradoxical form of self-parody and self-appreciation—a way to celebrate sexual and gender differences, to deflect the hatred of a hostile society with humor and self-mockery, to build a culture on shared pain, to laugh at misfortune to keep from crying. Many gay men used bits and pieces of popular culture—Art Deco, Cole Porter's songs, lines from *Gone With the Wind,* Billie Holiday's blues, Carmen Miranda drag, Tallulah Bankhead's way of saying "Darling!"—to create distinctive campy styles rich with irony, wit, artifice, theatricality, gender reversal, and sexual ambiguity. These styles reflected the self-consciousness of some gay men as sexual or gender outsiders and helped them define themselves as "insiders" of their own secret world. When they could identify each other—even covertly in the presence of others—they could "let down their hair" a little, find some camaraderie, even have fun with the masks they wore as everyday camouflage to lead normal lives. Gay men developed camping to create and expand a little social space for themselves within a society that tried to keep them invisible, isolated, and silent. In the decades following the war, camping slowly became less necessary as gay life became more open, politically organized, and tolerated.[55]

Ironically, the propaganda that portrayed soldier actors as masculine, combat ready, and essential to the war effort served as a camouflage that protected gay GI performers on the military stage, giving them greater freedom there than in other areas of military life to camp it up. But at the same time, the expanding antihomosexual policies discouraged gay GI performers from taking their freedom too far. These tensions between freedom on the stage and the military's antihomosexual policies were evident even in the Blueprint Specials prepared by Special Services. For a campy scene in the soldier show *About Face*—in which three gossiping Army cooks compliment each other's aprons, trade recipes, whisper secrets, and comment on each other's figures—the Army manual's stage directions warned the actors that "at no time do any of the characters mince or speak in an effeminate manner," hoping to prevent the soldier-actors from playing these roles as homosexuals. In a drag scene in *Hi, Yank!* where the main character, Sad Sack, "leaps daintily out of bed" to join a dance sequence of male ballerinas, the stage instructions also warned performers that "Sad Sack should never appear to be effeminate."[56]

Despite the danger of going too far, gay GI performers could become extremely bold on the stage. Some even created campy routines that included identifiable homosexual characters. After Pvts. Woodie Wilson and Norman Sansom successfully auditioned for parts in *Private Maxie Reporting* at Hunter Field in Georgia, they discovered that the soldier-playwright had written a gay character into the script. Private Wilson played "Pfc. Bloomingslip," an Officer Candidate School (OCS) appli-cant who, according to the program, "wears a green carnation"—the symbol for homosexual aesthetes inspired by Oscar Wilde. "Whoever wrote it [into the show] wanted to show a homosexual," Wilson recalled, "and I certainly volunteered to be Private Bloomingslip! So here is Norman being one of the OCS board. I skip in with this little cap and the green carnation and say to the OCS board, 'My name is Private Bloomingslip. I was told to report in here. I think to be an officer would just be too, too queer!' I remember that was my line!'' Other gay drag performers got away with sex jokes that were clearly homosexual when performed by two men. In one burlesque scene in a South Pacific island soldier show, Frank Jacober, dressed in drag, went up to his comic partner and said, ''Your motor's running.'' ''Yes,'' the comedian replied, ''and how're you going to stop it?'' ''Well,'' Jacober suggested, ''you back it into my garage and I'll show you how to stop it!''

But GIs—whether they were gay or not—more commonly brought gay culture and double entendre to the military stage in more subtle ways. In the ''Stage Door Canteen'' number in *This Is the Army,* soldiers impersonated not only women, but also Noel Coward—who was known to be gay—and Lynn Fontanne and Alfred Lunt—who, although husband and wife, were rumored to be living discreetly gay lives.[57] The song that the soldiers sang as canteen ''hostesses'' about the rules and regulations that prohibited them from fooling around with soldiers also had a parallel meaning about the military's antihomosexual prohibitions on these same soldiers as men. The World War II soldier show scenes in the 1949 musical *South Pacific* similarly incorporated coded gay slang into the drag numbers. During a show within the show, a female nurse plays a man who sings and dances with a male sailor who plays a woman. The nurse's stage name as a man is Butch—lesbian slang for a masculine woman—which plays off her given name Nellie—gay male slang for an effeminate man.[58] Such coded references and parallel meanings appeared in many soldier shows throughout the war.

The soldier shows that perhaps had their clearest origins in gay camp were the popular all-male GI productions of Clare Boothe's all-female satiric play, *The Women.* The play—and the 1939 Hollywood film directed by George Cukor, who himself was gay [59]—became staples of gay male culture for the next half century. Its cattiness, barbed lines, and bitchy characters—especially Joan Crawford as Crystal Allen—both represented and became models for gay camp. Yet enthusiastic reviews of the GI productions of *The Women* at Lowry Field, Colorado, and at Camp Lee, Virginia, made no direct reference to the camp undertones and instead merely laughed at the awkwardness of seeing men playing female characters and praised the men for not making the show into a joke. *Life* gave the show a favorable review. ''Despite their hairy chests, size-16 shoes and bulging biceps these 'actresses' did a good job with the play, present[ing] it as straight comedy. . . . After the first hour, the audience forgot that 'the women' were men, remembered only when they talked about having babies in bass voices.'' The men's talent, in fact, prompted the playwright herself to interpret the GI production as an important wartime critique of traditional gender roles. At the end of the show's three-day run in Virginia, Clare Boothe made a personal appearance to support the men's efforts. "She stood on the stage," the *Life* reporter wrote, "and said: 'This play shows that, after all, there is very little difference between men and women.' " The gay subtext of the soldier productions of *The Women* went unacknowledged in the press, although the GI drag performers photographed by *Life* displayed the gestures and poses that were classic examples of gay camp.[60]

The female character most impersonated by GIs, whether they were gay or not, was also the campiest movie star of the early 1940s—Carmen Miranda. Featured in the 1943 Technicolor film *The Gang's All Here* as a South American singer with full skirts, bare midriff, huge dangling earrings, and headdresses of fruit piled several feet high, Carmen Miranda became the idol of gay drag queens and soldier-performers alike. "If you've got a lot of signal flags around," explained Tom Reddy, "lots of pins—and Marines always carry needles and threads to repair things, so you have a lot of help on board ship—eventually you turn into Carmen Miranda. Because you've got multicolors, you can make the big flouncy skirt, and you've got the tropical fruit everywhere." In 1944 Army Service Forces produced a "Blueprint Special" for the soldier show *Hi, Yank!* which included five pages of patterns for a drag impersonation of Carmen Miranda (renamed Conchita for the show). The same year, the 13th Army Air Force Combat Camera Unit prepared a newsreel called *Guadalcanal Interlude*, which featured "Madame Latrine," an Air Corpsman done up in Carmen Miranda drag. Performing before an audience of heavy-bomber crewmen fresh from a mission to the north, Madame Latrine sang "I Can't Give You Anything But Love, Baby" while doing a slow striptease. The Carmen Miranda drag routine was so common in GI shows that it became a tired cliché and the subject of parody. Moss Hart's Air Force play and film *Winged Victory* (1944) featured a soldier decked out in forks, ammunition shells, Army blankets, and frying pans in a burlesque of the typical GI Carmen Miranda drag.[61] In April 1944 a writer for *Theatre Arts* magazine in New York reported that "cries of anguish can still be heard from harried Special Services officers" who were tired of "impersonations of Carmen Miranda" and who saw a "desperate need" for more variety.[62]

Gay GIs who did Carmen Miranda could easily slip a gay sensibility into their acts. Marine Corporal Tom Reddy played Carmen Miranda in *SoPac Follies* for marines and Navy men all across the South Pacific. After playing the New Georgia chain of islands, Reddy earned the drag nickname Georgia from New Georgia. His act combined gay camp with butch burlesque to make the men laugh and to loosen up stone-faced officers. In drag, moreover, he could get away with antics that the men might not have otherwise tolerated from another man. "We'd play a camp," Reddy recalled, "and I'd always say, 'Who's the commanding general of the camp?' and they'd say, 'Oh, the big, fat guy sitting there' or 'that young, little whippersnapper' and I'd say, 'Just get the fruit. We'll fix him.' [I'd] jump down off the stage and sit on [his] lap and sing 'Ayayayayayay love you verrrry much!' and jam a banana in his mouth. If he didn't open it, he got a banana all over. And I'd stay with him until he laughed, because [otherwise] no other officer would laugh. The rest of the place would be hysterical, but the officers would be frozen. Which you can understand. And if necessary, I'd even say into his ear, 'Oh, be a sport! Make 'em laugh. Help me.' And he would. They were great about it. Then he'd laugh hysterically and everybody would laugh and roar and applaud. Most of the time for Carmen Miranda I wore my Marine Corps combat boots so I could tromp around the stage and kick the fruit at people. Then I'd jump up and put my hands up in the air and they'd scream and throw their hats in the air and carry on. I had a flair for doing that type of thing. If I was making them laugh, God, it made me feel great! It may have been the only laugh they got before they died."

Impersonations of the Andrews Sisters—the most popular singing trio of the war years—became another military drag convention.[63] One of the trio's signature songs, "Three Little Sisters" from the 1942 film *Private Buckaroo,* was rich with gay double entendre when performed by three male GIs in drag:

> There were three little sisters, three little sisters,
> And each one only in her teens,
> One loved a soldier, one loved a sailor,
> And one loved a lad from the Marines.[64]

Privates Norman Sansom and Woodie Wilson and an MP friend created their own campy version of the "female trio" number for *Private Maxie Reporting* at Hunter Field, Georgia. Their drag style was comic burlesque rather than serious impersonation—mop wigs, GI boots, and comic makeup. But the song that they wrote and sang used gay slang and ended each verse with increasingly mocking and ironic questions about "camp," a gay word that was not yet known to outsiders. The song's ending suggested that the three men thought the audience's naïveté was even campier than the gay drag act itself. The trio sang:

Here you see three lovely "girls"
With their plastic shapes and curls.
Isn't it campy? Isn't it campy?

We've got glamor and that's no lie;
Can't you tell when we swish by?
Isn't it campy? Isn't it campy?

Those GIs all stop and stare,
And we don't even bat an eye.
You'd think that we were shy.
Now isn't that campy? Now isn't that campy?

So now drink a toast to these lovely "girls,"
Doing their utmost to upset you most.
Now who do you think is campy?
Now who do you think is campy?

The next day a reporter at the *Savannah Morning News,* either missing or covering up the gay meanings of this song, reported that "the 'female trio,' who almost stopped the show on the opening night, were again received by a roar of ovation. Clad in clinging evening dresses, the three drew howls from the audience, which mounted when they returned on roller skates for an encore. Lyrics sung by the three were composed by themselves." [65] The men had pulled off their gay performance with nothing but public praise for their talent and humor.

When gay GIs broke taboos to wear dresses, kiss men, and jump into officers' laps, they had to anticipate and monitor the reactions of the other men and officers so that they would not get into trouble. Many servicemen like Reddy, Sansom, and Wilson successfully used the protective camouflage provided by the military approval of drag to get away with their outrageous routines. It was a balancing act that demanded sure footing. Some gay soldiers who put on these campy drag routines did slip and fall—they lost their cover of legitimacy and were exposed as queer.

Ben Small created an Andrews Sister drag role for himself in an Army Air Corps revue on an island off New Guinea. "We did a beautiful show," he recalled. "I was singing 'Rum and Coca-Cola'—that was the big number with the Andrews Sisters—and 'My Heart Belongs to Daddy.' Just bringing the house down. We did the show everywhere but our home base and we did it there one night, and there must have been 1,500 guys. But it caused me to be thrown off the island. Because doing a number and doing it fairly seriously—I was the only serious drag queen. Although the numbers were funny, I wanted to look good. The next day I got called into the office and they said, 'You're being transferred to Manila.' I said, 'Why?' They said, 'Well, the island commandant was there last night with his nurse girlfriend and she was upset by what you did. She doesn't want any fags on this island.' And off I went to Manila.''

Another risk faced by GIs who performed in drag, whether they were gay or not, was getting unwanted sexual propositions from other men. A drag performer's stage roles could inspire some men to give him affectionate feminine nicknames off stage or to spread rumors that he was sexually available. ''Being Carmelita Ack-Ack kind of did me in a little bit,'' Robert Fleischer recalled. ''There were a couple of USO Clubs in some of the surrounding towns. They had heard about the show and every once in a while they'd ask us to entertain. So after a while I got a bit of a reputation in that corner of Texas.'' The private jokes among men in the 473rd Battalion about Fleischer's ''reputation'' became public gossip in the El Campo newspaper review of the show. '' 'Carmelita' Bob Fleischer,'' wrote the Camp Hulen press agent for the local newspaper, ''with his dancing of the South American Ack-Ack proved to be a good substitute for Carmen Miranda and was besieged by the boys for h'er' address. Much to their regret they learned that 'Carmelita' was a member of Battery C.'' But some men were not discouraged by Carmelita's true identity. ''What started to happen,'' Fleischer explained, ''is the tough guys in the outfit started to tease me quite often. I didn't know quite how to handle it. Sometimes they would show up in the hutment after hours and literally sit on my bed and try to play with me—half-heartedly joking and half serious. You couldn't tell whether they really wanted to have sex or they were just being teasing and showing how macho they [were].''

But other GIs who performed in drag played with or even welcomed the sexual attentions of these ''stage door Johnnies.'' After the shows they found that they had achieved a new status as the company pinup.[66] *Stars and Stripes* ran an article about a GI drag stripteaser in the 8th Air Force who was ''selected by his station as Pinup Girl of the Week,'' with Betty Grable coming in second. Following one show he was visited backstage ''by a colonel, armed with a bouquet of flowers'' asking ''her'' out for a date until he found out that ''she'' was a man. This GI drag artist enjoyed ''kidding the boys along.'' ''If they are interested,'' he told the *Stars and Stripes* reporter, ''I can cook, too.'' [67] After Ben Small's Andrews Sister routine, he recalled, ''guys would come along after the show and say, 'Do you have a way back to your tent? I've got a truck out there.' Suddenly, you were making it with these big husky guys who were married and some who were very tender, very kind, and I'm sure would never do it again once they were out of that situation.'' [68]

More than sexual opportunities, soldier shows gave gay GIs a chance to meet other gay men as friends, often for the first time in their lives. The friendships that resulted helped the men put together their own discreet social life on the bases. During rehearsals for *The Colonel Wants a Show*, recalled Robert Fleischer, ''some of the guys turned out to be gay. A lot of the guys in the show got more friendly, and when we could get weekend passes we went away together.'' Army Air Corps Privates Sansom and Wilson not only first met each other during auditions for the men's chorus in *Private Maxie Reporting* but also by chance discovered a gay hotel bar in downtown Savannah. The show had a ''Chorus of Girls'' made up of local women volunteers. Because the entire cast had to ''rehearse into the night,'' Sansom explained, the women were not permitted to come onto the base. ''So it was arranged to put the soldiers up at the De Soto Hotel in town.'' The Municipal Auditorium was ''across the street from the De Soto Hotel, which meant we could rehearse in the auditorium and then, in order not to be arrested for being out after hours, we could cross the street and go right back to the De Soto Hotel and stay there and sleep. That's how we found out that the bar at the De Soto Hotel was really the 'closeted' gay bar of Savannah. That's where we did our drinking and had our fun.''

The friendships among gay men in the shows, however, were not always so open. Sometimes men in the same drag routines never ''came out'' to each other. ''I knew these other two guys were gay,'' recalled Frank Jacober, a chaplain's assistant who choreographed a French cancan number in drag, ''but they would never admit it. And I thought to myself, 'Who's kidding who here? All three of us are gay. Let's just get on with this life.' But no, we couldn't do that. But we had a great friendship, all three of us. We had a good time. We did that show for quite a while while we were in New Guinea.''

While female impersonation could boost morale, in combat missions another art of illusion—camouflage—could save lives. These two arts required similar skills. Robert Fleischer remembered ''going out on a training mission and after a while, after forced marches and bivouacs and night campaigns, we had to do an overnight kind of dig-in and camouflaged the area with simulated antiaircraft equipment. And I went with who I was assigned with and I kind of got involved in doing the camouflage. I thought it was kind of fun to put the trees and everything around. I said, 'My goodness, this is just like stage sets, what the hell!' And I was very good at it. And the guys that were in charge were astounded because they figured that [it would be] a real drag with a sissy along. [But] I turned [out] to be the one that really accomplished [something].''

The easy transition from costume and set design to camouflage design for combat was not overlooked by classification officers. Many GIs who were classified as camoufleurs had as civilians worked in the decorative arts as window dressers, display artists, fashion designers or set and costume designers—professions that were stereotyped as homosexual. These men were equally capable of outfitting female impersonators and disguising matériel. At March Field, California, the 4th Air Force Engineer Camouflage School, which included some of the cast and crew from *This Is the Army,* produced a GI show called *You Bet Your Life,* with which the Air Force taught the men "the art and science of deceiving the enemy and saving the soldier's own life." At the end of the show, the song the camoufleurs sang about their craft had parallel meanings that described other artists of illusion as well—including the GI female impersonator and the gay GI who passed as heterosexual. "It's so confusing," the camoufleurs sang to their soldier audiences,

> But so amusing,
> The ruses
> One uses
> Are nature's own scheme. . . .
> Though we're like mirages,
> We're all camouflages—
> Things Are Not What They Seem. . . .
> No,
> Things are never quite what they seem! [69]

Both camouflage and female impersonation could serve gay GIs as metaphors for the fine art of "blending in"—their everyday use of protective "ruses" to keep from being exposed.

In remote combat areas, camouflage and makeshift entertainment were part of the realities of everyday life. After securing an area but when conditions were not yet safe enough for planes to fly in civilian entertainers, GIs had to put on their own shows. When his infantry unit in the South Pacific was not in combat, Frank Jacober recalled, "then the general would have me put shows together. When we'd finish the campaign, I'd get a week's break, and then he'd send me back to rehearsal to get a show together and we'd go do shows." But during their combat missions the men "had to stop all the shows. Then combat, we'd have a campaign, then we'd do another show. The guys just loved them. And always the chorus line had to go on, the cancan number always had to be done.''

As the Allies won victory after victory in 1945, the U.S. Army and Navy expanded their soldier show campaign, as they had done in World War I, to boost the sinking morale of the millions of anxious men and women stationed overseas waiting to go home. But even in this stepped-up effort to mobilize soldier entertainment, signs already indicated that the military's own golden age of female impersonation— begun in World War I and revived in World War II—was coming to an end.

By August 1945 a vast soldier and sailor show campaign that rivaled that of 1919 was in full gear on military bases, ships, and hospitals in Europe and across the Pacific, supplementing similar efforts by the USO. To organize soldier shows in each theater of war, the War Department sent Broadway producer Mike Todd to Europe, actor Melvyn Douglas to the China-Burma-India (CBI) Theater, Hollywood director Elia Kazan to New Guinea and the Philippines, and others to the Far East. The Army established a new Special Services Battalion in Europe, and the Navy, for the first time in the war, set up its own entertainment headquarters in New York, modeled after Army Special Services, to organize and coordinate sailor shows around the world.[70] Dubbed a "battle against boredom'' by Sgt. Daniel Schorr in the *New York Times,* these shows were particularly crucial in areas of nonfraternization and in the remote and lonely places where, Elia Kazan wrote from the South Pacific, "soldiers have no diversions; no towns to visit, no girls to see." In these isolated places, GIs continued to perform as female impersonators. "It's like playing prisoner of war,'' a GI stationed in Germany wrote to *Variety,* "so to overcome the boredom I'm staging and appearing in burlesque shows (with boys as strippers)." [71] In Melvyn Douglas's team of soldier-actors that toured the CBI Theater by jeep, truck and DC-3 planes, GIs still impersonated the Andrews Sisters.[72]

But in most other areas, as the fighting wound down, the status of GI female impersonators gradually changed. Many appeared to be out of place as they performed with women who played female roles; some were replaced altogether. Early in the war, the *Collier's* reviewer of *This Is the Army* had explained that GI female impersonation was necessary because it "was before the days of the Waacs and Waves, and the female dancers had to be men." But toward the end of the war this was no longer the case. Army officials first experimented with integrating soldier shows on home posts, allowing women and men to perform together but under strict supervision. Army policy then eased a little more to allow Wacs to appear in shows at nearby posts with all-military audiences if they were away from their home base not more than twelve hours and were accompanied by a WAC officer. In late 1945, when the occupation troops faced the severest entertainment shortage, the Army finally allowed Wacs longer periods of absence from duty to perform, but only for Army hospital patients. As the fighting stopped and a larger percentage of soldier shows entertained hospital audiences rather than combat troops, Wacs, including lesbians, enjoyed more opportunities to perform and to replace GIs in drag.[73]

Army officials developed a way to replace female impersonators with women without using Wacs by employing civilian actresses to play the women's roles in overseas soldier revues. In July 1945 the Army Special Services Division in New York City issued a call for "talented actresses" between the ages of twenty-one and thirty "to participate in soldier-acted and soldier-staged dramatic, variety and musical shows" in the European Theater of Operations. In August the first contingent of one hundred civilian actresses, some of them veterans of USO Camp Shows, arrived for training at Camp Shanks, New York. The same month Special Services launched a recruitment drive to employ seventy more female actresses, singers, and dancers "to play feminine roles in soldier shows in the Pacific." As Special Services stepped up its soldier show program for occupation troops and hospital patients, these and other women replaced female impersonators on military stages, a change "roundly welcomed by top brass and buck private." Because most of these Civilian Actress Technicians—nicknamed "CATs"—had theatrical experience, they also began to take over the theatrical "women's work"— sewing, makeup, hair styling, and dress design—that, when performed by male GIs, was stereotyped as homosexual. In the last year of the war, Army nurses as well as female Red Cross workers, soldiers' wives, and local civilian women also began to fill the female roles on stage.[74]

As GI entertainers and their audiences returned home during demobilization, the need for such a vast soldier show campaign gradually disappeared. At the same time the relaxed gender roles that women enjoyed during the war became more rigid as they returned to domestic life and traditionally female jobs. Soldiers continued to play with spontaneous drag as they had done before the war, using makeshift materials but with no official military sponsorship, training, organization, and publicity. Without a protective public relations campaign that used the rhetoric of combat preparedness, patriotism, female scarcity, and military tradition to legitimize GI female impersonation, GIs who continued to don women's clothes were more easily stereotyped as homosexual and were left to face the military's expanding antihomosexual policies on their own. At the same time a small postwar renaissance in gay drag balls and drag nightclub acts began, and—as they had done in the 1930s—reporters in the popular press began once again to discuss homosexuality explicitly whenever they reported on female impersonation.[75]

During the war the military stage had offered gay men a temporary platform on which they could express themselves in public at a time when few such platforms existed, especially in the armed forces. They could have fun and display their camp sensibilities while genuinely contributing to the morale of their outfits with the official approval of the highest-ranking military officials, including President Roosevelt. Reveling in dresses, makeup, and wigs, they called up the magic of drag and double entendre to subvert the moral order that otherwise rendered them silent and invisible. Their language was coded, their faces disguised, and their friendships covert, but they nevertheless chipped away at the barriers separating them from each other and their heterosexual buddies.

Most importantly these men had discovered and populated another niche for themselves in the military organization where, at least for the duration of the war and in the shadow of expanding antigay policies, they could enjoy the satisfaction of drawing on their own gay culture to contribute to the war effort. "You are entertaining soldiers," General Eisenhower said in a backstage speech to the all-male cast of *Yard Bird Review,* a soldier show in Algiers that included many GI female impersonators. "You are not fighting with machine guns—but your job is just as important. As long as you are doing your job well—and you are doing it extremely well—you will be rendering a service, and a great one, to your fellow soldiers and your country." [76]

CHAPTER
4

"The Gang's All Here"
The Gay Life and Vice Control

Passes into the bustling war-boom cities promised gay male and lesbian GIs the allures of fun, romance, and sex—a chance to let down their hair, let off steam, and take part in the wartime excitement of civilian life. "There was a hysteria that ran underground," wrote John Horne Burns about Washington in June 1943, "from the Pentagon to the Statler, Mayflower, and Willard hotels. . . . WACs tore efficiently through the streets. Thousands of sailors and marines were on the loose with cameras strapped to their shoulders. . . . Everybody beamed at everybody else, particularly on Pennsylvania Avenue after dark. . . . They all thought of themselves as part of an adventure, so for the first time in a decade they were united, proud, and rather gay." [1]

The "live-for-today" spirit in the wartime cities spilled over into gay life. "People sort of did with their gay behavior," explained Stuart Loomis, "what they did with everything else. Which was take chances and risks and try to enjoy things because who knows where you might be sent tomorrow." With less supervision than their parents had provided at home and with more money than many had seen during the depression, young gay GIs enjoyed a new freedom, looking for each other and a good time. "I have no one to answer to," wrote one gay GI to his buddy during the war, "as long as I behave myself during the week and stay out of the way of the MP's on weekends. . . . If I go home . . . how can I stay out all night or promote a serious affair? . . . My parents would simply consider me something perverted and keep me in the house." [2] Gay male and lesbian GIs took advantage of their freedom to create their own social life on base and to explore the flourishing gay nightlife in nearby cities.

Early in the war, however, military officials set out to bring this wartime boom in gay life under their control. While they perceived homosexuality in the service to be a problem of morale and discipline, in the cities they saw it as a form of vice. They used wartime vice control powers, which had been developed to eliminate heterosexual venereal disease and prostitution, to regulate the gay life as well. Military police (MPs) went everywhere GIs went, including the gay nightspots, making sure soldiers behaved themselves, followed the rules, and stayed out of forbidden places off base. Torn between the danger of getting caught by military police and the pain of being alone, gay male and lesbian soldiers still risked hanging out with each other in public and in private. They were acutely aware that at any moment they could be arrested, turned in by someone they mistakenly trusted as a friend, or assaulted by "queerbashers," and then thrown out of the service in disgrace.

Although the fear of exposure trapped some gay men and women in a world of solitude, many longed to have a sexual or romantic life and to meet others like themselves. They generally found each other by stages, realizing step by step that they were not the only ones in the service. Sometimes a person's first gay acquaintance would become a lover, but more often a buddy who might bring him or her into a circle of gay friends on base. With these new acquaintances, someone who was lonely and scared could feel a sense of belonging. When GIs went off base with their new friends to the cities, they explored the private gay world of civilian parties and the more public gay world of commercial bars, nightclubs, and bathhouses; discovered the diversity among gay people; and learned some of the rules and styles of gay life. With each of these experiences, a soldier met more people and became more deeply socialized into gay culture.

Many GIs made their first gay acquaintances on military bases. As millions of young men and women entered the service, bases grew almost overnight into small cities, some with populations approaching 100,000.[3] On most bases, personnel from the USO, American Red Cross, Special Services, and other agencies set up recreational facilities and activities—segregated by race, rank, and sometimes gender—to help newcomers meet each other and to give them something to do in their leisure time. GIs and officers could go to films every night at the post theater, buy items at the post exchange (the PX), and hang out with their peers at the service clubs for enlisted personnel or the NCO and officer clubs. The service clubs, which were staffed by civilian employees and volunteers, became the social centers of bases, with the best equipped having a coffee shop, snack bar, dance hall, pool room, library, music rooms, and meeting rooms.

Gay male and lesbian GIs easily blended into the crowd at social events and recreational activities. They played sports, danced in male-female couples, went to the movies, listened to records or the juke box, and joined their friends in the snack bar. But the loneliness that came with hiding one's sexuality led many to seek the companionship of others living through the same situation. "When you got to a camp," recalled Ben Small, "you just immediately sought out other gay guys just for the reinforcement of knowing you were not alone."

Gay GIs carefully put out feelers and used subtle eye contact to identify each other without exposing themselves to those who, in gay slang, were not "wise" to gay life. Phillis Abry cautiously revealed her interest in women by dropping hints and monitoring her friends' responses. "You'd start talking about anything," she recalled, "and then you'd start talking about women. Pretty soon it [becomes] obvious that you're only talking about women—where you went with other women or what you did with other women. And pretty soon it's becoming obvious that you're not mentioning any men. And so then you get a little bolder, and the next thing you know they're telling you about their love life. It certainly took many days to get to the point of feeling, 'OK, I can be open with this person'—that they're not going to run and turn me in." Bob Ruffing met his first gay friends at the Sampson Naval Training Station service club through eye contact; then slowly, he recalled, "you'd meet their friends, and they'd meet yours and it would spread. That's how I met everybody—they knew a friend who knew a friend who knew a friend." [4]

GIs who looked "queer"—women who acted butch and men who were effeminate or campy—were easier to identify and even became magnets for those looking for a circle of friends. Pat Bond knew on her first day that there were other lesbians at Fort Oglethorpe when she saw the butch women in the mess hall. As she walked to her barracks, she "heard a woman from one of the barracks windows saying, 'Good God, Elizabeth, here comes another one!' I thought, 'Well, at least they recognize that I am another one.' " Woodie Wilson's first gay friend at Keesler Field in Biloxi, Mississippi, was a campy MP. "We always queued up to go to the War Department theaters on base to see the first-run movies," Wilson recalled. "I remember standing in line and the MPs would come along. This very tall, absolutely blond but balding young man came up, and he would swing his club, and obviously he was a gay fellow! And he kept saying 'girls' to whoever was standing in line. And there would be a lot of giggling and a lot of horseplay— 'Oh what do you want, you fairy!'—but he was still part of the MP division on that base. So very easily I started to talk to him one night.''

Similar interests brought many gay GIs together. When Elizabeth Freeman was stationed at Leemore Army Air Force Base in California, she discovered that the small library on base had the book *Diana,* a 1939 lesbian novel. To check it out she had to sign her name in the back of the book. After she returned it, she was visited by a gay GI who subsequently had checked it out and noticed her name above his. A woman's interest in sports or in motor vehicles might also signal to others that she was gay. Betty Somers, who enlisted in the Women Marines, remembered that the women in the motor pool at Cherry Point, North Carolina, were "really a sort of up-front, out-and-out lesbian group" who also formed their own softball team. Offices where gay GIs worked sometimes gave them and other gay soldiers unexpected meeting places on base. When Woodie Wilson was assigned to glider school at Sheppard Field, Texas, he discovered that a gay crowd hung out at the chaplain's assistant's office in the chapel. "He would have parties over there in his office at night," Wilson recalled, "which I believe his chaplain even knew. We'd bring our canned foods over, our cookies or our cakes. We'd have a gay party, sitting in his office.''

Gay men and women hung out at the service clubs for some of the same reasons they went to gay bars. Service clubs were public places where they sometimes "cruised" (looked for prospective partners), where couples spent time together, or where both couples and individuals hung out with a gay crowd, usually in the company of others who were not gay but "wise." Woodie Wilson's gang of gay friends, who he met through his MP friend, hung around the service club at Keesler Field in Biloxi. "We all played cards together," he recalled. The crowd was "just swishy, giddy, gay, from all over the United States. They didn't all like one another, but they all knew one another." They weren't "pointed out at the club," and they weren't worried about being seen together or that others might think they were gay. When he was transferred, Wilson found an even larger gay service club gang at Sheppard Field, Texas.[5]

Some men used the service club piano and music rooms, where a phonograph and 78 rpm records were available, to create a gay "cocktail bar" ambiance, playing records or piano tunes that were popular among gay men. The music room "was just a quiet room," Woodie Wilson explained. Gay GIs went there "and sat and listened to long-hair music and wrote letters home—or you were supposed to be doing that, but you were really eyeing each other over." At the service club at Camp Beale, California, Marty Klausner pounded out "The Man I Love" on the piano to try to attract other interested men. His buddy Cpl. Tommy Martz described in a letter to a gay friend how his own service club romance began. In the snack bar Martz "kept watching and was being watched by the cutest thing you have ever seen. Later while listening to the radio he came over and asked me if they had a music room (they don't), and from there to records, to books etc, and finally we got some Coke and went down to his barracks and got a quart of bourbon and spent the time up 'til 3:30 AM talking, talking, and talking. . . . He is from LA, has been overseas 34 months and is returning soon. . . . We spent the nite in an empty barracks—and all was wonderful." [6]

Lesbian GIs also made the service clubs their home base. At Fort Oglethorpe, several Wacs testified that girlfriends and butches sat at the same tables together, talked about former lovers, pointed out other "dykes," cruised or were cruised, danced with each other, smoked, and drank beer. One private, who had been the girlfriend of a butch woman in the crowd, described an encounter with a Wac one night who tried to talk to her about the gay life. "She was at our table," the private testified, "all the rest of them were dancing . . . and she began to tell me about how different they were from other people; they couldn't ever find happiness. . . . She didn't put any name on it; she just said 'People of my kind.' " This private described other women at the service club who would point out a Wac and say "Well, she is another one of us" or "She is just like me." [7]

Both lesbian and gay male GIs who hung out together at the service clubs faced the danger of being turned in, especially if they kissed or necked in public. One night at Fort Oglethorpe, testified a WAC private, when two women started to kiss on the service club dance floor, "somebody, the hostess, I suppose it was, reported it, and they were called before their CO." [8] But the service club staffs sometimes were protective of their regular gay crowds. In the service clubs of most large bases, the rest rooms were convenient central locations for sexual activity between GIs, whether they were gay or not. [9] At Sheppard Field, Woodie Wilson recalled, the two hostesses, instead of reporting the men, would simply go into the men's room periodically and say in a friendly tone " 'Come on, boys, out of the booths!' " At Fort Oglethorpe the resident counselor had heard that at the South Post Service Club, "it got to be the fashion for those girls to stand over there and say to the new recruits as they came up: 'Are you in the mood?' " Her Wac informant told her that "if you say, 'Yes, I am in the mood,' then you go into the latrine with them." Instead of recommending disciplinary action, the resident counselor advocated giving lectures to the hostesses on the "scientific basis" of homosexuality so they would better understand what was going on.[10]

The gay "crowds" or "gangs" or "cliques" on military bases ranged from stable, tight-knit in-groups that shunned outsiders to loose bunches of "gay guys" or "gay gals" and other hangers-on who enjoyed each other's company and gained or lost members from week to week. In March 1943, Jerry Watson, a GI stationed in Coolidge, Arizona, described in his letters how he became part of a gay crowd. At first, he noticed that "the gay ones here seem to segregate, undoubtedly due to certain fears." A week later he had already "met several outstanding queens here, but fate seems to split us up, goddam!" But in the next two months, he found his own clique of eight gay GIs who gathered "several times a week in one of the local 'souse huts.' "[11] An apparently heterosexual truck driver at Fort Oglethorpe complained about a lesbian clique in the Extended Field Service that did not welcome newcomers. "Those groups of girls get in a group by themselves," she testified. "The majority of time they wouldn't let another outsider in that group, and it is hard to break into that group. They have just got their own set friends. . . . The majority of them wear short hair. . . . I think they are called 'Lesbians.' "[12] While Pat Bond felt left out of the lesbian sports crowd at Fort Oglethorpe, the college crowd was more open and included heterosexual women who "didn't give a shit what anybody else was." Gay men's cliques at Camp Crowder, Missouri, and Sheppard Field, Texas, also included fellow-travelers who were not gay but were "wise" to gay life or who had not made decisions about their own sexuality.[13]

People in each clique had their own rules and customs. Women often paired up into butch/girlfriend couples or remained unattached, although some lesbian cliques were made up only of butches. Adhering to their own sexual folkways and taboos, butches rarely dated each other and had to be careful about dating other butches' girlfriends in the same crowd. Rusty Brown, who was a Navy mechanic during the war, "automatically went to the table with the butches" so that she could "find out who was going with who—I didn't want to get my head knocked off.'' Couple relationships stabilized a lesbian clique but breakups, rivalry, and jealousy caused tensions and fights that sometimes tore a group apart.[14]

Gay men in cliques generally obeyed a taboo that prevented them from coupling with any of their buddies. ''We used to meet every night,'' Stan Carlow said of his gay clique on a U.S. Army base in Australia. ''We were friends. There was no sex or anything, just friends.'' ''Nobody wanted to go to bed with anybody,'' concurred Woodie Wilson about his gay gangs at Keesler and Sheppard fields. ''It was more camaraderie.'' Possibly because many gay GIs had been socialized as young men to pursue sex for its own sake and to feel that sex would destroy a friendship that hadn't started sexually, many had to work hard to figure out how to form intimate relationships with each other. As a result, they engaged more easily in one-night stands or pursued romance with gay and ''normal'' men outside the group while creating devoted but asexual friendships with their buddies. A gay GI's clique often served him as an emotional home base where friends welcomed his reports about his sexual adventures or romantic affairs.

Both men's and women's cliques spontaneously developed two important rules of thumb that protected them from exposure—not to talk directly to anyone about homosexuality and not to reveal anyone else's homosexuality, especially to military authorities. Gay male and lesbian veterans alike recall that the fear of being stigmatized was so great that they rarely heard other gay GIs directly refer to the subject in their conversation or say that they were gay or ''put any name on it,'' [15] even when they were speaking intimately with their lovers. Although Sarah Davis had a ''mad, mad love affair'' with another Wave in Florida, the two women never described their relationship as lesbian or homosexual.

Whether or not they openly discussed the gay life, people in each local clique often identified with each other as members of a secret club with their own meeting place, slang, signals, and nicknames. At Fort Oglethorpe, Wacs testified that women in one lesbian clique wore a particular ring, while women in another covertly identified themselves in the service club by whistling the tune of the ''Hawaiian War Chant.'' Rumors circulated that some butch Wacs had membership cards that designated them as ''one of the 'boys.' '' [16] At Camp Crowder, male GIs in one gay service club crowd gave each other nicknames based on the female characters in the 1939 film, *Gone With the Wind,* and the 1944 film, *Jane Eyre.*[17] A clique of gay male GIs in Arizona had their own campy identification signs—White Rose perfume, a secret handshake, and the name Legion of the Damned.[18]

Although the pressures of wartime service encouraged gay GIs to form their own cliques, they also split these fragile groups apart. In 1943, Woodie Wilson and his MP buddy, to stay in touch with their far-flung Air Corps buddies, put out a newsletter from Myrtle Beach, South Carolina. Most bases had official GI publications, ranging from glossy magazines to handmade newsletters stapled together.[19] Using these as models, the two soldiers produced a mimeographed newsletter called the *Myrtle Beach Bitch*, one of the first gay publications produced in the United States and possibly the earliest newsletter by and for gay servicemen. Woodie Wilson described how he and his buddy put the *Myrtle Beach Bitch* together. "We just started having a ball in the orderly room typing up these things, and then running them off on the mimeograph machine. We were saying, 'Guess who's still alive! The two that you knew at Keesler, Sheppard, and Hunter Field at Savannah! We're still around, and we haven't jumped off yet!' and 'What's happening to you?' Some of them did write [back] and say, 'I'm at Indio, California, at the Desert Training Center and I'm going into town every night to the canteen where the Hollywood stars are.' Those things got into our paper." "It was almost like receiving a newsletter from home," explained Norman Sansom, who received copies in Georgia, "because it was the only communication we had about people we had met in other bases. It let us know who was overseas and where they were." [20]

The gay crowd found a little more freedom off base than they could in the barracks or service clubs. When couples or the whole gang got passes together, they went into nearby towns to rent hotel or motel rooms for some rare privacy or to throw parties for their friends. Woodie Wilson's gay crowd at Sheppard Field, Texas, went to a hotel in nearby Wichita Falls, where they would "get a suite of rooms with what money we had," he recalled, "and sit up and get drunk." At Sampson Naval Training Station, Bob Ruffing and his bunch would go on weekend passes to hotels in Rochester and Ithaca or, in warm weather, rent cottages together on the Finger Lakes. Pat Bond remembered that the lesbian couples at Fort Oglethorpe went into Chattanooga for weekend passes. "When we got a pass," recalled Phillis Abry about the time she and her lover were stationed in Lubbock, Texas, "we went to a hotel and made love and stayed in the hotel most of the time, because that was something we couldn't do in the barracks. Our primary interest was getting somewhere where we could have privacy." Unlike many heterosexual couples, Abry and her lover never had trouble checking into the same room because, she explained, "[we] were two nice-looking women. Who would suspect [we] were going to go up and make love! People didn't think about it then."

In most parts of the country, hotels and motels, as well as the military bases, were racially segregated, at times making it impossible for black or interracial couples or groups to rent a room. During the Fort Oglethorpe investigation, one Wac testified that she had asked a "dyke" from Fort Jackson, South Carolina, if the white and black lesbians were able to mix. "I asked her how they managed there, and I knew they couldn't go to hotels together . . . and she told me they would meet in town, get a cab, and go out to this Savoy Inn." She described the Savoy Inn as a tourist campsite outside Columbia, South Carolina, that allowed both black and white customers to rent cabins.[21]

Gay male and lesbian GIs went into small towns to hang out on the streets or in taverns, at times becoming bold and daring. One night in March 1943, Jerry Watson's crowd "invaded the dime store" in Coolidge, Arizona, where they bought cheap perfume and "went down the street discreetly applying it behind our ears." Two weeks later Watson and his gay pal went into town again but "had time only for a few drinks and a quick look-see about town and we had to start back. . . . I'm surprised we weren't picked up [by MPs]—the way we carried on. Even necking in the tavern booth and on the bus back!" At Mitchell's tavern in nearby Florence, he wrote to a pen pal, he spotted "the most handsome corporal drinking at the bar" and they both began exchanging "very attentive glances." Watson ordered a beer, stuck a nickel in the juke box and, to express his interest, he wrote, selected the song "If you only loved me a little more." The corporal checked out the record title, then Watson selected another song, "Why don't you do me right," after which the corporal played a song to express his own intentions— "Heaven for Two." [22]

No matter where GIs did their training, it was likely that at some time during their military service they would be stationed near one of the nation's many port cities—Chicago, Washington, Seattle, San Francisco, San Diego, Philadelphia, New York, Miami, New Orleans—that were ringed with military bases and filled with the excitement of a nation at war. Millions of civilians arrived in the cities looking for defense work. Every night their numbers swelled as GIs and officers left their bases to invade the entertainment districts on temporary passes. By the summer of 1942, 50,000 soldiers and sailors were pouring into Chicago's downtown "Loop" each weekend looking for a good time.

The freedom that GIs found in the cities, however, did not liberate them from the strict rules and regulations of military life. Passes were privileges that could be denied at the last minute to those who had misbehaved or could be cut short during an emergency. Before leaving base, men were lectured to use condoms and to stay away from prostitutes and off-limits establishments. Lectures to female GIs focused less directly on sex and vice, warning them instead to be on their best behavior in public to protect their reputations as women soldiers. But being a lesbian, recalled Phillis Abry, made it "very easy to be a proper lady and not go around flaunting yourself at the men." Military police followed both male and female soldiers on passes into town; whenever they left their bases or returned, soldiers had to report themselves so their officers knew where they were at all times, otherwise they would be declared AWOL (absent without leave) and disciplined.

Once they had qualified for passes, GIs got away from their bases by taking special buses or hitchhiking into the cities. Each day thousands of servicemen lined roadsides thumbing rides. Civilians were told that it was their duty to pick up these men. "You would want the break if you were in their shoes," explained a columnist writing in the *San Francisco Chronicle* in late 1943. "Why not give it to them? Why not give them a ride?" [23] Routes between military bases and the cities became cruising areas where civilian men with cars picked up men in uniform. Many gay male soldiers and military employees welcomed these erotically charged roadside offers. "Decided to hitchhike home," Donald Vining wrote in his diary in May 1942 after leaving his job at the Fort Dix canteen, "hoping to be picked up by that Norwegian. Somebody else beat him to it, however, and what a somebody!" [24] Civilians who picked up soldiers and propositioned them, however, had to develop a cruising style that protected them from getting beaten, robbed or blackmailed by offended GIs. [25]

Arriving in town, men and women in uniform hung out with other GIs of their own sex, feeling an easy camaraderie and often seeing the sights with each other. When gay male GIs went into town with buddies who weren't gay, they stuck together or split up, some looking for female companionship, others hoping to find interested men, often in the same parts of town. The crowds of lonely men in uniform wandering the streets looking for companionship in the cities created what one veteran called a "gay ambiance" where gay GIs didn't feel out of place.

Lesbians moved about more freely on the city streets than before the war. Even late at night, they joined other women on their way to or from work walking in each other's company wearing slacks, coveralls, or a wide array of uniforms. Lesbians and their female friends went into bars, cafés, restaurants, and movie theaters unescorted by men without raising eyebrows, everywhere meeting other women who had replaced men as bus operators, streetcar conductors, taxi drivers, and bartenders in hotels and taverns.

GIs arriving on their own in a strange city did not have to be lonely with nothing to do and nowhere to go. Civilians were ready to greet them, give them directions, take them out on the town, invite them to dinner or parties, or offer them a place to stay overnight, even if it was on the floor or the sofa. Local citizens notified housing registries that they had a spare room or bed to offer a serviceman for the night. "It was 'Be nice to GIs' during the war," recalled Ben Small, who served in the Army Air Corps, "regardless of their orientation. Let them have a good time. If they're gay, fine. Just so long as they didn't embarrass anybody or do anything on the premises."

Civilian organizations set up canteens, clubs, and lounges, such as the Stage Door Canteens in many cities, where GIs went to relax, visit, dance, and be entertained by famous stars. Magazines, newspapers, posters, and radio programs all encouraged special treatment for men and women in uniform, asking civilians to give them preference in lines, at hotels, and on buses and trains. Men and women in uniform were given free or discount tickets to films, plays, concerts, the opera, the ballet, and other cultural events. In the most overcrowded cities, public facilities including movie theaters, bowling alleys, high school gyms, hotel lobbies, and bathhouses stayed open all night to offer servicemen places to sleep.[26]

Although some of these cultural events and emergency accommodations welcomed all Americans in uniform, others in every part of the country excluded servicemen because of their race or referred them to their own facilities, sending Chinese American soldiers, for example, to a Chinatown Servicemen's Club. In the middle of the war, when the Army gave male soldiers several weeks of rest and recreation at government expense, it shipped white GIs to hotels in coastal resort towns, sending black GIs to second-rate hotels in Harlem and on Chicago's South Side.[27] Minority soldiers, both men and women, couldn't enter segregated parts of town or apartment buildings for parties or overnight housing, nor could they go to segregated hotels, movie theaters, and other ostensibly public accommodations. As a result, gay nightlife for these soldiers often evolved distinct from white gay nightlife during the war.

Enormous crowds of GIs on the move infused some cultural events and emergency facilities with opportunities for gay romance and sex. Because young civilian men became scarce, women at public dances paired up with each other to jitterbug or fox-trot to big-band music, putting a premium on butch women who could lead their partners.[28] Intermission at the ballet in many cities turned into a sea of furtive glances as gay male soldiers and civilians cruised one another. Male GIs who packed the standing-room section in the Metropolitan Opera House in New York City, which for years had been a gay male cruising mecca, pressed their bodies together several deep against the rail. Balconies of cheap movie theaters, such as those on New York's 42nd Street at Times Square, harbored civilians and servicemen of various races looking for male sexual partners.[29] The differences between cruising and wartime hospitality became blurred as strangers invited servicemen into their homes for the night.

The needs of lonely and transient GIs for intimacy transformed servicemen's hotels, residence clubs, and dormitories into covert sexual resorts. These were often the first places where a new soldier in town spent the night. Hotel rooms were so scarce in most cities that GIs were lucky to double up in the same room or even the same bed with another man, which they could do without raising eyebrows at the front desk. The servicemen's residence clubs usually had several floors of small single and double rooms or larger rooms with bunk beds or cots, public showers, a common lounge, and sometimes a cafeteria and swimming pool. Covert sexual activity was lively in many of these crowded facilities, such as the Pepsi-Cola Servicemen's Canteen dormitory in San Francisco and the Seven Seas Locker Club in San Diego, where gay civilians "borrow[ed] servicemen's uniforms just to gain admission and make the scene."[30]

In the YMCA hotels especially, gay and GI life merged, with men cruising each other in the showers and climbing into and out of each other's beds. In 1943, Donald Vining began work as desk clerk at the Sloane House YMCA in Manhattan—one of the best known in the nation for its clandestine sexual activity—where most of the 1,200 possible guests each night were servicemen. One night in 1942, Vining described in his diary a typical encounter at the Y. "Just as I put on my robe to leave the shower room, in comes a nice-looking well-built boy. . . . Something destroyed my usual timidity and I walked right up and ran my hands over him. 'Do you mind?' I asked, without a quaver in my voice. 'No,' he said casually, as he went on drying himself. I would have had him come to my room but he had a double room with a fellow, who came to hunt him up.'' One night after a sailor complained that a resident had made a pass at him, Vining was relieved to find that the protection office took no punitive action. Although YMCA administrators did not condone sexual activity on the premises and occasionally conducted crackdowns that led to arrests, the staff often looked the other way if the men were discreet. YMCA hotels in nearly every city, from Harlem to Honolulu, from Tacoma to St. Louis and Miami, were active cruising grounds throughout the war.[31]

GIs, particularly enlisted men who were without money, too young to drink in bars, or excluded from white establishments, filled public parks in the cities, hanging out day and night, talking to each other, looking for a good time, mingling with civilians. These were often the same cruising parks where men had been picking up other men long before the war—Lafayette Park in Washington, the Public Gardens in Boston, Lincoln Park in Chicago, Central Park and Riverside Drive in Manhattan, Union Square in San Francisco, Pershing Square in Los Angeles, Old Plaza Park in San Diego. Soldiers with no place to stay cruised the parks and went home with other men to have sex for pleasure, money, companionship, or a bed for the night. "The best trick to get was a civilian," explained Burt Miller, who served in the Navy, "because he had someplace to go to."[32] Donald Vining was one of the many civilians who frequently cruised Central Park and Pershing Square during the war, taking home soldiers, sailors, marines, and Coast Guardsmen for the night.[33] One evening at Pershing Square, a soldier asked Vining "for the time and then commented on the weather. Since his purpose was obvious, I gave him the onceover and found him attractive. He gave me all the openings, saying he had five more days left of his leave and was broke, would have to spend the nite in the park, etc. I couldn't let the poor boy wear himself down so said he could come out with me, to which he immediately agreed."[34] In parks and along public beaches on warm nights, dimouts and blackouts gave homosexual as well as heterosexual couples, especially those with no place to stay or no privacy at home, the opportunity to neck without being detected.[35]

Each gay serviceman or civilian based his cruising techniques in all of these places on his own sexual folklore about men in uniform. Generally they believed sailors to be the most available and marines the least. Sailors acquired this reputation because they were out at sea without women for long stretches of time, they were younger than men in the other branches and their tight uniforms looked boyish, revealing, and sexy.[36] Marines were a challenge because of their tough image. "Marines were very bad," recalled Haviland Ferris. "You had to watch out for them. Sailors were very gentle. There were so many soldiers that you had to take your luck. The preferred group of the time were the sailors." "The marines had a reputation of being closeted gay," recalled Stuart Loomis. "The idea was that all marines were available, but they never wanted to talk about it and would hit you in the nose if you brought it up. That wasn't really quite true. There were lots of very obviously gay marines during the war." Each man's sexual experiences and the stories he exchanged with friends and sex partners either confirmed or contradicted these stereotypes, keeping the folklore alive. The danger, however, of making a mistake and being turned in to MPs, discharged, blackmailed, robbed, beaten, and even murdered was ever present, as "queer bashers" and thieves hung around cruising areas to prey on both military and civilian gay men.[37]

Parties in civilian homes offered gay GIs safer and more private surroundings where they could be themselves and escape the drab regimentation of military life. "It was just easier to let your hair down," Stuart Loomis recalled, "and be comfortable in a gay crowd in a private setting than it was in most of the public places." Some parties were thrown by gay hosts while others were held in the homes of people who enjoyed the company of a gay crowd. "The people who lived here in San Francisco," Bob Ruffing recalled, "the natives, were awfully good to servicemen. I remember a woman up in that area around Mount Davidson. She used to have a party around once a week that turned out to be very gay. There were many of them all around the city." In Columbus, Ohio, Martin Stow and his "college crowd" buddies from his infantry regiment would go to an afternoon tea at the home of "a wonderful woman named 'Miss Peach.' It was very classic—half of the young men there had to be gay, there was no question about it." Both lesbian and gay male GIs heard about these private affairs through word of mouth or from personal invitations.

Gay parties ranged from formal sit-down dinners to all-night raucous affairs with drinking, dancing, and sex. "There was a man who was sort of the queen of gay society in Louisville," Burt Gerrits recalled. "He had wonderful parties for both gay men and women. That was the first time I ever went to parties where there were gay women also. Everybody knew him or knew of him." "What we think of as a wild party in a bar now would only be done in the privacy of the home," Ben Small explained, "which was kind of nice because you could pass out right there, wake up the next morning, and continue on." In Biloxi,

Woodie Wilson met a dentist, "a wonderful old fellow," who "loved gay people around him in his own home." Wilson and his gay buddies from Keesler Field "were always going over to his house" for dinner parties where they would "stay over occasionally" and used the privacy of his home to bed with men they had met in town or at the party. Sometimes gay hosts rented hotel suites for grander affairs. In May 1943, Jim Kepner wrote that he had gone to the "maddest party" at San Francisco's elegant Mark Hopkins Hotel—a gay midnight wedding ceremony with more than a hundred guests, many in drag. "The largest gay gathering I have ever seen." [38]

When gay civilians threw wartime parties to entertain the new GIs in town, they drew on a long tradition in gay life. In the 1920s and 1930s, the private gay circles that existed in every city were often multigenerational, stable, and organized around a single man, woman, or couple who opened their home for get-togethers, ranging from "rent parties," which charged admission to raise the rent, to elegant affairs in the penthouses of the rich. In black neighborhoods between the wars, certain social circles welcomed "daggers" (butch lesbians) and "sissy men" (effeminate gay men) into their private worlds, such as that of heiress A'Lelia Walker in Harlem.[39] At all of these private gatherings, newcomers who had just moved into town or who had been recently discovered or "brought out" by someone in the group were socialized into the gay life. Private parties were especially important for teenagers who could not drink in bars and in small towns and cities where there was no commercial gay nightlife. In Nebraska in the late 1930s, Stuart Loomis and his college chums would drive from Omaha to a mansion in Lincoln called Magnolia Manor, which was owned by "an older gay gentleman" who rented rooms to gay students and let them use the house and gardens for parties on weekend nights.[40]

The war mobilization, however, disrupted gay circles as much as it split up other social networks. "It all went completely apart," recalled Bob Ruffing of his social crowd in Manhattan. "People left, like I left." The war "came as a kind of frightening and somewhat exciting event for those of us who were part of those particular gay circles," Stuart Loomis explained. "Our little group was going to be broken up. What would happen to us if we went off to some strange city or some strange place? Where would we find other gay people?" While military service depleted local gay circles of their youngest members, the gay social circles in war-boom towns widened as transient servicemen stationed at nearby bases dropped by. Some of the gay civilians who stayed

The labeling of homosexuals as unfit for military service began in World War II, when psychiatrists persuaded Selective Service to screen selectees for mental disorders. Dr. Harry Stack Sullivan *(top left)* and Dr. Winfred Overholser *(top right)* designed and promoted the screening procedures. *(bottom)* An Army doctor examines recruits at Camp Blanding, Florida, before they are interviewed by a psychiatrist.

Despite psychiatric screening, few lesbians or gay men were excluded from military service. Lesbians who enlisted in the armed forces included *(top left)* Phillis Abry, radio "repairman," and *(top right)* Pat Bond, medical technician, both in Women's Army Corps; *(center left)* Sarah Davis, machinist's mate, WAVES; *(center right)* Elizabeth Freeman, clerk typist, Women's Army Corps; *(bottom)* Helen Harder, synthetic flying trainer instructor, Women's Army Corps.

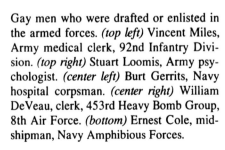

Gay men who were drafted or enlisted in the armed forces. *(top left)* Vincent Miles, Army medical clerk, 92nd Infantry Division. *(top right)* Stuart Loomis, Army psychologist. *(center left)* Burt Gerrits, Navy hospital corpsman. *(center right)* William DeVeau, clerk, 453rd Heavy Bomb Group, 8th Air Force. *(bottom)* Ernest Cole, midshipman, Navy Amphibious Forces.

This is no time to be FRAIL

(top) Illustration from a Fleischmann's Yeast advertisement proclaiming that "the dainty days are done for the duration." Lesbians who were interested "men's work" fit into the armed forces as mechanics, drill instructors, and motor vehicle operators. *(bottom left)* Phillis Abry driving a jeep at South Plains Army Air Field in Lubbock, Texas. *(bottom right)* Sarah Davis, aviation machinist's mate, at Naval Air Station, Vero Beach, Florida.

Most women and many gay men were channeled into the clerical and service duties that increased as the military expanded. *(top left)* A WAC poster designed to persuade women to enlist so they would release male soldiers from "women's work" to fight in combat. *(to right)* Gay men who served as clerks included Maynard Smith, in the Army Recruiting Service in Columbus, Ohio. *(bottom)* William DeVeau, stationed in England with the 8th Air Force, where he played piano in soldier shows.

An active soldier show campaign, coupled with an Army policy that prohibited Wacs from performing in musical shows with men, encouraged female impersonations on military stages. *(top)* GI dancers from the "Dream Ballet" scene in *This Is the Army,* the most popular soldier show of the war. *(bottom)* Black GIs in *Jumping with Jodie,* a musical produced by men of the 3966th Quartermaster Truck Company, near Regensburg, Germany.

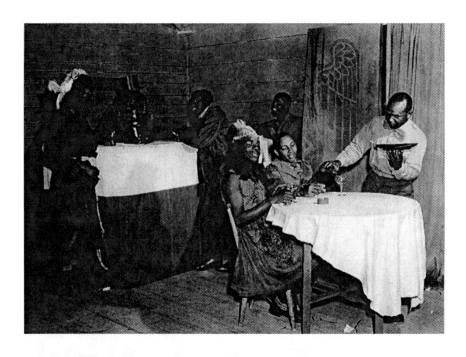

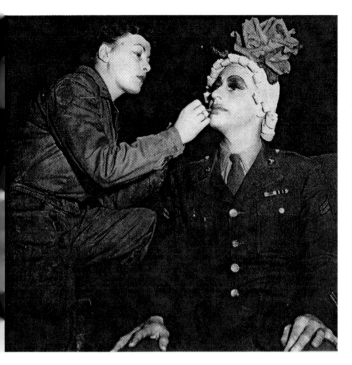

(top left) A Wac lieutenant teaches a soldier audience "how to create a female for a soldier show" at a workshop in London. Soldier shows became a haven for gay GIs. *(top right)* Pfc. Woodie Wilson holding a poster for *Private Maxie Reporting,* a 1943 show at Hunter Field near Savannah, Georgia, in which he played a homosexual officer candidate named "Bloomingslip." *(bottom)* Cpl. Thomas Reddy as "Georgia from New Georgia" performing with a Marine Corps troupe that entertained men in combat areas throughout the South Pacific.

Life in sex-segregated quarters created homosexual tensions as well as opportunities. *(top)* A magazine advertisement illustrates how young recruits were placed "two in every lower berth" on troop trains. *(bottom)* Army booklet "The Story of Mack and Mike" instructed soldiers to talk over their troubles with an officer, advice that caused some GIs to reveal their homosexuality and then be reported for discharge.

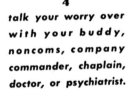

THE KID IN UPPER 4

THE NEW HAVEN R.R.

SERVING THE GREAT INDUSTRIAL STATES OF MASSACHUSETTS, RHODE ISLAND AND CONNECTICUT

Training is Mack's life work now!

Training is Mack's life work now; he should get it well—it may mean the difference between his life or the enemy's. Remember, the duty of the American Soldier is *not* to give his life for his country, but rather to make the enemy give his life instead. If Mack is confused, troubled and physically upset, he CAN snap out of it—HERE'S HOW!

1
Be honest with yourself; figure out exactly what's worrying you.

2
remember, everyone is going through the same thing.

3
resolve to do something about it – then DO it!

4
talk your worry over with your buddy, noncoms, company commander, chaplain, doctor, or psychiatrist.

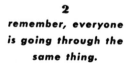

5
make yourself carry out the advice you get!

behind in Manhattan, recalled Bob Ruffing, "kept up these parties and they'd spread the word among their friends who were in town for the weekend. They got to be a little bit wild, because this war spirit was starting to invade everything." In Washington, private gay cocktail and dinner parties flourished to accommodate the military personnel and government workers who flooded into the city, enabling many to come out for the first time into middle-class gay life.[41] As old friends went away and new people arrived each week, the gay social circles in the cities were thrown into a state of continual change and adaptation.

One of the most dramatic changes brought about by the war mobilization was that gay bars moved closer to the center of gay life. Sometimes with only a few hours in a big city, gay male and lesbian GIs were forced to rely on commercial establishments near the heart of the city to find the gay life quickly. As a result, bars, cocktail lounges, cafés, and nightclubs that catered to the gay crowd flourished during the war, stretching the prewar gay nightspots to their limits and beyond. These establishments often were clustered in the parts of town that were flooded with GIs, introducing the gay life to a wider population of young men and women.

Some cities and states, however, in wartime efforts to discourage prostitution, prohibited women from drinking at a bar, tending a bar, or even from entering a tavern unescorted by a man. Cities clamped down on women's public heterosexual activity, barring those who appeared to be "Victory Girls" (wartime prostitutes) from hanging out in bars, hotel lobbies, and bus stations.[42] Partly because of such restrictions, lesbian GIs rarely found a predominantly female bar in any city, although "men only" bars were common. Instead, together with lesbian civilians, they carved out their own social territories in corners of bars frequented by gay men, such as the Black Cat in San Francisco or the Howdy Club in New York City, and often went out on the town in the company of their gay male friends. "Gay boys and girls mixed quite freely," recalled Helen Weinstock of the wartime bars in New York City. "Only a small minority confined themselves solely to their own sex" socially.[43] A bar that served a mixed crowd of lesbians, gay men and their friends more easily camouflaged its gay character than a bar that had only women or only men. The small number of bars nationwide that did cater to a lesbian clientele included nightclubs such as Mona's in San Francisco and, in Los Angeles, the if Club and the Lakeshore Club, which featured an "all-girl" band on weekends.[44] But because most bars were male domains, many lesbians, like other women, preferred to socialize with each other in the privacy of their homes.

Gay servicemen found the most discreet gay crowd in the men's bars and cocktail lounges at posh hotels, where patrons were officers or civilians in jackets and ties, although enlisted men generally were not excluded. Three hotel bars world famous for their wartime gay ambiance were the Astor Bar in New York's Times Square, the Top of the Mark at the Mark Hopkins in San Francisco, and the Biltmore men's bar just off Pershing Square in Los Angeles. These were so popular that servicemen sometimes had to wait in long lines to get in. Burt Miller, a twenty-one-year-old naval officer from Seattle who was stationed just outside Los Angeles, described how he first discovered the hotel bars. "Frequently I'd eat dinner at the Biltmore Hotel," he recalled. "One night, after dinner, I walked through the bar—about 75 percent of the men were in uniform—and I asked myself, 'Can what I think is going on here *be* going on?' I stopped to find out and sure enough it was! I was in that bar every night." By 6:00 P.M. every night at the Biltmore bar, recalled another gay man, "the guys would be packed three-deep, the servicemen among them hoping to find a reason to make America worth coming back to." [45] Most cities had their own versions of these bars, from the Mayflower and Statler Hotels in Washington to the Royal Lounge in Milwaukee's Royal Hotel and the Hotel Bentley in Alexandria, Louisiana. [46]

Gay cruising in hotel bars was quiet and covert, but still charged with erotic possibilities and an awareness that there was little time to waste. "The approaches were all extremely indirect," recalled Burt Miller. "I didn't know what the folkways of gay bars were, so I had to wait till somebody approached me and then I had to try to figure out what the nuance was." The self-policing of gay patrons—conservative clothes, no touching, no obvious propositions, no loud campy shrieks— enabled these hotel bars to lead successful double lives, so that patrons who were not gay might never know that they were in the presence of a great number of gay men. "You really had to behave yourself there," Ben Small remembered. "Play like a little gentleman. But you knew that the guy on your right and the guy on your left were gay, and [you went] through all of this nonsensical straight conversation: 'Hi. Where are you stationed? Where do you come from? Where are you staying while you're in town?' 'Well, I'm at the Y.' 'Oh, so am I. I'm in room 222. Drop by for a drink.' And that was the extent of it. There was certainly nobody running up and putting their arms around each other or, the greatest sin of all, groping in public." Bartenders and hotel management may not have been happy about their gay customers but did not bother them so long as they were "gentlemanly" and blended in.[47]

The Astor Bar, because of its location at Forty-fourth Street and Broadway at Times Square, functioned as one of New York City's primary meeting places. The hotel's advertising slogan was "Meet Me At the Astor," and many gay men did.[48] "One side of the large oval bar was gay," recalled Stuart Loomis, "and the other side was straight. It was pretty obvious what was going on." Daphne, one of the Astor Bar's cigarette girls, who was wise to the gay life, moved through the crowd of men on the gay side crying "Cigars, cigarets, hairpins. . . ." Because Norm Sansom, who had been discharged from the Army as a homosexual, worked across the street at a shoe store, he visited the Astor Bar daily. "I used to bring the bartenders free nylon stockings, which was like gold! And so I could have anything I wanted. I never paid for a drink in my life at the Astor Bar." Other veterans recall that they were able to give the bartender messages to pass on to gay GI friends. "It would be impossible to calculate the contribution of the Astor Bar to the war effort," wrote a wartime habitué when the hotel shut its doors in 1966, "impossible to estimate the number of one-night romances which brought comfort to the tense fighting men and reassured them that the things worth fighting for were still with us." [49]

Gay male and lesbian GIs with a little money to spend also found each other at certain nightclubs and cabarets. Although nightclub entertainment was never publicly identified as gay, such performers as Hildegarde and Tallulah Bankhead attracted a devoted gay following, sometimes dropping veiled hints or singing lyrics with double meanings directed at their admirers. During the war Beatrice Lillie sang "There Are Fairies at the Bottom of My Garden" in New York; the "whimsically naughty" Dwight Fiske—promoted as the "master of the double entendre, the hint and innuendo"—sang his songs at the Oval Room at Boston's Copley Plaza Hotel and the Clover Club in Los Angeles; Hope Emerson sang her campy, outlandish, and risqué songs at Manhattan's One Fifth Avenue; and the more ribald Rae Bourbon sang "He's Got the Cutest Little Dinghy in the Navy" at Miami's Five O'Clock Club.[50] Female impersonation night clubs such as Finocchio's in San Francisco, the Flamingo Club in Los Angeles, the Howdy Club in Manhattan, the My O' My in New Orleans, and Danny's Jewel Box in Tampa, attracted mixed crowds of GIs, tourists, curiosity-seekers, gay men and lesbians. They featured such artists as Walter Hart, Harvey Lee, Arthur Blake, Francis Blair, Nicki Callucci, Niles Marsh, and the traveling Jewel Box Revue, all of whom kept camp drag culture alive and public during the war.

Often within walking distance of the elegant hotels was another part of town where GI and gay recreational life overlapped. These were the "tenderloins"—Scollay Square and the Combat Zone in Boston, Ninth Street in downtown Washington, Times Square in New York, the Tenderloin in San Francisco, the French Quarter in New Orleans, Broadway in San Diego. They included an array of businesses that catered to servicemen's needs and pleasures—bus stations, penny and movie arcades, tattoo parlors, burlesque houses, "locker clubs" where GIs illegally checked their uniforms and rented "civvies" to go to off-limits joints, tailor shops where soldiers and sailors customized their uniforms, credit jewelers, cafeterias, newsstands, bathhouses and brothels (some of them gay), and cheap hotels.[51] In these parts of town were the sailor bars and servicemen's bars—which middle-class GIs called "rough" bars—that catered to enlisted men of many races, gay civilians, and "trade" (enlisted men and working-class civilian men willing to go with gay men). These included the Blue Jacket and Bradley's in San Diego, the Cavalier in Long Beach, the Silver Rail and the Old Crow in San Francisco, Pearl's in Oakland, the Silver Dollar in Boston, the Pink Elephant in New York's Times Square, and Carroll's on Ninth Street in Washington.[52] A soldier or sailor, whether he was gay or not, easily stumbled into pickup situations in these bars and in other places throughout the tenderloins, from the toilets in the bus station to the muscle magazine section of the newsstand.

While many commercial establishments were "whites only," minority gay GIs found their own places where they could get together.[53] Black GIs stationed near New York City discovered one of the nation's most developed black and interracial gay cultures in Harlem. It had begun to flourish in the 1920s and 1930s during the Harlem Renaissance and continued to evolve during the war.[54] In December 1942, Lucky's Rendezvous in upper Harlem opened its doors, a "narrow, smoky bar," according to Ebony, that catered to an interracial clientele in an atmosphere "steeped in the swish jargon of its many lavender [gay] customers." [55] The Mount Morris Baths in Harlem also catered to a gay crowd and accepted both black and white patrons.[56] Public drag balls, despite their decline in many cities, stayed alive during the war in Harlem and other black urban neighborhoods. Huge interracial "costume balls" and "fashion contests" were sponsored by Finnie's Club in Chicago beginning in 1939 and by Phil Black's Fun Makers Club in Harlem beginning in

1944.[57] Bars in other cities, like the Circus Inn in Rock Island, Illinois, also served racially mixed gay crowds.[58]

All these wartime changes—the sprouting of cliques on bases, the thriving bars and party life in the cities, the easy availability of covert sexual activity among servicemen—gave an enormous boost to gay life and culture. A growing population of displaced young men and women on the move learned to think of themselves as gay, located gay nightspots, met each other, formed relationships, used a new language, followed new codes of behavior, and carved out places for themselves in the world as gay men and lesbians.

Running through the nightlife of the cities was fragmented conversation about the gay life—"pillow talk" after sex in bed, secrets told over drinks, in taxis, on street corners, at parties, with bunkmates, by mail, on the walls of public toilets—among people on their way somewhere else. An encounter in the park led to a party invitation; a chat at the party identified the currently popular bar. "If you went to someplace," Bob Ruffing recalled, "and had a success, you always told somebody else." GIs on passes sent each other postcards with the names of places they had discovered. "Most guys devoted a rear section of their address book," recalled a veteran of the wartime gay life, "to city-by-city listings of action spots and people to contact. . . . One was forever up-dating his information to keep it current, crossing out closed bars or adding new ones." [59] The constant exchange of information among people on the go helped to standardize gay slang in the United States. "It was not until after Pearl Harbor," wrote homosexual rights pioneer Donald Webster Cory in 1951, that the word *gay* became "a magic byword in practically every corner of the United States where homosexuals might gather. . . ." [60]

In the temporary refuge of the bars, where they experienced what it was like to be "normal" because they were in the majority, gay servicemen talked about their common situations, developed a gay point of view, and pursued love and sex with each other. "It was there I learned that there could be a camaraderie," recalled Burt Miller of the wartime bars in Los Angeles, "that people who initially had nothing but their homosexuality in common could get together and like one another and talk." To fit into gay bar life, Miller had to "learn what the language was." It was there that he first heard the words *gay, queen, dyke,* and *cruising.* "It took me some time," he explained, "I was quite a greenhorn for a while, [but] I came back again and again. I was quite willing to learn!" [61]

Fear of exposure, however, threatened this wartime camaraderie and led to serious disagreements over whether to live the gay life and how gay one should be. The strongest criticism was leveled at the "swishes"—the most flagrant, loud, effeminate, and campy "queens"— and at the butches. Some lesbians afraid of being exposed felt threatened by the boldness of the butch women. "I never fraternized with them," Betty Somers recalled of the butch clique in the Women Marines at Cherry Point. "I didn't like them, particularly. [I thought], 'I'm not one of those.' " When a male GI was first coming out, his gay friends sometimes advised him to be careful "not to become too obviously gay" by acting "swishy," as one GI counseled his young friend.[62] Because they fit popular stereotypes and did not hide their homosexuality, the butches and swishes often blew a gay crowd's cover and became scapegoats for any trouble with outsiders. Gay-bar patrons often blamed the swishes and butches for raids, arrests, crackdowns, and even for society's hatred of homosexuals. "They're the kind who make it so rough on the rest of us," explains a technical sergeant to a lieutenant at a gay bar in the war novel *The Invisible Glass*.[63] Yet some gay men and women enjoyed the presence of swishes and butches because they livened up the gay life and made its more conservative majority seem normal by comparison.

Conflicts over sex, love, and romance were at the heart of wartime gay life, alternately raising and dashing young GIs' hopes of ever settling down with a lifemate. Popular beliefs portrayed all "queers" as "perverts" obsessed with sex who could not love and were not worth loving. Such a powerful stereotype robbed many gay men and women of the self-esteem and mutual respect upon which they could build long-term commitments and reinforced the notion that they were condemned to a life of loneliness and one-night stands. Some lesbians, because of their socialization as women, were able to build a culture around butch/girl-friend couples, some of which were monogamous, while other women had affairs on the side or between lovers. "I never did go for one-night stands," recalled Rusty Brown, a butch lesbian who worked for the Navy. "I wanted somebody I could count on to be there a while." [64] Only when her lover was away did Phillis Abry have a few "brief flings" with other women.

By contrast, gay male GIs found one-night stands or casual sex to be easily available and satisfying but had to work hard at developing couple relationships. Sometimes finding and keeping a lifemate seemed an unattainable goal. As a result, gay men felt a mixture of gratitude and bitterness about casual sex—gratitude when sex was fun and affirmed their sexuality and desirability in a hostile world; bitterness when they believed that the gay life offered them no other choice. Gay GIs sometimes cautioned each other not to get stuck on one man, not to fall in love, not to get one's hopes up. "It's the only thing to do," warns one gay soldier to another in the war novel *The Invisible Glass,* "or you'll go through life with one heartache after another. None of us really finds, and keeps, his ideal. That's the tough thing about gay life." [65]

One-night stands made sense for gay men during a war, when everyone was on the move. More serious love affairs could end with painful separations and heartbreak. "It was hard to have relationships of a lasting nature," recalled Ben Small. "Sometimes you made it with who you could in the bushes or under the blankets or whatever. But it was really hard to establish any kind of affair or real relationship." The vagaries of military life constantly separated men from each other. "I could easily fall in love with Matt," wrote Donald Vining in his diary about a sailor he picked up in Pershing Square, "but he's off to sea again tomorrow. I was restless and depressed when Matt left. When I really like them, I feel let down after they leave." [66] When one GI finally met a fellow he had "long desired to know" and "fell hard and fast" for him, he found himself in the same situation. "Our friendship was developing more beautifully than I dreamed possible," he wrote to a gay friend, "when—dammit—he transferred out today. I held back in anguish—and found another notch carved beautifully in the lace shawl I call a heart. It wasn't going to happen again—But, well what can you do to stop it?" [67]

Despite the warnings, bitterness and separations, many gay male and lesbian GIs, like their heterosexual counterparts, did fall in love. Couples tried to stay together and build relationships against what seemed to be impossible odds. With the right contacts, some pulled strings to make sure they were not split apart. Phillis Abry's lover "got very friendly with one of the officers in the administration office and told her that we really would like to be sent to the same base. And we were. I'm sure this woman was probably a lesbian and understood." Others who couldn't stay together during the war kept their relationships alive nevertheless. In 1944 Bob Ruffing met a man in Jack's Baths in San Francisco whom he dated several times before they were shipped to different parts of the Pacific. But "it seemed so good to each of us that we decided to get together after the war and give it a whirl." They kept in touch, survived the war, and reunited in California, where their relationship "turned out to be a fifteen-year love affair."

Other couples were not so fortunate. When Burt Miller was sent to midshipman's school at Columbia University in New York, he and his boyfriend Jack, who was in the infantry in Philadelphia, wrote letters and visited whenever they could get passes or furloughs. After Miller graduated and before he shipped overseas, he arranged to spend a half day with Jack on a stopover in Chicago's Union Station. But Miller's train was twelve hours late. "I was absolutely frantic," he recalled. "I raced around the station and I finally found him as he was getting in line to get his train. We simply had fifteen or twenty minutes to talk. That's the last time I ever saw him." Jack was killed while fighting in Germany.

Love letters affirmed men's commitments to each other, especially when one partner was sent away to combat areas. "To fall in love literally on the eve of your going overseas," explained Ben Small, "made it very, very hard to go. But it carried with it a lot of good things, going knowing that there was somebody that really cared about you, and not just saying good-bye to everybody, see you later." Small's civilian boyfriend, like many heterosexual spouses and sweethearts, was religious about his letter writing.

But gay men and lesbians writing love letters faced the problem of wartime censorship. To prevent information leaks to the enemy regarding a soldier's whereabouts, the military censored all overseas letters. In 1942 the Army even prohibited soldiers from using any Xs at the end of their letters because "the number and arrangement of 'kisses' might constitute a code." [68] To get around this censorship, gay male and lesbian GIs and their loved ones befriended sympathetic censors, used their own secret codes or gay slang, or changed the gender of names and pronouns. Ben Small's boyfriend's name was Don, he explained, "so I addressed his letters to 'D.' When I used affectionate terms, there was no way [the censors would suspect], because I was just saying 'My darling D.' and then going on with the letter. So we had a really hot and heavy thing in the mails." Just before Jerry Watson shipped overseas, he advised his pen pal to write to him "in guarded terms that only our kind can understand. Emphasize the word girls and no one will be the wiser. And if you mean Gene, say Jean, and Joan for John . . . etc." [69]

Overshadowing and threatening the wartime boom in gay life were the military's efforts to control vice. Wherever GIs congregated, MPs were not far behind. The military's antivice activities—giving lectures to men before they went on passes, placing establishments off limits, using MPs to keep track of GIs off base—had originated in a campaign not to suppress homosexuality but to prevent heterosexual prostitution and venereal disease in order to protect the health and morals of heterosexual male GIs.[70] Sex educational materials discussed neither lesbians nor gay men as sources of venereal disease, a problem described exclusively as a consequence of heterosexual behavior.[71] But the military's antivice efforts led MPs to places where gay men or lesbians gathered and gave officials a reason to extend their antihomosexual procedures even further—to protect the morals of the nation's soldiers from the additional "vices" of sodomy and sex perversion.

The military's wartime power to control vice was derived in part from laws passed by Congress that allowed the Army and Navy to regulate recreational activities near their bases. The most far-reaching of these laws was known as the May Act, which Congress passed in 1941. It gave the military the power to police a city and to close businesses if local authorities did not clean up prostitution and other forms of vice. The military used the May Act only twice during the war to clamp down on prostitution around military bases in Tennessee and North Carolina.[72] But whenever soldiers began to flood a city, the mere threat to enforce the May Act pressured municipal authorities to crack down on vice or lose their power to govern. During the war more than seven hundred municipalities closed down their red-light districts.[73] In some regions, Army and Navy officials worked with state and local authorities to set up emergency vice control boards to coordinate their efforts. These boards issued wartime regulations for serving military personnel. If liquor establishments failed to comply, they were declared off limits to military personnel and the owners' liquor licenses were suspended or revoked by state alcohol beverage control agencies.

The military had its own police forces—the Army's Military Police and the Navy's Shore Patrol (SPs)—who answered to the provost marshal and whose members patrolled civilian areas to supervise armed forces personnel. The requirement that soldiers and officers wear their uniforms at all times prevented them from blending into civilian populations, helping MPs keep better track of them. GIs had to obey military police, who could arrest them for being out of uniform, being AWOL, patronizing off-limits establishments, disorderly conduct (including black GIs entering a "whites-only" establishment), fraternization, engaging in homosexual activity, and other military offenses.

Military police deterred vice with their mere presence. "When MP's enter a bar," explained a writer in the *Saturday Evening Post,* "they prefer using a back door. They stay a few minutes—just long enough to let the grapevine start spreading the word they've been there.'' [74] MPs harassed gay bars in particular by threatening to have them declared off limits. ''You're getting away with murder in this joint,'' an MP warns a gay-bar owner in John Horne Burns' war novel *The Gallery*. ''Either you get rid of most of these people or we'll put you off-limits. And you know we damn well can, don't you?'' [75] MPs walked through parks and other public cruising areas to scare gay men away. When Burt Miller and his boyfriend Jack, after a springtime stroll together in New York, stopped to sit together on a bench in Central Park, MPs came by and told them, Miller recalled, ''we had to get out of there and get out immediately. We both asked why and they wouldn't answer. Just 'Get the hell out of here right away!' Apparently we were near some kind of fairly notorious homosexual meeting ground.''

Military police were the most visible arm of a surveillance system that expanded during the war to regulate more efficiently the private activities of gay GIs. When MPs on their rounds discovered a local gay nightspot, they reported it to intelligence officers. When MPs arrested soldiers in gay bars or cruising areas, they turned their prisoners over to intelligence officers, who interrogated them for the names of other gay people and places. After the interrogation of a suspected homosexual in the 750th Tank Battalion in December 1943, a commanding officer dispatched a memo to the provost marshal's office in Washington with a list of people and places in Ohio that the suspect had named—including a man ''known only as 'Queenie' [who] is working at the soda fountain of Service Club No. 3, Shenango, Ohio,'' and a tavern known as ''the 'Steel City Club' located near the square in Youngstown, Ohio,'' which the memo described as ''a rendezvous of men with peculiar habits.'' [76] Commanding officers, in turn, placed the newly discovered gay night spots under surveillance or declared them off limits. MPs then posted lists of off-limits establishments at the exits of military bases and nailed warnings outside each bar to keep soldiers and sailors away. To enforce these restrictions, an MP was placed on guard duty outside or even inside a gay bar. [77]

Ironically this expanding antivice system helped resourceful and daring GIs to find the gay life. Servicemen used the posted off-limits lists and signs as handy guides to gay bars. They patronized these places by exchanging their uniforms for civvies at ''locker clubs,'' or by taking the chance that their ID cards would not be checked or that no MP would be on duty that night, or by waiting until the off-limits restrictions were lifted after a crackdown had run its course. Lesbian GIs better evaded MPs in gay bars than did gay men because women more easily got away with wearing civilian clothes. ''There were so few women in the service," Betty Somers explained, that if she was out of uniform, "nobody's going to come up and ask me to show my I.D." In routine antivice lectures to their men, officers sometimes warned them to avoid specific places where civilian "queers" hung out. When William Manchester and others in his Marine Corps unit were stationed at Linda Vista, California, before being shipped to Guadalcanal, they were warned about the civilian gay life in Los Angeles. "We were solemnly told that all queers in California wore red neckties and hung out at the corner of Hollywood and Vine, a myth we all accepted." [78] Such warnings piqued the curiosity of many men, particularly those most eager to find the gay life.

The summer of 1942—the first after the declaration of war—was a season of widespread antivice crackdowns as servicemen flooded the nation's cities. When thousands of GIs descended on Chicago each weekend, the city council, under pressure from military officials, passed a law to prevent women from drinking at bars to "protect servicemen from being victimized by women." [79] In Philadelphia police raided nighteries that served drinks to under-age sailors. [80] In Miami Beach, military and civilian officials inaugurated "the most stringent liquor and nitery regulation ever instigated in this resort area." [81] Army officials in Washington stepped up their supervision of Ninth Street and warned nightspots on lower Pennsylvania Avenue to clean up or MPs would be posted at their doors. [82] In Atlantic City, where the Army was taking over dozens of hotels to house trainees, an "Army-inspired campaign against vice" turned the city into a "militarized resort," forcing the mayor to call in state troopers to back up the local vice squad and military police. [83] In New York City, the public military crackdown on nightspots didn't occur until the fall of 1944, when a joint Army-Navy Disciplinary Control Board was formed to suppress "conditions inimicable [*sic*] to the morals and welfare of service personnel." [84] Each campaign put into place new codes and penalties, new joint military-civilian vice agencies, and more police patrols.

Although gay night spots were rarely the primary targets of these antivice crackdowns, they were frequent casualties. Military officials and local police especially zeroed in on female impersonators during antivice campaigns, believing them to be homosexual themselves or likely to attract a gay crowd. The summer 1942 crackdown in Atlantic City began with attacks on that resort city's burlesque and drag shows. "Female impersonators as entertainers 'are out,' " the police chief told reporters. "They must not appear in any local entertainment places." In October, Detroit's Club Frontenac was forced to close its female impersonation show when police arrested most of its performers during a vice raid on a private party. During a 1943 crackdown in San Francisco, Finocchio's—the premier female impersonation club in the country—was cited for liquor law violations and was declared off limits to military personnel.[85] Military police and intelligence officers had no trouble equating female impersonation performances with "queers" when they were outside the protective confines of the wartime soldier shows.

Alternating periods of crackdowns and openness, combined with the massive influx of military personnel and war workers, put urban gay life through major cycles of disruption and reorganization.[86] In Washington, D.C., draftees who swarmed into Carroll's bar so disrupted its patrons' established cruising patterns that it drove many away. Before the war, recalled Haviland Ferris, who was a steady patron from the late 1930s through the 1940s, Carroll's was quiet during the week and busy on weekend nights. Its customers—only white men in this segregated city—were gay government workers who went there to meet enlisted men. Soldiers and sailors were willing to spend the night with someone in exchange for drinks, dinner, and a ride back to the base in the morning. Rose and Betty, the bar's waitresses, were "affectionate intermediaries" who "took good care of their gay or military customers." They warned regulars against any soldier, sailor, or marine who might be dangerous and they made hostile intruders feel unwelcome. The waitresses had "very solid relations" with the Shore Patrol, who came into the tavern frequently to check for drunken sailors. But during the war Carroll's was flooded with new and younger military men unfamiliar with its unspoken customs. Fights broke out, and civilian regulars risked getting beat up or robbed by newcomers offended by their sexual offers. At the same time new gay places in other parts of town drew away those civilian patrons who wanted safer surroundings.[87]

Cliques of gay servicemen sometimes adopted a particular bar as their own, converted it into a gay place with their presence, then stood their ground despite hostility from bartenders, patrons, and the police. In Denver during the war, Mary's Tavern on Broadway was suddenly packed with airmen from nearby Lowry Air Force Base. According to local historian Terry William Mangan, Mary's "was patronized by a group that went in repeatedly and was blatantly gay in behavior. At first they were thrown out or arrested. But they kept returning and eventually straight customers began going elsewhere."[88] In other gay night spots, whenever police successfully turned patrons out into the streets, the crowd withdrew and waited for the heat to cool down. They wandered about looking for new places that would accept them and their dollars, making their presence more strongly felt and staking out more public territory for themselves.

In San Francisco the gay night life went through several periods of disruption and reorganization during the war. From the summer of 1942 through 1943, a series of military-inspired antivice crackdowns resulted in the suspension of sixty-three San Francisco liquor licenses and the citation of twenty-five other nighteries, including at least three popular gay nightspots—Finocchio's, the Black Cat Cafe, and the Top of the Mark at the Mark Hopkins Hotel. The crackdown, according to *Variety*, was in response to the wartime revival of the "devil-may-care spirit of Barbary Coast days," which made San Francisco again into a "pleasure-seeking town" full of "navy and army boys" looking for a good time.[89] On New Year's Day in 1943, at the end of the five-month crackdown, the Army and Navy announced a more uniform and systematic "code of practices" to regulate the serving of liquor to servicemen who "must be physically capable of immediately manning their ships and stations at all times." With the new code in effect, the military removed off-limits signs from eight bars and taverns, including three that attracted a gay clientele: the Silver Rail and the Silver Dollar, both in the Tenderloin, and Finocchio's.[90]

A second wartime crackdown on vice conditions in San Francisco took place in May 1943 in response to a congressional investigation of moral conditions near Army camps, a California Assembly investigation of lax liquor law enforcement in San Francisco, and a Navy investigation into a rise in venereal disease rates among Bay Area naval personnel.[91] "Six or seven gay bars were closed simultaneously," wrote Jim Kepner in May 1943 to his Army pen pal, including "the Black Cat, the Subway, the Silver Dollar, etc." Displaced customers started to fill up Li-Po's, a discreet gay bar in Chinatown that until then had attracted "well dressed, handsome youths" including servicemen. But the crackdown on the other gay spots drove some of the "swish crowd" into Li-Po's, starting a second wave of crackdowns. "Within the last week," Kepner wrote, "the management has been refusing to admit a large number of the more swishy 'girls.' This is really a shame," he commented, torn between blaming and enjoying the campy queens, "as the place is beginning to get almost dull now, but I guess it was necessary" to prevent a raid.[92]

The same week police raided the Rickshaw around the corner from Li-Po's and arrested two dozen customers, including "a couple of lesbians [who] protested and were beaten up" in a fight that "led to a small free-for-all." "Dozens of arrests," Kepner's letter continued, "have been made in Union Square, popular cruising grounds in the downtown area," and "all of the places have been heavily watched."

The papers were filled with news of the crackdown, which was "really knocking what's left of San Francisco's gay world to hell." [93] The raided bars remained open but with very few customers as the displaced crowds withdrew, kept a low profile, and waited. "For a couple of weeks," Kepner wrote, "most of the belles [gay men] have been wondering where the crowd had gone. Then, last Saturday, everyone suddenly landed up at the Top of the Mark. The place was mad . . . everyone seemed to be surprised by it all. . . . And Techau's [a tourist cocktail lounge near Union Square] draws more of a gay crowd now." [94] By the spring of 1945, San Francisco's gay night life prospered once again in the old as well as in some new establishments.[95]

Ironically, the periodic crackdowns, together with the pressure from newcomers, helped the gay bars to evolve as new bars opened and closed, grew in number, and became more specialized. In medium-size war-boom cities such as Denver and San Diego, enough gay male and lesbian GIs and war workers arrived to sustain one or more predominantly gay bars, if only on weekend nights.[96] In larger cities like New York and Chicago, a process of multiplication and specialization developed by which more bars opened and mixed bars became more gay, each catering to a different clientele—"the Brilliant Crowd, the Swishy Crowd, the Empire Builders, and the Drugstore Cowboys," as John Horne Burns described them in wartime Washington.[97] At the same time other establishments responded to their new patrons by making it known that they would not admit or serve gay customers. Either way the powerful impact of the military mobilization on city night life forced increasing numbers of proprietors to determine exactly how they would manage the gay male and lesbian crowds they could no longer ignore. By uprooting an entire generation, the war helped to channel urban gay life into a particular path of growth—away from stable private networks and toward public commercial establishments serving the needs of a displaced, transient, and younger clientele.

The constant threat of raids, arrests, and police surveillance sent a clear message to gay male and lesbian GIs that the military and local governments did not want them to associate with each other in public and even in private. Some responded with self-blame, others with anger. Enraged by the 1943 attacks on San Francisco's gay nightspots, Jim Kepner asked his Army pen pal, "Why in the hell can't they let us have at least a few places where we can be free?" [98] "Some day," his Army pal replied, infuriated by what he called the Intolerance Squads, "I'm going to build a huge fortress with walls 10 feet thick and 5 sets of steel gates. *Then* let anyone try to invade our party!" [99]

But many gay GIs had already begun to fortify and police their own lines of defense. Their home bases were their friends, lovers, cliques, bars, and private parties. Their lines of communication were still underground but opening up. And they were teaching each other important defensive tactics—"camping," blending in, secret slang and signals, and most important of all, a stronger sense of camaraderie and mutual respect.

CHAPTER
5

The Fight for Reform

In 1941, strained by the demands of a massive war mobilization that included a large influx of gay soldiers, the military could no longer handle its homosexual discipline problems by sending all offenders to prison. Officers certainly had known that there were "queers" in their ranks long before World War II, but they had no mandate or approved procedures for getting rid of them other than by charging them with sodomy. To prevent additional strain on the already overburdened military prisons, an alliance of reform-minded military officials and psychiatrists proposed what they described as a more efficient system for handling homosexual offenders. Based on the belief that homosexuality was a mental illness, it provided for discharge without trial of homosexual personnel while allowing the retention of those whose services were deemed essential. Introduced in part as a humane gesture to rescue homosexuals from prison, the discharge system, ironically, greatly expanded the military's antihomosexual apparatus. While reformers fought with more traditional officers over the shift from imprisonment to discharge, gay male and lesbian GIs began to discover that being labeled deviant and undesirable carried its own burdens and punishments.

Army and Navy psychiatrists began their efforts to discharge rather than imprison homosexual servicemen in the spring of 1941, after Lt. Col. Ernest H. Burt, chief of the Military Justice Section of the Army Judge Advocate General's Office (the Army's legal department), toured the United States to assess how Army officers were handling their "sodomist" problems during the peacetime mobilization. Lieutenant Colonel Burt discovered "widely divergent" practices in different Army jurisdictions across the country. A "substantial number" of generals, he reported, had decided on their own to stop court-martialing sodomists and instead were discharging them for bad character. The generals told Burt that they considered sodomists to be medical or psychiatric rather than penal problems. Burt submitted to the judge advocate general a proposed directive that would establish a uniform policy requiring the discharge rather than trial and imprisonment of those who had engaged in an act of sodomy without the use of force. Burt's statement of the problem, his cast of critics, and his proposal for change sketched the early outline of a wartime reform movement that would dramatically alter military policy.[1]

The target of reformers was the military's penal approach to its homosexual problem. Whenever a soldier, sailor, or officer was caught or turned in for having sex with another man, the accused's commanding officer placed him under guard in a brig or stockade, where he stayed awaiting trial by a court-martial of commissioned officers. As a criminal defendant he had the right to be assigned counsel or could hire his own private attorney. During the trial the presiding officers read the charges, heard testimony, and delivered a verdict. They focused their attention on the details of sex acts, the admissibility and accuracy of evidence and testimony, and sometimes the reputation of the accused. When doctors or ships' surgeons were consulted, it was to provide medical evidence pertaining to the sex act or to establish the sanity of the accused, not to diagnose his homosexual tendencies or sexual identity. Under the Articles of War, the maximum penalties for Army enlisted men and officers convicted of nonforcible sodomy were five years' confinement at hard labor, forfeiture of all pay and allowances, and dishonorable discharge or dismissal. Under the Articles for the Government of the Navy, the maximum penalties for enlisted men were the same punishments but with ten years of confinement at hard labor, twelve for officers.

The case of James Ray Harwell illustrates how strong an impact this penal system could have on the lives of young men convicted of sodomy. A carpenter's son from Miami, Florida, Harwell enlisted in the Navy in 1917 when the United States entered World War I. He eventually achieved the rank of chief quartermaster, one of the highest ratings then available to enlisted men. In 1921 his commanding officer, using only a love letter as evidence, charged twenty-eight-year-old Harwell with sodomy and "scandalous conduct tending to the destruction of good morals" (oral sex) with another sailor in a YMCA room in Honolulu. He was convicted and sentenced to fifteen years' hard labor at Portsmouth Naval Prison in New Hampshire, with dishonorable discharge and forfeiture of pay. Despite repeated appeals from his mother that he had "killed no one . . . stolen nothing . . . destroyed no property," and that she and her ailing husband had depended on Harwell's meager pay to survive, the Navy Department refused to grant him clemency, defending their need to exact such a "heavy penalty" in order to bring about the "eradication of this evil" from the Navy.[2]

During the late-nineteenth and early-twentieth centuries, the conviction of Harwell and hundreds of other enlisted men for the crime of sodomy resulted, in the words of one Navy report, "in filling our places of confinement" with these "long-term offenders."[3] Their presence had a powerful impact on Navy prisons and federal penitentiaries, because of long sentences and the difficulty of controlling homosexuality among inmates. Prison administrators decided early on to set policies and establish procedures for managing their "sodomist" populations.

Segregation was the primary means of dealing with homosexuals in United States penitentiaries in the first decades of the twentieth century. In 1934, Joseph Fishman, a former inspector of federal prisons, noted that the policy of segregating known homosexuals into separate wings of prisons and forcing them to work and eat apart from other inmates was in place in "almost every big penitentiary" in the United States.[4] During the 1920s heads of Army and Navy prisons developed similar systems for isolating prisoners convicted of sodomy. In 1925 the Army adjutant general, intending to protect young inmates convicted of other crimes, ordered that all sodomy prisoners be transferred to the more secure federal penitentiaries and prohibited their confinement in Army disciplinary barracks. For a short time the federal penitentiary at Fort Leavenworth, Kansas, which housed many Army prisoners, in an effort to further punish and isolate sodomists, instituted the "barbarous practice," according to Fishman, "of putting a large yellow 'D' (to indicate degenerate) on the backs of prisoners actually discovered in an act of homosexuality. . . ." When the yellow Ds did not "stamp out the practice," they were abandoned.[5]

In the Navy, the commanding officer at Portsmouth Prison established a policy of segregating sodomists in a separate tier within the prison so that they could be "carefully watched." They were prohibited from doing any work inside the prison and were forced to labor outdoors on the rock pile. By 1929 the Navy judge advocate general, to further segregate and more carefully supervise sodomists, had specifically designated Portsmouth Naval Prison as the "place of confinement for moral perverts regardless of length of sentence." As a result, in the decade before World War II, more than 40 percent of all new admissions to Portsmouth were men convicted of sodomy, oral coition, and sexual crimes other than the rape of women.[6]

It was this system of prosecution and imprisonment that some Army generals, psychiatrists, and prison wardens early in the World War II mobilization judged to be archaic, inefficient, and cruel. Forming a temporary alliance, they promoted what they called an "enlightened" plan to convert the penal system to an administrative discharge system for handling known homosexuals. Their use of the clinical term *homosexual* rather than the legal term *sodomist* was symbolic of their reform. They were opposed by the hard-liners, many of whom were in the Judge Advocate General's Office, who defended the military's longtime practice of punishing sodomists with imprisonment and public disgrace. But both factions did agree that most or all homosexuals were bad for discipline, bad for morale, and had no place in the military.

When Lieutenant Colonel Burt submitted his report together with his proposed reforms, the Army judge advocate general, Major General Gullion, sent it through the chain of command, recommending that heads of other Army offices comment on it and study this "vexatious problem." The Surgeon General's Office, represented by the Army's chief psychiatrist Patrick Madigan, recommended adoption of the new policy. But objections from his own officers confirmed Major General Gullion's belief that Burt's proposal represented a minority position in his office. With support from top officials in the Personnel Division, Gullion asked the War Department not to abandon the policy of "trying sodomists" but instead to issue a strong directive to prohibit "the growing practice of [issuing] administrative discharges."

The adjutant general sided with Gullion and on July 15, 1941, by order of Secretary of War Henry L. Stimson, issued to all commanding generals the Army's first policy directive on homosexuality, entitled "Sodomists." It reminded all commanding generals that sodomy was a serious crime and that trial by court martial was the only acceptable way to remove sodomists from the Army. It ordered an immediate halt to the unapproved practice of discharging sodomists without trial and declared that such practice was "not only contrary to the War Department policy but to the express intention of Congress" in the Articles of War. Not only had reformers lost the first round in their fight for change, but the hard-liners had strengthened their punitive stand on sodomists by writing it into a new directive that demanded immediate compliance.[7]

But the July 1941 War Department directive brought about neither prompt nor uniform compliance. As the nation declared war and stepped up its military mobilization throughout the fall and winter of 1941–42, a more organized wave of challenges to the penal approach poured into Washington. Commanding generals argued that the speed and secrecy of administrative discharges were more efficient than the long, public proceedings of a trial. They argued that mandatory trials for all sodomy offenders deprived officers of the power to use their own discretion in special cases. Under the new "Sodomists" directive, the only official with authority to grant discharges to sodomists was Secretary of War Henry L. Stimson and his expanding centralized bureaucracy in Washington. Jealously guarding their turf, these reform-minded commanding generals found allies among their own medical and neuropsychiatric staffs, who offered them a medical rationale—that homosexuals were mentally ill—to justify the swift discharge rather than trial and imprisonment of sodomists.[8]

Wardens of federal penitentiaries and Army disciplinary barracks worked together with commanding officers and psychiatrists to advocate wartime reform, recreating an alliance that had earlier reformed prison policy. During the 1930s prisons had become the first federal institutions where psychiatrists, who conducted research on homosexual inmates to construct psychological profiles of "sexual psychopaths," had promoted understanding and management rather than punishment for homosexuals. They had won some prison wardens and other penologists over to their point of view that homosexual offenders belonged in hospitals rather than in prison.[9] Prison wardens and commanding generals began to pressure the judge advocate general to release convicted sodomists from their institutions, arguing that homosexuals should be treated as insane people rather than as criminals and that prison life created more "sex perverts" than it cured or deterred. They recommended that commanding officers be allowed to summarily discharge these men without trial rather than sentence them to prison. These early efforts at reform failed.[10] But prison wardens remained acutely aware of the problems caused by sending sodomists to prison. In 1941 they expressed a renewed concern that the huge wartime influx of citizen soldiers would overwhelm military courts and prisons with sodomy cases.

The judge advocate general, as head of the Army's legal department, was responsible for bringing offenders to justice and was interested in those areas of discipline related to law and crime. When federal prison wardens and commanding generals challenged the Army's imprisonment of sodomists, the judges advocate general consistently defended the penal system, using the military's traditional "prevent, punish and protect" rationale. Because common law punished sodomy severely as an infamous and unspeakable crime against nature, the military had the responsibility to prevent such crimes with severe punishment and to protect the morals of the nation's young men under its supervision. The military's strict penalties reflected a fear that leniency in such an all-male institution would lead to widespread homosexual activity. When psychiatrists in the 1930s began to argue that sodomists should not be imprisoned because they were mentally ill, the judge advocate general stuck to his guns. He responded that a "pervert" charged with sodomy could establish at his court-martial trial that he was deranged and could not "distinguish right from wrong." He would then be confined to a mental hospital instead of prison.[11] In 1941–42 administrators in the offices of the judge advocate general and adjutant general continued to defend the penal system with the new argument that discharges during a state of war would "open up an easy way of avoiding military service."

Medical officers, especially psychiatrists, were not swayed by such arguments. Using clinical terminology, they maintained that sodomists were in fact "homosexuals" and "sexual psychopaths" who belonged in the hands of the psychiatric profession as patients and that boards of medical officers should have the power to remove such men from the service with discharges. Although they disagreed whether homosexuals should be given honorable medical discharges rather than punitive undesirable discharges and how to classify homosexuals within psychiatric and administrative categories, nearly all psychiatrists in these discussions agreed that homosexuals who had not used force or violence did not belong in prison. Such a position was humane but also served their interests. The transfer of jurisdiction over homosexuals from the criminal justice system to a system based on hospitalization, diagnosis, and discharge promised to expand the psychiatric profession's power and authority in the military organization.

The most powerful voices representing the psychiatric point of view came from psychiatric consultants in the Surgeons General's Offices and in the National Research Council's Committee on Neuropsychiatry, which was headed by Winfred Overholser. These men worked closely with each other, were charged with advising policymakers and initiating new policies regarding psychiatry, and took a leadership role in promoting the discharge system for homosexuals.[12] In January 1942, when the Navy surgeon general asked the NRC committee for their advice in the case of a sailor convicted of a homosexual offense, Overholser used the occasion to attack existing military law as "antiquated" in regard to homosexuals, and recommended that "the question be fully studied by a selected group of lawyers, psychiatrists, and administrative officers." [13] During the summer of 1942, psychiatric consultants to the surgeons general, working with the NRC Committee on Neuropsychiatry, initiated their own systematic review of the military's penal approach.

These consultants' first success was to persuade top administrators in the Navy Department to consider reform. In July the chief of Naval Personnel circulated a proposed procedure for discharging homosexual personnel, which became the basis for discussions of reform. [14] In August a representative of the Bureau of Medicine and Surgery wrote to Overholser that Navy Surgeon General Ross McIntire, who also served as President Roosevelt's White House physician, strongly supported the discharge rather than imprisonment of "these unfortunate individuals." [15] Possibly through McIntire's connections, the psychiatric consultants' efforts at reform reached as far as the White House, where they also gained encouraging support.

Only a few days after the proposal to set up a homosexual discharge system started to circulate within the Navy Department, President Roosevelt, as commander in chief, commuted the five-year prison sentence of a Navy officer who had just been convicted of homosexual activity, ordering his dismissal instead. Roosevelt's action, however, did not indicate that he felt sympathy toward male homosexuals. In 1919, responding to reports from the Naval Training Station in Newport, Rhode Island, of "immoral" conditions involving homosexual sailors and civilians, Roosevelt, then assistant secretary of the Navy, initiated his own attack against what he called the "perverted" and "horrible practices" at the training station. To clean up Newport he secretly assigned undercover officers out of his own office who used young Navy recruits as sexual decoys to entrap civilians. [16] The next year Roosevelt took steps to prevent sailors convicted of sodomy from being restored to duty on Navy ships. [17] In May 1942, when the press accused Senator David I. Walsh from Massachusetts of visiting a male brothel near the Brooklyn Navy Yard, Roosevelt privately explained to a senator that suicide had been the traditional custom for handling such offenses among Navy officers. However, Roosevelt at times acted expediently in ways that protected gay men. He suppressed charges for two years that Under Secretary of State Sumner Welles, his friend and right-hand man in the State Department, was homosexual, until threats from Welles's enemies forced Roosevelt to ask for his resignation in the summer of 1943. [18] While clearly sympathetic with the traditional hostility among career officers toward sodomists, President Roosevelt also supported the expansion of psychiatry's role in the military during the war, thereby indirectly contributing to a more liberal policy toward homosexual offenders.[19]

While the reform movement gained momentum in the Navy Department, some hard-liners in the Army began to realize that the July 1941 directive prohibiting discharges had not solved the Army's homosexual discipline problem. The massive expansion for war threatened to overcrowd the prisons with unproductive sodomists and tie up valuable personnel in time-consuming trials and appeals. Signs of stress on the Army's penal system were evident when in November 1942 Army Chief of Staff George C. Marshall notified all commanding generals that the increasing number of courts-martial was unacceptable and reflected badly on the discipline of the citizen Army. "Reliance on courts-martial to enforce discipline," he warned, "indicates lack of leadership and faulty command." He directed commanding generals to instill stricter discipline and obedience in the millions of new soldiers and to rely on courts-martial only as last resorts.[20] Marshall's directive further pressured Army administrators to devise alternative procedures for handling homosexual cases.

Considering the long tradition in the Judge Advocate General's Office of defending the punitive system, it was a significant moment when, in late 1942, top JAG officials relaxed their hard-line position and considered reform. In a series of memos, Colonel John M. Weir, executive of JAG, explained his office's change of mind. "Past experience" and the recent "study of the subject," he wrote, now made it clear that "there is not and probably cannot be any entirely satisfactory solution of the problem of homosexuality in the Army." An "inflexible" or "rule of thumb" policy requiring courts-martial in all cases was no longer advisable. The only possible solution to the sodomist problem, he concluded, was to try different experiments and see how they worked.[21]

Once top administrators in both the War and Navy Departments accepted the idea of reform, a discussion was opened among medical, personnel, and legal officials, civilian psychiatrists, and other experts in the National Research Council and the American Psychiatric Association. In their correspondence and conversations with each other, they tried to define homosexuality and explain its origins, to classify the various types of homosexuals and establish corresponding bureaucratic categories, to determine why homosexuals were undesirable in the military, and to anticipate problems that might arise from discharging them.

Some psychiatrists were keen to prevent punitive assumptions from migrating to the new system, particularly through the language of crime, threats of prosecution, and a hostility toward homosexuals. Psychiatric consultants in the Navy Surgeon General's Office opposed a section of the proposed reform that called for drawing up criminal sodomy charges against suspected homosexuals as a threat to scare them into accepting a discharge rather than risk going to prison. "This still harkens back," Navy Surgeon General McIntire patiently explained, "to the out-moded way of handling homosexuals, because it implies trial and punishment." McIntire warned against using such terms as *specifications, offense, trial,* and *accused* in any directive on homosexuality.[22] Overholser and his NRC committee cautioned Navy administrators not to be influenced by the irrational intolerance toward homosexuals that was embedded in both the penal system and public opinion. "The emotional reaction of the public against homosexual activity," Overholser explained, "is out of all proportion to the threat which it represents to personal rights, or even to public order." [23] Psychiatric consultants in the Army Surgeon General's Office concurred with Overholser, explaining that homosexuals rarely posed a threat to anyone else because most of them engaged "in their chosen sexual activity with those of like tastes who, far from resisting, may seek such gratification." [24]

With these caveats the psychiatric consultants began to design a discharge system based on the assumptions of their own profession. The first step was to educate other administrative officials about the origins and definitions of homosexuality. Stating that their views represented the beliefs of "most authorities" in the field, they explained that homosexuality had psychological ("acquired") as well as biological ("constitutional" or "congenital") origins, putting forth a developmental model of human sexuality based on Freudian psychoanalysis. They described all people as "bisexual," explaining that at different stages in life any person had the potential to feel homosexual desires and engage in homosexual acts. The "normal" person passed through a homosexual "stage" and then on to heterosexual maturity. Some people did not advance into the heterosexual stage and remained homosexual. Even "normal" individuals retained a "homosexual residual" as a component of their sexuality that when "adequately sublimated" became the "foundation of social solidarity." But when "normal" people were placed in unusual circumstances such as prison or the military, they might "revert" to their homosexual stage of development, and even "might engage in homosexual practices." Three psychosexual categories emerged from this developmental model of human sexuality—the mature "normal" heterosexual, the immature "deviant" homosexual, and the regressive heterosexual who "reverts" to homosexuality due to unusual circumstances or the influence of others. Occasionally, psychiatrists used the terms *true homosexual* or *confirmed homosexual* to distinguish them from "regressive" heterosexuals when they both engaged in the same homosexual activity.

When psychiatrists applied these psychosexual categories to members of the armed forces, the issues of responsibility and self-control assumed primary importance. They explained that "true" homosexuals, whether their homosexuality was psychologically "acquired" or due to "faulty biological make-up," could not change their "perverse desires." "There is no known medical treatment which will successfully cure cases of this type," reported a team of Army psychiatrists at Brooke General Hospital in Texas. "Confinement is not a cure for sexual perversion" and "will not even act as an effective deterrent." Whenever the military imprisoned homosexuals, they explained, "the Government assumes the enormous expense of caring for these men for long periods of time with no possible return from the investment." The idea that "true" or "confirmed" homosexuality was incurable became a fundamental premise of the psychiatrists' campaign against prison and for discharge.[25]

If not all homosexual "offenders" were true homosexuals, and if true homosexuals were not responsible for their sexual desires, then how should the military handle "offenders" under a new system? Solving this problem involved matching the psychiatrists' psychosexual categories with the military's bureaucratic and legal categories. Military officials in the legal, personnel and medical offices developed three administrative categories for disposing of homosexual personnel: the criminal offender who would go to trial, the mentally ill who would be discharged, and the reclaimable offender who would be "salvaged." The criminal "sodomist" category was narrowed to include only those offenders, whether they were homosexual or regressive heterosexuals, who raped or otherwise coerced their same-sex partner into having sex, or who had sex with a minor. Those in the category of "true" perverts who had sex with consenting adults were to be considered for discharge as mentally ill. And only those "normal young men" who, in the words of the Army judge advocate general, were not "by nature homosexuals" but who "submit to the practice" through "intoxication or curiosity" or in response to "the strange environment of foreign service" would "be rehabilitated and retained in the service" without trial or discharge.[26]

The willingness both to reclaim and discharge some homosexual offenders because they might be important to the nation's defense reflected the wartime pressure to utilize all human resources in the most efficient way. The discharge of homosexuals, explained Colonel Weir to justify the judge advocate general's acceptance of reform, is useful "in time of war where the manpower of the nation is needed either in the Army or on the farm or in industry. . . . Under the present conditions, [the homosexual] may still be capable of at least some useful service in civil life instead of becoming a burden as a prisoner in some penal institution." [27] This acknowledgement that known homosexuals could temporarily serve the interests of both the military and the nation during the war emergency—either assigned to military duties deemed suitable for homosexuals or as a discharged civilian in defense jobs—ran counterpoint to the growing military belief that homosexuals threatened the morale and discipline of any organization, creating a tension that increased with the demand for more men as the United States stepped up its involvement in the war.

The question of who would have the authority to decide whether a suspected homosexual was a criminal, a mentally ill person, or a normal young man gone astray was a serious procedural issue confronting administrators. Proposals were circulated within both the Navy and Army to set up special boards of officers to review each case. Psychiatrists would have preferred boards of medical officers, but they settled for nonmedical boards so long as they included a psychiatrist. Navy Surgeon General McIntire explained that a psychiatrist was the officer most qualified to determine "whether the individual is in fact a homosexual." Which officers would have the final authority to decide how to dispose of each homosexual was the issue which would later destroy the alliance that psychiatrists and "lay" officers had created in these early stages of reform.

Once it was assumed that discharges rather than imprisonment would become official policy, the nature of the discharge became an issue. Overholser argued against giving homosexuals an honorable or medical discharge, but for practical rather than moral reasons. Honorable discharges during a time of war could encourage men to engage in homosexual activity, to malinger, or to declare themselves in order to escape compulsory service. The stigma of bad discharges, on the other hand, would conserve manpower by discouraging such practices and would set "offenders" apart from those who had successfully controlled their desires. McIntire added that, although the homosexual offender might no longer be prosecuted under the more "enlightened" military reforms, he had still "violated the civil and military law." "Obviously," he argued, "it would not be fair to award the overt homosexual an honorable discharge" because it would only equate him with the man "who had been wounded in action or has become incapacitated in some manner while in pursuit of his duty."[28] In the interest of military efficiency, psychiatric consultants in this stage of reform found themselves supporting the stigmatization of homosexuals with punitive rather than medical discharges.

If homosexuals could not be discharged honorably, the question arose as to what kind of bad discharge to use. Dishonorable discharges were part of the penal system and were used only for men who had been convicted of a crime and who had served their sentences. Undesirable discharges had been used to eliminate those social misfits—alcoholics, chronic liars, drug addicts, men who antagonized everyone—who psychiatrists described as psychopaths. But regulations governing undesirable discharges—such as Section Eight of Army Regulation 615-360, which permitted the discharge of men with "undesirable habits or traits of character"—did not include homosexuals and were not supposed to be used to discharge sodomists, who were to be brought to trial instead. As reformers redefined these men as "sexual psychopaths" in screening directives and in their memos, it was logical that they would want to match this psychosexual category with the administrative "undesirable discharge" category. Enlisted men had nicknamed undesirable discharges "section eights" or "blue discharges" and "blue tickets"—after the color of paper on which they were printed in the Army. Calling someone a "section eight" or an "eight ball" had meant that they were goofy or crazy, and now it would mean that they could be "queer" as well.[29]

In November and December 1942 reformers made steady progress. Toward year's end McIntire updated Overholser on how well the reform proposal was moving through Navy channels. It "begins to look as though it will be approved by the Secretary of the Navy," he wrote. "Just how it will be promulgated to the service, I do not know, but I shall keep you informed of the progress that is being made."[30]

Victory was swift. On January 19, 1943, Secretary of War Henry L. Stimson, who according to William Menninger was "cognizant" of psychiatry's importance,[31] issued a new Army directive entitled "Sodomists," a reversal of the July 1941 directive, that steered a compromise course between the reformers and the hard-liners. Rhetorically, it adhered to tradition by never using the word "homosexual" and by stating at the outset that sodomy was a serious crime and that all sodomists should be tried by court-martial. The directive then provided for exceptions that were applicable to offenders who did not use force or violence. One exception was the offender who was a "confirmed pervert." He was to be examined by a board of officers with the purpose of discharge under the provision of Section Eight. The other exception was the man who engaged in homosexual activity but who was not a "confirmed pervert." After examination by a psychiatrist and if "he otherwise possesses a salvage value," this type of offender was to be reclaimed and returned to duty after "appropriate disciplinary action has been taken." The officer exercising general court-martial jurisdiction would decide the disposition of each case, but he was supposed to consider the advice of a psychiatrist whenever possible.[32]

The same month, the Navy Department issued its first explicit policy on homosexuals.[33] On January 1, Secretary of the Navy Frank Knox dispatched a confidential letter to all ships and stations entitled "Procedure for the Disposition of Homosexuals Among Personnel of the U.S. Naval Service," which told commanding officers why reform had become necessary. The "[Navy] Department believes that heed should be given," the letter explained, "to the opinions of physicians and penologists who believe its treatment of homosexuals to be, to some degree, archaic." It had become "the generally accepted opinion that homosexuality in the majority of cases is a medical rather than a criminological problem. . . . The fact, however, that homosexuality is primarily a medical problem," he cautioned, "does not affect the criminal nature of the acts of certain homosexuals. . . . Socially dangerous homosexuals must be isolated."

Knox's letter outlined new procedures that, like Army policy, limited court-martial trials to violent offenders, allowed "habitual homosexuals" who committed in-service acts to be discharged without trial and gave psychiatrists the authority to diagnose suspects and advise disposition boards. But unlike the Army system, the Navy procedures made no provision for reclaiming homosexuals. Instead, disregarding protests from the surgeon general, it required officers to confront the offender with charges, then offer him the option of signing a statement accepting an undesirable discharge (or resignation for officers) "to escape trial by general court-martial." If the man refused to sign, he would be sent to trial.[34]

These new procedures appeased the most hardline officers by continuing to punish violent offenders and allowing dischargees to be stigmatized as undesirables. They satisfied reformers by requiring the psychiatric diagnosis of all suspected homosexuals, replacing the imprisonment of most homosexuals with prompt discharge, and, in the Army, keeping final decisions in each case with the local commanding general. Despite some compromises, reformers considered these directives to be important victories. Colonel Roy D. Halloran, who was Madigan's successor as chief consultant in neuropsychiatry to the Army surgeon general, praised the new policy as a "more enlightened and humane method of handling the homosexual problem." [35] The American Medical Association, in an editorial in its journal, stated that these reforms heralded in a new era in the military. "The crude methods of the past," the editorial explained, "have given way to more human and satisfactory handling of the problems of homosexuality. No longer is it necessary to subject cases that are so definitely in the medical field to a routine military court-martial." [36] The fundamental rationale and initial procedures for the discharge system based on the psychiatric model of homosexuality were now firmly in place.

Though the new procedures looked good to policymakers on paper, Army and Navy officers in the field soon discovered they weren't so easy to put into practice. Undefined terms in the directives, such as *habitual homosexual, pathic, sexual pervert, true sodomist, confirmed pervert* and *moral pervert* were confusing to commanding officers unschooled in psychiatry who had to sort actual people into administrative categories. Throughout 1943 inquiries from the fleet reached the Navy Department in Washington asking how to deal with homosexuals who admitted "tendencies" but who had not committed "provable acts" while in the service. These individuals did not fall into either the violent offender or "habitual homosexual" categories, and it was unclear how to deal with them. As for military psychiatrists, they were unhappy serving as mere advisers on disposition boards rather than as decisive actors. Generating much confusion and discontent, the directives provoked an even wider discussion of the military's homosexual problem and new efforts at policy reform.

During this third wave of reform, psychiatrists remained on the sidelines while legal and personnel officials ironed out procedural problems in order to ensure the most efficient use of manpower. They responded to continuing objections from hard-liners by reiterating that discharge was not a sign of moral weakness but of military efficiency during a time of war because it "rid the service of such individual[s] by the simplest and most expedient means." They raised the issue of the "recalcitrant" soldiers who would not accept blue discharges, recommending that they be threatened with trial to force their acceptance. They also proposed a clarification of the procedure for reclaiming what they called the "casual homosexual." These individuals would be hospitalized and treated before reassignment to another outfit because, in the words of one War Department official, "it is impossible to keep such a matter absolutely quiet within a unit." [37]

With the expansion of separate women's branches, policymakers had to decide how they would handle what they called "female homosexuals." Although sodomy was usually identified as a crime between men, the military defined it to include both oral and anal sex and technically could have pressed charges against women as well. Officers, however, were reluctant to prosecute lesbians for such sexual activity. In the Women Marines there were no courts-martial for sodomy or other homosexual acts during World War II. But unlike the penal system, the discharge system's focus on the homosexual person made it easier for the military to extend its antihomosexual apparatus to women and to define lesbians as a problem for the first time. The 1943 Navy directive had already noted that the policy applied to all personnel "including the Women's Reserve." In 1944 an Army Personnel Division report, once again following precedents set by the Navy, recommended that because "homosexuality occurs among women also," the discharge procedures should apply to them as well. The proposed changes would raise to the level of policy the already common practice of disciplining women through guidance first and discharge as a last resort, rather than through court-martial and imprisonment.[38]

At the beginning of 1944, Army and Navy administrators, after considering these and other recommendations, issued revisions of their 1943 directives. On January 3, Secretary of War Stimson—through Chief of Staff George C. Marshall—issued WD Circular No. 3, and three weeks later the Bureau of Naval Personnel issued a new confidential letter to all ships and stations. Each of these directives established the policies and procedures on the disposition of homosexual personnel that were to remain in effect for the rest of the war.[39]

As the crowning symbol of the Army's nearly complete conversion from a penal to a discharge system based on psychiatric principles, policymakers replaced the legal term *sodomists* in the title of WD Circular No. 3 with the clinical term *homosexuals*. The directive instructed commanding officers to begin admitting suspected homosexuals to Army hospital wards for psychiatric observation and diagnosis. Shortly before the directive was issued, the Surgeon General's Office had reported to the Personnel Division that medical staffs were ready to process suspected homosexuals as patients through "practically all" Army hospitals, both stateside and overseas.[40] Possibly in response to an increasingly acute personnel shortage, the circular broadened the category of "offenders" who might be reclaimed, extending it beyond the "normal" young men who had gone astray to the "true or confirmed homosexual[s]" whose "cases reasonably indicate the possibility of reclamation." The officer exercising court-martial jurisdiction, not the psychiatrist or any other medical officer, would still determine whether the patient would be discharged, court-martialed, or salvaged. Save this limitation, the hospital, the psychiatric diagnosis, and the administrative discharge together formed the core of the Army's new system for handling homosexual personnel.

The Navy's January 1944 directive introduced an important but controversial administrative category: the person who admitted homosexual "tendencies" or acts but who had committed no "provable" acts while *in* the Navy—"latent" homosexuals, as some officials began to call them. This firmly established the military's interest in homosexuals as a class, regardless of their sexual behavior. Ironically, the new category of "latent" homosexuals with "tendencies" made it easier for men—including those who had been drafted into the Navy for the first time beginning in February 1943—to declare or fake homosexuality to get out of compulsory service without being prosecuted for sexual acts. Under the 1944 Navy directive, whenever individuals voluntarily declared their own homosexuality to obtain a discharge, they were required to sign a statement "relative to such tendencies" and submit it to the Bureau of Naval Personnel in Washington, along with the psychiatrist's diagnosis and the commanding officer's report. The Bureau of Naval Personnel, rather than the local commander, was given the final authority to determine the disposition of each case, which generally was discharge as an undesirable.

The 1944 directives finally installed the system of discharge rather than imprisonment. Suspected homosexuals confronted the new system not only if they were caught in a sexual act or reported by witnesses but also if they declared themselves to an officer. Once identified, the suspect was placed on sick call or sent to sick bay and hospitalized for his condition. A psychiatrist interviewed him to identify his appropriate diagnostic and administrative category, the hospital staff observed his behavior, and a Red Cross worker compiled his life history and contacted his family. Intelligence officers might interrogate him to obtain the names of other homosexual personnel and sexual partners. A medical report, including the psychiatrist's diagnosis and recommendations for treatment and disposition, was compiled by the hospital staff and forwarded to an administrative board, which was required whenever possible to include a psychiatrist. The board determined whether the patient remained in the hospital, returned to duty, or would be discharged or forced to resign as an officer. The enlisted man was subject to the decisions of these boards of commissioned officers without benefit of counsel and with no right to be present, cross-examine witnesses, or obtain a copy of the proceedings. Consequently officers could conduct these hearings more swiftly and with more freedom than the more cumbersome court-martial trials.[41]

As soon as the system went into effect, men caught in the act of sodomy began to appear before the disposition boards. In January 1943 two Army Air Corps privates at Wendover Field, Utah, were turned in by men in their barracks who discovered them having oral sex. A psychiatrist diagnosed them both as sexual psychopaths. A Section Eight board of three officers, including the psychiatrist, was convened. The two men denied having sex with each other, but the board determined that both men had committed the act of "sodomy by mouth" and recommended that they be discharged under Section Eight.[42] In April 1944 at an Air Force base in the Southeast, a corporal and a PFC were observed having anal sex with each other on a bed. They were hospitalized and examined by a psychiatrist, who diagnosed each as "constitutional psychopath, sexual psychopath[. . .], homosexual." The two men denied being homosexual, claiming to have had satisfying sexual relations with their girlfriends and female prostitutes near the airfield. The disposition board recommended that, because it was each man's first offense and they both had been under the influence of alcohol, they were reclaimable and should be returned to duty.[43] Under the old system, men who had committed such offenses would have been court-martialed, found guilty, and sent to prison.

Although the discharge system rescued these and many other "sodomists" from prison, it supplemented rather than replaced the penal system. Imprisonment continued to operate as a powerful backup—a trapdoor that could be released at any time to swallow up recalcitrant gay soldiers. Homosexual patients could be charged with sodomy and other sexual crimes and, if they didn't accept undesirable discharges, they could be court-martialed and sent to prison. Sometimes known homosexuals who could not successfully be convicted of sodomy or other sexual offenses would be charged with other crimes, such as misconduct or being AWOL.

In 1944 Woodie Wilson and his buddy "Kate" were court-martialed in South Carolina for publishing the gay servicemen's newsletter the *Myrtle Beach Bitch*. They were convicted of misusing government property and sentenced to a year of confinement at the Army Disciplinary Barracks in Greenhaven Federal Prison in Stormville, New York. There they found a prison system that, as in the decades before the war, was crowded with homosexual prisoners who were segregated from the rest of the population. "There was a whole wing of that huge prison," Wilson recalled, two tiers "of declared homosexuals and convicted homosexuals. They all were isolated and they all wore 'A' on the back of their uniform and it was called the 'A' Block." Wilson worked as a typist and messenger inside the prison, which enabled him to visit the A tiers many times. "There must have been over a hundred people in there," he explained. "It's something I'll never forget, seeing some of the faces and the ages. The ages are what got me. They weren't just all young. There were old, old men with white hair. They looked like they were up there before we ever got in the war. When they came in to eat," Wilson continued, "they ate at a separate table in the dining room. If they came to the movies, they sat in a separate section. They were ostracized like crazy. Kate and I always said, 'Thank God we didn't come in here as homosexuals [convicted of sodomy].' "

As the focus of procedures turned away from criminal acts and toward the person, the military's commitment to defining and managing its homosexual problem deepened. Preliminary directives were superseded by longer, more specialized directives designed to solve the unanticipated problems created by the previous ones. Internal debates broadened the discussion of homosexuality, chipping away at the "conspiracy of silence" that had surrounded the "unspeakable" crime of sodomy. To discharge homosexuals, officials needed ways to identify them, distinguish them from others, and fit them into useful administrative categories. One of the most exasperating problems military officials faced was what to do with the large number of "latent" homosexuals who had engaged in no "provable" sexual acts while in the service.[44]

In May 1945 a representative of the American Medical Association, Dr. W. W. Bauer, wrote to Navy Surgeon General McIntire on behalf of a serviceman who had sought advice about his predicament in the Navy. The man was "an intelligent homosexual," Bauer explained, who "realized the implications of his trend," had married a woman, but in the Navy discovered "temptation assailing him again," found his situation in the Navy "practically intolerable," and was "trying to find a solution." The serviceman had asked medical officers for advice, but he "says that he finds them of the old-fashioned opinion that a homosexual is a criminal and should be treated as such. . . . What he wants is a discharge but he is reluctant to take a discharge that will be other than honorable. . . . What would you advise us to do in regard to this situation, which is not only bad for the individual but definitely bad for the men among whom he serves?" Frustrated himself at the complexity of this issue, McIntire replied that "it has given us great concern and is at present under close scrutiny.'' He advised the gay serviceman ''to try to carry on and not to do anything at all at the present time'' until the secretary of the Navy could come up with a better procedure ''which is satisfactory to all concerned.'' [45]

For decades psychiatrists had confronted the problem of how to define and what to do about different forms of homosexuality, at times calling it the ''riddle of homosexuality,'' and now the military faced it as well. By 1945 military officials had broken down the *sodomist* category into a confusing array of legal, psychiatric, and administrative subcategories. Homosexual personnel were identified as either latent, self-confessed, well-adjusted, habitual, undetected or known, true, confirmed, and male or female. There were homosexual nonoffenders who admitted only tendencies or acts; heterosexual malingerers and homosexual reverse-malingerers; normal offenders who were casual homosexuals, first-timers, curious, drunk, immature, submissive, or regressive; offenders who still possessed salvage value; the aggressors and willing followers, regardless of their sexuality; the sexual psychopath, moral pervert, and sexual deviate. With the multiplication of categories as the policies and procedures expanded, military officials began to comprehend the magnitude of the project they had taken on, which was to create a comprehensive system for classifying into administrative categories the varieties of deviant sexuality.

Although psychiatric consultants had intended the discharge system to be a humane gesture toward homosexuals, in practice it was humane only to the degree that it saved some men from prison. In September 1943 the Army had reported a total of fifty-two sodomy cases, while it reported only eleven in July 1944, after the new policy had gone into effect. This reduction occurred while the Army had expanded its forces to more than seven million men. The judge advocate general believed that the decrease in sodomy court-martial cases could ''reasonably [be] traced'' to the new procedures. [46]

But the most dramatic outcome of the new system was not humane—the widening of the net in which gay men and lesbians could be caught, vastly expanding the military's antihomosexual apparatus and creating new forms of surveillance and punishment. When previously only those men who had been caught in the sexual act and convicted in court were punished, now merely being homosexual or having such ''tendencies'' could entrap both men and women, label them as sick, and remove them from the service with an undesirable discharge. Because the discharge system punished both gay men and women even if they remained celibate, it demanded that they carefully police their social behavior and appearance as well, so that no one would suspect them of being homosexual. "There was this constant threat of being found out," recalled Stuart Loomis, "and being cashiered out of the service." If the eye of suspicion turned its gaze toward them, gay male and lesbian soldiers could no longer protect themselves by proving that they had engaged in no sexual acts. They also had to prove that they were not homosexual. Their new "crime" was belonging to a class of people that the discharge policies deemed "undesirable" while denying them the rights to which they would have been entitled had they been defendants formally charged with a criminal act.

The impact of this shift in policy was evident in the dramatic increase in the number of people it affected. More homosexuals could be discharged than could reasonably be sent to prison. From 1941 to 1945, more than four thousand sailors and five thousand soldiers—mostly men—were hospitalized, diagnosed as sexual psychopaths, and discharged from the service with the label of homosexuality appearing on their military records. By contrast, the total population of men in both the Army and the Navy who had been convicted of sodomy from 1900 to the beginning of World War II had numbered only in the hundreds.[47] Although neither the Navy nor the Army officially tallied the numbers of women discharged as homosexuals, Ruth Streeter, director of the Women Marines, reported that twenty women marines were given undesirable discharges for homosexual tendencies or overt acts.[48] According to official estimates, many more men and women were discharged with other primary diagnoses disguising secondary homosexual diagnoses. Still others were "treated," reclaimed, and returned to duty, "possibly less than 1,000," according to one Army report.[49] The grasp of the new system was far-reaching.

The increase in discharges and multiplication of sexual categories provoked a critical question regarding authority: Who had the final power to identify, categorize, and dispose of so many suspected homosexuals— the psychiatrist, the commanding officer, the officer in charge of courts-martial, personnel administrators in Washington, the secretary of war, or the suspected men or women themselves? With the shift in policy, the power relationships among psychiatrists, gay personnel, and the military command shifted as well. Psychiatrists, who claimed to know more about homosexuality than other officers, gained more power under a system they had partly designed. But they and other reformers had inadvertently given gay soldiers and officers the option of declaring their homosexuality, which some used for their own purposes, usually to escape mandatory military service or intolerably hostile environments. Confronting the military with their own homosexuality, they could demand a response the military was compelled to give. With challenges from psychiatrists and self-declared homosexuals chipping away at their power, military officials found it necessary periodically to issue directives to ensure that they retained the final authority in each case.

While for decades men convicted of sodomy had fought their individual battles to stay out of prison, psychiatrists in World War II had won a major victory against the penal system itself. Their reforms, however, didn't free "discovered" gay GIs. Now, instead of being locked up behind prison bars, they were forcibly committed to hospital psychiatric wards, sometimes under lock and key, and discharged as psychopathic undesirables. Gay GIs were still fighting a war within the service, but the battlefield on which they defended themselves was moving from the courts to the discharge boards, from the penitentiaries to the hospitals, requiring them to learn the lay of this new land and to develop appropriate tactics.

The discharge system not only expanded the military's antihomosexual apparatus in practice but strengthened the ideology that justified it, rooting it more deeply in the psychiatric conception of homosexuality as mental disease. As psychiatric screening had introduced this model into preinduction examinations, the discharge system embedded it in Army and Navy regulations and procedures. Forced hospitalization, mandatory psychiatric diagnoses, discharge as sexual psychopaths, and the protective sympathy of psychiatrists all reinforced the idea that homosexuals were sick people and that homosexuality itself was an illness. Ironically, the very fact that psychiatrists fought so hard to bring about a more humane military system for handling homosexuals only added to the notion that gay men and women belonged within the domain of abnormal psychiatry. "Homosexuals, in the opinion of the psychiatrist," wrote the sympathetic Army psychiatric consultant William Menninger about the basis for wartime changes in military policy, "have immature personalities which make them and their lives and some of their personal relations grossly pathological. Like any sick person, they deserve understanding instead of condemnation." [50]

CHAPTER
6

Pioneer Experts
Psychiatrists Discover the Gay GI

In the Washington offices of the War and Navy Departments, psychiatric reformers had the luxury of discussing and formulating homosexual policies in the abstract. But in the field and aboard ship, psychiatrists assigned to duty in military hospitals had to put these policies into practice. As psychotherapists they were inclined to understand their patients—nearly all of whom were men—as people who needed help. But as military officers having to obey orders, they were called upon to identify homosexuals and report them for discharge. The conflicting roles of therapist and informer presented psychiatrists with difficult ethical dilemmas and frustrating bureaucratic responsibilities. Some psychiatrists, hoping to improve the efficiency of the discharge system, tried to develop clinical techniques for more accurately identifying male homosexuals. Others who were more sympathetic to their patients began to question the fairness and rationality of the discharge system as soon as it went into effect.

In January 1943 nineteen-year-old Burt Gerrits enlisted in the Navy at a Sioux Falls, South Dakota, recruitment center. After completing courses to become a hospital corpsman, Gerrits was assigned to the Treasure Island Naval Base in San Francisco, where he worked as an aide on the hospital's psychiatric ward. "Most of the people on this ward," Gerrits recalled, "were being discharged from the Navy because they had been discovered to be gay." Dr. Wynn, the hospital psychiatrist, interviewed all the homosexual patients. "I don't know if the psychiatrist was trying to learn more about homosexuality by interviewing these people," Gerrits wondered, "or just what was going on. I don't know why they had so many interviews once it was determined that a person *was* homosexual. Why didn't they just get rid of them?" [1]

Dr. Wynn was one of the 2,400 Army doctors and 700 Navy doctors who served as military psychiatrists during World War II. Most of these physicians were inexperienced young white men—the Army included only sixteen female and seven black psychiatrists—who had been drafted fresh out of medical school with no training in psychiatry prior to their military service. Their job under the new discharge policies was administrative rather than therapeutic—to evaluate and diagnose suspected homosexuals so they could be discharged, court-martialed, or reassigned by other officers. But drafted medical students, doctors, and even practicing psychiatrists, whose previous clinical experience was essentially with severely disturbed individuals, were unprepared for the task of diagnosing homosexuality in healthy people. [2]

Dr. Allan Fredericks was one of the few gay physicians who served as military psychiatrists during the war. Born and raised in the Midwest, he entered medical school at the University of Illinois in Chicago in 1940, where he kept his homosexuality a secret because "if they knew you were gay, you might not stay in medical school very long." Upon completing his internship in early 1945 at the age of thirty, he was drafted into the Navy and did his basic training at Great Lakes Naval Station, where he served as a general practitioner, treating recruits who came down with the children's diseases that were so common among trainees in crowded barracks. After serving as medical officer on a North Atlantic convoy flagship, he was sent to the Naval Air Station in Memphis, Tennessee, where the Navy "drafted" him into psychiatry. "I liked it anyway," he recalled, "so I was very willingly drafted." In high school he had devoured books by Freud, Ellis, and Krafft-Ebing, trying in part to understand his own homosexuality.

To train Dr. Fredericks and other medical recruits to serve as military psychiatrists, the Army and Navy put them through crash courses in elementary psychiatry that taught much about military regulations and little about the complexities of human sexuality. The military's schools of neuropsychiatry were run by psychiatrists prominent in their profession. They shared a general bias with Menninger, Sullivan, and other policy-makers toward a psychodynamic orientation, but in their brief courses all they could do was present the symptoms within each diagnostic category. At the Army's School of Military Neuropsychiatry in Atlanta, headed by Col. William C. Porter, who had conducted some of the

Selective Service Seminars, the four-week intensive training course for medical officers contained only one hour on "Problems of Discipline and Morale" including alcoholism, drug addiction, and psychopathy, of which homosexuality was only a minor subtopic.[3] Most of Dr. Allan Fredericks's training at Memphis was in how to "survey" (process for discharge) psychiatric cases. His class was given no specific lectures on homosexuality other than instructions that such men were to be discharged as unsuitable for military service. When even these minimally trained officers were not available in the field, surgeons and general practitioners with no psychiatric training at all diagnosed homosexuals and served on disposition boards in their stead.[4] The wholly inadequate training and staffing of psychiatric personnel to administer the new directives concerning homosexuals made an ambiguous and unwieldy policy into a bureaucratic nightmare for all involved.

On the job in hospitals and clinics, doctors who had been trained in different schools of psychiatry sometimes made contradictory diagnoses of the same individuals, exasperating hospital staffs and confusing their patients. It was for administrative convenience alone that psychiatric consultants in Washington had decided to standardize the diagnosis of homosexuals in the military, despite their diversity, simply as "sexual psychopaths." Yet psychiatrists still argued over whether homosexuality was a personality disorder or a symptom of another disorder such as neurosis, psychopathy, or schizophrenia; a condition resulting from hormonal imbalance or other biological, hereditary, or psychological origins; a form of arrested or regressive emotional development; a willful and immoral act; or merely a unique personality type that occurred in otherwise well-adjusted people. A soldier who had engaged in a single homosexual act could be routed from one hospital to another and be assigned diagnoses ranging from "Constitutional Psychopathic State" and "Sexual Psychopath #1507" to "Emotionally Unstable," "Psychoneurosis," and even "No Disease." Like diagnosis, the disposition of homosexual cases aroused disagreement and disorder. "At one station," wrote Major Carl H. Jonas, who served in the Army Medical Corps, "a psychiatrist would recommend separation for all homosexual individuals, while at another station the psychiatrist would refuse to recommend separation for any homosexual individual." In practice, Jonas concluded, psychiatry during the war "was truly a ship without a rudder."[5]

To direct their course some psychiatrists and other doctors in military hospitals and clinics undertook their own wartime research projects. Rapid military expansion, the pressure of the war emergency, and the new discharge policies gave doctors the opportunities, motives, and populations for studying homosexuality. Menninger described the attitude in the Army toward research on soldiers as "not only liberal, but in most places encouraging." [6] The new discharge policies themselves, explained Navy Lt. Herbert Greenspan and Comdr. John D. Campbell, had made their particular research possible by placing in hospitals "a greater proportion of homosexuals . . . under the scrutiny of psychiatrists than ordinarily are observed in civilian life." [7] At least fifteen psychiatric studies of male homosexual soldiers and officers were conducted—eleven of them originating from hospitals and clinics—involving more than two thousand patients.[8] The large quantity of homosexual "clinical material" in military hospitals, in fact, so preoccupied psychiatrists that nearly every published psychiatric study of human sexuality that came out of the military during the war concerned male homosexuality. None were published concerning lesbians or other women in the military, and few were published concerning heterosexual soldiers.[9]

The research interests of psychiatrists reflected the range of their own attitudes toward patients, which ran from the punitive to the sympathetic.[10] Researchers tried to define or describe homosexuality more accurately. They examined patients' physiques, analyzed their urine, explored family backgrounds for hereditary evidence or developmental problems, applied a battery of psychological tests, and questioned patients about their sexual behavior and life history. Those who searched for biological markers, physical traits, or personality characteristics, hoping that they might help the military definitively identify the homosexual, were the least scientific in their research, relying on unexamined stereotypes of the "typical homosexual" that reflected popular prejudices about "queers."

Several doctors, hoping to improve the military's ability to identify homosexuals, tried to develop clinical tests for detecting men who had performed oral sex—an act that soldiers more simply called giving a blow job—on other men. In 1944 Dr. Nicolai Gioscia and his staff at an unidentified Army base inserted tongue depressors into the throats of 1,404 psychiatric patients at the clinic and hospital to test their reactions. The researchers observed that 89 percent of the patients who had been diagnosed as sexual psychopaths and who had "admitted fellatio" did not show a "gag reflex" due to "the repeated control of the reflex during the act of fellatio." Gioscia didn't explain why half of the psychoneurosis and one-third of the drug addiction cases he tested also showed no gag reflex. "Frequently," he reported, "the gag reflex test proved valuable in detecting the malingerer who attempted to obtain a discharge by professing homosexuality. Presented with the gag test findings the soldier would invariably change his story or admit having lied for selfish gains.'' The test, he added, was also ''a definite aid in screening candidates not only for the military services, but for positions where the sexual deviate must be eliminated.'' [11]

Another bogus test for identifying fellators used interviews rather than tongue depressors. Two Navy doctors, Comdr. A. C. Cornsweet and Lt. Comdr. M. F. Hayes, selected two hundred patients between the ages of eighteen and thirty who had been identified as homosexual through "psychiatric evaluation" at an unidentified Navy hospital. They wanted to separate these men into three categories: true homosexuals, latent homosexuals, and malingerers. They asked each man to describe his sexual responses when he had engaged in the "application of the mouth to the sexual organ" of another man. Their theory was that homosexuals, as they became more sexually active, reversed the process by which the child is weaned from the mother's breast and the bottle's nipple. True homosexuals, they theorized, had given so many blow jobs that their pleasure became localized in their lips and mouths, while their penises remained limp during fellatio and they rarely had orgasms. Latent homosexuals were in a transitional stage, still able to feel erotic responses in other parts of their body but well on their way to localizing their pleasure in their mouths. The malingerers weren't sophisticated enough to describe oral pleasure without orgasm, so they could easily be detected. Cornsweet and Hayes concluded that a soldier's description of having had oral but no genital satisfaction while giving a blow job was a "diagnostic sign" that identified him as overt and distinguished him from the malingerer who "apes homosexuality" to escape military service. [12]

Other psychiatrists tried applying to their patients recently developed clinical procedures such as the Rorschach ink blot test and sex-hormone urine tests to see if they could detect homosexuality. In 1945, Sgt. Martin S. Bergmann, a medical officer stationed at the Psychiatric Consultation Service at Camp Wheeler, Georgia, reported that his use of the inkblot test on twenty soldiers had been the first attempt to observe the responses of homosexuals in Rorschach literature. His inconclusive results led Bergmann to admit that the "Rorschach Test cannot be used as an infallible instrument for the detection of homosexuality." Yet he claimed that "our findings suggest that it could be of practical value to Army psychiatrists who may be confronted with simulators or soldiers accused of homosexuality which they deny." [13] The same year, two Navy researchers, Lt. Comdr. Floyd O. Due and Lt. (jg) M. Erik Wright, also reported that they had applied Rorschach tests to forty-two "homosexual subjects'' who ''had been brought to the attention of the psychiatrist either by being apprehended in overt homosexuality or by self-referral.'' They concluded that content analysis of the sailors' responses could serve ''to identify certain types of overt homosexuals'' and to differentiate them ''from other diagnostic categories.'' [14] Other researchers gave homosexual military prisoners an array of psychological tests to see if the results would be useful in detecting the male homosexual and even, according to one report, ''the homosexually inclined woman'' in the armed forces. [15]

Researchers who tried to develop biological tests hoped that laboratory results might convince military officers suspicious of the psychiatric discharge that homosexuality, even when ''latent,'' was a physical disorder. Hormone tests in particular, explained Army psychiatrist Maj. Isidore Weiss, would be ''of inestimable help'' to psychiatrists serving on discharge boards, because the results ''would be objective and acceptable by laymen who might not be receptive to the less tangible psychiatric concepts. . . . They want concrete evidence, not theory.'' [16] To this end, several researchers tried to develop reliable hormone tests that would clearly indicate, according to *Newsweek,* ''a higher degree of estrogens (female hormones) than androgens (male hormones)'' in homosexual soldiers, ''just the opposite of a normal male.'' [17]

Despite researchers' hopes that such clinical tests would be useful to the military, their results were neither reliable nor practical. The often elaborate testing procedures were time consuming and required laboratory space as well as special equipment and trained personnel that were not available at most Army installations. The problems inherent in trying to correlate hormone levels, Rorschach responses, and even gag reflexes with the varieties of human sexuality also made the test results suspect. The ''urinary hormone-secretion test,'' concluded *Newsweek* shortly after the war, ''was too uncertain and too expensive to try on every inductee.'' [18] In military hospitals most psychiatric examiners continued to rely primarily on direct observation and face-to-face interviews to diagnose homosexual patients.

Case histories constructed from interviews should have alerted military psychiatrists to the inaccuracy of generalizations about the homosexual soldier. The wartime pressure to streamline diagnostic procedures, however, led many psychiatrists instead to focus on character traits that they believed distinguished these soldiers from other men. To help speed up diagnoses of the psychiatric patients who occupied so many beds in military hospitals, they aimed for a shorthand description of the homosexual "personality type." [19] The published studies of case histories, based primarily on interpretations of interviews, life histories, Rorschach responses, and direct observation on the wards, tended to be wholly subjective. The weakness of any single profile of "the homosexual," however, became apparent as the hospital wards filled with an expanding and changing population of gay patients who challenged all pat formulas.

The published case histories did reflect some of the diversity of gay patients. But many psychiatrists saw only those characteristics that confirmed their stereotypes, while others were willing to use these new data to question their own assumptions. In 1945 Navy researchers Greenspan and Campbell published the case history of a gay sailor, "S. R. C.," whom they presented as the typical patient among the "large number of homosexuals" they had studied in Navy hospitals. Like many other gay GI patients, S. R. C. both fit and challenged the stereotype that the researchers expected to find.

Twenty-two-year-old S. R. C. was serving as a chaplain's assistant when he was pulled from his unit and hospitalized as a suspected homosexual. The son of a "reputable business man in a rural community," S. R. C. in his early years had "displayed a fervent interest for music" and had put himself through college by working as a church organist and choir director, being "particularly well-liked by women who met him at church and in their homes." In school he had had crushes on male teachers and students, but only in the Navy had he "actually indulged in homosexual acts," his admission to the psychiatric ward resulting "solely from the discovery of his sexual activity."

During the psychiatric interviews, S. R. C. remained unapologetic about his homosexuality. When asked to describe his first homosexual experience, "he became enthused and almost euphoric. He stated, 'I never knew that there were such people. I was very happy!' " When S. R. C. recounted his sexual history, the psychiatrist observed in him a "smug, superior complacency" and an "impatient petulance, suggestive of a spoiled child or a pampered female." He told the psychiatrist that he "regretted his stay in the hospital" but "offered no alibis, somatic complaints or other indications that he felt morally wrong. He rationalized that if his mode of sexual expression was satisfactory to him, and not a criminal act, then he could not appreciate society's criticism." On the ward the hospital staff perceived S. R. C. to be "uncomplaining, cooperative and resigned to his predicament." Greenspan and Campbell found him to be effeminate, conscientious, and without indications of psychopathy, neurosis, or psychosis. [20]

When military psychiatrists interpreted this and other case histories of gay male patients on hospital wards, they identified what they considered to be the three major traits of the homosexual personality—effeminacy, a sense of superiority, and fear. Effeminacy was by far the most common characteristic psychiatrists attributed to the typical homosexual. At a time when national survival depended on aggressive masculinity, military psychiatrists paid special attention to effeminacy as a sign of homosexuality, expressing on the hospital wards the same interest in gender characteristics that their colleagues had shown at induction stations. Researchers described their gay male patients as womanly in their bodies, mannerisms, emotional makeup, and interests.

Army researcher Major Carl H. Jonas admitted that identifying the degree to which homosexual men had female bodies was "the phase of the examination . . . which offers the most opportunity for subjective variation." [21] Many researchers lumped together what Greenspan and Campbell called the "physical as well as psychic traits of effeminacy" as if they were different manifestations of the same feminine nature. These two doctors reported that the majority of their patients displayed "an effeminate manner, appearance, temperament and interests," including "delicacy of speech and movement, high-pitched voices," and "feminine body configuration." Other researchers decided to separate effeminate bodies and mannerisms into two different phenomena. Major Jonas, in his study of sixty homosexual and sixty "normal" soldiers, concluded that although many in the homosexual group had effeminate mannerisms, their bodies were no more masculine or feminine than the control group of normal men, and that when other examiners observed differently, they were misinterpreting mannerisms as if they were biological. Jonas believed that most of his effeminate homosexual patients were not so by nature but "had cultivated feminine gestures, postures and gaits" as well as "a high-pitched voice" to fit in with other homosexuals and to be attractive to men.

"Sissy" interests and a strong "maternal attachment" in the patient's childhood were among other effeminate signs that psychiatrists identified as typical of the homosexual, often linking the two together. Greenspan and Campbell noted that one of their sailors had, from the age of five, "manifested an attraction for feminine interests and activities. He shunned the company of boys in preference for female companionship and participated in the 'sissy' pastimes of little girls." [22] A psychiatrist at the 298th Station Hospital in Miami, Florida, reported that his patient "never participated much in sports" and as a child had "stayed home helping mother with home cleaning, dish washing and running errands for her." [23] Researchers often perceived sissies as not being able to let go of their mothers' apron strings. Jonas was impressed with "how emphatic many patients are in professing their love for, and dependance [*sic*] on, their mothers." Others directly blamed mothers for the patient's effeminacy. Cornsweet and Hayes described the sailor "W. B." as "an extremely sensitive youth of 19 who had been over-indulged and over-protected by his mother." [24] Greenspan and Campbell believed that as these young, maternally attached boys reached adolescence, they demonstrated "a spirit of comradeship toward women that [would] characterize them for the remainder of their lives." [25]

This profile of the typical male homosexual as more womanly than manly described him as having a passive emotional makeup as well. "Several of our patients," noted Greenspan and Campbell, "demonstrated a feminine resignation without evidence of resentment, and when informed of a discharge from the service, resorted to such expressions as 'Oh, my goodness' or 'My dear, my dear' in characteristic female style." [26] One soldier, "W. L.," was described as an "effeminate, ineffectual youth of 24." [27] The stereotype of gay men as passive and womanly trapped them in a double bind. When they did act aggressively, they were dismissed, like women, as petulant, impulsive, or silly; when they complied or withdrew, they were perceived, also like women, to be characteristically weak, oversensitive, and unable to defend themselves. Either way, they were described as pseudo men who did not fit the profile of the masculine, aggressive soldier.

Another cluster of traits attributed to the typical homosexual was a sense of superiority both as individuals and as a group—they were artistic, smug, and cliquish. Military researchers found that gay men believed their interests and styles set them apart from other people as a special elite rather than degenerate and queer. "Many dabble in poetry, art, sculpture and drama," explained Greenspan and Campbell, and display a "feeling of intellectual superiority" as well as a "delicate appreciation of colors, fabrics and the arts." It was unusual, they added, "for a homosexual not to like music," and many "had their own pianos, whether or not they could play, and they frequently owned albums of fine recordings." [28] Observers explained that homosexual soldiers used their shared artistic interests and sense of superiority to justify banding together in opposition to the outside world.[29] Navy researchers Due and Wright, who studied Rorschach responses in homosexual sailors, speculated that their patients transformed their "failure to identify with normal people" into a "positive feeling of being set off as a part of a unique group" and that it led them to "seek out others who are in revolt against the etablished order." [30] Greenspan and Campbell described this process of creating a gay in-group as a "compensatory mechanism, behind which the homosexual barricades himself from a hostile society." [31]

Once in their own separate and secret society, reported Due and Wright, homosexual soldiers had a "tendency" to use their own "esoteric and stylized language," which further set them apart. [32] Greenspan and Campbell, possibly trying to understand some gay men's use of "camping," described the typical homosexual conversation as "pseudophilosophical, blasé, ultra-sophisticated and ethereal." They reported that an "egocentric, subtle, satirical attitude is developed" among them, growing out of the homosexual's need to feel superior to what he "considers to be a shallow-minded world, incapable of appreciating his mode of expression." Behind the security of this "cultural aloofness," the homosexual can create a protective world in which "he is comfortably adjusted." [33] In these awkward descriptions of how and why gay soldiers banded together, military researchers began to move beyond the clinical tradition of individual case histories toward an elementary sociology of gay life.

Nowhere did psychiatrists study the social life of gay patients more closely than at the Army's 36th Station Hospital in England, which served the European Theater of Operations and was designated by the Army as an "observation and recommendation center" for homosexual soldiers. [34] From February 1943 to August 1944, the staff, working under the hospital's commanding officer Lt. Col. Lewis H. Loeser, observed the social behavior of 270 "sexual psychopaths" on the wards. Loeser reported that "homosexuals tend to group together, and it is interesting to observe the speed and certainty with which they are able to recognize one another. Within a few hours after admission to the ward the homosexual will have located others of his type and becomes one of the group. They tend to stay grouped together," he added, "and rarely include heterosexuals in their activities." Loeser believed there was military value in studying the social behavior of these men. "It is wise to insist," he urged, "that these cases be hospitalized for observation." Learning how gay men reacted to one another and how they used their "knowledge of the homosexual 'lingo' " gave psychiatrists "valuable clues" that they could use to diagnose homosexuals more accurately. [35]

Fear was the other dominant trait that completed the wartime profile of the homosexual personality. Fear took various forms—nervousness, anxiety, paranoia, panic, terror. Some examiners merely observed that their homosexual patients appeared nervous during the interview. Cornsweet and Hayes noted that twenty-four-year-old "W. L." "appeared fearful, apprehensive and mildly dejected." [36] Another Navy doctor, after what he called his "interrogation" of a nineteen-year-old sailor, Michael O'Connor, reported that when the boy "walked into the office he appeared to be under a great deal of emotional tension and apprehension as characterized by fidgetiness and many unpurposeful movements." [37] Although patients had much to fear from the psychiatrist himself, their fear was more commonly interpreted as having other causes, depending on whether the man was an "overt" or "latent" homosexual. O'Connor, an "overt" homosexual who knew he was gay, was described by his psychiatrist as "decidedly suspicious of his shipmates, believing that they might know of his abnormal trend, this, of course, causing him to be under increased pressure at all times." [38] Due and Wright observed that the overt patients to whom they administered Rorschach tests displayed many "paranoid reactions." The homosexual, they concluded, "uncertain of his social status with others, constantly exposed to disapproving social attitudes . . . tends to develop a cautiousness and suspiciousness about people." [39] Psychiatrists believed that these states of fear and anxiety could lead to more serious conditions. O'Connor's psychiatrist described him as "overly apprehensive" and diagnosed him as being "in the earliest states of an escape mechanism whereby he would in all probability detach himself from reality and become overtly psychotic because of his professed homosexual makeup." [40]

Psychiatrists observed in some "latent" homosexual patients a more acute form of fear, which they called "homosexual panic." A case history of a twenty-four-year-old black soldier reported that wherever he went, he felt that the other men were spreading rumors that he was "queer." He believed that " 'instigators' were placed on the ward and they spread the tale about him. He insisted that his door be locked to keep them out of his room for they annoyed him. . . . He could tell by 'their' actions and attitude that 'they' considered him a 'queer' and threatened to kill the first man that made an advance to him." [41] Many men were hospitalized or imprisoned during the war after having gone AWOL to escape what they perceived to be such rumors and advances from other men. These panic reactions, as well as a patient's anxiety and nervousness during the interview, certainly had much to do with each man's own psychological makeup. But they might also have been responses to the real threat of being turned in by the psychiatrist or caught in the act, being taunted or assaulted by the other men, or getting a bad discharge or going to jail.

Sometimes researchers were surprised to find so little fear or anxiety among their patients. Greenspan and Campbell commented that "none of our homosexual patients expressed somatic complaints or other manifestations of anxiety, even though threatened with disgrace and an undesirable discharge from the service.'' They observed that the sailors they studied were remarkably ''patient, resigned, placid, philosophical and long-suffering,'' quietly bearing their ''burden, in spite of constant harassment and frustration.'' These and other gay GIs appeared to be model psychiatric patients.[42] Because they had been hospitalized for administrative processing rather than therapy, many gay patients were the best adjusted and best behaved on the psychiatric wards and had no desire to receive treatment for their homosexuality. Their mere presence on the wards challenged the assumption of mental illness underlying the discharge policies.

Seeking to amplify their profile of the homosexual personality, Army and Navy doctors constructed sexual histories of their patients by compiling information from the patient's interview and from the written statements of commanding officers, investigative officers, witnesses of the sex act, and the patient's sex partners. Psychiatrists assumed that clues leading to the patient's true sexual identity would be revealed in these sexual histories. Along with the developers of the gag-reflex and the fellatio-response tests, many psychiatrists believed that the ''true'' homosexual fit a typical sexual profile that showed that, unlike ''normal'' men, he did not sexually penetrate his partners. They assumed that homosexuals were active partners in oral sex or passive partners in anal sex—or in the soldier slang of the day, that all queers were cocksuckers or got fucked. Military psychiatrists also believed that true homosexuals, again unlike ''normal'' men, had had no sex or only unpleasant sex with women. Apprentice Seaman O'Connor's sexual history noted that he ''had his first homosexual contact with another young man approximately four years ago,'' and since then he had ''entered into many homosexual acts.'' He ''had had only one heterosexual experience in his life at which time he stated that he became quite nauseated and had never had any desire to go out with the opposite sex.''[43]

More problematic than the diagnosis of true homosexuals was the task of diagnosing the ''first-time offenders'' and ''experimenters''—the normal men who enjoyed sex with women yet were accused of homosexual acts. In their interviews psychiatrists tried to discover how these patients felt about sex with women, why and how many times they had sex with men, who initiated it, whether they were active or passive, what the sexual identity of their sex partner was, how much remorse and guilt they felt, and whether they were lying. First-time offenders who received only one blow job from a ''confirmed pervert,'' felt remorse, and still enjoyed sex with women were the most likely candidates for reclamation and reassignment rather than discharge. Women accused of being lesbians, especially the "girlfriends" who did not appear to be butch, were subjected to similar questions about sexual experience with men, active and passive sexual roles with women, orgasms, and remorse to determine their true sexuality and thus their reclaimability.[44] Any suspect, however, even men and women who had solid heterosexual histories, could be diagnosed as a sexual psychopath under the new regulations by virtue of having committed a single homosexual act.

The case of Pfc. Leo M. Koski illustrates how the complex sexual histories of individual soldiers could baffle psychiatrists who tried to fit them into simple categories, often leading doctors to make contradictory diagnoses of the same person. Early in 1944 Koski was admitted to the Army's 168th Station Hospital in the European Theater as a suspected homosexual following an investigation into the alleged homosexuality of his roommate. An intelligence officer had extracted a confession from Koski in which he "at first denied homosexual relationships" but "later admitted passive fellatio about once a month for eight months." After examining him for two weeks, the psychiatric staff at the hospital concluded that Koski was "really interested in women and had always enjoyed a normal heterosexual life." But because he had confessed to approximately eight acts of "passive fellatio," he was assigned the preliminary diagnosis of "constitutional psychopathic state." Koski then was transferred to the Army's 36th Station Hospital in Exeter, England, for further observation. After a month of more interviews, tests, and examinations, the psychiatric staff completed a more detailed sexual history, noting that Koski "enjoyed heterosexual experience" but, because of depression after basic training, had started drinking "with some friends whom he knew indulged in homosexual perversions, and whom he permitted to perform fellatio upon him because he 'felt sorry for them and got weak.' " Because Koski knew that "the abberant sex acts" were "abnormal" and had "a sense of guilt and fear of detection," the staff believed that there was a "good likelihood that he will not indulge in homosexuality in the army, again" and that "he could still render useful service." Deciding that Koski was not a "true pervert," the staff changed his diagnosis to "no disease," and recommended his return to duty.[45]

The psychiatrists' responsibility as military officers, however, was not to conduct clinical research but to diagnose suspected homosexuals for discharge or reclamation. This task presented them with a difficult ethical dilemma. Their professions had trained them to counsel, evaluate, treat, and sometimes study the troubled people who came to them for help. In civilian practice psychiatrists generally diagnosed patients to determine the cause of their suffering and to select the therapy that would restore them to mental health. In the armed forces, to their great dismay, these members of the helping professions discovered that sometimes when they performed their military duties, they hurt homosexuals more than they helped them.

Many obstacles blocked the way of psychiatrists who genuinely wanted to help their gay patients. There were medical doctors who dismissed psychiatry as unscientific hocus-pocus and officers who saw them as a little queer or crazy themselves—overprotective mothers who pampered sissies and cry-babies by permitting them "to hide behind the skirts of psychiatry." From their side, psychiatrists saw most officers as stubborn adversaries who defended their archaic and cruel prejudices against the humane, rational influence of psychiatry.[46] Their lack of authority to decide the ultimate disposition of each patient continually frustrated psychiatrists, sometimes breaking apart the temporary alliances they had formed with "lay" officers to bring about the new discharge system in the first place.

One of the thorniest issues between psychiatrists and lay officers was whether or not to discharge homosexual patients. Officers on discharge boards had many reasons for rejecting psychiatrists' recommendations to discharge gay patients. Those who had contempt for homosexuals did not want to reward them by letting them escape their military duty, even with undesirable discharges, and instead preferred to whip them into shape by assigning them to punitive duties or even sending them to prison. Army Chief of Chaplains Major General William R. Arnold believed that the homosexual soldier exerted "a vicious influence" on other soldiers, posed a "virulent danger to the Army," and should not be retained in the service. Yet Arnold thought that it was even more reprehensible that some homosexuals "are so without shame that they take advantage of their condition to bring about a discharge from our armed forces. . . . It is unfortunately true that some men do not consider it a privilege to fight for their country and for those ideals for which good men are willing to sacrifice so much." [47] Less hostile officers could be suspicious of psychiatrists' claims that "latent" homosexuals who had not been caught in the act were unfit to serve, choosing instead to keep the man, especially if he was vital to the unit.[48] Officers also refused to discharge these men because they wanted to discourage malingerers from posing as homosexuals to escape military service, some fearing that even undesirable discharges threatened to throw open the exit doors to a stampede of heterosexual slackers.

But malingering by faking homosexuality was a problem more imagined than real. During World War II—unlike the Vietnam War— few heterosexual soldiers pretended to be homosexuals to get discharged, probably because the taboos against both homosexuality and avoiding military service were much greater than in the 1960s. "Whether the problem of feigned homosexuality is serious elsewhere is not known," reported Lieutenant Colonel Loeser from the 36th Station Hospital, which processed most of the Army's homosexual cases in the European Theater of Operations. "Certainly it is not a serious problem in this theater." After "careful study" by the hospital's staff, all one hundred of their self-declared homosexual soldiers had without exception been "considered to be true homosexuals." [49] Menninger believed that the pervasive social stigma of homosexuality was sufficient to discourage this type of malingering. Those who "so heatedly condemn the homosexual," he reasoned, and "assume that feigning homosexuality to escape the service is a very common procedure. . . . fail to see that if a man does wish to malinger he has a far easier time of it if he chooses a simple expedient like a backache or headache." [50] Toward the end of the war, however, conditions for black soldiers became so intolerable at some posts that a few desperate men did claim to be homosexual as the only way out of the Army. [51]

Army psychiatrists who recommended that their gay patients not be discharged but be treated and reassigned to duty, citing the reclamation procedures outlined in the new policy directives, also met much opposition. They faced boards of officers who rarely approved requests to rehabilitate "true" homosexual soldiers, and they were limited by their responsibilities as military officers. Psychiatrists had been conscripted to win a war, not to provide therapeutic services to patients. "The Army does not and should not plan to provide prolonged clinical care," the Army's chief psychiatric consultant, Roy D. Halloran, explained to a 1943 convention of psychiatrists in Detroit, "since its purpose is to build and maintain a healthy and effective fighting force." The danger that long-term psychotherapy posed to the military mission was that, as combat casualties mounted, medical and surgical wards would be overwhelmed with homosexual and other administrative cases. If the psychiatrist could not quickly "fix" patients' problems and restore them to their units, Menninger complained, then his duty was to "give them a name and get rid of them!" [52]

Ironically, the bias of many officers against rehabilitating homosexual soldiers was reinforced by psychiatrists who fought against imprisonment by arguing that homosexuality was incurable. Since the late nineteenth century, experimental drug therapy, hormonal injections, hypnosis, psychoanalysis, testicle irradiation, and castration all had failed to cure homosexuality in civilian patients.[53] During the war such treatments as electroshock or Metrazol shock therapy were tried on a few homosexual soldiers who suffered from other disorders, including severe anxiety states and panic reactions.[54] Winfred Overholser and his colleagues at the National Research Council, however, specifically advised the Navy not to use hormonal treatments for homosexual sailors because they had not been proven effective.[55]

Whenever psychiatrists recommended "true" homosexuals for reclamation without treatment, military board officers generally denied their requests, preferring to discharge these men and reassign only the first-time offenders who seemed otherwise heterosexual. "It is not known how many homosexual offenders were salvaged for further duty under this system," Menninger reported, "but probably not a significant number. . . . The fact that any were salvaged seems surprising in the light of the prevalence of such strong prejudices."[56]

GIs who had heeded the standard advice in basic training lectures to talk over their problems with the chaplain, psychiatrist, or other officer were often shocked to learn that their request for help ended with an undesirable discharge without honor. Every soldier's trust in military doctors was "undermined," Menninger complained, when the Army required medical officers to "report even those statements given in confidence in a consultation room."[57] Dr. Francis Braceland, the Navy's chief psychiatric consultant, decried the same situation in the Navy, where psychiatrists also "had to betray the confidences gained in an interview" with a gay sailor or officer.[58] The psychiatrist's responsibility as a military officer was to act as a secret informer against his homosexual patients and to deliver them to military authorities.

The system for reporting suspected homosexuals under the new discharge policies penetrated every corner of the military organization. It even eroded the "sanctity of the confessional," which prohibited officials from forcing chaplains to report the confidences of their men. In August 1943 the post chaplain at Fort Bliss, Texas, who was sympathetic to the plight of gay soldiers, noticed that such men were coming to him for help and drew up guidelines which he asked the chief of chaplains in Washington to circulate to other Army chaplains in the field. ''What does the efficient Chaplain do,'' his proposed guidelines began, ''when a soldier comes to him and says, 'I am a homo-sexual!' Some Chaplains would be horrified. Some have treated the soldier with contempt and have said, 'You nauseate me.' Such a Chaplain is not very helpful to the man or the Army. . . . The Chaplain's responsibility . . . is to get the individual in the hands of the psychiatrist at the earliest possible moment.'' [59]

Such mutually supportive working relationships developed between chaplains and psychiatrists during the war. ''The chaplain should be capable of recognizing serious mental ailments,'' advised a sociologist who studied the role of the Army chaplain, ''and of explaining clearly to the medical officer just what he has found.'' If a troubled man mistrusted psychiatrists, he continued, a good chaplain told the man ''to speak frankly to the first medical officer in whom he could confide.'' [60] By working hand in hand with psychiatrists who were required to report their homosexual patients, chaplains unwittingly—or intentionally when they were hostile to homosexuals—helped military officers detect and discharge gay men and women who would otherwise have remained hidden in the ranks.

Because the consequences could be so severe, gay soldiers risked exposing their secret worries to chaplains and military psychiatrists only as a last resort. Over and over chaplains and psychiatrists were struck by how afraid the men who came to them were of what they called ''losing control''—doing anything at all that might make others suspicious enough to turn them in. In December 1944 Private ''L. B. F.,'' a black soldier serving with an engineer regiment stationed in England, ''became very apprehensive'' because ''he thought the men suspected he was a homosexual and expected that at any time they would either beat him themselves or turn him over to the officers for punishment. Finally, in desperation he went to the chaplain for protection and poured out his story.'' [61] At Camp Maxey, Texas, the commanding officer of the Army Regional Hospital reported that gay soldiers ''come to the clinic or the hospital because they are afraid of eventualities and feel that they are losing ability to control behavior.'' [62] The new antihomosexual policies, combined with the prejudices of officers and other soldiers, had placed these particular men in a nightmare of fear. At the end of their rope, some went AWOL or got drunk and were arrested for various offenses, while others desperately sought out chaplains and psychiatrists, hoping to find protection and someone to talk to. [63]

The psychiatrist's military duty, when confronted with a soldier claiming to be homosexual, was to assume that he was lying until interviews and clinical tests could prove he was telling the truth. Self-confessed homosexuals might actually be devious malingerers who faked homosexuality to escape military service; men claiming to be normal might be "reverse" malingerers who hid their homosexuality to stay in. Under such an intense climate of suspicion, the interview techniques researchers were developing became even less reliable tools for accurate diagnosis. The information gathered during an interview was based on the patient's sometimes deceptive or coerced statements under threats of punishment and on the psychiatrist's own attempts to protect his patients or to trick them into telling the truth.[64] When the psychiatrist diagnosed his patients correctly and performed his military duty properly, he discovered that he had become both an interrogator and an informer against his patients.

Many psychiatrists followed the rules, reported their patients, and recommended giving them undesirable discharges. In July 1943, according to the records of one Army board of officers, a soldier "went to the doctor to get help and advice," telling the doctor that he had been a homosexual since the age of fifteen. The doctor immediately diagnosed him as a sexual psychopath and told him that there was "no other solution" than to get a discharge. Although his patient didn't want to be turned in, his doctor reported him and "testified against him" at the board hearing, which resulted in an undesirable discharge.[65]

But other psychiatrists refused to play the role of informer, choosing instead to become quiet advocates for their gay patients. Psychiatric interviews, after all, were private encounters in which secret negotiations easily could take place. Psychiatrists found clandestine ways to get patients honorable discharges or even to disguise their homosexuality so they could keep fighting for their country. Some also openly defended their gay patients and spoke out against what they perceived to be "grave injustices" against them. In the process these sympathetic psychiatrists became the military's first advocates for individual gay soldiers and their rights as patients.[66]

The most common form of "subterfuge" was for the psychiatrist deliberately to misdiagnose his patient with a condition, often physical, other than homosexuality. Some of the highest-ranking psychiatrists in the Army and the Navy were aware that these secret actions were common practice among psychiatrists in the field and privately approved of them. Francis Braceland acknowledged that many Navy doctors, unwilling to help hostile officers take punitive actions against homosexual patients, had invented ways "to circumvent the stringencies of the directives and still rid the service of these people. The basic problem would be disguised and the man would be discharged with another diagnosis." [67]

William Menninger also knew that many Army doctors, to save the homosexual patient from procedures that "singled him out for punishment," developed, in his words, "a reluctance to call clinical entities by their correct designations." [68]

There were many ways for doctors to commit these "humane errors," as two psychologists referred to them.[69] One was to avoid the word *homosexual* in the patient's records. "Certainly many who were fundamentally homosexual," Menninger acknowledged, "were returned to duty with no mention or indication to commanding officers of the root of their difficulty." When a disposition board, on the other hand, had a reputation for refusing to approve discharges for any homosexual patient, "a subterfuge was the only course left for the hospital staff— to give the man a medical diagnosis and then discharge him with a certificate of disability." [70] Another form of subterfuge was secretly to advise the soldier or sailor himself to fake a medical condition for which an honorable discharge was mandatory. Even commanding officers could recommend this tactic to their homosexual men. "Some commanding officers," wrote the Army post chaplain at Fort Bliss, Texas, in August 1943, "wishing to avoid unpleasantness in such cases have told the man to wet the bed for a period of days in order that he might be released from the service on this account." This chaplain and other sympathetic officers disapproved of such deceptive practices, believing that it was "better to face the fact and deal with the case directly rather than resorting to subterfuge." [71]

Perhaps the most popular form of "humane error" was the diagnosis of homosexual patients as psychoneurotics rather than as sexual psychopaths. Such diagnoses automatically led to honorable discharges, because Army and Navy regulations considered most psychiatric ailments other than homosexuality to be medical disabilities. The psychoneurosis diagnosis could be used in this way because Army regulations defined it as a catch-all category that, according to Menninger, could be "attached to anything from a transient emotional upset to a severe hysterical paralysis." By 1944 it had become common practice for company commanders similarly to abuse this diagnosis by referring all troublemakers to the psychiatric section of the hospital and then pressuring the staff to diagnose them as psychoneurotics to get rid of them quickly with an automatic medical discharge. Commanding officers thus avoided the inconvenience of courts-martial and even of Section Eight board hearings. The abuse of the psychoneurosis discharge became so widespread in the Army— late in 1944 the number of discharges for psychoneuroses equaled the number of men inducted—that it caused a manpower crisis and forced the Army inspector general to order an investigation. In March 1945 the War Department finally ordered a halt to the misuse of this diagnosis for getting rid of unwanted men.[72] The real wartime exodus from the military, then, was not of heterosexual soldiers faking homosexuality but of troublesome soldiers being diagnosed, often at the request of their commanding officers, as psychoneurotic for quick discharge.

Dr. Allan Fredericks joined many of his colleagues in diagnosing gay servicemen as psychoneurotic, but as a gay physician he had to be careful not to draw too much attention to himself as someone trying to protect these men. He would state on the medical record that the patient was homosexual, but whenever possible he made the primary diagnosis "anxiety neurosis." There was "always some room for latitude of viewpoint in a diagnosis," Fredericks explained. "And even as I think some people stretched their diagnosis to kick queers out of the Navy, I leaned over a little bit in the direction of not penalizing them." Because he also sat on the disposition board, he had to be prepared to defend his diagnosis of these men, which was not difficult because some of them "just really came unglued" especially when they were thrown into the brig. But there wasn't much he could do to help the men whose sole diagnosis was homosexuality. His fellow officers on the disposition board generally accepted Fredericks's recommendations and granted the men honorable discharges. But his experience was unusual. Most military boards, especially in the Army, rarely gave any kind of honorable discharge to men they knew to be homosexual.[73]

When they couldn't cover up their patients' homosexuality, some psychiatrists tried to defend them by acting as their advocates. Seeing firsthand how individual soldiers could be hurt by the new discharge system, many agreed to act in their patients' behalf at meetings with commanding officers and disposition boards. One psychiatrist testifying at an Army hearing for a homosexual officer attacked punitive discharges as "archaic," claiming that they "helped to result in injustice to many people."[74] Many of his colleagues similarly appealed for leniency, humane treatment, fairness, and understanding, acting on their belief that homosexuals, as patients with mental disorders, had the right not to be called names, publicly humiliated, punished, or blamed for their illness. "Our consciences sometimes hurt," admitted the hospital staff at Camp Maxey, Texas, in their 1944 annual report, "when we recommend a discharge for undesirable habits and traits of character" for homosexuals. If these men had to be separated from the service, they protested, "we think that few of them should receive blue Section VIII's."[75]

The new discharge system was supposed to have corrected the

injustices of the penal system. But when psychiatric consultants in Washington, who had initially supported giving undesirable discharges to homosexuals to prevent malingering, began to see how such discharges harmed individual men and women, their voices of protest joined those of their colleagues in the field. Dr. Braceland believed that the Navy had done a "grave injustice" to homosexual enlisted personnel.[76] Dr. Menninger fought hard during his tenure in the Surgeon General's Office from 1944 to 1946, with only minimal success, to change Army regulations so that all homosexuals who had committed no criminal offenses would be discharged honorably.[77] In a letter to Menninger, Dr. Edward Strecher, the 1943–44 president of the American Psychiatric Association and civilian consultant to both the Army Air Forces and the Navy surgeon general, expressed the frustration that came with trying to bring about a nonpunitive military procedure for managing homosexuals. "In both the Army and Navy," he wrote in June 1946, "we failed to solve the important matter of how these chaps should be discharged. . . . The difficulty was that there was a good deal of real objection, in some instances, to a straight medical discharge. On the other hand, a blue discharge hardly seemed fair . . . since many of these fellows made an earnest effort of service. . . ." The inability of psychiatrists to solve this problem, Strecher concluded, "was not for want of trying, because in both services we tried very hard."[78]

The liberal position that some psychiatrists took toward the homosexual soldier, as startling as it may have appeared in the United States military during World War II, was not new. It had roots in early psychoanalysis, when Sigmund Freud had expressed his own compassion toward homosexuals and opposed discrimination against them. In 1930 Freud lent his support to the early homosexual rights movement by signing a petition circulated by gay emancipationist Magnus Hirschfeld to decriminalize homosexual behavior in Austria and Germany.[79] Elements of this liberal and activist humanism were evident in the wartime work of such top military administrators and consultants as Capt. Francis Braceland, Brig. Gen. William Menninger, Winfred Overholser, and Col. William C. Porter; in the published research of such psychiatrists in the field as Lt. Col. Lewis Loeser, Maj. Carl Jonas, Lt. Herbert Greenspan, and Comdr. John Campbell; and in the mostly undocumented work of psychiatrists who tried to protect their gay patients in their offices and before officer boards. Colonel Porter, who headed the Army's School of Military Neuropsychiatry, summed up the liberal viewpoint of top psychiatric consultants when he wrote in 1943 that there was "no problem confronting the military psychiatrist that calls for more kindly, tolerant, scientific understanding than . . . the field of the sexual psychopath." [80] A WAC psychiatrist, Capt. Alice E. Rost, exemplified how psychiatrists incorporated a liberal point of view into their everyday work when she described her lesbian patients to an investigative board in 1944.

As one of the Army's sixteen female psychiatrists, Captain Rost was ordered to examine several Wacs accused of lesbian activity at Fort Oglethorpe. In her testimony before an investigative board, she explained that homosexuality, though unfortunate, was only "a certain bent of character and is part of the personality, but not an illness" and could not be cured. She believed that such women were not necessarily detrimental to the Women's Army Corps, and that what two women did "to their mutual satisfaction in the privacy of their bedroom, is their own business." She stated that the "three girl-couples" under investigation "conducted themselves inconspicuously" and "handled their love with discretion" and need not be discharged. She interpreted the 1944 War Department Circular on homosexuality to mean that unless there is a violation of individual rights, homosexual relationships "should be met with tolerance." Only those "confirmed" (butch) lesbians who tried to pass as men, she maintained, and whose entire emotional and sexual interests "centered on girls," were detrimental to the service and should be discharged under Section Eight. But her report on one such lesbian indicated Rost's reluctance to recommend the Wac's discharge and revealed her concern for the Wac's welfare. She recommended psychiatric care not for the Wac's homosexuality, but because, as a result of accusations against her, "her attitude toward the world is now one of despair and bitterness, feeling that she does not have a friend in the world." [81]

Data collected by psychiatric researchers who shared Dr. Rost's point of view led them to challenge old stereotypes of the homosexual or at least to develop more complex stereotypes that allowed for a variety of exceptions. A common conclusion in their wartime studies was that, in the words of Maj. Carl H. Jonas, who studied fifty-three white and seven black gay men at Camp Haan, California, "overt homosexuality occurs in a heterogeneous group of individuals." [82] Dr. Clements Fry, director of the Yale University student clinic, and Edna Rostow, a social worker, who together studied the service records of 183 servicemen, discovered that there was no evidence to support the common belief that "homosexuality is uniformly correlated with specific personality traits" and concluded that generalizations about the homosexual personality "are not yet reliable." [83] At the 36th Station Hospital, Loeser and his staff had accumulated such a large population of male homosexual patients that they were able to conduct the first social survey of gay American soldiers, which revealed a wide range of occupations, family backgrounds, and other characteristics that similarly challenged the concept of the typical homosexual. [84]

One of the most powerful stereotypes that these researchers challenged was that gay men were poor soldiers. Sometimes to their amazement, they described what they called the "well-adjusted homosexuals" who, in Menninger's words, "concealed their homosexuality effectively and, at the same time, made creditable records for themselves in the service." [85] Some researchers spoke in glowing terms of these men. "The homosexuals observed in the service," noted Navy doctors Greenspan and Campbell, "have been key men in responsible positions whose loss [by discharge] was acutely felt in their respective departments." They were "conscientious, reliable, well-integrated and abounding in emotional feeling and sincerity." In general, "the homosexual leads a useful productive life, conforming with all dictates of the community, except its sexual requirements" and was "neither a burden nor a detriment to society." [86] Fry and Rostow reported that, based on evidence in service records, homosexuals were no better or worse than other soldiers and that many "performed well in various military jobs" including combat. There was no reason whatever for concluding that homosexuality itself "would make a man a poor military risk." The popular belief that homosexuals could not fight because they were effeminate, they pointed out, was a myth based on prejudice that did not stand up to the facts. The discharge policy was based on the erroneous assumption that every homosexual lacked "the capacity to make a socially productive adjustment to the particular group in which he might be placed in the service." [87]

Fry and Rostow were particularly concerned with how antihomosexual prejudice harmed these men and caused waste in the military organization. In one group of forty-eight homosexual soldiers they studied, the six who were discharged for homosexuality had been "doing their job well. They were discharged in circumstances which should raise questions about the rationality of the rules, and the rights of individuals. Other things being equal," Fry and Rostow continued, "should a man be discharged on the basis of censorship of letters or for being picked up when on leave for homosexual activity with a willing partner, when a heterosexual episode in similar circumstances would not be grounds for discharge?" They maintained that there was no rational basis for enforcing this kind of double standard. "If the general situation requires that all manpower be used most effectively and economically," they asked, "how do our prejudices affect this purpose?" [88]

Loeser, Fry, and Rostow had seen in their studies how the new discharge system, as soon as it had been put into practice, had reinforced prejudice and created inefficiency by wasting manpower. They proposed reforms designed to eliminate antihomosexual prejudice and to formally integrate these soldiers into the military organization. They backed up their proposals by documenting the service records and skills of more than 450 homosexual servicemen, including the growing number of men identified as such by the new discharge procedures.

Lieutenant Colonel Loeser's proposal for reducing prejudice was to create even more centralized facilities, like his own hospital, for processing such personnel. On the wards of the 36th Station Hospital, he and his staff had been able to examine large numbers of homosexuals "coldly, without emotions or prejudice" and had discovered that, "alone and by itself," homosexuality was "probably less dangerous to society than sexual promiscuity, adultery or prostitution." If the Army could route all homosexuals through such centralized hospitals, then more military officers would have exposure to the diversity of homosexuals, would similarly overcome their prejudices, and would no longer insist on punishing these soldiers. Loeser's plan for conserving homosexual personnel was outlined in a section of his report entitled "Utilization of the Sexual Psychopath in the Military Service." He suggested that "intelligent and calm study of the individual homosexual, followed by careful reassignment would result in conservation of man power and salvaging of a large percentage of this group." He used his statistical data about his patients' work histories to suggest how these men should be reassigned. He recommended that the homosexual soldier "will usually be found of most value in clerical work and do best in large metropolitan areas where sexual taboos and prejudices are less forceful." Male homosexuals, like women, were ideally suited to serve as soldiers in the rapidly expanding "paper" Army.[89]

Fry and Rostow believed that such a system for using homosexual personnel was already operating as an unofficial but widespread practice and should be adopted as official policy. Their examination of service records led them to conclude that the military rarely enforced its discharge policy and that in reality both the Army and Navy permitted nearly all homosexual personnel to remain in the service, where most succeeded in keeping their sexual behavior private and many became exemplary soldiers and officers. The relatively few who were detected were discharged late in their careers.[90] Even if it could be proved that homosexuals did have particular personality traits, their unique skills and talents still might "be appropriate for different functions within the services."[91] The assumptions underlying the regulations to eliminate homosexuals, they concluded, were based on prejudice alone and could no longer be justified in light of the good service records of most of these men. They argued that "homosexuals should be judged first as individuals, and not as a class" and "like other people, should be individually differentiated and placed purposefully so that they may contribute fully to the common work." They recommended that military officials "examine the question as to whether the military service should be interested in homosexuality as such, or only in the individual's ability to perform his duties and adjust to military life."[92]

These proposals for integrating gay personnel into the military organization were never implemented or even taken seriously by policymakers in Washington. When Loeser, Fry, and Rostow completed their studies in 1945, the climate was no longer right for such reform. The military was demobilizing, and the wartime pressure to conserve manpower was off. Liberal psychiatrists were a tiny minority within the military organization whose voices were lost or suppressed as the armed forces continued to expand their antihomosexual apparatus in peacetime. They were a minority on the homefront as well, bucking trends in their own profession, especially among psychoanalysts, whose public voices in the late 1940s began to express an increasingly unsympathetic, intolerant, and cure-oriented approach to homosexuals.[93] Possibly for these and other reasons, the proposals to integrate homosexuals into the armed forces were not taken seriously by military officials.

Though unsuccessful at bringing about reform, the handful of psychiatrists who studied the largest groups of gay soldiers did develop the first substantial critiques of the assumptions underlying the military's antihomosexual discharge policy. From evidence obtained in their wartime research, they came to believe that gay men and women were neither rarities, criminals, nor military threats. They maintained that both male and female homosexuals were merely different rather than sick, or that even if they were sick they were not disabled and could still function well in the military. Willing to question stereotypes, they saw gay men and women as diverse members of a despised social group who banded together for mutual protection, even creating their own secret language and style in response to the prejudice and hostility they found both inside and outside the military. These conclusions led them to become foes of prejudice, proponents of reform and advocates for gay and lesbian soldiers. It is an irony of history that the first public challenges to the military's antihomosexual policy came not from the homosexual rights movement but from psychiatrists who studied gay soldiers, sailors, and officers during World War II.

CHAPTER
7

Comrades in Arms

On February 28, 1945, Pfc. Robert Fleischer, who had just turned twenty, found himself crossing the English Channel into France. He was to become a replacement in an antitank company in the 42nd (Rainbow) Infantry Division, which was making its way across France toward Germany. Wading through the icy waters from their landing craft onto the bombed-out beach at Le Havre, Fleischer and his terrified buddies were greeted by French children lined up on the beach offering them bouquets of flowers. From Le Havre the Army transported Fleischer by boxcar and truck to the Harz Mountains, where he joined his antitank company and was assigned to a platoon that proceeded in advance of the troops to locate mine fields. When their equipment turned out to be faulty, Fleischer and his squad had to crawl through the fields on their hands and knees, poking the ground with their bayonets. "If it blew up," he explained, "you were in a mine field."

In March the Rainbow Division broke through the Siegfried Line and headed toward Würzburg. When they reached the Main River, Fleischer and the three other men in his squad rowed across under heavy machine-gun fire. Landing on the other side, according to his Bronze Star Medal citation, Fleischer "proceeded, under intense fire from tanks, machine guns, and mortars, to assist in building road blocks and laying mines," contributing "materially to halting an enemy counter-attack launched that same night." Fleischer had come a long way from designing costumes and playing Carmelita Ack-Ack at Camp Hulen, Texas. "I don't know how I did it!" he recalled. "It's like climbing the mountain because it's there. You just keep going on." [1]

Despite the new screening and discharge policies that designated gay soldiers as unfit to fight, gay men served in combat areas during World War II as disciplined, trusted, and courageous soldiers. As the war heated up, manpower needs, the inability of any screening system to filter out most homosexuals, and the desire of gay soldiers to see action led thousands into combat zones around the world. There, like their buddies, they had to prove themselves as fighting men. Their performance in combat challenged the policies that stereotyped them as weak, passive, and incompetent. And in the lands where young men had to kill, risk their lives, and protect one another, soldiers on the battlefield, aboard ship, and in the air had to find ways to put their antigay prejudices on hold until the fighting stopped.

The main purpose of the military organization was to wage war. The combat soldiers were the people who did the job of killing the enemy. Every male soldier, regardless of his assignment, had to be trained and ready to fight. Men who were deemed unfit for combat were not supposed to become soldiers.

The screening and discharge policies that branded gay men as unfit for the job of killing were based on exaggerated stereotypes of both the combat soldier and the sissy "queer." The combat soldier was portrayed as everything a sissy was not—aggressively masculine and sexual, brave, strong, and tough—he had guts, determination, nerves of steel, and a taste for battle. The popular caricature of the sissy described him as everything a combat soldier was not—passively effeminate and asexual, timid, weak, and soft—he was a frivolous mama's boy, a crybaby, and fought "like a woman." [2] Like most stereotypes, each of these portraits had contradictory counterparts. Fighting soldiers were also innocent boys; homosexuals were dangerously aggressive psychopaths. But it was the simplistic equation of male homosexuality with effeminacy that led to the general belief that "queers" could not become fighting men.

The mixture of folklore and fact that made up these profiles did not reflect the reality of either the typical soldier or the gay GI. [3] Most American soldiers never served at the fighting fronts. In the Army only one of every four soldiers actually saw combat. [4] Even among these two to three million men, it would be difficult to describe the typical combat soldier. Possessing a wide range of personalities, motives, skills, family and cultural backgrounds, sexualities, and reactions to stress, what they had in common was minimal: They were able-bodied men, mostly citizen-soldiers in their teens and twenties, who had been trained for combat and sent into battle. [5]

The data that exist on the performance of American soldiers in combat during World War II portray them differently from the wartime media's heroic image of the American fighting man. The soldier's minimal obligations in combat were to obey orders, carry his weapon, fire it when necessary, and not run away. GI culture encouraged the men to face these obligations with cynical resignation, to gripe about their misfortune, and never to stick their necks out or volunteer for anything. While most soldiers would and often did risk their lives to protect their buddies, they shunned heroics and often used the term *hero* as an insult rather than a compliment. *Hero* described the undependable man who displayed a foolhardy bravado that could get him killed or endanger the lives of his buddies.[6]

America's young soldiers were, on the whole, reluctant to kill. One wartime study concluded that at least three out of every four armed soldiers never fired their weapons at enemy positions or men during any one battle. GIs resisted their combat roles because of what Col. S. L. A. Marshall called the "fear of killing" so prevalent among the "average and normally healthy" men who otherwise were able to "endure the mental and physical stresses of combat."[7] Some soldiers could not endure such stresses and "broke down," becoming the psychiatric casualties of war. During the first eight weeks of the Normandy invasion, 12 to 14 percent of the twenty-eight thousand combat soldiers in four U.S. Army divisions suffered from these "nonbattle casualties." (In a few companies the rate was as high as 50 percent.)[8] Psychiatric studies of combat veterans concluded that these breakdowns were more the result of the intense "environmental stress" of combat than of any predisposition to failure because of personality traits.[9] Combat was exhausting, terrifying, and relentless. Any man, regardless of his sexuality, could fall apart in such extreme circumstances.[10]

The stereotype of the gay GI obscured the reality of the many gay men who were sent to the fighting fronts. They served in combat zones in all branches of the military as riflemen, field artillery men, tank drivers, medics, signal corpsmen, intelligence officers, war artists, members of bomber and fighter control squadrons, gunnery officers aboard destroyers, field artillery men, cryptographers, members of amphibious forces, and in numerous other capacities.[11] Like their buddies, some were bad at being combat soldiers, and others received medals for their fighting skills and courage.[12]

Gay soldiers went into combat with all the fear, griping, and fighting spirit of their heterosexual fellows. Some had tried to get assigned to noncombat duties and went overseas reluctantly, resigned to their fate.

Others did whatever they could to be sent to the fighting fronts. When the Army put Robert Fleischer through specialized training at Louisiana State University, he recalled, "I realized I was stuck on a campus and I really wanted to be overseas in combat." So he deliberately flunked his exams and was transferred to an infantry unit. As a rite of passage that defined manhood, combat offered many gay trainees the masculine legitimacy they sought. It was a chance to prove that they were no longer boys, that they were not sissies, and that they could be "men among men." The painful injuries of being labeled less than a man left deep emotional scars on many gay teenagers and young men that combat duty promised to heal. Ted Allenby, who enlisted in the Marine Corps in Dubuque, Iowa, became unbearably impatient during his training because, he explained, "I wanted to fight. Like every other young American, I was superpatriotic. And, being a homosexual, I had that constant compelling need to prove how virile I was." Allenby ended up fighting at Iwo Jima.[13]

Some gay men felt especially compelled, as homosexuals, to join the fight against the Nazis. Few Americans knew until after the war that the Nazis had sent tens of thousands of homosexuals to the death camps, forcing them to wear pink triangles, as Jews were forced to wear the yellow Star of David. But as early as the mid-1930s some gay men read American newspaper reports about Nazi antigay attacks,[14] while during the war rumors of German atrocities against homosexuals circulated through the gay underground in the United States. Midshipman Burt Miller heard about them from a man he had sex with one night before shipping overseas. Other gay men, recent refugees from the Nazi regime, knew what was going on firsthand.

Richard Plant was one of these refugees. He had reached New York City from Switzerland, knowing that many of his gay friends in Europe had already disappeared. Plant tried to enlist in the Army but couldn't because although he was Jewish, he was German-born and had to register as an "enemy alien." However, he knew other gay refugees in New York City who had joined the United States Army, hiding their homosexuality from military examiners, hoping to do "everything they could" to fight Hitler. In the 1930s the vehemently antifascist novelist Klaus Mann (Thomas Mann's son) fled Germany for the United States, where he continued to write and lecture against the Nazi regime, taking on Richard Plant as his personal secretary. After trying unsuccessfully to enlist in the United States Army, Mann was finally drafted, took part in the invasion of Italy, and reentered Germany as an American combat soldier. Another of Plant's gay refugee friends became a flamethrower in an infantry unit, while yet another served as "a parachutist who was dropped behind German lines with a false identification as a spy" and "transported valuable information to American intelligence." [15] These gay men made the U.S. war against the Nazis into their own fight to save Hitler's chosen victims from the death camps.

As gay recruits found their places in the ranks of combat units, manpower shortages forced Army officials to relax the enforcement of their antigay policies, recognizing that they could not afford to lose men who had become good soldiers. Military officials made many such wartime exceptions to their own rules, designating the previously disqualified as temporarily fit for duty. In 1942 the Army began to reexamine men rejected for venereal disease, choosing to treat them instead on induction. This reversal of policy added two hundred thousand men to Army ranks.[16] In October 1943 Selective Service announced that it would begin drafting fathers. In 1944 it began to draft Japanese American men from the internment camps and reversed its practice of calling blacks last in each draft board, inducting them instead at a rate equal to their percentage in the population. The same year the Army integrated blacks into combat units for the first time instead of using them for auxiliary services only. The Marine Corps began to take some of its black soldiers out of service units and assigned them to combat units as well.[17] Although reluctant to engage in social experimentation, military officials placed necessity above traditional practices to raise a fighting force large enough to win the war.

Expediency, too, led Army officials, despite their expanding antihomosexual ideology, to decide by stages that some homosexuals were fit for military service. Shortly after the declaration of war, the adjutant general ordered the commanding general of the West Coast Air Corps Training Center at Moffett Field, California, to review the cases of seven convicted sodomists "to determine their respective availability for military service" with "the view of conserving all available manpower for service in the Army." The commanding general complied, cancelling the men's dishonorable discharges and making them eligible for reassignment after completing their prison sentences.[18] In July 1942 the Adjutant General's Office issued a letter to commanding generals warning them that they should not use Section Eight to discharge any soldiers who were doing their jobs well.[19] In November the War Department added more wartime restrictions on issuing Section Eight discharges for "undesirable habits or traits of character." Such men (and, by 1943, women), including homosexuals, were to be discharged only if their rehabilitation was "considered impossible after repeated attempts to accomplish same have failed." [20]

By 1945, when major combat offensives were taking place in Europe and the Pacific, the Army considered more extreme measures to conserve homosexual personnel. At the end of March, Secretary of War Henry L. Stimson ordered a review of the cases of all self-confessed homosexuals who had been given blue discharges. If investigation revealed that they had not committed any in-service acts, they were to be reinducted into the Army.[21] The same month, some officials in the War Department even considered recruiting convicted sodomists along with other general Army prisoners into separate volunteer combat units.[22] Under the pressure of escalating manpower shortages, the War Department sent out conflicting messages about homosexual personnel—they were unfit for military service, but they should be "salvaged" whenever necessary.

Accompanying these measures to conserve all available personnel was a willingness to relax prohibitions on some homosexual behavior. Army directives sometimes mixed harsh condemnation of sodomists with an unusually tolerant understanding of young soldiers who might become involved in homosexual activity during the war. In January 1943 the War Department directive on sodomists acknowledged that because "the Army will be serving during the period of the war in many parts of the world where the standards of morality may be at variance with our own," it was to be expected that some men "will submit to unnatural practices." At least one medical officer interpreted this to mean that, "particularly for soldiers overseas . . . homosexual relationships should be tolerated" if they didn't involve force or hurt the morale of the group.[23] This cautiously tolerant approach was especially true in the Women's Army Corps, where the personnel shortage was most acute. "I found there was a tolerance for lesbianism if they needed you," recalled Johnnie Phelps, who served as a WAC sergeant. "If you had a job to do that was a specialist kind of job or if you were in a theatre of operations . . . where bodies were needed, they tolerated anything, just about." [24]

Combat conditions themselves led officers to relax their enforcement of antigay discharge policies on the battlefields. "There was a war on," explained Ted Allenby, who fought at Iwo Jima. "Who in the hell is going to worry about this shit?" [25] Although some such discharges did take place in active combat zones, where a few cases of self-declared or caught-in-the-act homosexual soldiers in submarines, on the beaches, and in the jungles of the South Pacific were reported,[26] many commanding officers held on to their good men even if they were homosexual. "The problem of homosexuality," concluded the Army's history of psychiatry in World War II, "was not conspicuous in most combat divisions. There were undoubtedly a great many homosexuals throughout the military services, but, for the most part, they carried out their assignments conscientiously and exercised sexual restraint. In the 38th Division," the report continued, "four or five men were referred to the psychiatrist for making unwelcome homosexual advances. The routine of management was to assign them to another regiment, and in each instance, this was the last that was heard of the case." [27]

In Alaska, as in most isolated combat areas, commanding officers had to devise makeshift procedures for handling homosexual personnel without discharging them. The tens of thousands of men stationed for the duration of the war on the Aleutian Islands—a "bleak, desolate land of snow, rain, fog and wind"—endured some of the most severe morale problems of the war. [28] The men bitterly joked that there was "a girl behind every tree" in this treeless land. [29] Under such conditions, gay soldiers became more visible. "Overt homosexuals were found in groups," explained Maj. Frank Gelbman, an Army physician who was stationed at Adak Island, which had a military population ranging from four thousand to thirteen thousand men, "at least one group on each island in the Aleutians." But he and other commanding officers realized that the discharge of any homosexual soldier would threaten morale because it rewarded him "with a trip home," causing "great resentment" among the men left behind. Major Gelbman believed that "every attempt should be made to eliminate homosexuals" before they were sent to such isolated areas as Adak. But "after arrival," he maintained, "it is doubtful if morale is served by evacuating homosexuals. . . . Each man seems to identify himself with the person who is fortunate enough to go back to the United States, regardless of cause." [30]

One pragmatic commanding officer stationed at a post near Atka Island in the Aleutians found that he could best utilize known homosexual personnel by keeping them under his close supervision. This Regular Army colonel "of capacity and wide experience," noted an Army report, "became aware, unofficially, of a number of homosexuals in the troops under his command. No difficulties had been reported in connection with these men. By careful assignment and by attention to problems before they became serious, these men were kept on effective duty over a long period of time. Some of them were gradually moved to a somewhat isolated area of the post where they would not be disturbing to other men on the post." In these outposts, the discharge of homosexuals was more disruptive to troop morale, provoking envy and a sense of injustice, than the practice of retaining them or even assigning them to segregated areas.[31]

The constraints placed on the discharge of gay men by the demands of combat thwarted the attempts of some GIs to avoid action by declaring their homosexuality. Soldiers who tried to take this escape route often learned instead how much they were needed. In 1941 Jim Warren had been pleased to be assigned to Cooks and Bakers School because he "wanted to get into something that would keep me away from the front lines if we did get into war." But after being stationed in Hawaii as an officer's cook for more than a year, he discovered that he was going to be sent to combat areas in the South Pacific and started thinking of ways to get out. "Of course, I was afraid of dying," Warren explained. "But I was afraid I would run—of being yellow in front of my friends— more than anything else." Warren finally decided to declare his homosexuality to the base psychiatrist. The psychiatrist interviewed him about his sex life for twenty minutes, then dismissed him, saying, "I'll let you know." Warren expected his commanding officer to say " 'Take your bags, Warren, we don't want you!' " but "it didn't happen. The next thing I knew, my ass was on Eniwetok and I [was] fighting Japanese!"

After the Eniwetok campaign, Warren was sent to Saipan, where, he recalled, the fighting was "gut-wrenching. Seeing your friends die and not being able to do anything about it. And so after the Battle of Saipan, I just said, 'I don't think I can go through another one of these.' " He again went to the medical officer, who had known since Hawaii about Warren's homosexuality, and asked him "Why am I still here?" "The men like you very much," the doctor replied. "You're good with people. We need you. If you were getting razzed or hazed or if you had done something that would be brought to our attention in an unseemly fashion, we would do something about it. You like what you're doing, don't you?" "Yes," Warren admitted, "but I'm scared to death of combat." "We all are," the doctor said. "All I can say is, have a good time. Do whatever you want to do, but *just don't get caught.*"

Ben Small, who fought with the Army Air Corps in the Philippines and New Guinea, wanted to avoid combat duty, he recalled, "not because I was afraid of the war, [but because] I was afraid I couldn't cope with what I had to cope with as a homosexual. So I went to the psychiatrist and told him I was a homosexual." Seeing on the record that Small had been married, the psychiatrist asked him questions about his sex life with men. He decided that Small was probably trying to get out of combat by faking homosexuality and refused to discharge him. "What the hell do I do now?" Small asked himself. "I told him I'm queer."

No longer fearing discovery, he went overseas "with this attitude that 'If they don't care, I don't care.' If they catch me, all they can do is send me back. And that means I won't get killed.'' As a result, Small began to lead a more openly gay life for the rest of his combat duty until he was discharged honorably after the war ended.

When Greg Aarons, a gay draftee from Los Angeles, heard that his infantry unit was headed for the South Pacific, he, too, got scared. "I told a priest that I was a homosexual," he recalled, "and I thought I should get out of the army. He really laid it on me. He told me how much money the government had spent to train me, how human beings had to be expendable in times of need. By the time I left I was practically in tears. If it had been a recruiting office, I would have signed up for another hundred years." [32]

Despite the belief that their work was "womanly" and "soft," gay men who performed duties that were sometimes stereotyped as havens for homosexuals also did not escape assignment to the fighting fronts. Male nurses and medics usually found themselves marching down a road that led to the battlefield. Chaplain's assistants, some of whom were trained as riflemen or cannoneers, aided medics as they evacuated the wounded and dying. Clerks and yeomen served on ships and in combat infantry units, keeping notes on the day's actions and firing their weapons when necessary. Many were wounded and killed. Special Services men who could throw together a soldier show at the drop of a helmet were cheered on by exhausted, demoralized troops who were beyond the reach of civilian entertainers.

Despite their ostensibly noncombatant roles, male nurses, pharmacist's mates, medics, and hospital corpsmen, like female nurses, were widely respected as brave and courageous in combat. They were unarmed yet served under direct fire, and their casualties were higher than those of most other men. "A very special fortitude," wrote an Associated Press war commentator in 1945, "is needed by the man who goes into battle as a noncombatant. . . . These unarmed forces—trained to defend themselves with their bare hands in emergency—form a vital part of Uncle Sam's mighty fighting-machine. They are the paradox of war, for their mission is to save human life, and not to take it. This labor of devotion they perform with few headlines, though their deeds are epic.'' [33]

Gay men who served as medics were acutely aware of the dangers they faced and the important function they served. In June 1944 nineteen-year-old George Dohmann, who grew up in the Bronx, had been trained as an Army surgical technician and assigned to the 3rd Medical Battalion of the 9th Infantry Division, which took part in the Normandy invasion.

"Medics weren't lasting more than a few days," he later wrote, "and most combat units didn't even have an aid man apiece." Dohmann believed that all the combat medics in his battalion, including many who were gay, were wounded and only three survived. He was wounded at Cherbourg and again in the Battle of the Bulge, for which he received a Purple Heart and a Medical Combat Badge.[34]

Chaplain's assistants and medics were often assigned to the same companies in combat units. "The chaplain and the medics were together all the time," recalled Martin Stow, who served as a chaplain's assistant in France and Germany. Under fire the medics "would go out and if a man was shot, bring him back in again to the regimental aid center. There emergency surgery or whatever would be done. I can remember, though, men who had to have legs amputated. Then I would just in essence become one of the medics, holding plasma bottles and [being a] 'go-fer.' Fetch this and get that and help."

Martin Stow believed that the Army was right to assign him and other gay men to these service duties. "In the Chaplain's Corps in combat," he explained, "in the medics in combat, you're taking care of people who are hurt. And that's the thing that we did best. I had to draft letters and write letters to families whose sons had been killed, and I think that I wrote very, very sensitive letters. I mean, I think I did a better job than perhaps someone else might have." Researchers who studied homosexual servicemen during the war came to the same conclusion. "For a certain kind of sensitive, intelligent individual," they suggested, "it is certainly possible that the emotional experience of helping, directing and caring for men in danger, may be a satisfaction about which we know too little." [35]

Even gay soldiers who looked and acted "queer" could fit well into combat units. Many outfits had at least one flamboyant soldier who did his job especially well, was protected by a superior officer, and, despite the talk behind his back and the joking and teasing, won respect from the other men. Gay veterans tell many stories about these men. Jim Warren described a mail clerk at an Army post in New Guinea who "was very blatantly gay. He swished—I mean, he just laid it right out! He said he had a lover back on the mainland that he intended to go back and live with. [The other guys] joked about him all the time but he did his job. I was always surprised that none of the officers reported him. They liked him! He was a nice guy. He was a smart man, and somehow they seemed to respect his abilities and they didn't care what he did with his sex life." Robert Gervais described a torpedo officer aboard his destroyer "who walked around the ship in a bathrobe, hair-net and slippers. He was what I'd call a real 'Nellie Queen'—but he was the best torpedo officer in the 7th Fleet! Our captain put the word out that if he heard any gossip about his torpedo officer, they would hear from him! He later personally decorated him (silver medal) with the entire crew standing at attention.'' [36]

Gay men who did female impersonations had an indispensable role to play in combat. Some of these soldiers entertained the troops as soon as an area was secured. Marine corporal Tom Reddy performed his Carmen Miranda and Andrews Sisters drag routines on Bougainville, Guadalcanal, and the New Georgia Islands during combat missions. "We were the only entertainment the Marine Corps had," he recalled. "When part of the island was secure, the guys in the front, as soon as they could get the bulldozers in, would dig a gigantic foxhole. Then they would bring in as many troops as they could, get them into the foxhole, and they'd be standing there with their rifles and their helmets, and they'd 'chute us in and we'd play on the edge of the foxhole."

During all of these shows, Reddy continued, "we carried our carbines. I think I'm probably the only drag star in the world that went on the stage with a gun sitting right there alongside of him!" At times the shows were strafed in surprise attacks by Japanese planes. "We were doing the 'Three Little Sisters' number," Reddy said, "and all of a sudden, over the treetops, it came: *Rrrrrrreh-eh-eh-eh-eh-eh!* [We] three guys in dresses jumped into this gigantic foxhole with about 500 Marines in it. And they were really very nice. They even reached up and grabbed us so that we wouldn't fall and then they made a semicircle around so we had plenty of room. The three of us stood there looking at these guys saying, 'I don't know how the hell we got into *this!*' "

These flamboyant, campy, and funny men helped bring their buddies through the hardest of times. Even when he was wearing a dress, Reddy explained, the other men "weren't going to turn on me. Something inside of me was saying, 'This is the way you're going to survive,' [which] didn't mean I didn't go to the front. I fired a gun, too, besides wearing dresses. That's one of the things the Marine Corps was famous for. You don't give up and you survive. You survive any way you can." For his service in combat, nineteen-year-old Corporal Reddy received a Letter of Commendation from the commanding general of the 3rd Amphibious Corps. "Your ambitious and successful venture into the field of stage entertainment," the letter read, "is an example of what may be accomplished even in adversity. I hope it will inspire others to follow your fine leadership."

Relaxed enforcement of antigay policies in combat areas corresponded to relaxed prejudices among the men. It is likely that in nearly every combat unit—Army companies were generally made up of a few hundred men—there were several gay soldiers. Many enjoyed the "live and let live attitude" [37] and even the respect from other men that could develop into a strong camaraderie as the men survived battle after battle together. Commanding officers knew that such camaraderie reinforced morale and discipline and was as essential to the men's fighting effectiveness as training, weapons, and ammunition. [38] Under the extreme conditions at the fronts, the boundaries that ordinarily separated men based on race, rank, sexuality, age, and other differences weakened as men dealt with their dependence on each other, their sexual desires, their fears, and their grief. As a result gay soldiers, whether or not their fellow soldiers knew them to be gay, could feel less out of place and less "queer" in a world of imminent danger where they could protect, rely on, and be needed by their comrades-in-arms.

In battle GIs judged a man first for his loyalty, know-how, and teamwork more than for his personal life. "We have learned the hard way that no man is an island," wrote World War II veteran activist Charles G. Bolte in 1945. "In this comradeship we learned to judge the men we loved as brothers by what they were and by what they did, not by the clothes they wore, the house they lived in, the accent they spoke with, or the place where they worshipped." [39] The outcast was the unreliable loner who didn't do his part. The combat soldier's pragmatic check on his prejudices could be reluctant and temporary, but that did not make the gay soldier's sense of belonging and being needed any less real.

Veterans of all kinds describe the love they felt for each other with a passion, romance, and sentimentality that often rivaled gay men's expressions of their love for other men and made gay affections seem less out of place. "You're dealing with excesses of love and hate," explained Marine Corps veteran William Manchester, who was not gay, "and among men who fight together there is an intense love. You are closer to those men than to anyone except your immediate family when you were young." [40] "War binds men more tightly together than almost any other branch of human activity," observed Jack Belden, another veteran who wrote about seeing action in World War II. "To share your last crumb of bread with another, to warm your enfeebled body against another's in the bleak and barren mystery of the night, to undergo shame, fear and death with scores of others of your age and mental colouring—who, indeed, would trade these comrades of the battlefield for friends made in time of peace." [41]

In combat, gay soldiers won a hard-earned acceptance from their buddies as men and as soldiers that sometimes repaired the damage to their self-respect caused by stereotypes that portrayed them as silly, unreliable, and "not one of us." "I was a combat medic," recalled George Dohmann, who at eighteen enlisted in the Army and saw action in the Normandy invasion and the Battle of the Bulge. "No one asked me if I was gay when they called out 'Medic!' and you went out under fire and did what you were trained and expected to do." [42] "I enlisted in the Marine Corps," recalled Tom Reddy, "and they accepted me. And once they did that, I was one of *them*. I was welcomed with open arms." "I know a lot of guys in my company suspected me," recalled Greg Aarons, who served in the Army in the South Pacific. "I think that they wanted to catch me, yet there was also a degree of respect for me because I was a rifleman. They thought, 'Whether he's a homo or gay or a fruit or a fag he's still one of us.' " [43]

Heterosexual soldiers who felt such deep camaraderie with their gay buddies that they risked their lives to save them in battle could further strengthen a gay GI's sense of self-worth. Gay veterans are reluctant to "brag" about the men's lives they saved, but they willingly express their gratitude for the men who saved their own. Robert Fleischer and the three other men in his mine platoon squad were "inseparable" on their way through Germany in 1945. During one mission Fleischer was "pinned down by mortar fire and had fallen. I wasn't hit, but I was petrified and I couldn't move and shells were all around. I could see in front of me the dust coming up from bullets and blades of grass actually being cut right in front of my nose." One of his squad buddies saw him, went over to him, and "lifted me up and carried me for a while. And once or twice he literally saved my life. Those experiences," Fleischer explained, "there's no way to pay it back. The closeness that develops between men is more than love. It's an understanding that unless you've been in combat—it's hard to put into words. I think only being together that way at the very abyss of your life, constantly, can create the closeness." This desire to fight for the men who saved one's life lay at the heart of military morale.

While the respect, loyalty, and reliance of their comrades could strengthen a gay soldier's sense of self-esteem and belonging, the "buddy system" could affirm a gay man's desire to be close to other men, at times even providing a protective camouflage for lover relationships. [44]

In some Army and Navy outfits, commanding officers instituted an official "buddy system" in which they formally organized men into pairs. This system, especially on large ships and during dangerous attacks, protected each man by ensuring that he had at least one other man looking out for his welfare. A more informal buddy system also operated in combat units in which two men of equal rank or rating chose to pal around because they liked each other. A pair of buddies could be Army friends or men who came from the same town; they could be cousins or brothers or boyfriends or an experienced soldier who took care of a more dependent "kid." The two buddy systems often overlapped.

By encouraging men to pair up, the buddy systems gave a respectability to devoted male couples, whether or not they included gay men, that was unusual in civilian life. Even constant companions were protected from harassment by temporarily narrow definitions of deviant relationships. "The choice of a buddy," explained Stewart Stern, who after the war was screenwriter for the film *Rebel Without a Cause*, "was as or more critical than that of a bride. You'd be living in a kind of physical intimacy which was unlike any other. The classic David Duncan photos of buddies consoling each other, those who had lost their buddies, was very expressive of this. And what greater love song in those days than 'My Buddy'? Men were having the experience of never having been so close to other men." [45] Buddies watched out for each other, prayed for each other, did their best not to let each other down.

To outsiders the open affection that buddies expressed toward one another, which was captured in wartime photographs, can appear to be surprisingly "gay." Gay civilians at the time clipped buddy photographs from magazines, such as one from *Life* of two GIs sleeping with their bodies intertwined on a park bench, as rare keepsake images of male intimacy.[46] In the 1980s the popular wartime song "My Buddy" became a signature piece for many gay men's choruses, who recognized in its lyrics an open expression of male love that was rare in American society outside of gay life. But during the war the combat soldiers' acceptance of one another's pairing and physical intimacy was more a recognition of their need for closeness in life-threatening situations than any conscious tolerance of homosexuality.

Buddy relationships easily slipped into romantic and even sexual intimacies between men that they themselves often did not perceive to be "queer." "You'd get a buddy," explained Maxwell Gordon, who served in the South Pacific on a Navy carrier, "and you'd look out for each other and pretty soon you started exchanging clothes. And you ate together, usually bunked close together, went down to the head and showered together, and shared everything together. Went to the dentist together, for God's sake! A lot of friendships became intense and men were getting closer and closer. People ended up lovers. The ship was crawling with them. It was an accepted thing." Most of these men were teenagers like himself, Gordon continued, who "didn't consider themselves gay or homosexual. You had a buddy and if you carried on, why, that was that." Gordon had several steady boyfriends aboard ship during his service in the South Pacific.

Even heterosexual men could find themselves abandoning the norms of civilian life as they had to rely on each other for companionship and affection. Burt Miller, a gay Navy officer who served aboard an LST (landing ship, tank) in the Pacific, was astounded one night to find that some of the crewmen, who had been overseas for more than a year and had seen women only once in the Philippines, were pairing up in the dark while watching movies on the tank deck. Standing at the back of the rows of cots where the men sat, he began to notice from their silhouettes against the screen that they were holding hands. After a month or so they had their arms around each other, then "after another month you'd see them kissing." What the men were doing was "obvious to one another," Miller emphasized. "It was not only the back row." But they remained out of sight of the officers who sat in the privileged front-row seats. Miller believed that the fifteen or twenty men he saw necking were not necessarily gay and probably didn't have sex with each other. They merely had become "very close, inseparable" buddies on board ship.

Under such conditions, gay lovers managed to live, work, and even sleep together without raising suspicions. Fred Thayer and his lover Phil were both company clerks and shared the same tent in Noumea, New Caledonia. Oren Myerly, who served as medical stenographer and ward attendant at an Army hospital in France, recalled that a staff sergeant and corporal were "together practically constantly" and managed to share the same pup tent together every night. Others in the hospital would refer to them as the staff sergeant and his "boy." "You teamed up in combat," explained Frank Jacober, who fought with an Army mobile artillery unit in New Guinea and the Philippines, "and if you had a chance to camp, you put your shelter halves together and you camped together and slept together. This is when the guys who were gay would have their sexual thing. Most of the lovers were teams. They actually slept together and they teamed together on whatever their jobs were." A man could arrange to leave his own squad to be with another tent buddy by telling his superior officer that he " 'didn't like that guy and that squad leader, but I'd rather be with that squad leader because I like him.' What he really wanted to do was to get next to his lover.''

Gay soldiers who were determined not to expose their homosexuality while in the service had mixed feelings when they saw other gay men with lovers. "They took real good care of each other," Frank Jacober recalled of two pairs of lovers in his outfit. "They really loved each other. I thought, 'Well, now, this might not be so bad. This would really be nice to have someone that would care for you like that.' But I didn't do it. I found that scary. What's in your mind is, 'What if someone catches us? It's all over. It's curtains. You're in prison. The whole thing.' " Instead, Jacober found a gay buddy to tent with who was also trying to be celibate. "Neither of us [was] expressing [his] homosexual side at all," Jacober explained, "We talked about the situation, the way it was." The two men were able to help each other abstain from sex with men by confiding in each other whenever they faced sexual temptations.

Officers who saw their men pairing up into intimate couples had to decide how to deal with them. A few officers terrified their men by keeping them under close scrutiny, trying to catch anyone engaging in homosexual activity. But others, especially on board ship, allowed the men to pair up so long as they acted with discretion. On hot tropical nights in the Pacific, when men who hadn't seen women in months slept on deck in their underwear or nude to keep cool, the erotic charge in the air could be electric. Some men risked coupling with each other in private, especially if they sensed that the officer on duty was not out to get them. Robert Gervais recalled that during his late watch one night on his destroyer, the lieutenant commander came by "to chat a little about the signals or stuff like that. I had him pegged as a strict disciplinarian. And so both of us looked down in number two turret there and two guys were having sex. You could just see it in the moonlight. So I looked down there, and he looked, and he looked at me and said, 'Gervais, would you go down there and tell those men to move underneath the turret out of sight of the bridge.' Not to get their names or stop what's going on or bring them up to the bridge! So I went down there and I just stamped my feet as I went by and of course they shoved off. Nothing said, you know. I thought, 'You old son-of-a-bitch! You're not as bad as they think you are.' " On a similar night, Burt Miller went up to the conning tower of his LST to read, switched on the light, and "here was one of my radar men and one of my signal men in a '69.' " Miller "immediately switched the light off again" and never reported the men.

Enlisted men could express their own, spontaneous form of toler-ance, reacting to each other's trysts with joking and teasing. Such re-sponses enabled them to release the tension surrounding these homoerotic bondings without creating a climate of fear and hostility that would inhibit their own expressions of intimacy for each other. Maxwell Gordon recalled what happened on his carrier when two men were caught sleeping together. "Early one morning in chow line I was standing with some friends and there was a commotion ahead, and we all looked over the rail, and there was a gun tub down below. The canvas had blown back, and there [were] two fellows down there. I knew one of them. And they were naked, except the older one had on black socks. And they were wrapped in each other's arms, front to back. They'd obviously been screwing all night long. People started throwing pieces of bread down on them till they woke up. They were very embarrassed—hundreds of people saw them. [The other men] were whistling and saying 'Oh, wake up! It's morning!' The one fellow who was a bos'n's mate was kidded for weeks and months after about his socks. They said, 'Hey, we're all going to take a shower. Do you want to put your socks on and come along?' Because that's all he had on."

Many GIs assigned to the fighting fronts began to engage in a kind of situational bisexuality as combat life chipped away at civilian sexual taboos. Some gay soldiers had sex with women while heterosexual soldiers had sex with men, each suspending their normal inclinations under abnormal conditions.[47] When gay GIs discovered that some of their heterosexual buddies occasionally behaved in this way, they began to understand that their own homosexual desires and behavior were not so unusual, making them feel even less like outsiders.

Combat soldiers, including those who were married, had their own folk wisdom to justify the recreational sex they had overseas. They believed that healthy young men needed some kind of sexual outlet. Danger and deprivation could take away their sex drive but the exhilaration of surviving a combat mission could restore and increase their hunger for sex. Sex and intimacy with women was supposed to be the best solution to their sex problems. Many GIs, however, thought that a man about to go into combat had a right to take sex and seek intimacy however it came his way because it might be his last chance. Some hostile men, however, if they thought a "queer" was approaching them for sex, beat them up to defend their own manhood.

In the red-light sections of European and Pacific cities that became the recreational playgrounds of combat soldiers, sex between GIs and women sometimes had homosexual overtones. GIs accompanied each other to visit female prostitutes in brothels, where some gay men went to establish that they were masculine and normal, to get sexual release, to enjoy female companionship, or to have sex next to the men who attracted them.[48] Because Raymond Mailloux spoke French, he helped his buddies pick up women in Rheims and Paris, becoming their interpreter at the brothels, where the next morning he compared notes in French with the women about his buddies' sexual performances. Similarly, heterosexual combat soldiers on leave discovered bars, brothels, and cruising areas where men were available for their pleasure, such as the Pink Elephant in Manila, the "cottages" (public toilets) in London, Shepheard's Hotel in Cairo, and similar spots in Paris, Naples, Algiers, and other war-torn cities. These were often located in the same parts of town where GIs hung out looking for sex with women and where the most violent GIs were likely to beat up "queers."[49] Even when female prostitutes were available, some heterosexual soldiers thought that sex with men in these places was safer because, after seeing the military's graphic but exclusively heterosexual hygiene films, they wrongly concluded that only sex with women could give them venereal disease and that sex with men, though taboo, could not.[50]

But combat soldiers rarely had the chance to explore the nightlife of these cities. Most of the time their only source of comfort, reassurance, affection, and sexual release was other soldiers. Sex itself could become one of many expressions of affection and camaraderie among the men, even between strangers who would never see each other again. "The pressures in the military were horrendous," recalled Greg Aarons. "You were in a strange situation like in the Solomon Islands, your only outlet was each other—a situational type of homosexuality. A lot of these guys would ordinarily never think of doing such a thing in their hometowns, but they would there because it was the only thing to do other than masturbate."[51] Such situational sex with a man did not necessarily make a soldier feel "queer." He could believe that if he ever got back home alive he would once again date women, marry, and have a family. On board ship Bob Ruffing overheard two GIs talking about a mutual friend who had been having sex with men. "He's going to be Okay when he gets back to Arkansas," one said to the other. "He's just getting it out of his system."

Many officers were well aware that the homosexual behavior aboard ship and in isolated combat areas was an occupational hazard that was difficult to eliminate. "Such conditions will crop up occasionally," a Navy doctor in Washington advised the commandant of the Marine Corps regarding the homosexual activity in the South Pacific, "especially in areas in which the men have been isolated from female companionship for long periods of time. Under these circumstances," the doctor continued, "latent homosexuality is liable to become overt, should occasion present itself." [52] Two doctors at the 9th General Hospital on Biak, a coral island in the South Pacific, reported much homosexuality among the soldiers and noted that men in a black company—who were prohibited from dating the white women on the island—organized Saturday night parties "in which many men appeared dressed as women and at which homosexual practices were common." [53] These reports only confirmed the Army's reminder in its 1943 directive on sodomists that such activity would be likely among some American soldiers stationed in foreign lands.

Although medical officers knew that this homosexual activity was taking place overseas, neither the Army nor the Navy surgeon general issued any official policy or procedures for the prevention of venereal disease transmission between men. Assuming that any man might have sex with women while on leave, officers routinely issued all men prophylactic kits and required them to report to a "pro station" for examination and treatment before returning to their base or ship. But such preventive measures were rarely taken when women were not around. Despite the lack of official instructions on the matter, one conscientious gay pharmacist's mate, who served on a destroyer that was at sea for months at a time, developed his own unofficial plan for preventing the spread of venereal disease on board ship. He discreetly gave the men condoms, telling them to use one whenever they had anal sex. [54]

Out of their need to find private hideaways for their clandestine homosexual activity, soldiers and sailors created a kind of sexual geography aboard ship and on remote islands. Large ships and carriers, some of which had populations of more than three thousand men, provided more secluded corners and more available men than smaller ships and submarines. Maxwell Gordon identified the ammunition ready rooms on his carrier as the favorite trysting spots for romance and sex. Encircling the carrier were quad mounts—each holding antiaircraft guns—behind which were ammunition ready rooms. During combat these rooms housed the shells the men had taken from the magazine before loading the guns. To prevent the shells from hitting steel and exploding prematurely, the ready rooms were lined with carpeting and thick pads. When the carrier wasn't under attack, the rooms were empty. "People started using these ready rooms for lounges," Gordon recalled. "A lot of them were just under the flight deck and had a nice view of the sea. And you could go up there in the evening and sit and watch the sea and have a cigarette or take a buddy there. And when twilight came, you'd go inside.''

On some destroyers, the underwater sound room in the hull of the ship served a similar purpose. "We had a little clubhouse set up down there," recalled Robert Gervais. "We listened to music. I had a phonograph. It was known that it could be used for sex, too. We had mattress covers down there. The guys that wanted to use the place for sex, we just figured, 'Well, it's time to get the hell out of here.' So we'd leave a couple of guys behind. Just close the hatch and silently leave. It never got out. It was probably the safest place on the whole ship. You could hear anybody coming down the ladder, so it gave you a chance to get your clothes on." Officers with their own quarters had more privacy than enlisted men for similar encounters. Other men used gun turrets at night, linen storerooms, and similarly secluded corners for moments of sexual privacy. "The captain one time called the gun turrets 'cribs,' " laughed Robert Gervais. "[He said,] 'What's happening back there in number 5 crib?' "

Beaches on islands where soldiers rested between combat missions also became cruising spots, especially when men from different units or services were stationed there at the same time. In the Solomon Islands, recalled Greg Aarons, "they had a little place in the jungle called 'vaseline alley.' I used to go there and pick up all kinds of trade and tricks." [55] In the Philippines, reported another Pacific veteran, "daytime sexual relief could be obtained at a spot on the seashore marked by three reddish rocks soaring up like phallic symbols at the beach where many units went bare-ass bathing." [56] Some men remained totally unaware that such activity went on. "It was very secretive but open," explained Jim Kuzell about sex between men in the New Hebrides. "It was definitely there. I suppose there were guys that didn't even know it was going on."

Occasionally the MPs or SPs would police these beaches, as they did gay bars and park cruising areas in the stateside cities, to discourage men from having sex. Between combat missions in the South Pacific, recalled Robert Gervais, the men in his task force "had these little R & R things on these islands. They'd pick out a hell of a good spot [with] a lot of palm trees and undergrowth. Why, they'd have the MPs walking around and beating the bushes trying to find the guys! They'd pick them up and take them back to their ships with a full report and the whole damn thing." But other officers who were aware of the sexual activity on the beaches ignored it unless specific problems arose. Hal

Call, who commanded an infantry battalion on Okinawa, was present at a battalion meeting where officers discussed the "goings on under the cocoa trees." Call remembered the colonel asking, " 'Has anyone any complaints about it?' Everyone said no. Then the colonel said, 'Well, we'll just overlook it.' " [57]

No matter what he did between campaigns, the combat soldier's job was to kill and risk being killed. Gay soldiers going into combat, like other young men, were reluctant to kill and wondered how they would perform under fire. But unlike many of their comrades, gay GIs had to overcome the stereotype that portrayed them as unmanly, weak, and cowardly.

Some gay soldiers and officers, particularly those with a college education, carried with them a mythology, developed from reading the classics and in conversations with other gay men, about "armies of lovers," such as the "Sacred Band of Thebes" in ancient Greece, and heroic military leaders, such as Alexander the Great, Julius Caesar, Frederick the Great, and Lawrence of Arabia, who like themselves had had male lovers. This folklore provided them with romantic historical images that could help allay self-doubts before their first combat missions. It confirmed that there had always been gay warriors who fought with courage and skill, sometimes spurred on by the desire to fight bravely by the side of their lovers. [58]

Most soldiers, not only gay GIs, were kept going in battle by a strong desire to protect their buddies and not let them down, as well as to get the war over with. Few were motivated by anger, revenge, or hatred of the enemy. [59] The concern for one's buddies that mobilized so many soldiers to fight, however, had a particular poignancy for gay men. American photographer Minor White, who was drafted into an Army infantry unit at a time when he was struggling to understand his own homosexuality, was afraid of how he would hold up in combat. To build his fighting spirit, he consciously tried to cultivate a hatred for his future enemies on the battlefield. "I have an inkling of a way I might do it," he wrote in a letter to a friend, "by a deep regard for the men in my outfit. A regard that must be as deep as love at least. I am told that seeing your mates hurt makes a man blistering mad, but that is a little late. This rage of retaliation must be present early, so that I will eagerly destroy whatever threatens them long before a hair of their heads has been damaged. I am fairly certain that the only way I can acquire a semblance of hatred is by the backdoor method of learning a love for my mates." [60]

No matter what motives kept them fighting, gay combat soldiers, like their heterosexual comrades, did kill enemy soldiers, as they were trained to do. Although gay veterans make the painful effort of remembering their buddies who were killed, they are more reluctant to talk about how they killed other men. Ted Allenby simply explained that he was a machine gunner at Iwo Jima.[61] "I would kill if I had to," recalled Ernest Cole, who led the first wave of boats onto the enemy shore of Rendova in the New Georgia Islands, "but to rejoice in it was not my cup of tea." Frank Jacober, as a mobile artillery cannoneer in the 63rd Infantry, 6th Division, fought in the South Pacific for two years and was in the first wave of GIs that attacked Japanese troops at Leyte. To this day he has been reluctant to talk about his experiences with anyone but his combat buddies. "They condition you to kill well," he explained, "but they don't condition you how not to, and you have to find your own way." With the 44th Bomb Group, 8th Air Force, Robert Ricks flew bombing missions over air bases in Sicily and southern Italy, unable to see the enemy airmen who may have been blown up in the raids. These and other gay soldiers thrown into life-and-death situations proved that their homosexuality did not prevent them from doing the most difficult task the combat soldier was called upon to perform.

Any soldier's resolve, however, could weaken whenever the enemy took on a human face, often jarring the GI into seeing the absurdity of war. A married GI who searched the body of an enemy soldier he had killed was often stunned to find a photograph of the man's wife and child that reminded him of his own family. A gay soldier could be shocked when he found himself identifying with or even attracted to the man he had just killed. After Ernest Cole and his shipmates shot down a couple of Japanese planes at Rendova, they went over in a boat to inspect the wreckage. "I saw this Japanese floating in the water," Cole recalled. "He was good-looking, too. He was still warm from death. And he was floating, ebbing in the water. And I thought, 'How can I think that this man who tried to kill me is attractive?!' But he was. I thought, 'In another day, in another time, we might have been friends.' " When Robert Fleischer came across the bodies of three dead German soldiers, he, too, realized that, despite his hatred of what the Nazis were doing, each of these soldiers was "still a man. You think that you're firing at an enemy, and you're firing at another human being." It was to prevent this identification with individual enemy soldiers, which could make a man even more reluctant to kill, that in many units combat soldiers were not put on burial squads.[62]

Among the bodies lying dead on the battlefields and floating in

ocean waters during the war were those of gay American soldiers who
had been killed in combat. Sometimes the only people who knew that
these men were gay were their own lovers or buddies. One Army veteran
remembered that a friend who had declared his homosexuality to his
officer was sent into combat and "was killed in Normandy, soon after
we invaded France. . . . His body was hit by a mortar shell. He is
buried in the U.S. Military Cemetery in Normandy." [63] Frank Jacober
remembered a gay soldier he worked with at a headquarters company
in the South Pacific who "wanted to have sex and I wouldn't do it."
When they were sent out together on the same campaign, Jacober's
friend "pulled me out from under fire two times. I would have been
killed but he saved my life. And then the third time he was just riddled
right through the middle with machine gun [fire]. I was eternally grateful
to him." Fred Thayer's lover Bob, who was separated from him when
they were drafted into different outfits, was shot down and killed in a
bombing raid on a Nazi submarine installation in France. Burt Miller's
lover Jack was fighting with an infantry company in Europe, where he
volunteered to go on a scouting party to pin down a Nazi machine-gun
nest and was shot and killed. The Army awarded him the Silver Star
medal posthumously. The number of gay combat soldiers who were
killed in World War II can never be documented and will never be
known.

Combat soldiers often responded to each other's personal losses
with the deepest respect and understanding, allowing many gay GIs to
express openly their grief over the deaths of boyfriends or lovers. Jim
Warren's boyfriend was hit while trying to knock out a machine-gun
nest on Saipan. "They brought him back," Warren recalled, "and he
was at the point of death. He was bleeding. He had been hit about
three or four times. I stood there and he looked up at me and I looked
down at him and he said, 'Well, Jim, we didn't make it, did we.' And
tears were just rolling down my cheeks. I don't know when I've ever
felt such a lump and such a waste. And he kind of gave me a boyish
crooked grin and just said, 'Well, maybe next time.' And I said, 'I'm
going to miss you. And I'll see your mother.' There were people standing
around, maybe seven or eight people standing there, and I was there
touching his hand and we were talking. Somebody said later, 'You
were pretty good friends,' because I had been openly crying and most
people don't do this. I said, 'Yes, we were quite good friends.' And
nobody ever said anything. I guess as long as I supposedly upheld my
end of the bargain, everything was all right."

Ben Small was even less able to control himself when his boyfriend was killed in the Philippines. But he, too, was surprised by the other men's compassion toward him. "We had a funny freak attack of a Japanese kamikaze plane," he recalled, "and I guess he was getting rid of his last load of these baby cutter bombs, these little bombs that explode at about three feet high so if they went through a tent they exploded at bed level. I had just been in the tent of a guy I had been going with at the time. He crawled into bed, and I said goodnight and walked out of the tent. And this plane came overhead and all we heard was explosions and we fell to the ground. When I got up to see if he was all right, the thrust of the bomb had gone through his tent and he was not there. I went into a three-day period of hysterics. I was treated with such kindness by the guys that I worked with, who were all totally aware of why I had gone hysterical. It wasn't because we were bombed. It was because my boyfriend had been killed. And one guy in the tent came up to me and said, 'Why didn't you tell me you were gay? You could have talked to me.' I said, 'Well, I was afraid to.' This big, straight, macho guy. There was a sort of compassion then."

Gay combat veterans describe the quiet empathy that sometimes pervaded battle areas, especially toward men who embraced one another in moments of loss or joyful reunions, as powerful experiences that affirmed their love for men. When Ted Allenby's buddy Barrett ran into him on board ship after believing that he had been killed at Iwo Jima, he "grabbed hold of me," Allenby recalled, "hugged me, and couldn't let go. He was crying uncontrollably. . . . If Barrett and I [would] have done the same thing in the street in San Diego—Oh, a couple of queers." [64] After a raid in the Philippines, Ben Small remembered, a lieutenant who had been injured was being shipped back to the States, so the men "all went to the plane to see him off that night. It was an amazingly touching moment, when he and his lover said goodbye, because they embraced and kissed in front of all these straight guys and everyone dealt with it so well. I think it was just this basic thing abut the separation of someone you cared for, regardless of sex." Small described this tender parting as "a little distilled moment out of time" when the men's "prejudices were suspended" and gay soldiers "could be a part of what this meant."

But the fear of being exposed, punished, and sent to jail was so great in some gay soldiers that they tried to accomplish the seemingly impossible task of hiding all their grief, even when their lovers were killed. When Ernest Cole took part in the invasion of Iwo Jima, his boyfriend was sent ashore where the beach "was absolutely alive with fire. Oh my God, boy, did I pray for that kid." When Cole's boyfriend didn't come back that night, "I just went out of my mind. I kept thinking about that beautiful boy bouncing around on the fucking beach. I was bawling in my cabin." The next day, as Cole was hanging around the gangway where the boats returned with the casualties, he saw his boyfriend coming off the boat, his face black and dirty, unhurt but looking "like he'd been through hell." Cole "didn't dare go to him, because I was afraid I'd cry. So I turned around, and I went back to my cabin and I cried. The next day I saw him, and I put my arm around him and I was under control by that time. How glad I was to see him!" When Burt Miller received a message on board ship after the invasion of Okinawa that his lover Jack had been killed in Germany, he "couldn't talk to anybody for the rest of the day. I couldn't cry and I couldn't tell anybody. Just alone. No way that I could release any of the emotion or express any of it. It was the most terrible day I've spent [in my life]."

Some gay combat survivors tried to protect themselves from immobilizing sadness by throwing themselves into their next task. "When you've had death all around you," explained Ernest Cole, "you do your job anyway. I did whatever was required of me." Others relied on the memory of their lover or buddy to keep going, rededicating themselves to fighting for their own survival and to bringing the war to a quick end so they all could go home. "One of the people I was very attached to got killed," recalled Marine Corps veteran Tom Reddy, "which kind of wrecks you. It either wrecks you or makes you say, 'I'm going to survive, goddamn it! I'm going to keep on living, because that's what Tommy would have wanted.' " Still other gay combat soldiers found strength in their faith in God. "The whole time the fight was going on," recalled Vincent Miles, who fought in Italy and North Africa with the mostly black 92nd Infantry Division, "it didn't seem to really get me panicky." His religious upbringing had prepared him to believe that "it's all in God's hands. What's going to happen is going to happen."

Many gay soldiers who survived combat, however, did not necessarily escape other hardships and dangers. Some, like George Dohmann, Minor White, and Vincent Miles (who was hit in the side by shrapnel), were seriously injured. Others were captured by enemy forces and thrown into German, Italian, or Japanese prisoner-of-war camps, where they stayed for the rest of the war.[65] Robert Ricks, a gay man who grew up in North Carolina, served as a navigator on a B-24 bomber in the 8th Air Force, flying missions over the Ploesti oil fields in Romania and over air bases in southern Italy, where, near Potenza, his plane was shot down in August 1943. He and the pilot were able to parachute to safety, but the copilot and most of the crew were killed by enemy fire.

Ricks was captured and transferred from one prison camp to another as the Allies moved up the boot of Italy. He spent the last three months of the war in a compound with other American officers imprisoned at Dachau. By April 1945 he had lost forty pounds, his hair had turned white, and he could barely walk, conserving energy by staying on the shelf-bed of his barracks.

Gay GIs were forced to consider the meaning of their own survival not only when they were wounded or imprisoned but also when they were among the liberated or themselves served as liberators. On April 28, 1945, Robert Ricks and his fellow prisoners, hearing gunfire, looked out the window of their prison barracks and could see the Germans "come down the guard towers and nobody went back up." When the shooting stopped, American troops came into their compound and "started bringing us in food, and took out a few fellows who were really sick." It was from American GIs that Ricks first learned that Dachau had been an extermination camp for Jews. One of the soldiers who liberated the inmates of Dachau was Robert Fleischer. "As we traveled on the road in the truck," he recalled, "the roads were clogged with walking skeletons in those striped uniforms. They could hardly drag themselves along. I tried to talk to them, and they didn't know any English. All of a sudden it dawned on me to ask, 'Du bist Juden?' 'Are you Jewish?' One man nodded, 'Ja' and I said, 'Me, too.' A [prisoner] came up to me who wore a British uniform. He was about my own age, and he took my hand when we started to speak, and he started kissing my hand. I was so upset, I said to myself, 'How dare the world do this to two human beings! Who am I that he should kiss my hand because he's free?' "

By the time the fighting ended, the lives of gay soldiers who survived combat were changed in fundamental ways. The closer they had come to combat, the more they understood how much they were needed and valued—by the people they liberated, the military organization, and their comrades-in-arms. On the battlefields, some of these men had the chance to experience what it would be like to live in a world where prejudices against male-to-male love, affection, and sex were suspended, if only temporarily. Simply by doing what they were expected to do, they powerfully challenged the stereotypes that portrayed homosexuals as poor soldiers, proving to their heterosexual buddies, other gay soldiers, and themselves that they would not let each other down. It is one of many tragic ironies of the war that gay soldiers and officers had to kill, risk their lives, and see their buddies die in order to gain some respect and a sense of belonging as "men among men."

CHAPTER

8

Fighting Another War

In combat, gay GIs pointed their guns at enemy soldiers. But some gay servicemen also found American guns pointed at
them. Those who were caught having sex, or who were rounded up in
systematic witch hunts at stateside or overseas bases, or who were asking
for help coping as homosexuals in the service, found themselves fighting
a war for their own survival. As officers began to discharge homosexuals
as undesirables, the gay GIs who were their targets had to learn how
to defend themselves in psychiatrists' offices, discharge hearing rooms,
hospital wards, and "queer stockades." There they were interrogated
about their sex lives, locked up, physically abused, and subjected to
systematic humiliations in front of other soldiers. Although only a fraction
of all gay and lesbian GIs—approximately ten thousand, the vast majority
of whom were men—became the victims of such extreme measures,
their persecution and expulsion from the service had an impact far greater
than their numbers reveal.

The discharge system could drag any GI whose homosexuality
became known or even suspected into a seemingly endless maze of
unexpected humiliations and punishments. Some gay male and lesbian GIs
first entered this maze when they voluntarily declared their homosexuality,
fully expecting to be hospitalized and discharged.[1] But others, following
advice in basic-training lectures to talk over problems with a doctor,
psychiatrist, or chaplain, were shocked when medical officers betrayed
their confidences by reporting them for punitive action as "self-confessed" homosexuals, or were disappointed and frustrated when more
sympathetic psychiatrists could not help them at all. Caught during their

processing for discharge in battles between friendly and hostile officers, they found themselves thrown around like footballs in a game over which they had little control. They were "kicked into the hospital," explained William Menninger, "then sent back to assignments, shoved back into the hospital, returned to their assignments, and so on, until someone weakened." [2]

Expecting to be harassed by all military officers once their homosexuality was known, some gay patients were initially relieved to find that psychiatrists turned out to be understanding. After Pfc. Marty Klausner and his best friend Cpl. Tommy Martz declared their homosexuality in early 1945, Klausner wrote to their friend Howard Taylor that the psychiatrist and psychologist at the Army station hospital in Torrance, California, "are both extremely nice and all in all we have been exceedingly fortunate because everyone has been kind." But they and other gay patients needed more than friendliness. Some became disillusioned when they discovered that psychiatrists with good intentions actually knew little about homosexuality, could not offer them any useful therapies, or ignored their problems altogether. After several months of psychiatric interviews that seemed to lead nowhere, Martz lost his patience with what he called "these 'understanding' psychiatrists." "He is very nice," the frustrated corporal wrote about a psychiatrist at Camp Beale, California, "though—of course I think they all are—it's part of their act." [3]

Realizing that even the most sympathetic psychiatrists could not help them with their personal problems, gay patients instead began to exchange information, negotiate, and compromise with them to achieve the best outcome in a bad situation. While psychiatrists began to study them on the psychiatric wards, gay GIs learned how to deal with psychiatrists and, in the process, with the military's new discharge system. "As I look back," explained Chuck Tarrance, "I was just using [the psychiatrist] as a channel to get where I wanted to go. That was the only way I could do it without going through my commanding officer, and then it would have been a dishonorable discharge." Step by step, gay patients grew adept at managing the system that was designed to manage them. Some were tempted to concede mental illness, at least on paper, in order to escape the military, and even asked to be diagnosed as psychoneurotics to get automatic honorable discharges. They discussed administrative loopholes with their psychiatrists and persuaded the most sympathetic to serve as their advocates in meetings with hostile officers.

But even when they successfully enlisted the support of their psychiatrists, gay patients rarely received the honorable discharges or returns to duty they sought. When Fred Thayer and his buddy Arnie were committed to a locked psychiatric ward at O'Reilly General Hospital in Missouri after an antigay purge in the Army, they demanded to see the psychiatrist. "Our main point," he recalled, "was to say 'We don't want to be thrown out.' " Knowing that the psychiatrist was a Jewish refugee from Germany, Thayer said to him, " 'You must understand persecution,' and he agreed. I said, 'That's what we feel. We had fine service records.' " Thayer believed that the psychiatrist tried to use his connections to help them, but with no success. At an Army hospital in California, Private First Class Klausner and Corporal Martz convinced their psychiatrist to diagnose them as psychoneurotic, but the colonel rejected the diagnosis and ordered a blue discharge for sexual psychopathy instead. "Both of the psychiatrists were very sorry," Klausner wrote to their friend Howard Taylor, "and it seems as though everyone has stuck his neck out for us and will probably get into trouble with the colonel." [4]

Their frustrating encounters with psychiatrists, however, did give gay patients a private forum for telling military authorities that they didn't want to give up their homosexuality despite the hardships and humiliations they had to endure—a message that psychiatric researchers later made public in their writings. All of the two hundred gay patients in one Navy hospital were aware of "the universal disapproval of their perversion" but they "nevertheless made little or no attempt to channelize their sexual expression into normal paths." [5] Each of twenty gay Air Corps patients at Truax Field in Wisconsin "had participated apparently without conflict in a wide variety of homosexual practices" but none "requested or desired" therapy to change their homosexuality.[6] At the Army's 36th Station Hospital, Lieutenant Colonel Loeser noted that "very few homosexuals who do not have a neurosis will ask for or cooperate in treatment." [7]

Unlike many psychiatrists, officers who conducted interrogations were neither friendly nor understanding. Their job was to extract confessions and the names of other homosexuals by systematically destroying a suspect's emotional defenses. Confessions were the proof needed to issue a discharge, and names helped interrogators round up more suspects and unravel the cliques of gay friends and sexual partners that formed everywhere in the service. Interrogators wrestled with gay suspects in a terrifying power struggle over the surrender of each sexual detail and over what it meant to be homosexual.

The interrogation usually began with some form of confinement or restriction to barracks, often under armed guard. Mail was opened and visitors were limited or prohibited. Those who weren't confined were kept under continuous surveillance. One by one MPs removed gay men—and occasionally gay women—from their barracks, hospital wards, or queer stockades and took them to a truck, tent, or office where they were interrogated by intelligence officers or members of hospital disposition boards, Section Eight discharge boards, or secret investigative teams. Suspects and witnesses who were forced to testify under oath before formal boards were ordered not to discuss the proceedings with anyone and did not have the right to legal counsel. These measures ensured that the interrogators had control over the suspect's mobility and communication and provided a cover of secrecy that protected the proceedings from outside interference. "It was so cloak and dagger," recalled Fred Thayer of his interrogation in Noumea, New Caledonia, "hidden up on a hill in an old deserted farmhouse like they didn't want anyone to know what they were doing."

Once the questioning began, interrogators tried to catch suspects off guard, employing some of the same techniques that basic training instructors used to break down the recruit's civilian identity. Many of those questioned did not know beforehand that the investigation was about homosexuality. They were stunned when asked bluntly about their sexual practices and shocked to find that interrogators had already obtained information about their private lives. Interrogators made false promises of immunity and threatened to tell family members that the suspect was homosexual. They used these threats and promises like precision tools, taking turns in good-cop/bad-cop roles to exhaust the suspects and chip away at their defenses. Interrogators successfully forced suspects to talk about their sexual desires, pleasures, positions, orgasms, relationships, language, correspondence, or friends by stages, taking advantage of each humiliating exposure to make their victims even more vulnerable to further questioning.

Sexual humiliation was one of the interrogators' most powerful weapons for getting at the "naked truth" beneath the suspects' denials. "They do make it horribly embarrassing," wrote a gay infantryman to a buddy after his interrogation by a disposition board at Camp Livingston, an infantry replacement center in Alexandria, Louisiana. "There's one board, for instance, where the victim is placed on a block, quite nude, in front of a table full of assorted colonels and majors, and made to answer the most intimate questions. We call it the 'slave mart.' Then there are the interviews, and questionnaires, and consultations, and accusing looks." Such humiliations could make gay suspects feel as if they were the enemy or were pieces of garbage to be thrown away. "How do you recommend I be disposed of?" the infantryman at Camp Livingston wrote to his friend. "Gas? Firing squad? Weighting with chains and casting into the sewerage canal? I'm bucking for cremation. I've been burned up so many times in the past two years that it would be a pleasure to be burned up once and not feel it." [8]

The systematic violation of their dignity and trust made many GIs talk, but at a terrible cost to their self-respect. David Barrett, who in 1943 was held with dozens of other suspected homosexuals in a Navy "queer brig" in Noumea, New Caledonia, described how interrogators used the good-cop/bad-cop technique to break him down. Taking him from the brig to an office, both the judge advocate and a lieutenant worked on Barrett while a yeoman took notes. They began the interrogation by telling him about his family and his former employers. " 'My God,' " Barrett wondered to himself, " 'how did they learn all this?' They scared the hell out of me." Then the judge advocate threatened him with criminal prosecution. During a break in the interrogation, the lieutenant took Barrett "out to a station wagon and we sat out there. He put his arm around my shoulder and he said, 'For the good of the service, you should go.' And I said, 'Well, if you feel that way, and if I've done something wrong and it hinders the service, I suppose I'll go.' He said, 'You go in and tell them that.' So he softened me up." Back inside the office Barrett agreed to talk once he got assurance that nothing would happen to anyone he named. He named two men. On his confession Barrett had to sign that he was " 'not under duress' or 'I was not coerced.' Then the judge advocate looked at his yeoman and said, 'For Christ's sake, I didn't think he'd break.' And that hurt terribly. I was heartbroken." The men he named were rounded up for interrogation and discharged.[9]

The interrogation of a twenty-four-year-old corporal at Fort Ogle-thorpe demonstrates how officers could barrage a suspect with sexual questions in a kind of psychological rape until they broke her unwillingness to expose herself, her partner, and her friends. When the line of questioning approached the corporal's sexual pleasures and orgasms, the interrogation was turned over to a female officer. "Are you and Lt. Foster closer than just friends?" the officer asked the corporal. "No ma'am," she replied, "I think a lot of her but we are just close friends."

Q. Are you in love with her?
A. No ma'am.
Q. Is she with you?
A. I don't think so. . . .
Q. Which one of you first made love to the other one?
A. We don't make love to each other ma'am. . . .

[Interrogator] informs witness of allegations against her and explains to witness that she understands about people like her.

Q. Now do we understand each other better . . . ?
A. Yes ma'am.
Q. Has Lt. Foster ever made love to you?
A. Yes ma'am. . . .
Q. What do you do when you and Lt. Foster get together and make love?
A. We just love each other.
Q. How? Describe it to me.
A. We put our arms around each other and love each other.
Q. Do you feel various parts of one anothers bodies?
A. Yes ma'am, I have. . . .
Q. Have you ever touched her sexual organs?
A. No ma'am.
Q. What physical reaction do you get from kissing Lt. Foster and petting her?
A. I would say I would get the same reaction that I would get from kissing a man. . . .
Q. Does making love with Lt. Foster make you nervous?
A. No ma'am, it doesn't make me nervous. . . .
Q. Is it a pleasure?
A. Yes ma'am. We always get such funny feelings.
Q. Do you continue until you get relief in the form of an orgasm?
A. Yes ma'am. . . .
Q. Do you kiss long clinging kisses?
A. An average one I would say. . . .
Q. Have you ever heard the term "to come" expressed—meaning someone has been relieved physically, that one has had a physical reaction as a result of being made love to?
A. Yes ma'am.
Q. How do you love one another to get this reaction?
A. We are very close to each other.
Q. With your clothes on?
A. In bed with our pajamas on.
Q. Did you learn it from her?
A. I think we learned it together. . . .
Q. Besides being the finest person you have ever known, is she sexually gratifying?
A. Yes ma'am. . . .

[Here the male interrogator takes over and threatens to tell the Wac's brothers, sisters, parents, and Baptist minister about what she has just admitted.]

Q. We are here to eliminate from the Army people who practice this kind of thing. If you know anything about these kinds of people that you haven't told [the female officer], we want you to tell us.

A. . . . Do I have to drag other people into this?

Q. You are under oath to tell us the truth and tell us what you know.

A. Yes sir. [Witness names several pairs of women.] [10]

Trying to destroy this woman's devotion to her lover, the interrogators played on her self-doubts. The purpose was to get her to admit that her relationship was both wrong and a threat to the Army, possibly making her available for reclamation and reassignment. "It isn't quite normal for two women to get such strong reactions from physical contacts as you say you get," a female officer lectured the Wac after completing her sexual interrogation. "I feel so funny because it is so unusual," the Wac replied. "I have never come in contact with anyone that made me feel like this. It has always worried me."

Q. Does it still worry you?

A. Yes ma'am, it does. . . .

Q. Do you feel that it is wrong?

A. In a way it is. We have talked about that a lot. I don't know whether it is or not. . . .

Q. Do you feel guilty about it?

A. Yes ma'am.

Q. Is the feeling [of guilt] so awfully strong that you don't want your family to know it and crying as you are now and you feel that they might know it, is the feeling so strong that you don't want to break [your relationship] up?

A. I don't want it broken up. . . .

Q. Do you know that the Army wouldn't approve of a friendship that exists between two women like your friendship with Lt. Foster?

A. Yes ma'am. . . .

Q. As much as you don't want [your mother] to find it out, do you still say you would rather take a chance at that than give up Lt. Foster?

A. I would hate to give her up.
Q. If you had a choice, which would you take?
A. My family. . . . They mean everything in the world to me.[11]

Signed confessions were the suspect's ultimate act of surrender and the prize of the interrogation. A typical signed confession was composed by the interrogator after the questioning ended. "It's not even my own words," explained Fred Thayer, who signed one in New Caledonia. "It's words dictated to me." The confession verified consent to the confession even when the signer was coerced, and described his or her sex acts and relationships in the awkward language of military regulations. The confession of a sailor interrogated at the Naval Air Station in Jacksonville, Florida, began:

> I have since March 15, 1943 attended six "gay parties" at Jim BELL's home. Jim BELL was at that time a civilian and is at present a private first class in the U.S. Army. I have also attended two parties at Doris', a "dike" living in Jacksonville, Florida, and on several occasions I have been present at "gay parties" which were held at the Mayflower Hotel, Jacksonville, Florida. By "gay parties" I mean those parties were attended by sexually perverted individuals and were usually held on Saturday nights with practically the same crowd present. I have seen Bob SMITH, Bob KNOWLES, Stan CASELLI, Doug MARKS, Lt. N. R. BURKE USNR, Richard GIANNINI, "Buddy" WILSON, Steve DUNN, and Manuel MIRANDA. All but the last three are serving in the U.S. Navy, the others are serving in the U.S. Army. Drinking, singing, dancing and the playing of suggestive records occurred at these parties with the exchange of kisses upon greeting each other.[12]

The threat that such confessions would be used to charge suspects with criminal offenses was present during most interrogations, investigations, and psychiatric interviews. Gay male and lesbian suspects often disclaimed their sexuality during the interrogations not because they believed what they said but to avoid criminal prosecution. Many who broke down under questioning did not know that they were not on trial.[13]

Gay men and lesbians who held up under such intense grilling devised on-the-spot tactics to defend themselves. Some denied knowing other gay people or used evasion to delay naming names, hoping their endurance would outlast the interrogators' persistence. During a purge at the Naval Air Transport station at Patuxent, Maryland, a group of

War boom cities were flooded with lonely GIs on passes. *(top)* A wartime cartoon captures the "gay ambiance" in train stations. *(bottom)* Gay GIs found camaraderie in bars but risked getting caught by police and MPs. The Black Cat Cafe in San Francisco, a bohemian hangout that attracted a gay crowd, was declared off limits to military personnel. In upper left two MPs stand guard to make sure only civilians enter the premises.

"Lost, Sweetheart?"

Drawing by Garrett Price; © 1941, 1969 The New Yorker Magazine, Inc.

Despite the official belief that homosexuals could not become good combat soldiers, the military sent many to the fighting fronts. *(top)* Pfc. Robert Fleischer was awarded the Bronze Star for laying a mine under enemy fire at Würzburg, Germany. *(bottom left)* Cpl. Oren Myerly, a ward attendant and medical stenographer, outside a hospital tent in Carentan, France, in 1944. *(bottom right)* Second Lt. Robert Ricks, a navigator in the 8th Air Force, whose plane was shot down near Potenza, Italy, in August 1943. Photo is from German records captured at Dachau, where Ricks was imprisoned.

Although the military prohibited women from fighting in combat, many, including lesbians, gave vital support to the combat effort. *(top)* Cpl. Helen Harder, who instructed male pilots in instrument flying at Gardner Field, California. *(bottom)* Sgt. (T/4) Jacquelyn Beyer, attached to the Army Security Agency in Arlington Hall, Virginia, worked on experimental photo processing techniques that helped break Japanese codes.

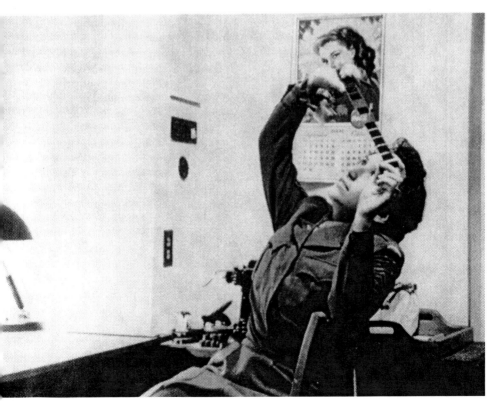

ART. 93 · Any person... who commits manslaughter, mayhem, arson, burglary, housebreaking, robbery, larceny, embezzlement, perjury, forgery, sodomy, assault...

In World War II, psychiatrists reformed military policy so that personnel diagnosed as homosexual would be discharged as undesirable rather than go to prison. *(top)* In 1943, Lt. Dave Breger drew a series of *GI Joe* cartoons for *Stars and Stripes* to simplify the Articles of War for soldiers. Article 93, pictured here, established sodomy as a military crime. *(bottom)* Brig. Gen. William C. Menninger, neuropsychiatric consultant to the Army surgeon general, tried to change policy so that homosexual soldiers would receive honorable rather than punitive undesirable discharges.

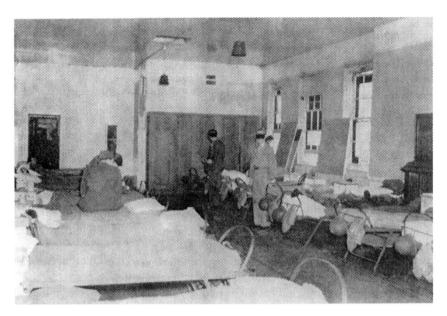

The new policies filled psychiatric wards of military hospitals with gay patients being processed for discharge. *(top)* A psychiatric ward in the 36th Station Hospital in Devonshire, England, which the Army designated as an "observation and recommendation center" for homosexual soldiers. [Eye masks are in original Army photograph.] *(bottom)* Lt. Col. Lewis H. Loeser, commanding officer of the 36th Station Hospital, in his office. Loeser and his staff, in a study of 270 homosexual patients, concluded in 1945 that most homosexuals were effective soldiers and should be integrated into the armed forces.

Some officers used the new discharge policy to conduct witch hunts and imprison homosexuals without trial in "queer stockades." *(top)* An exercise yard attached to an Army psychiatric ward in Brisbane, Australia, of the type used to segregate groups of suspected homosexuals during purges. *(bottom left)* Pvt. Norman Sansom, who received a "blue" undesirable discharge for homosexuality at Columbia Army Air Base, South Carolina, in December 1943. *(bottom right)* Pharmacist's Mate Second Class Robert Plant Armstrong, who was "undesirabled" out of the Navy as a homosexual in San Diego in 1942.

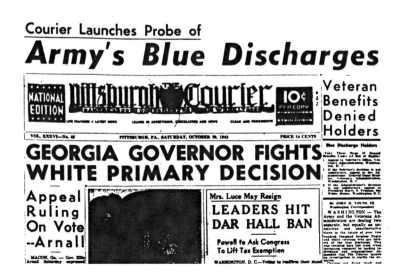

Discharge from
The Army of the United States

TO ALL WHOM IT MAY CONCERN:

This is to Certify, That* NORMAN F. SANSOM

† 12203359, Private, Walterboro Base Detachment, Walterboro, South Carolina

THE ARMY OF THE UNITED STATES is hereby DISCHARGED from the military service of the UNITED STATES by reason of ‡ Section VIII, AR 615-360, not eligible for reenlistment, induction, or reinduction, per 2nd Ind. Hqs. Columbia Army Air Base, Columbia, South Carolina dated December 21, 1943.

Said Norman F. Sansom was born in Bridgeport , in the State of Connecticut

When enlisted he was 20 8/12 years of age and by occupation a IBM Operator

He had Blue eyes, Brown hair, Ruddy complexion, and was 5 feet 11 inches in height.

Given under my hand at Walterboro Army Air Field, Walterboro, S.C. this 8th day of January , one thousand nine hundred and forty-four

William M. Prince

WILLIAM M. PRINCE

Colonel, Air Corps

Commanding.

See AR 345-470.
* Insert name; as, "John J. Doe."
† Insert Army serial number, grade, company, regiment, and arm or service; as "1620002"; "Corporal, Company A, 1st Infantry"; "Sergeant, Quartermaster Corps."
‡ State fully actual cause of discharge, giving number, date, and source of order or full description of authority therefor.
W. D., A. G. O. Form No. 56
April 1, 1940

Because officers could use blue discharges to eliminate soldiers they didn't want, a disproportionate number of GIs discharged as "undesirable" were gay. Most were denied honor and benefits despite good service records. *(top)* Norman Sansom's blue discharge. *(bottom)* In October 1945, the *Pittsburgh Courier*, the nation's largest circulation black newspaper, launched a campaign to stop the use of blue discharges as instruments of prejudice against both black and gay GIs. In response, Congress held hearings and issued a report sympathetic to the plight of blue-discharge veterans.

Courier Launches Probe of
Army's Blue Discharges

Pittsburgh Courier

NATIONAL EDITION

VOL. XXXVI—No. 48 PITTSBURGH, PA., SATURDAY, OCTOBER 20, 1945 PRICE 10 CENTS

Veteran Benefits Denied Holders

GEORGIA GOVERNOR FIGHTS
WHITE PRIMARY DECISION

Appeal Ruling On Vote --Arnall

Mrs. Luce May Resign
LEADERS HIT
DAR HALL BAN

Powell to Ask Congress To Lift Tax Exemption

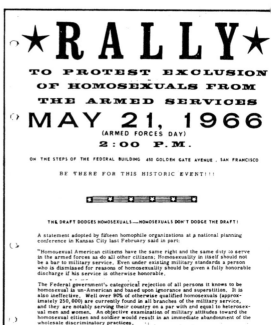

Beginning in the 1950s, a gay movement emerged which in part fought for the recognition of lesbian and gay male soldiers and against the military's antihomosexual policies. *(top left)* ONE magazine was one of the many movement publications to feature articles on homosexuals in the military. *(top right)* Flyer from a 1966 Armed Forces Day rally to protest exclusion of homosexuals from the armed forces. *(bottom)* In the 1980s lesbians and gay men began to form their own veterans' groups. The predominantly gay Alexander Hamilton Post 448 of the American Legion marching in the Veterans' Day Parade in San Francisco, November 1986. World War II veteran Martin Stow is third from left.

men named only military personnel who already had been discharged and claimed not to know any others.[14] One gay GI reportedly took revenge on a hated officer by naming him during the interrogation.[15] But most often such evasive tactics did not work. Suspects were outnumbered, caught off guard, and overpowered by interrogators who seldom quit until they extracted at least some names or sexual details.

Interrogators tried, with some success, to weaken suspects by making them describe their relationships as an addiction rather than as a form of love. "True" or "confirmed" homosexuals were the addicts, their sexual practices the "habits," and their partners the innocent victims seduced into a sexual underworld that threatened to destroy their lives. "Are you addicted to homosexual practices?" was a common way to phrase the opening question during an interrogation.[16] The lesbian couple that consisted of a "butch" and a "girlfriend" partner was redefined by interrogators so that the butch was the "addict" and the girlfriend was the seduced "victim." Officers used these categories not to judge who was guilty and who was innocent, as in a trial, but to determine who was more likely to be a confirmed pervert. The "addict" then became responsible for the sexual "habits" in the relationship, making the "victim" available for reclamation. Interrogators generally assumed that the addicts were those who initiated sex, had previous relationships, were the most promiscuous, "went down on the other," were the more masculine (for women) or effeminate (for men), and, among women, paid the bill on a date.[17] The drug addiction and aggressor-victim models allowed little room for understanding a mutually responsible relationship.

Some gay men and women defended their ability to love their partners by steadfastly describing their lives in their own and not military terms. During an interrogation at Wright Field near Dayton, Ohio, a first lieutenant, when pressed to explain why he thought two other officers under investigation were homosexual, did not give the interrogators the descriptions of effeminacy or sexual perversion they expected. Instead, he told them that he thought the men were homosexual because of the "very fact that they admire each other very greatly. . . . They enjoy being in one another's company, they enjoy doing things together. They are pleased when they are around each other. It is something to me that seems quite nice." [18] When two men in a couple were questioned separately how many times each had engaged in "copulation by mouth" or "masturbation by hand" with the other, each partner tried to place his sexuality in the context of their relationship. "Colonel, there is more to this business than just sex," offered one of the partners. "There is companionship. It is the same thing as a husband finds in a wife, as far as I can see." "It may sound funny to somebody else," the other partner added during his interrogation, "but I love him." [19]

Not all suspects evaded or redefined the questions they were asked. A few angrily defied their interrogators, despite their training to obey orders. A WAC lieutenant at Indiantown Gap, Pennsylvania, refused to answer questions about her sex life and categorically denied the interrogators' accusations. "Every time you kiss somebody," she snapped back at them, "you are classed as a homosexual, is that it?" The interrogation halted when she offered to submit her resignation from the Corps in protest. [20] Another WAC lieutenant grinned when she was accused of having an "abnormal relationship" with a WAC corporal. "About the only thing I want to do," she interrupted her interrogators, "is take all the blame for and clear the kid." [21] In New Caledonia, Fred Thayer at first refused to write out a confession, asking the officer " 'Have you ever sat down and written out all the details of the sexual relations with your wife?' " When discharge board officers started "firing questions" at John Hall "and just bugging me to death," he initially denied everything, but "finally I got to the point where I just thought, 'Oh well, to hell with it.' I said, 'Yes, I am a homosexual. I suck cock. I sucked every air force boy's cock on the grounds,' and I just read the riot act to them. That is what they wanted to know, so I told them." [22]

Psychiatric wards of military hospitals were the approved facilities for holding suspected homosexuals until their discharge. Because the military during the war discharged few women for homosexuality, it was rare for groups of lesbians to gather on psychiatric wards. [23] But so many gay men were hospitalized as homosexuals that in some psych wards they outnumbered all other patients. There they established new lines of defense against the military's actions against them. Sometimes drawing on their ability to "camp," gay patients developed a sense of camaraderie, privately helping each other overcome the demoralization and boredom of psych ward life.

Military hospitals ranged from mobile tents behind front lines, and the hundreds of station and general hospital buildings constructed during the war, to massive psychiatric institutions such as Saint Elizabeths Hospital in Washington, D.C. Small facilities placed their psychiatric patients on the same wards as medical and surgical patients, while larger hospitals placed them on separate psychiatric wards. Open wards were reserved for patients with mild conditions such as neuroses, epilepsy, bed-wetting, personality disorders, and homosexuality. Hospital staffs often allowed open-ward patients, including homosexuals, to walk around the grounds at designated times and even to leave the hospital on temporary passes. Locked wards housed patients who were considered dangerous to themselves or others.

But hospital administrators sometimes assigned homosexual patients to locked wards as a punishment or when open wards were overcrowded. "To make matters worse," William Menninger observed, "general prisoner patients (with their guards) were often housed in the closed psychiatric wards while awaiting transfer or examination. Another unwise practice," he added, "was the use of the closed-ward section as a detention ward." Closed wards were usually located off an isolated ramp to the rear of the hospital. "It was the exceptional visitor," noted Menninger, "or even inspector, who reached that far corner of the hospital." [24] Many patriotic gay soldiers and sailors felt betrayed by their government when they were thrown into locked wards with violent psychotics, suspected criminals, and prisoners of war.

Gay patients filled the long hours in the hospitals by writing letters, playing cards, listening to the radio or phonograph, reading out-of-date magazines, talking, arguing, or just staring out the window. Meals in the mess hall, inspections, discharges, new admissions, visits from Red Cross volunteers, and changes in the nurses' and ward attendants' shifts were the only breaks in the dull routine of each day. Because they were "sick," these patients had to exchange their uniforms for robes and pajamas, which they wore wherever they went.

Lax supervision enabled some gay patients to slip away from the hospital to join their friends. Pvt. Howard Taylor, who was admitted to the hospital at Camp Crowder, Missouri, knew that his conspicuous blue robe and pajamas would have prevented him from leaving the ward undetected. So, in his effort to become a "Service Club Commando," he wrote to a gay pal, "I swipe the ward boy's clothes and make for Service Club 2 to get a fresh supply of Tareytons and to watch Tony, Marty, Daniela, and the rest [of the gay crowd] go through their routines." [25] "Every evening," Corporal Martz wrote to Taylor several months later from the station hospital's Ward D-5 at Torrance, California, "we dash down to the Special Service department and play 'cocktail lounge' for Marty's sake, and Sheila Barrett records for mine!" [26]

When they couldn't meet at the service club or were transferred to other bases, these and several other gay GIs from Camp Crowder kept their tight-knit group together by writing letters, sometimes daily. Howard Taylor, one of the first in his crowd to be hospitalized, wrote to his pals to explain how the homosexual discharge system actually worked, inspiring some of his friends similarly to declare themselves.

While he awaited word from his disposition board, he received a letter from his friend J. D., who was stationed at Camp Livingston in Louisiana. "What technique did you use to get into the hosp.?" J. D. asked. "Don't be afraid to divulge any trade secrets," he added, hinting that he too was gay, "I've joined the trade. . . . Perhaps I'll follow in your feetsteps and go from here to the hospital . . . and eventually get a discharge." Five months later, after Taylor had been discharged, J. D. wrote that he had finally declared himself. "I am now in 4-D— Psycho—Pending Disposition," which was "so easy," he added, "I'm sorry I didn't try it a year or so ago." [27]

In their letters to each other, these gay patients shared the pain and despair over their common plight as well as the fate of all young men as soldiers during a time of global war. "Sometimes I think our lives are always going to be a hell," Marty Klausner wrote to Taylor from his hospital ward at Torrance, California. "You can't blame it on the army—it's the whole damn world and we were just born at the wrong time. God knows I have no flag-waving patriotism. I only love the land and my heart goes out to the youth—the virile youth who dies a thousand deaths hourly. . . . I would like to clasp all those boys to my heart and comfort them and I don't mean sexually. . . . Howard, we must remain friends and someday, God knows when, but some day we can help each other." [28] "Never forget," Taylor replied to a friend from his hospital bed, "that our bunch is going to get someplace if it kills us! Parents, . . . morals, conventions, money be damned. Agreed? Love, love, love, and here's to us all." [29] Few others than fellow gay patients could give these GIs such affirmations of friendship, love, and courage while they were incarcerated on psychiatric wards.

The humor, irony, and drama of "camping" helped some gay patients relieve tensions, escape the drab regimentation of the military hospital and strengthen their bonds with each other. Privately acting out the roles of famous stars and movie queens, they created an illusion of glamor and even power that lifted their spirits from depression. "Marty and I," Tommy Martz wrote to Taylor, "currently playing Ward D-5, are doing a revival of 'The Gay Sisters'. . . . Sunday, according to the Red Cross Schedule, some group is going to present 'The Women' here—God I would love to do Sylvia [Rosalind Russell's role] for them, but in this blue robe I am dressed more for a part in 'Boy's Town.' " Martz even dramatized his and Klausner's interviews with psychiatrists as if they were auditions for Hollywood films. "Marty is terribly burned up," Martz wrote after his first interview, "because I have done more 'story conference' with the psychiatrist than he. . . . Marty is in conference with the Sam Goldwyn of Ward D-5, the man in full charge of the entire production, so now neither of us have anything to look forward to other than the, as yet, unwritten finale, and a few well deserved curtain calls." [30] Gay patients sometimes broke out of these private conversations to indulge in more outrageous campy antics in public. Private First Class Klausner was amazed at how bold some of the other gay GIs had become in the hospital at Camp Anza, California. "One called Terry," he wrote to Taylor, "would scream out loud all over the place. . . . 'I'm getting cornholed by my country.' " [31]

Ironically, thrown together on psych wards because of their homosexuality and no longer having to keep up the charade of heterosexuality, gay patients had great opportunities to flirt and even have sex with other men. Army chaplain Chuck Tarrance led an active sexual life on the officers' psychiatric ward at the Army hospital in McKinney, Texas. "I met this one officer," he recalled, "who had a room across the hall from me. We played tennis and got talking. He wanted to know what my problem was so I told him. He invited me over to his room that night. I just did him. And then the next night he came over to my room and did me. And then another night or so later I went to the movies. Of course we didn't wear uniforms, so we wore robes and pajamas. [I] sat next to a young man and all of a sudden we were rubbing knees, and he wound up in my room later that night. And then we had a few sessions down by the pond on the grounds."

In the locked wards, where patients could not escape for nightly visits to the service club, the movies, or romantic trysting spots, some gay GIs found themselves outnumbered by psychotics and even German and Italian prisoners of war. To maintain their self-esteem under such humiliating conditions, they banded together, sometimes trying to organize campy activities with other inmates. When, in December 1943, Pvt. Norman Sansom was admitted to a locked psychiatric ward at Walterboro Army Air Field in Georgia, he discovered that all the other 'patients' were German prisoners of war except for two other gay American soldiers. Making the best of a bad situation, the three gay patients cheered themselves up by teaching the Germans how to sing "This Is the Army, Mr. Jones," Irving Berlin's catalog of the discomforts of Army life. "I can still hear them now on the ward," Sansom recalled. "Every morning we'd have our little 'musicale.' They couldn't speak any English at all, but they were able to sing, 'Dis is dee Army, Mister Shones.' "

During outbreaks of antigay witch hunts and purges, suspected homosexuals were locked up, sometimes for months, in what GIs called "queer stockades," "queer brigs," and "pink cells." These ranged from pup tents and psychiatric restraint rooms to entire Quonset huts (prefabricated shelters made from arches of corrugated metal), barracks, and sections of brigs or stockades. More punitive than even the locked psych wards, these makeshift homosexual detention facilities were outgrowths of the penal system, although their gay inmates were seldom put on trial. Unlike patients in the psych wards, men in the queer stockades were often placed under armed guard in full view of other GIs rather than hidden away in the back wards of hospitals.

By the middle of the war, the witch hunts and purges that filled these queer stockades erupted at many military installations overseas, even as policymakers in Washington were making efforts to better utilize homosexual personnel. These occurred in part because the military's expanding antihomosexual apparatus enabled hostile officers in the field to round up large numbers of gay soldiers without putting them on trial. Morally vigilant chaplains, intelligence officers, and MPs took it upon themselves to initiate antihomosexual crusades, casting the eye of suspicion on ever-widening circles of suspects in witch hunts that were difficult to contain. A single rumor that someone was gay, if not put to rest by a commanding officer, could spread like wildfire and lead to a full-scale purge, filling the stockades with suspected "queers" who were held for interrogation. Witch hunts were also set in motion when police pressured civilians and military personnel arrested in bar raids to name their friends and sexual partners in exchange for their own release. During such roundups, by spreading fear and panic, antihomosexual crusaders often sacrificed valuable personnel and seriously threatened order and discipline in an outfit or a whole region.

Secret proposals to incarcerate homosexuals more systematically in formal detention camps rather than in makeshift queer stockades were discussed by Navy officials at least twice during the war. The earliest proposal came in 1942 from Comdr. F. M. Harrison, a liberal reformer in the Navy Surgeon General's Office who actively promoted discharge rather than the imprisonment of homosexuals. Writing to Winfred Overholser, Harrison raised the theoretical problem of whether to discharge homosexual officers who had access to secret codes and who might reveal them to the enemy out of resentment for their discharges. He suggested that "confinement . . . in the interest of national security" was indicated for these men.[32] Six weeks later, Navy Surgeon General Ross McIntire suggested that members of the proposed officer boards charged with reviewing each homosexual case should determine whether the man was a threat to military security. If so, he would be "committed into protective custody for safety purposes, not punishment, and placed in a suitable detention camp for the duration of the war." [33] This was the same national security argument used to intern West Coast Japanese Americans who, like homosexuals, had been convicted of no criminal act. Fortunately, the Navy's 1943 homosexual policy directive included no provision for setting up such camps.

In 1944 the more hard-line commandant of the 8th Naval District in New Orleans, A. C. Bennett, who wanted to imprison rather than discharge homosexuals, reopened the discussion of homosexual detention camps. In July Bennett dispatched a confidential letter to Secretary of the Navy Frank Knox reporting on a purge in April of thirty Navy officers and enlisted men in New Orleans. Bennett warned that the discharge of these and other homosexual servicemen posed a moral threat to civilian society. He wanted the Navy to establish a separate institution where "homosexuals and/or perverts should be segregated . . . for the duration of the war . . . for the good of the military service but also [as] an obligation which the Navy owes to society generally." In response Knox asked his bureau chiefs for their comments. Randall Jacobs, chief of Naval Personnel, argued against the idea. The Navy's job, he maintained, was to win the war, not to protect civilian society from homosexuals. "The interest of the Navy in these cases lies first in punishment for violence and secondly in speedy elimination." Navy Surgeon General Ross McIntire concurred. Secretary Knox rejected the proposal.[34] However, commanding officers at bases where witch hunts broke out still had to decide where to put the growing number of suspected homosexuals who were rounded up.

Because antigay witch hunts were conducted under a cloak of wartime censorship and secrecy, it is difficult to determine how widespread they were, where they took place, and how many men or women were targeted. Gay GIs exchanged and embellished their own stories about what they had seen or heard. They told how thousands were rounded up at staging ports in New Caledonia and Australia, where men were stationed for long periods of time awaiting transfer to combat areas in the South Pacific. They told stories of how General MacArthur's staff was shaken by a purge, how Axis intelligence triggered witch hunts at American bases in England before D day and in the South Pacific during the troop buildup in 1945 to disrupt troop morale, and how hundreds of gay troops were rounded up on Midway Island, in the Aleutians, and on various naval vessels. Many of these stories described hundreds of men packed onto "queer ships" and sent back to the States for discharge. "The Australian one supposedly included between 300 and 500 military personnel," recalled Stuart Loomis. "They rounded them up and put them in stockades, in concentration camp kind of conditions, and jammed them onto ships and shipped them back to San Francisco." [35]

While these stories may have been exaggerated as they became part of the gay folklore of World War II, many were based on fact. The few military records that do refer to local witch hunts, at times not even naming the location, confirm that they targeted anywhere from a dozen to hundreds of GIs and officers in any one purge. In November 1943 the commandant of the Marine Corps, Joseph H. McDowell, reported that ten marines and "thirty-odd officers and men of the naval service" stationed at an unidentified South Pacific base were rounded up and issued undesirable discharges as homosexuals. [36] In April 1944 a Navy investigation into homosexual activities in New Orleans concluded with the arrests and discharges of forty-seven men: seven Navy officers, ten Army officers, twenty-three sailors, and seven soldiers. [37] Also in 1944, the Army provost marshal USASOS (U.S. Army Services of Supply [Southwest Pacific]) reported that twenty-one officers and 201 soldiers— many of them black—stationed in Australia were discharged as homosexuals. [38] Investigations and discharges of pairs of women also took place at WAC training centers in Daytona Beach, Florida, in 1943 and at Fort Oglethorpe, Georgia, in 1944. [39] Victims of the purges, however, tell a more detailed story than these mere numbers reveal.

Gay GIs were often shocked when military police arrived unannounced at their barracks or posts, seized them, and took them away to be locked up. In 1943 Bill Thompson was assigned to the base communications office as radioman on Admiral Halsey's COMSOPAC (Commander of the South Pacific) staff in Noumea, New Caledonia. Part of his job was to file dispatches, including SOSs from ships in trouble. "I was in the office," he recalled, "and glanced up and there was an MP officer with his gun and a marine guard. And they called out, 'Is there a Thompson here?' And I said yes. 'Will you come with us, please?' I said, 'Well, what for?' 'We just want to ask you some questions.' They just whisked me away! It was like the SS coming in the middle of the night in Germany." When Woodie Wilson and his buddy "Kate" were rounded up and charged with misusing government property to publish their clandestine gay newsletter, *The Myrtle Beach Bitch,* military police arrested them at their posts and escorted them to their barracks. "The provost marshal was there," Wilson recalled, "with two MPs apiece at our bunks. And right in front of us, they picked up our footlockers, took them away, and put us into the stockade, surrounded by barbed wire.''

As they were thrown into the makeshift stockades, gay prisoners immediately faced the terror of not knowing what was going to happen to them. Some were locked up at first in small cells by themselves. It was in a small wooden cell in New Caledonia that Fred Thayer, frightened and alone, first had thoughts of killing himself. ''I had a sweatshirt with me,'' he recalled, ''and I tried twisting it around my neck until it hurt, and [I] said, 'This is pointless. I don't want to do this,' and I didn't.'' Through the little square hole in the door he looked out and saw a friend from a cavalry company in another cell. As their number increased, inmates were transferred to larger facilities. Bill Thompson was in his brig cell in Noumea ''for a day by myself,'' he recalled. The guards then moved him in with other suspected homosexuals at another brig. ''We were in single little wooden cells. We could call out to each other and find out who was down there. 'Oh God! Did they get ''her'' too?' The cells were all full, and there were seven or eight across from me and I was in one of the seven or eight on this side, with a little pathway between the two sides.'' When these cells were full, guards moved Thompson and the other men to a large Quonset hut on a hill, where they were kept under twenty-four-hour armed guard. David Barrett, a storekeeper first class who was seized in the same purge, recalled that he was ''number 24 that arrived in the Quonset hut and the other men said, 'Oh, there's another one arriving.' Two more came after that.'' Barrett remembered staying in the Quonset hut for thirty-four days; Thompson remembered being there for two months or more.

When more men were rounded up than a Quonset hut, stockade, or locked psychiatric ward could hold, barbed wire fences were erected around buildings to cage the extra men.[40] Stan Carlow and dozens of other men seized during an Army purge in Australia were admitted to a series of hospital wards as mental patients. As their number grew they were transferred to a large hospital outside of Brisbane. ''By this time there were twenty to thirty men all in this hospital,'' Carlow recalled. ''Part of us were put into a ward for nervous cases and mental disorders, and the others were put into a unit behind barbed wire and treated just like insane people.'' Frank Jacober, a cannoneer who served in New Guinea and the Philippines, also recalled seeing at another Army hospital in the South Pacific a compound surrounded by barbed wire which was full of ''twenty-five or thirty guys'' who were suspected homosexuals. Inside were Army cots with blankets. ''It was the bare minimum they gave them for survival," he explained. "They could walk around the compound behind the wires and that was about it as far as I could tell."

As in the psych wards, gay prisoners in the stockades who could "camp it up" were a welcome relief from boredom. But as the conditions of their incarceration grew more severe, "camping" became more than comic relief and those who could camp often assumed leadership roles. David Barrett believed that Bill Thompson's campy sense of humor literally saved him from total despair. "He was such a wit and so very good," Barrett explained, "we're all indebted to him—or 'her'—for keeping our spirits up." "I did a lot of camping," Thompson admitted, "and carrying on and joking and kept things going." It was Thompson's idea to name "a lot of the kids" with drag nicknames, in the process welcoming newcomers into the group. When a very young and "nelly" black sailor was thrown into the Quonset hut, he too asked for a campy name, so Thompson named him "Hildegarde." "He loved it!" Thompson recalled. "At the time, Hildegarde was that café society singer, sophisticated and all. And I explained who Hildegarde was and it just made him love it even more." Thompson named himself "Rebecca." "I got my name from the movie, which had come out before the war. 'The Lovely and Ever Gracious Rebecca de Winter,' as they say in the film." [41]

In the stockades gay inmates not only used their theatrical flair to lift their own spirits but also directed it toward the armed guards, wielding it like a weapon to taunt their tormentors. Outdoor shower stalls sometimes became the stage for their most outrageous acts. "We used to have to go take showers daily," Barrett recalled, "and we would astound the guards around the shower. We would soap Hildegarde down, just cover her with soapsuds except for her little nitty-gritty, and scream and holler. We were the talk of the whole base. They wondered how in the name of God those queens [could] have such a great time!" Behind these taunts were reservoirs of suppressed anger. "I was getting madder and madder and gayer and gayer!" recalled Woodie Wilson about his incarceration in South Carolina. "I didn't give a shit. I was just giving hell to everybody. When we showered, I carried on, 'screaming' like a queen. The guards kept saying, 'That Wilson, watch him. He's our problem.' I was called in to the provost marshal several times. He said, 'Will you quiet it down? Quit screaming like a sissy.' I had been locked up in a cage in that stockade. I felt very humiliated. Yet I don't think I was ever gayer! I must have made more wisecracks in that stockade and had more fun. Kate would scream out, 'Oh shut up, Woodesia!'

She called me Woodesia and I called her Kate. You see," he explained, *"we kept it up!"*

The men in the stockades used some of their time together to devise common strategies for dealing with the interrogations. Woodie Wilson and Kate made a pact with each other not to give away names. "The investigation went on slowly," Wilson recalled. "We would be interviewed one day, then we'd work for two weeks. Then we'd be interviewed three times in one day. We never gave them the names of anybody. We refused. We said we didn't know." Navy interrogators in Noumea also took the men out of the Quonset hut one by one to get them to confess. The inmates would talk among themselves, Thompson recalled, "and try to determine what there was to be done. And there was nothing to be done. We were all told individually that if we didn't confess we were just going to stay in the brig forever. And as soon as we signed our statements that we were homosexuals, we would be processed and freed. Well, some did it right away and they disappeared. A lot of us just held on and tried to fight it all off. But there was really nothing to do. So finally, I just signed."

Gay inmates had mixed feelings toward other gay GIs in the stockade who succumbed to the pressure to name names. "It hurts to say," David Barrett recalled, "but the ONI [Office of Naval Intelligence] used to come and take that yeoman out and take him someplace in the jeep during the daytime and interrogate him [and he would name someone else]. Then we'd have one more [suspected homosexual] added to the group." Bill Thompson was careful about condemning the others who "sang" (named names), especially "Dottie," the enlisted man whose confession Thompson believed began the witch hunt at Noumea and who was locked up with the rest. "Had she not sung," Thompson explained, "why, a whole lot of this would never have happened. But she was still part of the crowd."

To punish as well as control the inmates of queer stockades, commanding officers, provost marshals, and MPs segregated them into special work details and during meals in the mess halls, as well as in their living quarters. "Every morning," Stan Carlow recalled, he and his fellow gay inmates at the hospital in Brisbane "were all called out together as a little group and given some little work detail to do like raking leaves or picking up cigarette butts. We were all kept together in one group away from the other men." The segregation of suspected homosexuals in stockade living quarters, however, was controversial.

Some officers feared that homosexual men sleeping in the same barracks would have sex with each other, while others believed that heterosexual men needed protection and should not be housed with homosexuals. In April 1944 the Prisoner of War Division of the Provost Marshal General's Office in Washington asked the Surgeon General's Office for advice concerning the "segregation of homosexuals" in stockades. The surgeon general replied that the "general policy of segregation in work details is approved" for homosexuals, but that segregation "as a group in quarters is undesirable," recommending instead "individual isolation." [42]

The physical isolation of each suspected homosexual, however, particularly in large roundups, was impractical. At most queer stockades, the provost marshal or other officer in charge put gay men together in segregated quarters but kept them under twenty-four-hour guard. Frank Jacober recalled that at the compound of suspected homosexuals he saw in the South Pacific, armed guards were stationed inside the barbed wire so that the men were "never allowed to touch each other. I mean they couldn't even help each other. It was terrible." David Barrett remembered that when he was incarcerated late in 1943 in a queer barracks attached to a receiving hospital at Camp Shoemaker, near Pleasanton, California, the guards thought the gay inmates "were going to be pairing off with one another." Their solution was to make the men "sleep with the lights on all night long with guards patrolling outside" to make sure they didn't have sex. "To this day," Barrett recalled in 1983, "I cannot sleep with any light on."

The provost marshal at Myrtle Beach, South Carolina, did physically isolate Woodie Wilson and his buddy Kate from the other men in the stockade barracks. A work detail "built two special cells," Wilson recalled, "out of two-by-fours around our beds. That gave us just enough space to turn around and pass cigarettes through the bars. We were kept there at night because they wouldn't trust us with the rest of the prisoners. Real caged pigeons," Wilson added, "only I guess we were called the peacocks. We were not allowed to go around from bunk to bunk, like all the other prisoners and visit and talk. But we could talk to them through the bars and they'd talk to us. We were treated rather good by the inmates themselves. They didn't ostracize us. But that was the nearest to segregation I have ever in my life known as a white man." He believed that Kate and he "were in that stockade over three and a half months awaiting trial."

Gay men who were locked up sometimes were terrorized by sadistic guards who, in the private areas of the stockades, subjected them to psychological torture. "They treated us like scum," recalled Bill Thompson, who was placed with other men from Noumea under Marine Corps guard in the brig at Treasure Island Naval Station in San Francisco. "The head of the brig said, 'You sons of bitches are going to eat out of garbage cans! Get the fuck out of here!' That's what they said to us. It was terrible to go through that when you are basically genteel and fun-loving and you didn't rob somebody or hit him with an axe or shoot him or kill somebody's wife." "You wouldn't believe the treatment in the brig," added David Barrett, who was also shipped to Treasure Island. "There was a guy called Big John. He lined us up in front of all the inmates there who were murderers, rapists, thieves—everything you could think of. He lined us up and he just tore us apart. He told all the rest of them that he thought more of them because we were the scum of the fucking earth." [43]

Some guards threatened the men's lives. As David Barrett and his gay brigmates were transferred from Treasure Island to Camp Shoemaker, in Pleasanton, California, they were thrown into the back of a truck. "Two young marines got in the truck with us," Barrett recalled. "They said, 'Don't open your mouth!' And they sat there with their finger on the trigger of the gun aimed at us the whole drive over there. When we got out of that van, there was a lieutenant there and he said, 'Why didn't you shoot the motherfuckers!' That's how we were greeted."

Some guards stationed at the stockades believed that homosexual inmates were available to them for sexual services and abused their power accordingly. At Treasure Island, Bill Thompson recalled, the "marines would come by and they'd get a detail from the brig to go do something. There were three marines; they picked three of us. The marines just took them off somewhere and got blowjobs. Then their buddies would come by. The thing is, the kids that were doing it had to do people they didn't want to do. I managed to not be near the cell bars when the guards came by." David Barrett reported similar sexual abuse at the Quonset hut in Noumea, where the Marine guards nightly escorted one man to the outdoor latrine to use him for their own pleasure. "The guards were all getting done," Thompson explained, "and then guarding the people that were blowing them! How do you like that! So if it came down to it, they could have put the whole goddamn armed forces in the brig!" [44]

While this kind of abuse took place under cover, other officers more openly subjected homosexuals to public humiliation. Their strict segregation stigmatized gay inmates as a group, especially on the way from their barracks to the mess hall. When the men in Noumea had to walk the quarter mile from the Quonset hut to the mess hall, David

Barrett recalled, "we folded our arms in front of us. The rest of the hillside was lined with thousands of guys waiting to go to chow, and the minute we'd start down, there'd be whistles all over the place. 'Oh, here come the girls!' And it was a rough experience to go through." When the men finally reached the mess hall, Bill Thompson added, "they cleared the chow hall at a special time for us to eat." After their meal the men again ran the gauntlet outside. " 'Hey, fuckin' fruits! Hey, queers!' " Thompson remembered them saying. "It was just humiliating to go through that three times a day." Norman Sansom remembered such an experience in Georgia as "one of the most traumatic things in my life. I just felt all of these eyes upon me and could hear 'fairy,' 'fruit,' 'cocksucker,' and I just wanted to block it out of my mind. It was almost like being in front of a firing squad." Such open displays of hatred destroyed whatever live-and-let-live tolerance the soldiers may have felt toward gay soldiers in combat and other isolated areas.

Although segregation itself humiliated these men, officers on some bases devised especially sadistic ways to intensify the degradation of gay GIs in front of the other men. Veterans who were stationed in the South Pacific during the war described seeing outdoor pens, some with signs that said QUEER STOCKADE or QUEER BRIG, that caged one or more servicemen awaiting discharge for homosexuality, sometimes exhibiting them for months at a time. Fred Thayer was thrown into one of these pens when he was returned to his original outfit while the authorities were deciding what to do with him. This particularly cruel form of abuse, together with the routine parading of homosexual inmates to and from their stockades, not only punished these men but also dramatized the military's power over them and used them as examples to teach everyone not to associate with homosexuals or become known as homosexual. Such rituals terrified other gay GIs into deeper isolation and discouraged sexual relationships between any servicemen.

Some eyewitnesses responded to such public degradations by taunting the men; others reacted with shock and fear. Gay onlookers sometimes resolved never to have sex again. "Imagine what that did to everybody looking at the fellow!" declared Army Air Corps veteran Richard Bernstein, who saw such a "queer pen" on a Navy base in the South Pacific. "The other guys laughed about it and ridiculed him. I just didn't cotton to that kind of oppression at all. It was intimidating, to say the least." Men saw gay GIs dragged away in chains. "Whenever we pulled into a port," recalled Navy veteran Tony Isaacs, "everybody that wasn't on duty would always crowd along the rail and watch what was going on on the dock. Suddenly they took this kid O'Reilly off in chains.

Word was out that O'Reilly [a hospital corpsman] had sucked off a patient. . . . I never saw such a sad looking boy in my whole life when he went down that gangplank with his chains on. So that definitely strengthened my resistance to playing around in the navy." [45] Frank Jacober was also terrified when in the mess hall of an island hospital he saw a table of twenty-five to thirty gay patients sitting under armed guard. "I thought, 'Shit. I won't have sex with anyone. Forget it. I don't want to be treated like that.' "

The stigma created by these public humiliations placed gay inmates in a no-man's-land where it became difficult for anyone, including their friends, to defend or even visit them. When Ralph Davidson learned that his former boyfriend had been thrown into the stockade in Hawaii but didn't know why, he asked his commanding officer for permission to visit him. The CO, trying to protect Davidson from guilt by association, refused to give him a pass, knowing that the prisoner had been accused of homosexual activity. William Johnson put himself in jeopardy when he tried to console one of the gay men in the stockade at Tuskegee Army Air Field in Alabama. "I went up to him one morning," he recalled, "and I put my hand on him and said, 'It's terrible what's going on,' and he said, 'Stay away from me, or you'll be called one, too.' "

Although the risks were high, some men did visit the inmates of queer stockades. David Barrett recalled that at Camp Shoemaker, "no one came near the queer barracks except one chaplain. He was a sweetheart. He befriended us as much as he could." Frank Jacober used his status as a visiting soldier show producer with Special Services to go inside a queer stockade on a South Pacific island to talk to the men because he "felt so bad. I felt [it was] so inhumane to treat people this way. I just went past the guard," he recalled, "and he tried to stop me and I said, 'I'm not gay, I just want to talk to this man.' He said, 'What are you going to do, make fun of these queer guys?' I said, 'Yeah. Would you like that?' And he said, 'Yeah, that'd be fine. Go in and talk to them.' But I didn't really do that, ever. I didn't stay there that long. If you made more than one contact, you were suspected of being queer yourself."

Occasionally an officer risked his own reputation to reduce the humiliation these men had to endure. One commanding officer who had heard about the jeering of the gay inmates in Noumea intervened on their behalf. He gave the order, David Barrett recalled, that when the inmates went to the mess hall, "anyone that spoke to us out of line or said a word to us, we were to stop our line and tell the guards and that person who made the remark to us, he was to be brought in our line and marched into chow with us." As a result of his order, the jeering stopped.

The taunts, humiliation, and degradation took their toll on the men inside the stockades. David Barrett remembered that at Noumea, one of the sailors, a farm boy from South Dakota, had crying spells during the night. Some of the other "kids would cry and break down and withdraw from the rest and just stay in their bunks," Bill Thompson added. "I'd go and talk to some of them and do what I could. Some were really mentally scarred from the experience. I remember David [Barrett] was down. I mean, he just couldn't handle it. He had a kind of frightened, hunted look on his face." Thompson, trying to describe the emotional conditions in the stockade, explained that "it wasn't a concentration camp, but psychologically it was. We weren't going into ovens [and] we ate, but the rest of it was all there." He found strength to take care of the other men "from watching the people that were breaking down, if that makes any sense. I just didn't want to get like that and I decided I was going to handle it. And I did. There were times at night in my bunk when I was upset, but no one saw it or heard it."

When they were humiliated in public, gay GIs began to direct their "camping" not only to their guards but to the crowds of taunting onlookers, trying to defuse the hostility directed toward them by making the crowd into their audience. Performing as "queers" on these degrading stages, they danced a fine line between self-contempt and outrage, between acting the victim and surviving. A gay man's ability to "camp it up" in such desperate situations could be his last defense against hopelessness and even suicide.

When Fred Thayer and his gay buddies who had been rounded up in Noumea were shipped back to the States, they were thrown into the fo'c'sle of a passenger ship and kept under continuous armed guard. On their voyage across the Pacific, Thayer remembered one night "going out to the john and staring down the fo'c'sle and saying, 'Maybe it would be nice just to slip into that. It's all over.' Then I'd go back into bed." Every day, when he and his fellows in the ship's makeshift queer brig were taken out for "airings" under armed guard, the other men would "all come to the front of the deck to look down at the faggots." For someone in a deep depression, such humiliation could have put him over the edge. But Thayer's friend Arnie would not let him give in. Arnie "would usually put on his Mae West and he would do dance numbers and sing for them all. He said, 'They know we're a bunch of faggots. They want to look at us, so let's show them something! We can't just walk here and look like anybody else.' He was cheering me up and cheering everybody else up.''

When Jim Kuzell's ship landed at Noumea on the way to Espiritu Santo, he saw in the middle of the receiving station a ''queer compound'' surrounded by barbed wire with twenty or thirty men inside. He was distressed by their campy behavior. ''They'd come out around their fence and they would prance and be prissy. It hurt me to see it, because they were making fun of themselves. They swished up a storm and pretended to have big chandeliers and were just doing it like wild.'' So long as they still could ''camp it up,'' the men in the stockades were able to show everyone—and themselves—that the military was not yet powerful enough to make them give up being gay.

The placing of gay GIs on public display, as well as the secret disappearance of gay suspects in the night, taught other GIs and officers to be terrified of getting too close to each other and of associating with known ''queers.'' These fears deeply affected many more of the nation's young men than the several thousand who were discharged. James Michener, who served in the Navy in the South Pacific during the war, described in his 1947 collection of short stories *Tales of the South Pacific* how the fear of being accused could affect everyone in a Navy unit, causing them to fight ''against expressing friendliness or interest in any other man. From time to time horrifying stories would creep around a unit. 'Two men down at Noumea. Officers, too. Dishonorable discharge! Couple years at Portsmouth!' And everyone would shudder . . . and wonder.'' [46]

Private fears fueled public rumors of witch hunts that broadcast the harsh treatment of some homosexuals even further. Rumors could be as effective as public humiliation for inhibiting homosexual behavior. But the spread of fear was hard to control and easily backfired on military officials. It threatened morale and discipline by encouraging individual episodes of homosexual panic, self-declarations, suspicion, false accusations, and more witch hunts. As a result of their own policies and practices, military officials increasingly had to confront not only the disorder they perceived to be caused by the presence of known homosexuals, but also the disruption caused by antihomosexual fears that got out of hand.

Military authorities in Washington were well aware of how witch hunts could damage the effectiveness of the armed forces, displacing valuable manpower essential for fighting enemy forces. ''The War Department is concerned with the wholesale discharge of soldiers under the circumstances shown in these cases,'' the Army adjutant general in 1942 wrote to the commanding general of Moffett Field after the arrest of eight air corpsmen for sodomy. "The primary consideration should be . . . the preservation to the service of men possessing a salvage value." [47] The wartime constraints on witch hunts were perhaps the strongest in the Women's Army Corps, whose officials were acutely sensitive to the need to conserve personnel and to protect the Corps from "smear campaigns" that damaged its reputation and ability to recruit women. Lecturers warned officers not to "indulge" in such "witch hunting or speculating," and threatened them with punishment if they did. [48] WAC officials believed that rumor spreading and false accusations were more serious threats to the Corps than were lesbian relationships. [49]

Gay servicemen had their own folklore to explain how witch hunts were stopped. The basic story had many variations. One, according to Allan Fredericks, who served as a Navy doctor, was that the purge in New Caledonia ended when "a high-ranking admiral told ONI to 'Lay off my district because you're taking some of my best people away and we've got to win this fucking war. Now back off!' " Burt Miller heard the story that General MacArthur, to stop a purge in his headquarters, "handed down the order: 'No more discharges for homosexuals because I do not want my staff ruined, and we have to win the war!' I'd hear that story over and over again, from one gay person to another." Miller believed that such stories were so popular because they proved to gay GIs and officers that, in his words, "We are indispensable. We are men. We *are* good fighters."

During a war in which American propaganda condemned the evils of fascism and intolerance, the men who had to endure brutal treatment for being gay—most of them draftees, some of them having risked their lives in combat—perceived the military as acting in ways that resembled the fascism they were supposed to be fighting. Whenever gay veterans, especially those locked up in queer stockades under armed guard, compared themselves to victims of the Nazis, they did not do so lightly. As Fred Thayer and his fellow inmates—who were labeled with tags hanging from their shirts that said "Psychopathia Sexualis"—were being transported from the hospital in New Caledonia to a ship's queer brig, the truck stopped at a disciplinary barracks to pick up Thayer's friend from the cavalry company, whom he hadn't seen in weeks. "He crawled into the back of the truck," Thayer recalled, "looking like something from Dachau. I'll never forget it. He took one look at me and fell in my arms and cried for the next hour and a half." From his own ordeal, Thayer weighed "only 112 and I looked like a skeleton, like I'd been through hell. In a way I suppose I had. But it wasn't [from] the Japanese and guns.''

Although they remained patriotic Americans, many gay GIs and officers who were interrogated, incarcerated, and publicly disgraced during the war wondered why they were treated as if they had become the enemy. Forced to fight two wars, the several thousand gay servicemen, and at least dozens of lesbians, who were caught up in the new discharge system had to learn how to defend themselves with either declarations or denials of their homosexuality. Whenever the military waged its sporadic little wars against them, some of these men and women were broken in defeat and others managed not to surrender, but few saw victory.

Ironically, the extreme and sometimes violent measures taken against gay men and women, especially when they had been convicted of no crimes, often forged bonds of comradeship among them as victims of injustice that strengthened their sense of being members of a persecuted minority. Despite their defeats, the inmates of queer stockades still rattled their prison bars with outrageously campy behavior and used their segregation to help one another get through each day. Backed into corners by the military's growing obsession with identifying homosexuals, gay male and lesbian dischargees learned a hard lesson—their ability to defend themselves, and to remain ''gay'' despite what they had to endure, held the key not only to their survival but also to who they were.

CHAPTER
9

Rights, Justice, and a New Minority

Gay male and lesbian veterans returned home having undergone their own sexual revolution during the war. Many had overcome their sense of being alone—they had formed cliques, found the gay life, and discovered the situational homosexuality of their heterosexual peers. At the same time the military had reinforced their gay identity by beginning to manage them as homosexual persons in its screening, antivice, and discharge policies, as well as in the practice of utilizing them in stereotyped jobs, sending them to the fighting fronts, and tolerating them where necessary. Coming home with a stronger sense of themselves as gay men and women and feeling closer ties with each other, they had new expectations as they reentered civilian life.

The gay veteran's change in outlook after the war was most dramatic among those who had received undesirable discharges for homosexuality. As participants in a public campaign to end the stigma and discrimination they faced as civilians, many of these men and women helped shape the idea that homosexuals had rights, could engage in their own fight for justice, and constituted a political minority.

Gay veterans with "blue" or undesirable discharges, as they left behind the abuse and humiliation they had undergone in the military, faced additional punishment when they returned to civilian life. In the Army the gay male blue-discharge veteran was put through a series of humiliations from the moment he left his base. He was stripped of his service awards, medals, rank, and uniform and taken by bus or truck to a discount men's clothing shop where, sometimes still wearing his hospital pajamas and robe, he was allowed to buy a cheap suit of clothes. Then he was brought to a train or bus station and given a one-way ticket home, where he had to report to his local draft board to present his discharge papers. Stan Carlow, who was shipped with dozens of other men from an Army queer stockade in Australia to Fort Lawton, Washington, was stripped of his Coral Sea badge and told that if he ever tried to serve his country in uniform again, he would be put in federal prison. The Navy gave similar treatment to its men.

The stigma attached to these discharges was not an accident of bureaucratic oversight. It had been instituted by hard-line military officials to punish homosexuals and to prevent masses of well-adjusted gay soldiers and heterosexual malingerers from escaping compulsory military service by "confessing" homosexuality. Army and Selective Service requirements that the veteran report to his draft board ensured that his community would find out the nature of his discharge because the clerk and board members did not have to keep this information confidential. Gay blue-discharge veterans thus were faced with the sometimes all-consuming task of hiding the nature of their discharges. They lied, altered their papers, and forged new ones. When their efforts at covering up failed, they were forced to come out to their families and communities, often in fear, humiliation, and self-contempt. "The only effort in life of many people with this type of discharge," noted Navy psychiatric consultant Francis Braceland, "is directed to removing the stigma." [1] Wherever blue-discharge veterans lived, employers, schools, insurance companies, veterans' organizations, and other institutions could use their bad discharge papers to discriminate against them on the basis of their undesirable status or their homosexuality. Sometimes their lives became so unbearable as exposed homosexuals that they had to leave home or tried to kill themselves.

One of the most vindictive punishments meted out to these veterans was the denial of GI benefits. In June 1944 Congress had passed the Servicemen's Readjustment Act, better known as the GI Bill of Rights, in a spirit of generosity and gratitude toward American men and women in uniform. The bill's provisions, together with legislation passed on state and local levels, entitled World War II veterans who had not been convicted of a military crime to receive a large package of benefits. They were eligible for federally subsidized home loans; college loans with allowances for subsistence, tuition, and books; farm and business loans with access to surplus government property; unemployment allowances; job training and placement programs; burial allowances; subsidized life insurance; disability pensions and insurance; hospital care; personal adjustment counseling; physical rehabilitation; and cash bonuses. These benefits were far more extensive than those the federal government had granted to the veterans of World War I.[2]

Top officials at the Veterans Administration were responsible for denying blue-discharge veterans these benefits. Charged with implementing the GI Bill, the VA did so in a discriminatory manner. It allowed employers to give job preference to white veterans over black, generally denied all blue-discharge veterans GI benefits, and in April 1945 issued an instruction that singled out gay blue-discharge veterans for ineligibility. "An undesirable or blue discharge issued because of homosexual acts or tendencies," the instruction read, "generally will be considered as under dishonorable conditions and a bar to entitlement." This discriminatory practice was at odds with the Army's policy of issuing dishonorable discharges only to personnel convicted of a military crime, and at odds with the GI Bill of Rights, in which Congress had specified that only veterans with dishonorable discharges could be denied benefits. The VA's moral judgment of each blue-discharge veteran and its antihomosexual bias drew the wrath of Congress and many citizens, including gay veterans and their friends. Nevertheless the VA renewed its antihomosexual instruction in October 1946 and again in October 1949.[3]

Such calculated stigmatization and discrimination made it even more difficult for blue-discharge veterans to adjust to civilian life. When they applied to the Veterans Administration for unemployment insurance and small business, housing, or college loans, they were usually denied assistance. They faced similar difficulties in college admissions offices and personnel offices. "Many of them kind of crumbled," recalled Stuart Loomis of the gay blue-discharge veterans he knew, "and didn't find a place for themselves in the world." This discrimination took place while other World War II veterans—a generation that had grown up during the depression—were beginning to use the GI Bill to improve their lives.

The ordeal of Marty Klausner after he was discharged, which he chronicled in letters to his friend Howard Taylor, exemplifies some of the problems gay blue-discharge veterans faced in trying to readjust to civilian life. By June 1945 Klausner had returned home to Pittsburgh to live with his parents and find work. He first reported to the local VA office with his blue discharge, where he was "more or less interviewed and made out an application for schooling. I then casually asked whether I would have any trouble getting it and they said I would." Klausner believed that when the VA found out the "real reason for my discharge" then "the jig will be definitely up." He called his friend Tony, who had also received a blue discharge, to see how the VA had responded and found out that Tony's "education was stopped and that now he is paying his own way."

At the same time Klausner had started job hunting and faced new problems. He applied for "a terrific job at the largest hotel in P[ittsburgh]. the William Penn—night room clerk—11 to 7AM—easy work and $120 a month." But when the personnel officer "asked to see my discharge— she studied it for a while and then copied down 615-368 and sent me to see another man who after about two words sent me back to the woman who said she was terribly [sorry] but I simply wouldn't do because she had called the Vets Ad and had of course found out that I was an undesirable." [4]

In September Klausner decided to apply to the University of Pittsburgh to get his music-teaching certificate, although he knew that he risked being denied admission, a teaching certificate, and a job. "Nevertheless," he wrote to Taylor, "I thought it out from all angles and it seems sensible to take these risks because if it does work I will at least be able to earn a living and that is something that I can't adequately do at present." Despite the obstacles Klausner was accepted into the university and got a job working at a department store.[5] But in April 1946 he lost his job because the department store replaced him with "returning service men who had [formerly] worked there." His blue discharge made him ineligible for unemployment compensation, "so at present I have no income." Unable to earn money, he spent his time "helping my mother with the housecleaning." [6]

Klausner's chronicle of discrimination revealed how deeply the stigma of the blue discharge had affected him, filling him with frustration, anger, and despair. "Now what I want to know is this," he confided to Taylor after he was denied the hotel job. "Aren't we even going to be permitted to make an honest living[?] I have never been confronted with such a difficult problem before and I simply have no decent solutions." "It does seem that we're blocked every way we turn," he wrote three months later when he was afraid the university would also reject him, "and if it were something you could fight it would be different because I have it in me to fight but you simply can't. Surely to God there will be an answer some day. . . . You don't have a leg to stand on and how can you keep saying you won't let this lick you—I swear suicide is the only ultimate answer unless you could manage being a hobo and not give a damn." By January 1946 the uncertainty he faced was overwhelming him. "You asked me if I were really happy—" he wrote to Taylor, "hell no—I'm terrifically unhappy and I am constantly in a state of utter confusion as to what to do and where to turn. I find myself more and more taking consolation from the idea that this too shall pass away. . . . Why they don't round us all up and kill us I don't know." [7]

Among the earliest organized attempts to defend the rights of homosexuals in the United States were efforts to correct the injustices against the tens of thousands of blue-discharge veterans, including homosexuals. These efforts came not only from gay male and lesbian veterans themselves but from such institutions as the United States Congress, the Army Surgeon General's Office, the American Legion, the Congress of Industrial Organizations (CIO), the National Association For the Advancement of Colored People (NAACP), and the military and civilian press.

At first, blue-discharge veterans had no way of knowing how many others were going through the same ordeal. But by 1945 the press started publishing preliminary estimates of their number that helped these veterans realize they weren't the only ones. "The blue ticket has been issued to 47,000 men in the Army alone," reported the *Pittsburgh Courier* in November 1945.[8] By 1946 the government had released official estimates of Army blue-discharge veterans that ranged from forty-nine to sixty-eight thousand, a group that was mostly male and disproportionately black (ten thousand) and/or homosexual (five thousand). In addition the Navy gave tens of thousands of its veterans undesirable discharges, including four thousand homosexuals.[9] Most had been discharged for vague "undesirable traits of character" by officers who wanted to get rid of "problem" soldiers—blacks, homosexuals, and psychopathic personalities (alcoholics, drug addicts, liars, "troublemakers")—without giving them a court-martial.[10] Their number and the nature of their mistreatment triggered an organized campaign from late 1945 to early 1947 to protect their rights, promote their welfare, and abolish the blue discharge.

Concern for the rights of veterans with undesirable discharges was first expressed in Washington as early as 1944 when, during the debate over the GI Bill of Rights, members of Congress set up discharge review boards to "correct any inequity in the blue-discharge procedure." Congressman B. W. Kearny of New York, himself a retired Army major general, stated that men with blue discharges "in many instances were of excellent character, but the possession of such a discharge will brand them for life. . . . The provision of reviewing boards is an excellent one and will result in correcting many a rank injustice." [11] In 1945 this concern for blue-discharge veterans continued, spreading to GIs and various organizations as millions of veterans began to return home.

The postwar campaign to correct the injustices of blue discharges was initiated by advocates for black civil rights. From October to December 1945, the *Pittsburgh Courier*, the most widely read black newspaper in the United States,[12] started a "fight in behalf of veterans who are holders of blue discharges," making it clear that it was "fighting for the rights of the 37,000 white veterans involved as well as for those of the 10,000 Negroes involved." Branding the blue discharge "a vicious instrument which should not be perpetrated against the American Soldier," the *Courier* criticized the Army for "allowing prejudiced officers to use it as a means of punishing Negro soldiers who do not like specifically unbearable conditions." Some officers had interpreted "bona-fide resentment to racist treatment" as an "undesirable trait of character" among black soldiers and had discharged as many as fifty at a time. Army conditions were so "intolerable" for some black GIs that they were "feigning . . . homo-sexuality just to get out of the Army." [13]

The *Courier* listed homosexual veterans among the " 'unfortunates' of the Nation" who were "being preyed upon by the blue discharge" and asked "why the Army chooses to penalize these 'unfortunates' who seem most in need of Army benefits and the opportunity to become better citizens under the educational provisions of the GI Bill of Rights." The newspaper harshly criticized the VA for acting on its own to disqualify these veterans from GI benefits, accusing it of embarking on a "witch hunt" against blue dischargees. "There is no twilight between honor and dishonor," the *Courier* proclaimed, and challenged "the Nation to solidify its opinion on what should happen to the holder of the blue discharge. These are our forgotten men. The spirit of the GI law demands that Congress should make its position clear." [14]

The *Courier* reported that its campaign "brought an avalanche of letters from holders of the blue discharge and interested citizens who considered the situation an outrage." The newspaper wired Secretary of War Patterson requesting that he "abolish the blue discharge" and submitted a brief to United States Attorney General Tom Clark, who agreed to investigate the actions of the VA. The same week the CIO decided to "place its full strength behind the fight to place the blue discharge holder's case before the Nation." In early November an American Legion official told the newspaper that his organization would take up the matter in mid-November. By December 1, the *Courier* reported, a member of the White House staff "promised that President Truman would request that the Veterans' Administration issue clarifying instructions on those to be barred from rights under the GI Bill when holding the blue discharge. The President himself,'' the newspaper added, ''is said to have expressed interest in the move to help holders of the blue discharge.'' [15]

The crusade launched by the *Courier* quickly reached the halls of Congress. On November 8 Senator Edwin C. Johnson of Colorado, chairman of the Senate Veterans Committee, had the *Courier* editorials read into the *Congressional Record* and condemned the blue discharges from the Senate floor. ''There ought not be a twilight zone between innocence and guilt,'' he declared, adopting the *Courier*'s rhetoric. ''Blue discharges are certain to be a headache for Congress from now on.'' [16] In late November a representative of the *Courier* was called into conference with a member of the House Committee on Military Affairs, which subsequently appointed a special committee, chaired by Congressman Carl T. Durham of North Carolina, to study the inequities of blue discharges. On January 30, 1946, the committee issued its report. [17]

The House Report, ''Blue Discharges,'' expressed the same spirit of generosity and gratitude toward veterans that had informed Congress's passage of the GI Bill of Rights in 1944. It used a rhetoric of rights and injustice that explicitly mentioned gay dischargees as among those who had been treated unfairly. Although focusing on the male veteran in general, the report implicitly appreciated the predicament of gay male and lesbian dischargees. The House committee's description of the opposing risks of exposure and isolation faced by each blue-discharge veteran identified the same social forces that kept most homosexuals from speaking up in their own behalf. The congressmen were surprised to find that any blue-discharge veterans had risked exposing themselves to further stigmatization by protesting their mistreatment. ''It should be borne in mind,'' their report began, ''that even a moderate amount of complaint in a matter of this sort is significant. For a person to make such a complaint in his own case implies that he feels a sense of injustice so great that he is willing to risk publicizing the stigma of having been discharged from the Army under circumstances which savor of disgrace. For each complainant,'' the report added, ''there are many more persons who feel the same sense of injustice but prefer to bury their hurt in as much oblivion as possible.'' [18]

The committee staunchly defended the right of all citizens not to be persecuted by their government, suggesting that military officials had used blue discharges to avoid the more cumbersome court-martial procedures that better protected the rights of the accused. Because the Army wielded such tremendous power over so many individuals, Durham's committee cautioned, it bore a special responsibility not to use that power to ruin the lives of its veterans. "The Army is part of the Government of the United States," the congressmen explained, and "is, at the present time, the largest employer in the country [with] some 8,000,000 employees. Almost one-tenth of the entire population has been in the Army. . . . The condemnation or quasi-condemnation of this vast organization carries tremendous force against the individual. This force should not be used to crush the individual" who had been convicted of no crime. The committee reserved their harshest criticism for the Veterans Administration's mean-spirited handling of blue-discharge veterans. "It seems fairly clear that the generosity which Congress intended is being restricted" by the VA, which should be stopped "from passing moral verdicts on the history of any soldier." [19]

The Durham committee called for treating all blue-discharge veterans with "humaneness and even charity," particularly because most had been drafted and were very young. "They had no choice not to enter," they explained. "The Nation required their induction in the service." This fact "implies a responsibility in the treatment of those men even beyond that which might be called for in a completely voluntary army." If some of these men turned out to be "not readily adapted to military life" or "succumbed to temptations they never met until they entered the Army," then the nation "has a special obligation to see that they are dismissed with as little prejudice as possible." The Army "has the duty of ejecting them; but it has no right to make the remainder of their lives grievous" by discharging them "with what amounts to a disgrace for life." The report recommended abolishing the blue discharge.[20]

During the debate over blue discharges, some gay male and lesbian veterans watched hopefully as Congress conducted its hearings. In January 1946 Marty Klausner wrote to his friend Howard Taylor, also a blue-discharge veteran, that "we are considered to be in the 'twilight zone' " and that many public officials were saying that "something would have to be done" about the discrimination against them.[21] Other gay dischargees began to raise their voices in their own behalf, privately and even publicly. To make a case for their rights and to appeal for help from others in correcting the injustices against them, they wrote letters to newspaper editors and columnists, to their senators and congressional representatives, to the Red Cross, to Eleanor Roosevelt (who had a reputation for being the champion of the downtrodden, including black Americans and servicemen in trouble),[22] to the surgeons general and other military officials, and to doctors and psychiatrists. In these letters they spoke for themselves in less-constrained voices than they had used to defend themselves during psychiatric interviews and interrogations on the psych wards and in the queer stockades. Their letters followed similar patterns. They generally began with a declaration of their patriotism and an account of their service; then they described the military's injustices against them and concluded with an appeal for advice or support.

"Emmanuel" wrote such a letter asking the Red Cross for help in appealing his discharge. "The day I was inducted for service will long be remembered," he wrote. "I can well recall the tingle of proud excitement that filled me when I stood bareheaded under the glaring sun, repeating the oath of allegiance to our country. That oath I never once repudiated. From my rookie days to my very last day in the service, it was with respect for my fellow men and my officers alike. Yet I was discharged from the service without honor." After a year in the service, Emmanuel was hospitalized for a long period for a physical ailment. He became lonely and depressed, he wrote, and "needed someone very badly to confide in." He talked to his nurse, who betrayed his confidences by telling her superiors about his homosexuality. He was ordered to report to his chaplain, who "said he knew the reason for my distress, and I broke down and confessed my true self. The result was that I was given a blue discharge from the Army."

Emmanuel expressed his sense of injustice when he described the problems he faced as a blue-discharge veteran. "I found that my battle was just beginning," he wrote. "I couldn't go home without honor, and yet my desire to see my family was too strong to overcome. I came home with the lie that my discharge paper was to be forwarded. But my struggle continued. I couldn't face my draft board, and I couldn't apply for my ration book. All these people knew me and respected me. I had always been well liked in the community. I had taken part in our community drives and my friends had sought my advice. I had left home a somebody, and I came back a nobody—without honor." [23]

One lesbian veteran was so outraged by her treatment that she wrote a letter of protest for publication. In late 1945 the Army weekly *Yank* was filled with letters from GIs protesting the injustices of dishonorable and undesirable discharges. Among these was an anonymous letter from a former WAC officer who lived in Columbus, Ohio. "I firmly believe recipients of discharges other than honorable are, in their own unique way, branded for life," her letter began. "I feel I know wherein I speak, for my case is one of many who received the in-between discharges 'Without Honor'. . . . I served well for approximately three years," she continued, "as an officer in the WAAC and WAC. My efficiency ratings were 'Excellent,' and in due course I won my promotion.'' A brief affair with another woman, however, led to her forced resignation, a bad discharge, and the resulting hardships. "I am rather shocked and saddened to see my life in ruins at my feet," she explained. She had been unable to find a job because "most application forms require information on military service" and without showing her discharge she could not account for her work during the war. "The public in general is uneducated in the psychology of handling my type of discharge," she continued, "hence I find it embarrassing and impossible to elucidate upon just why I left the WAC." Her letter concluded with an appeal to the GI reader's sense of fairness. "Many Army medical doctors," she wrote, "believe strongly concerning the injustice of this situation. If only people would realize this and help us with understanding rather than casting us out with condemnation!" [24] The publication in *Yank* of this lesbian WAC officer's letter was remarkable for the mid-1940s. But it was possible because the public debate about undesirable discharges provided her with a broader context for expressing her sense of being a victim of injustice.

These two letters were representative of many written by veterans discharged for homosexuality. In his 1948 book on psychiatry during the war, William Menninger reported that he had received many similar letters. "Throughout the war," he wrote, "and increasingly in late 1945 and 1946, reports came to me of individual soldiers who had given months or even years of good service and had then received a blue discharge because of homosexuality. Many soldiers wrote me; many physicians wrote me. It was apparent that the blue discharge had sometimes been punitive and unfair, certainly nonmedical." These gay veterans correctly perceived Menninger to be an ally in their efforts to seek a redress of their grievances. In an aside in his book, he gave gay blue-discharge veterans some practical advice, assuming that they and their supporters would be among his readers. "An appeal for a reconsideration of their discharge," he suggested, "can be addressed to the Secretary of War Review Board. It may be well for these men to recognize, however, that the odds are against them; the prejudice still exists!" [25] Blue-discharge veterans also asked doctors, senators, congressional representatives, and veterans' groups to write letters to the Army and Navy inquiring if their discharges for homosexuality could be changed. In June 1947, Senator C. Wayland Brooks of Illinois wrote to the Navy surgeon general on behalf of a gay veteran from Chicago whose appeal of his bad discharge had been rejected by the Navy Board of Review. [26]

Such letters threatened to open up a public debate over the injustices of the Navy's antihomosexual policies. In response the Bureau of Medicine and Surgery drafted a standard reply that, its representative privately explained, was "pointedly made as vague as possible in order to avoid subsequent correspondence." [27] Another way to contain a public debate was to redirect the flow of letters to the review boards. When Navy Surgeon General C. A. Swanson received one such letter from a doctor in Suffern, New York, he recommended to the doctor that "if your patient feels that any injustice was done, he may present a petition to the Chairman of the Board of Review, Discharges and Dismissals, Navy Department, Washington, 25, D.C. It is possible that that Board will be able to take some action favorable to his case if the circumstances so warrant." [28] By having to route such gay protests through the discharge appeal channels that had been established by Congress under the GI Bill of Rights, top military officials, while delaying a public discussion of the problem, could not help but strengthen the legitimacy of gay veterans' claims of injustice.

When gay dischargees began to ask veterans' organizations to help them appeal their discharges for homosexuality, these agencies were forced to develop their own policies and procedures for aiding homosexual veterans, further extending the controversy over the military's antihomosexual discharge policies into the civilian world. Among the organizations authorized by Congress to advise and represent veterans in their discharge appeals were the American Red Cross, the Jewish Welfare Board, and the NAACP, as well as veterans' groups such as the American Legion, Disabled American Veterans, Veterans of Foreign Wars, American Veterans of World War II, Catholic War Veterans, and others.[29] Some of these organizations adopted their own antihomosexual policies, while others assisted gay dischargees in their fight against injustice.

Officials in some veterans' organizations, when they wrote to the military for advice regarding their homosexual clients, questioned the fairness of the military's antihomosexual policies. In November 1946 the director of the Kent County Veterans' Counseling Center in Grand Rapids, Michigan, wrote to the Bureau of Naval Personnel on behalf of a "responsible official in the community" who had asked the veterans' center to tell him why the Navy had such a strict antihomosexual discharge policy. "What prospects are there for liberalizing the Navy's viewpoint on the subject?" the veterans' center inquired.[30]

Officials in other veterans' welfare agencies were more reluctant to assist homosexuals in their appeals. As soon as the GI Bill was enacted, the American Red Cross began to tackle this problem. In October 1944, at a Washington meeting of the Red Cross Policy Committee on Service to Veterans, the question was raised of the advisability of the Red Cross assisting in preparing evidence in cases "involving charges of moral perversion, etc." The committee discussed the possibility of accepting veterans' cases on a selective basis by "eliminating those in the group involving morals" but did not reach a decision. They instead sent a representative to discuss the matter with the presidents of the Army and Navy discharge review boards, who explained that the Red Cross, as an authorized veterans' agency, could not decline to assist any veterans, including homosexuals, who exercised their right to appeal. But the Red Cross did adopt a discriminatory policy that prohibited its chapters from conducting character investigations or social histories that might assist those whose cases involved "questions of moral turpitude." [31] By having to take sides either for or against their gay clients, veterans' agencies were drawn into the growing debate over how homosexual persons should be treated by the military.

Many gay veterans made their discharge appeals on their own, afraid to reveal their homosexuality to anyone, including veterans' groups or their families. But others, because they did not or could not hide the nature of their discharges, asked their parents for help. Advice books that told families how to prepare for their sons' return suggested how parents should respond to their sons' undesirable discharge. Social service agencies also sponsored lectures to teach social workers and home nurses how to help families handle their sons' return home. One such lecture, sponsored by the New York Red Cross chapter, told a group of home-nursing instructors to tell parents, including those whose sons were discharged as "homosexuals and sexual perverts," not to "condemn the psychopath, but . . . not [to] make apologies to him either. . . . Above all, family and friends should not pry into tragic military experiences; give him a chance to forget. Do not ask if he feels the need for speaking; he will in his time. . . . Be sympathetic with intelligence and restraint. . . . There must be family teamwork, which will make or break the family as well as the soldier." [32]

Certainly some parents rejected, abandoned, and disowned their sons and daughters who had discharges for homosexuality, but many parents did not. When Army chaplain Chuck Tarrance, after his discharge, told his seventy-five-year-old mother that he was in love with a man, "she just sat in her rocking chair," he recalled, "and she rocked a little bit and she said, 'Well, you know, I read in the paper a few years ago about two women up near Chicago that were living like a man and wife. Was that the way they were?' And I said, 'I'm sure it was.' 'O.K.' That was the only thing that was ever said. But I had three lovers only, and my mother just loved them all.'' After Jerry Watson got his blue discharge, he went home to Wisconsin to live with his mother, and one night, on his birthday, he "broke down and confessed. She has become very understanding and sympathetic,'' he wrote to a gay friend. '' 'All I want is for you to be happy . . .' she said, and I feel so much better now.'' [33]

Families not only found their own ways to accept their gay sons and daughters but even rallied behind them. Regardless of how any one parent responded, the exposure of a blue-discharge veteran's homosexuality forced thousands of families to weigh their love for their children against their feelings about homosexuality. Despite any aversion they may have felt toward homosexuality, many parents also felt protective toward their children and angry toward the military for denying them benefits. They could have believed that homosexuals did not belong in the military yet still have shared the same outrage expressed by the congressmen in their report about the unfair treatment of these veterans. As a result some parents chose to work together as a family to remove the stigma from their child's military records. When Howard Taylor told his mother why he was being discharged, she urged him to "fight for your full rights and privileges'' and reassured him that she and his father would do everything they could to help him. [34]

Gay blue-discharge veterans sometimes received unexpected help. When Tommy Martz arrived home in Kansas City and reported to his draft board, he showed the clerk his military papers. "She took down some notes,'' he wrote to a friend, "after writing 'Honorable Discharge—Martz' at the top of the page,'' altering his records to make him eligible for benefits. Martz "didn't say anything—after all I wasn't supposed to be reading across the room.'' [35] After David Barrett returned home with his blue discharge, which said "homosexual,'' he started to look for a job. "There was a lovely woman in the California State Department of Employment,'' he recalled. "When I gave her the discharge, she [said], 'Oh. You know, a lot of this is happening nowadays. I don't see why that should prevent you from getting employment.' And she falsified whatever I wrote there. I sent the woman flowers later on. I didn't forget her gesture.''

While these veterans were often forced to rely on parents, office workers, doctors, public officials, and the kindness of strangers to defend them, many also relied on each other. Small groups of gay male veterans with blue discharges sometimes moved to the same cities to be near each other or, if they were far apart, wrote to each other about how they were doing. They even gave their small fraternities nicknames that acknowledged their common stigma as well as their loyalty to one another. "Two other homosexual friends of mine got discharges," recalled John Hall, himself an Army blue-discharge veteran. They called themselves "The Three Musketeers," moved together to Los Angeles, lived in the same rooming house, and went out to the gay night spots together.[36] As many as twelve of the men David Barrett got to know during the antigay roundup at Noumea moved to Los Angeles after they were discharged. They called themselves "Daughters of the French Revolution" because the purge had happened in New Caledonia, a French colony, and the name of the ship on which they had been sent back home was the *Rochambeau*. Just before receiving his discharge in April 1945, Tommy Martz dubbed the six men in his crowd from Camp Crowder who had received blue discharges the "Blue Angels," after the title of the 1930 film starring Marlene Dietrich.[37]

These small groups of buddies supported each other and shared experiences of appealing their discharges, dealing with the VA, facing discrimination, and keeping track of others in their crowd. Even those who were isolated from friends could learn from GI newspapers at Army bases as well as local newspapers how to appeal blue discharges. In a March 1945 article in the Camp Beale, California, newspaper, an Army counseling branch officer wrote a column urging these veterans "not to delay their return home" because of their bad discharges and gave instructions on how to file an appeal with the Discharge Review Board in Washington. In October 1945 the *Pittsburgh Courier* not only published on their front page similar instructions to "Blue Discharge Holders," but also printed this warning to all soldiers still in the Army, particularly black GIs: "Do not accept the Blue Discharge as a quick means of getting out of the Army. You will be losing Army benefits and benefits under the GI Bill of Rights." Veterans clipped these articles and sent them to each other to spread the word.[38]

Large numbers of gay blue-discharge veterans availed themselves of their right to appeal. They traveled from all over the country to Washington, D.C., sometimes with the support of their families and friends, to present their cases to the Army and Navy Discharge Review Boards. They "accumulated in little groups" in Washington, explained Navy psychiatric consultant Dr. Francis Braceland, "attempting to get their discharges changed because they were afraid to return to their homes."[39]

The popular and congressional crusade against the injustices of the blue discharge, together with the flood of letters and appeals from gay male and lesbian veterans, did have an impact on military policy.

From late 1945 until early 1947, there was a tense period of tolerance during which many homosexuals were granted honorable discharges or had their bad discharges upgraded. During its first year of operation through 1945, the Navy Discharge Review Board, with the approval of the judge advocate general and the secretary of the Navy, routinely upgraded on appeal the undesirable discharges of homosexuals who had committed no in-service acts, changing them to honorable instead. In the Army, after months of conferences, the Surgeon General's Office, under the initiative of its psychiatric consultant William Menninger, successfully persuaded the adjutant general to issue on October 31, 1945, a memorandum directing that homosexuals who had committed no in-service acts be granted honorable discharges.[40] This memorandum coincided with the beginning of the *Pittsburgh Courier*'s crusade and the congressional hearings opposing blue discharges. From 1945 through 1946, then, the political climate both inside and outside the military was moving toward a liberalization of discharge policies toward homosexual personnel.

But at the same time hard-liners were mobilizing to stop this trend. In the Army strong opposition came from the Discharge Review Board. Unlike the Navy board, the Army board had refused to upgrade blue discharges, although one dissident board member consistently voted to give honorable discharges to men and women who appealed. The board's president, Brig. Gen. James B. Crawford, wrote repeatedly to the Personnel Division arguing against discharging any homosexuals honorably, warning that such a policy would lead to a more "lenient" attitude toward all homosexuals, an approach he claimed was opposed by "the vast majority of all officers of the Army and Navy except psychiatrists." In the Navy strong opposition to a more liberal policy came from the Bureau of Naval Personnel, whose assistant chief, Rear Admiral W. M. Fechteler, argued that unless the Navy Discharge Review Board stopped reversing the bureau's undesirable discharges for homosexuals, the "discipline and the high morale expected of the Naval Service" would be threatened.[41]

In May 1947 Army officials took action to solve both the problems of blue discharges and the controversy over the liberalization of policy toward homosexuals. In response to "much Congressional criticism," reported the *New York Times*, the Army decided to "scrap its controversial 'blue' discharge practice" and to replace most undesirable discharges with general discharges for unsuitability. None of these would be printed on blue paper, and these veterans would now "meet all qualifications for an honorable discharge."[42] At the same time, the Army revised its discharge regulations to prevent homosexuals from getting these general discharges and to make it nearly impossible for them to get any kind of honorable discharges. As a result gay men and women remained among the few veterans who continued to be discharged without honor as undesirables. The new regulations also reversed wartime policy by designating homosexuals as unreclaimable.[43]

Because the hard-liners within the Army had halted the postwar trend toward a liberalization of homosexual policies, gay veterans who were discharged for homosexuality were once again stigmatized as undesirables and continued to be denied benefits by the Veterans Administration. Having staked their hopes on the successful campaign to abolish blue discharges, gay dischargees could not themselves enjoy the benefits of victory.

The minor sexual revolution regarding homosexuality that gay veterans had experienced during the war brought about more changes than the effort of blue dischargees to fight discrimination. The vast majority of gay male and lesbian veterans who received honorable discharges returned home with a sense of pride and accomplishment for having done their part in winning the war and a sense of entitlement to the GI benefits that awaited them. With heightened awareness of themselves as homosexual persons, familiarity with gay social life, and stronger bonds with each other, they adjusted to postwar civilian society with raised expectations of how they should be treated as homosexuals and as veterans.

The sexual tensions and opportunities of military service had caused many veterans, not only those who were gay, to think about homosexuality as an issue of personal concern. A 1946 survey of American occupation troops in Germany suggests that male veterans left the service with many burning questions about the subject. From January to July, the Lecture Bureau of the Information and Education Branch of the occupation army sent out from its headquarters in Frankfurt teams of three to four men to address groups of servicemen on social, political, and economic topics. These lecture teams included one panel that addressed more than twenty thousand troops on the topic ''Sex: Fallacies, Facts and Problems.'' During their entire lecture tour, the panel received more than twelve hundred anonymous questions on sex. Despite the fact that the lecturers never initiated a discussion of homosexuality, questions about the subject were the fifth-most-frequently asked out of sixty-four topics and were of more interest to the men than questions about venereal disease and pregnancy.

Fred Brown, clinical psychologist at Mount Sinai Hospital in New York and one of the three panel members, wrote after the war that he and the other panel members were struck by "the absorbed intensity with which our military audiences reacted to open discussions of this perplexing and tabooed topic." Questions about homosexuality, Brown continued, "were asked in virtually every group before which we spoke, and attention remained sharply focused throughout the discussion." The men asked questions about "the causes of homosexuality, its prevalence, effect on character and personality, possibilities for cure, and, most persistently, whether homosexual practices were to be considered 'natural' or 'harmful.' " The panel members believed these questions to be spontaneous inquiries that reflected the personal needs of the men rather than expressions of "idle curiosity." They attributed this intense interest to the men's anxieties about "the emergence of repressed homosexual tendencies" in military life and to the soldier's "penchant for discovering the haunts of sexual deviates of both sexes in his free time excursions" in Europe.[44]

Veterans who had formed their first gay relationships or discovered gay social life while in the military had an even stronger need to resolve questions regarding their own homosexuality. They had to make important life decisions about marriage and partners, education, where to live and work, how much to reveal about their sexuality to their families, and how deeply to become involved in a gay social life. They often had to choose between their families' expectations and their own needs. Some based their civilian life decisions on their loyalty to their families and home communities, while others embarked on lives organized around their homosexuality. After brief visits home, many lesbian and gay male veterans left their parents, abandoned small towns, and joined the majority of other veterans who headed toward the more expansive and tolerant conditions in American cities after the war.

The choice between staying in their hometowns or moving to the big city was for many veterans the choice between heterosexual marriage and the gay life. Some eagerly chose the gay life. "I can't change," wrote a gay GI in a letter shortly before his discharge in 1946, "have no desire to do so, because it took me a long, long time to figure out how to enjoy life. . . . I'm not going back to what I left." [45] Others who did go back faced deep conflicts between their love for their hometown and their attraction to the urban gay life they had discovered during the war. "Naturally I was afraid to return to Maysville," wrote one gay veteran to another about his trip home to Kentucky, "a town of ten thousand that I had left as a fair youngster. . . . Yet I have found the same things which always gave Maysville its charm are still here. I have my little circle of admirers—the river still flows—and drives on country roads are still as restful. . . . As far as really gay life," he continued, "there will be none here. At least not for a long while. I have spotted a few sisters—but in a town of this size—and being as well known as I am . . ." [46]

A great many gay male, lesbian, and bisexual veterans got married, settled down, and raised families after the war, putting their homosexuality on hold or finding ways to have homosexual relationships within the context of their marriages. Robert Gervais got married, raised three children, and was "happy I didn't make it a completely gay life," yet for decades after the war he remained the occasional lover of the communications officer he met aboard his destroyer. "My wife knows," he explained, and "understands when he comes to visit with us." Other bisexual veterans had clandestine sex with men in bathhouses, public toilets, and parks, while hiding their homosexuality from their wives. Some lesbian veterans who got married after the war waited until their children were grown or their husbands died to resume a lesbian life; others remained part of a lesbian circle of friends or had a female lover throughout their married life. With so little support for maintaining gay relationships, the temptation to lead a more acceptable married life was always present, as was the fear that one's lover would abandon one to get married, leaving the gay life behind.

Gay male and lesbian veterans who moved to the cities found an anonymity, independence, and safety in numbers allowing them to lead gay lives without the scrutiny of unsympathetic family members and small-town neighbors who could condemn them or threaten their livelihood. They created their own circles of friends and risked going to the growing numbers of postwar lesbian and gay bars. Some used the GI Bill to go to school. "If it hadn't been for the Army, I probably wouldn't have been educated," explained Robert Fleischer, who used the GI Bill to go to fashion design school in New York City. Many used GI loans to open their own small businesses as florists, antique dealers, hairdressers, and shopowners, protected from the antigay prejudices of employers. Others worked for the government, universities, industry, private corporations, and other employers, where they could be fired if their homosexuality was discovered. Those who had found lovers during or after the war often settled down into quiet private lives, even joining the postwar migration to the mostly white suburbs. Sometimes reuniting with wartime buddies, they socialized with friends, neighbors, and other couples in their homes and avoided gay bars where they would risk public exposure and arrest.

Many poor and working-class veterans who had been raised in minority neighborhoods or on Indian reservations had to choose between trying to fit their homosexuality into the extended family life of their home cultures or trying to fit as minorities into the gay culture of white society, where people had more economic resources and privacy to live independently gay lives. When Todd Grison, who had had his first gay experience in the Army, returned home to his mother in Alabama, he at first married a young woman he got pregnant, although he really wanted to go to Detroit to live with his aunt, which he eventually did after divorcing his wife. In the racially segregated city of Detroit, he discovered other gay black men and female prostitutes who hung out with the gay crowd in their own bars. One night he ventured into a white gay bar to see what it was like, but he "really got the cold shoulder, no one would even talk to me." When his black friends found out, they accused him of "goin' hiking on us," of thinking that he was better than they were. Todd Grison, living with his aunt, faced much social pressure to keep his gay life within the black community.[47]

The camaraderie in combat that both heterosexual and homosexual veterans missed after the war had been especially important to those gay men who had not previously felt themselves part of an all-male community. The gay life in the civilian world offered them a camaraderie that approximated what they had known in the military. Maxwell Gordon was such a veteran. In the spring of 1946 Gordon felt a restlessness and a nostalgia after being discharged from the Navy in San Francisco. "I hated it when the war ended," he recalled. "Everything stopped too quick. I felt very uncomfortable." Gordon hitchhiked across the country, "sort of looking for something," and ended his journey in New York City. "When I got there," Gordon recalled, "I found out that literally there were hundreds and thousands of people just like me, who'd been in either Europe or the Pacific," veterans who had gone back home but discovered that they didn't fit in. "So they all ended up in New York for one more party. They didn't want it to end." Gordon began working as an office clerk and lived at the Sloane House YMCA, which was notorious for harboring clandestine homosexual activity. All of his friends were honorably discharged veterans his own age who also were trying to come to terms with their homosexuality. They ate meals together, went out to the gay bars together, and slept on each other's sofas when it was too late or too expensive to take the subway home.

Gordon described the difficult process he and his veteran friends went through to decide who they were sexually and where they belonged. They would "express it in different ways," he explained, "but they would go home, [after having] had an experience or a friendship in the service with a man. They'd say, 'Well, the war's over and I'll put that behind me. Now I'm going home and I'm going to marry and we're going to settle down.' They'd go home and they could not fit in. Everything was too odd. They had responsibilities and there was a lot of peer pressure: get married, have kids, start a home. They just weren't ready. Then they'd come back to New York. We would say, 'Well, you can go back all you want, but it won't work. Because you're gay.'" Gordon recalled getting calls in the middle of the night from friends who had returned home to get married. They would say, " 'Hey, you remember me? Can I come over and stay?' So we'd take them in. A lot of them knew they would never fit in again. So they stayed in New York."

Some gay veterans tried to resolve their conflicts over their newly discovered homosexuality by seeking professional help. After the war psychotherapists set up agencies in most cities to help veterans readjust to civilian life. The treatments they prescribed for homosexuality ranged from electroshock therapy or marriage to encouraging the veterans to accept their homosexuality. A therapist at the Veterans Rehabilitation Center in Chicago reported that "Louise," a twenty-two-year-old Wac, had sought help just before her discharge because she "was at a loss as to what she would do after discharge from the Army." She "wore her hair in a boyish bob," her therapist noted, "walked with a mannish swagger," and "frequented low class taverns where often she picked up homosexual girls." She agreed to undergo therapy only after the therapist told her that "the purpose of treatment would not be to change her from a homosexual into a heterosexual." [48] Three staff members from the Veterans Rehabilitation Clinic of Mount Zion Hospital in San Francisco reported on how they handled the case of a veteran who asked for help with his guilt over "his strong homosexual impulses." During a series of five sessions, the counselors encouraged him to find work that would help him sublimate his homosexuality and advised him to marry a "masculine woman." Another therapist reported that he gave a gay veteran ten treatments of electroshock therapy, but failed to "alter his homosexuality in the slightest degree." [49]

"Tony" described his own experience seeking professional help as a gay veteran after the war. When he was discharged from the Army and went home to Boston, he "felt very strange. I was used to this male ambience [of the Army] and I liked it. [By this time], I knew I was gay but had had no experiences except for one [brief] one with a German. I thought it was something to be cured! So I went to [a therapist.] Finally, after three sessions, he told me, 'My advice to you is to express yourself sexually as you must—but keep yourself out of the hands of the police.' I didn't accept it. I wanted to be cured, so I went to the veterans hospital and [the therapist] said, 'What's your problem?' and I said, 'Inversion.' He said, 'What's that?' By the time I explained it to him I was so thoroughly disgusted that I finally accepted it then and have accepted it ever since. I realized that my first therapist was right.'' [50]

Gay men and lesbians relied on each other to smooth their transitions from soldiers to civilians. They wrote letters and visited each other in their home towns, hung out with each other in the cities or became roommates or lovers. ''I want to hold the best of the friends I've met in the army,'' wrote one gay veteran in late 1945, ''to ease my way into what will be a new era in my life.'' [51] Burt Gerrits, who served as a Navy hospital corpsman at Treasure Island, moved to Oakland to live with the lesbian head nurse of his ward and her lover. Pat Bond moved in with lesbian roommates and immersed herself in the gay night life that flourished in San Francisco's North Beach after the war. Betty Somers and Phillis Abry each set up households with the women who had been their lovers in the service. When Bob Ruffing returned from the Pacific, he reunited with the gay GI he had met at the baths in San Francisco during the war, and they set up house together as life partners. Others drifted apart from their wartime buddies as they let go of the past and made new friends rooted in their lives as civilians.

Many lesbians and gay men believed that they had learned a great deal from their military service about living as homosexuals. Some believed that, despite the military's antihomosexual stance, it had left them emboldened as gay men and women. ''You lived a lifetime of experiences in four years'' explained Ben Small, ''that you would never have lived ordinarily in your own hometown. And to get some awareness of yourself and also, being a homosexual, to learn to be crafty, to be careful, to have fun when you can, be careful when you can't. So that I think I was much more prepared to be an upfront homosexual once I settled here in San Francisco.'' Because of her long-term affair with another woman in the Women Marines during the war, Betty Somers felt ''more homosexual'' when she left the Marines. Tom Reddy, who performed as a female impersonator in combat areas throughout the South Pacific, believed that his experience in the Marine Corps ''was one of the best things that ever happened to me. I was never rejected, [so] when I got out, the rest of my life I have never asked anybody to accept me being gay. I've never denied it; I have never paraded.''

As they tried to adjust to their new lives as civilians, some gay veterans realized that their identity as homosexuals was integral to the way in which they lived. The military, ironically, encouraged gay veterans to assume a stronger gay identity when it began to identify and manage so many people as homosexual persons rather than focus narrowly on the act of sodomy. Their shared memories of the war helped them to identify more closely with each other's struggles as veterans and as members of a homosexual minority. Having served their country well in a time of national emergency, gay veterans, especially those who had fought in combat, felt a heightened sense of legitimacy as citizens, entitlement as veterans, and betrayal when denied benefits. The rhetoric used and the actions taken to appeal blue discharges and bring about reform in the military's antigay policies reinforced their sense of legitimacy. A few began to speak of rights, injustice, discrimination, and persecution as a minority, expressing a hope that the war had led to social changes that would improve their status in American society.

A handful of gay veterans tried on their own after the war to bring about improvements in their social status as homosexuals. In New York City, four honorably discharged gay veterans reached beyond their immediate circle of friends to form an organization of and for gay veterans, called the Veterans' Benevolent Association. Like many other veterans' groups that proliferated across the nation in 1945, the VBA attempted to meet the needs of veterans who felt out of place in established organizations.[52] Its seventy-five to one hundred members met regularly for social gatherings, attended by as many as four or five hundred additional guests. Through informal networks, its members assisted gay veterans in matters concerning the military, the law and employment. Edward Sagarin, a sociologist who in the early 1960s interviewed former members of the VBA, explained that its leaders came to the organization unapologetic about their homosexuality because ''the hardships they had endured'' as soldiers during the war had made them believe that they were entitled to some respect. They expected that their status as veterans would help protect them from persecution as homosexuals. The Veteran's Benevolent Association existed until 1954, and was the first major gay membership organization in the United States.[53]

Some gay veterans, who had met in the military so many others like themselves, began to feel more normal than ''queer'' and to sense that there might be power in their numbers. "The real revelation was when I went to London," recalled Bill Wynkoop, who served in the medical corps and was stationed in England during the war, "and saw the large number of servicemen of all nations and ranks cruising each other in Piccadilly and Leicester Square. Here were thousands of female prostitutes wandering around, but these men were choosing each other. This was far beyond anything I had known before, and I began to think there would have to be some kind of social revolution because too many good people were homosexual . . . for there to be anything wrong with their relationships or for them to remain perpetually suppressed and oppressed." [54] The publication of the Kinsey Report in 1948, which the press interpreted to mean that 10 percent of the United States male population was homosexual, only added to this sense of being normal, one of many, and potentially powerful.

Other gay veterans began to feel less deviant after the war—and wondered if society might develop a new morality that would be more tolerant toward them—because the war's atrocities began to make the charges of immorality thrown against homosexuals seem weak in comparison. "How can we speak of sin," asks a gay soldier in John Horne Burns's 1947 novel *The Gallery,* "when thousands are cremated in German furnaces . . . ? This [gay bar] is merely a polite kind of anarchy . . . just a bunch of gay people letting down their hair. . . . Big issues are much more important. . . . Perhaps some new code may come out of all this . . . I hope so." [55]

Having survived fear and death on the battlefield, some gay combat veterans began to cast off the veil of secrecy that so seriously constrained their lives. For them, "coming out" to family and friends was not nearly as terrifying as facing an armed enemy in battle.[56] Frank Jacober explained that, having survived combat, his fears about coming out were nothing like "the time we went in the first wave. Nothing like that, boy." Robert Fleischer believed that it was his combat experience that enabled him to come out to his family after he returned home to Manhattan. "The first six months," he recalled, "my family was trying to get me dates. They were getting me the most eligible Jewish girls in New York. Finally one day at my sister's home, the entire family practically was there for a summer weekend having a barbecue in the back yard. I lined everybody up and I said, 'Listen. Enough!' And I stood up and made my speech. I said, 'I prefer men and I'm not going to accept any more blind dates with women. Leave me alone! Let me live my life.' And all it did was make my life much easier and much happier."

Poet Robert Duncan took an even bolder step and came out publicly in a political magazine. After receiving a blue discharge from the Army for homosexuality, he had written to a friend, "I am an officially certified fag now." In August 1944 he published an extraordinary essay in Dwight Macdonald's monthly review *Politics* entitled "The Homosexual in Society." Duncan insisted on signing his name to the piece, telling Macdonald that it was "only by my committing myself openly that the belief and the desire of others for an open and free discussion of homosexual problems may be encouraged." His plea for homosexual liberation reflected a lesson that many others believed they had learned from the war. Liberation could not be achieved through an allegiance to any special group or minority, he argued, including "nations, religions, sexes, races" and even the "outcast society" of homosexuals. Such groups forced their members to "surrender their humanity" and only encouraged the patriotism, bigotry and sense of group superiority that had fanned the flames of war. Liberation could be achieved only through a larger "devotion to human freedom" and "human aspirations" that disowned all special allegiances. Homosexuals should come out as individuals, he suggested, but not form separate political organizations. Their freedom depended on the liberation of all humanity.[57]

Duncan's coming out, and his critique of forming separate homosexual groups, anticipated a political discussion that began to appear in gay novels immediately after the war. Their authors, some of them veterans, addressed from many points of view a new conflict that had arisen in gay life—whether or not homosexuals in the United States constituted a political minority. In her popular 1946 novel *The Wasteland,* Jo Sinclair portrayed a lesbian character, Deborah, who was acutely aware of her ties to other minorities. During the war, she donates blood to the Red Cross "as a way of warding off, and fighting evil: the sins of society against minorities, the evil of society's segregation of Jew, Negro, homosexual." In his 1947 novel *The Gallery,* John Horne Burns cited the "four freedoms the Allies were forever preaching"—the freedoms of speech, of worship, from want, and from fear—as a basis for accepting homosexuals as "a minority that should be let alone." [58]

Articles in the popular press gave the minority issue even wider exposure. From June 4 through October 8, 1949, a heated debate surfaced in the letters column of the *Saturday Review of Literature* with the heading "Homosexual Minority." The opening letter referred to homosexuals as "another minority which suffers from its position in society in somewhat the same way as the Jews and Negroes." The previous month, *Cosmopolitan* magazine had run a feature article about homosexuals entitled "The Unmentionable Minority." [59] In June 1947 *Newsweek* magazine, in a remarkable article entitled "Homosexuals in Uniform," broke the press's silence about gay veterans. It reviewed the history of the Army's wartime policies against homosexuals and revealed that many blue discharge veterans had been homosexual.[60] The growing public perception that homosexuals might be members of a persecuted minority contributed to a climate increasingly favorable to the emergence of a gay political movement.

The war experiences of black and gay veterans ran parallel in more ways than suggested by the rhetorical comparisons in postwar literature. Both groups had received a disproportionate number of blue discharges, and both had experienced overseas an unexpected acceptance, respect, and relaxation of prejudices. This, together with the rhetoric of war propaganda that condemned fascism and promoted freedom, democracy and equality for all, raised their expectations for a better life as civilians. When they returned home to find discrimination, violence, and arrests based on their color or sexuality, many felt a heightened sense of injustice and betrayal. As a result some black veterans, both heterosexual and homosexual, became a force for social change within their already-existing movement for civil rights.[61] A few white gay veterans, beginning to imagine the possibility of a similar movement for themselves, wrote about their own sense of injustice and hope for change, even arguing passionately that tolerance and equal rights were the things they had fought for in the war.

Gay men and women often tried out these new ideas in letters, sometimes stating their case with a righteousness not usually associated with homosexuals before the beginning of the gay rights movement in the 1950s. In July 1946 Henry Gerber, who served in the Army during the war, wrote to the director of the Mental Hygiene Bureau in Washington, D.C., to protest proposals to increase the prison sentences for "sex perverts." "Shall these thousands of homosexuals," he asked, "who fought in this war have come back to this country to find that they fought in vain and that persecution of them is still going on as before in the land of ours, disgraced by the presence of stupid and hypocritical fanatics?" [62] Jerry Watson, who also served in the Army, envisioned a future when the nation's homosexuals would fight back against bar raids, arrests, discharges, and prison sentences with anger and even revenge. "Our perversion is our destiny," he wrote to a friend, "our right. And we'll fight for what we know to be our right." Someday, he imagined, homosexuals would take their fight to "the newspapers, magazines and radio programs from coast to coast. . . . The fear that the world has given *us* will soon be *their* fear, for the fight will be one of monstrous proportions.'' [63]

The WAC officer from Ohio who in November 1945 wrote to *Yank* ended her letter with her own vision of a better future for gay people, one she based on the ideals for which the war had been fought. "I use the word us," she admitted, "for I have voluntarily drunk from the Lesbian cup and have tasted much of the bitterness contained therein as far as the attitude of society is concerned. I believe there is much that can and should be done in the near future to aid in the solution of this problem, thus enabling these people to take their rightful places as fellow human beings, your sister and brother in the brotherhood of mankind.'' [64] The idea these veterans all agreed on was that homosexuals were human beings who belonged side by side with others in society and had a right to be left alone.

Such visions for the future and anger at injustice indicated that the changes brought about by the war were leading to a redefinition of homosexuality as a political issue. Those veterans who appealed their discharges were engaging in an early form of protest, as individuals and in small groups, against the government's discrimination against them as homosexuals. The fact that the military now had procedures for guiding their protests through new administrative channels only affirmed and strengthened their cause. The GI Bill of Rights, which was meant to protect veterans from the inequities of the discharge system, together with the campaign against blue discharges, introduced the concepts of "rights," "injustice," and "discrimination" to public discussions of homosexuality. Popular magazines and novels began to publicize the notion that homosexuals constituted a persecuted "minority." This was the language of politics, not the language of therapy or military efficiency that had dominated the discussion of homosexuality in the military during the war. Such changes in political awareness and action began to anticipate the emergence of a movement for homosexual civil rights.

The existence of a period of relative government leniency toward gay veterans from 1945 to May 1947—when the Army and Navy discharged homosexuals honorably and when Congress tried to correct the injustices of blue discharges—suggests that the antigay hysteria of the 1950s, rather than being inevitable, was a departure from more liberal social changes that had been set in motion by the war. The gratitude and generosity of a nation during these two years were powerful forces that, by temporarily diminishing some prejudices against homosexuals, helped to raise their hopes and expectations and to reduce the sense of shame and worthlessness many had learned to feel about themselves. These personal changes held strong political possibilities, but they also had a powerful impact on veterans' private lives.

Until he died in 1985, Robert Fleischer saved a personal letter that President Harry Truman had sent him and other veterans upon their return from the war. "To you who answered the call of your country," the president wrote, "and served in its Armed Forces to bring about the total defeat of the enemy, I extend the heartfelt thanks of a grateful Nation. As one of the Nation's finest, you undertook the most severe task one can be called upon to perform. Because you demonstrated the fortitude, resourcefulness and calm judgement necessary to carry out that task, we now look to you for leadership and example in further exalting our country in peace." Such words of thanks were difficult for Robert Fleischer and his generation to forget.

CHAPTER
10

The Legacy of the War

The massive mobilization for World War II propelled gay men and lesbians into the mainstream of American life. Ironically the screening and discharge policies, together with the drafting of millions of men, weakened the barriers that had kept gay people trapped and hidden at the margins of society. Discovering that they shared a common cause, they were more willing and able to defend themselves, as their ability to work, congregate, and lead sexual lives came under escalating attack in the postwar decade.[1]

Long before the war a chain of social constraints immobilized many gay men and women by keeping them invisible, isolated, silent, ignorant, and trivialized. As young people they learned to hide their homosexual feelings in fear and in shame, helping to perpetuate the myth that people like them didn't exist. Locked in a closet of lies and deceptions, many people with homosexual desires mistakenly believed that they were the only ones in the world, often not even knowing what to call themselves. Isolated from each other and kept ignorant by a "conspiracy of silence" in the media, they lacked the language and ideas that could help them define themselves and understand their often vague feelings and desires. When publicly acknowledged at all, they were caricatured as "fairies" and "mannish" women, freaks whose lives were trivialized as silly and unimportant, so that many lesbians and gay men learned not to take themselves or each other seriously. Such insidious forms of social control worked quietly below the surface of everyday life through unspoken fears and paralyzing shame, coming into view only in sporadic acts of violence, arrests, school expulsions, firings, or religious condemnations.

255

Ironically the mobilization for World War II helped to loosen the constraints that locked so many gay people in silence, isolation, and self-contempt. Selective Service acknowledged the importance of gay men when it drafted hundreds of thousands to serve their country and broke the silence when examiners asked millions of selectees about their homosexual tendencies. The draft, together with lax recruitment policies that allowed lesbians to enter the military, placed a whole generation of gay men and women in gender-segregated bases where they could find each other, form cliques, and discover the gay life in the cities. Classification officers assigned even the most "mannish" women and effeminate men to stereotyped duties, recognizing that these previously marginal people were useful and even indispensable to the war effort. Officers confirmed the competence, value, and courage of gay soldiers when they sent many into combat, some to die, even after they had declared their homosexuality.

Changes in policy brought about similarly dramatic effects. Military officials intensified the significance of homosexuality by building a special bureaucratic apparatus to manage homosexual personnel. In the process, they inadvertently gave gay inductees and soldiers the option to avoid compulsory military service by coming out. Psychiatrists, as the military's pioneer experts on homosexuality, gave soldiers as well as military officials a biased but useful new language and set of concepts—such as the word *homosexual* and the idea of a "personality type"—that some did use to categorize homosexuals, understand homosexuality, and even define themselves. During purges interrogators terrorized suspects into breaking their protective silence, forcing them to describe their homosexual lives, to make confessions, and to name their friends and sexual partners. Officers who aggressively rooted out homosexuals and exposed them to their draft boards, company mates, and families further destroyed their ability to hide in the closet, forcing them to lead new lives as known homosexuals. As these soldiers were thrown together into psych wards and queer stockades, they endured the same hardships together in small groups, better able to perceive themselves as compatriots who were victims of the same persecution. When they were discharged as undesirables without benefits and without having been charged with any crime, gay men and women gained a cause, a target to attack, and new avenues of appeal to defend their rights as gay GIs and veterans.

Disrupted and exposed by the war, gay life in the postwar years seemed to be growing at an unprecedented rate. Gay men and lesbians often saw this growth as a sign of hope, while government officials and the press saw it as a dangerous threat. The proliferation of gay bars, the broadening of public discussion of homosexuality, the formulation of the idea that homosexuals constituted a minority, the widespread acceptance of the psychiatric model of homosexuals as sexual psychopaths, the emergence and growth of federal antihomosexual policies and bureaucracies, and the opening of new avenues through which gay citizens could appeal government injustices against them were some of the many legacies of World War II. These changes had a powerful impact on how a nation and its people would respond to homosexuality long after the war.

The veterans of World War II were the first generation of gay men and women to experience such rapid, dramatic, and widespread changes in their lives as homosexuals. Their common experience and shared memories as a generation helped determine how they would fit into this new world. Having grown up during the depression under New Deal reforms, many had learned to view the government as a provider of social welfare programs, a tradition that continued with the 1944 Servicemen's Readjustment Act. These men and women had matured at a time when the government was waging a war against fascism and when President Roosevelt's "Four Freedoms" had come to embody the principles for which the United States and its allies were fighting. In many ways their attitudes resembled those of second-generation immigrants who were passionately pro-American and who gained legitimacy as Americans by serving in the armed forces.[2] Despite their griping in the military, gay veterans were patriotic and proud of their service to their country. They took advantage of the GI Bill and the postwar prosperity to try to settle down as civilians into stable, secure lives and to fit into American society whenever and wherever they could.

But beneath their desire to assimilate loomed an uneasiness, a sense of possibility mixed with fear. They saw the gay life begin to grow while the military, the federal government, and the press increasingly focussed public attention on them. Like the Nisei generation of Japanese Americans, who had been interned by the government that questioned their loyalty but from which they sought approval,[3] this generation of gay Americans felt deep conflicts during and after the war. Often blaming themselves for being arrested or losing their jobs, they retained a strong faith in their government and a desire to fit in. Yet they felt a growing sense that as veterans they were being treated unfairly when singled out for persecution and should instead be able to live their lives in peace so long as they did their jobs and didn't hurt anybody else.

By the late 1940s, however, the ability of gay men and lesbians to blend into normal life became increasingly difficult as the attention of the nation's media, government officials, and church leaders turned toward issues of conformity and deviance. As families were reunited and struggled to put their lives back together after the war, articles, books, advertisements, and the media promoted idealized versions of the nuclear family, heterosexuality, and traditional gender roles in the home and in the workplace. Accompanying this preoccupation with conformity was a fearful scapegoating of those who deviated from a narrowing ideal of the nuclear family and the American way of life. Lesbians and gay men, many of them unable or unwilling to conform to such a narrow family idea, stood out more than they had during the war as "queers" and "sex deviates."

The media and government propaganda associated homosexuals and other "sex psychopaths" with communists as the most dangerous nonconformists—invisible enemies who could live next door and who threatened the security and safety of children, women, the family, and the nation. From 1947 to 1955 twenty-one states and the District of Columbia, following local panics over child murderers and rapists, enacted sex psychopath laws. Supported by psychiatrists interested in extending the authority of their profession further into the criminal justice system, these laws targeted personality types, including homosexuals, more than their crimes, allowed their indefinite incarceration in institutions for the mentally ill until they were cured, and often required their registration as sex offenders with police departments wherever they lived.

During the nationwide campaigns against sexual psychopaths, the terms *child molester, homosexual, sex offender, sex psychopath, sex degenerate, sex deviate,* and sometimes even *communist* became interchangeable in the minds of the public, legislators, and local police.[4] In such a hostile climate, gay blue-discharge veterans could feel especially threatened because the military had diagnosed them on their military records as sexual psychopaths. The local panics that followed violent sex crimes, especially those against children, sometimes ended in rounding up gay men as potential suspects. "I suppose you read about the kidnapping and killing of the little girl in Chicago," wrote Marty Klausner in a letter to a gay friend in January 1946. "I noticed tonight that they 'thought' (in their damn self-righteous way) that perhaps a pervert had done it and they rounded up all the females [gay men]—they blame us for everything." [5]

The press added to the national hysteria by portraying gay men as molesters of children, corrupters of youths, and even perpetrators of violent sexual crimes; lesbians were sometimes portrayed as malevolent seducers of women and girls. Some pulp magazines ran antigay articles in nearly every issue with titles such as "Homosexuals Are Dangerous" and "Lesbians Prey On Weak Women." Such an image of the homosexual as a dangerous sex pervert suited the paranoid political climate in the 1950s in which the national enemy was seen as lurking within.[6] When America had needed its men and women to fight powerful enemies overseas during World War II, the military organization had found it more useful to project the image of the homosexual man as an effeminate weakling who was incapable of fighting or killing and of the aggressive, masculine woman as a patriot.

The enforcement of sex psychopath laws had the greatest impact on gay men and lesbians who led sexual or social lives outside their homes. While arrests for violent sexual crimes did not increase significantly in the postwar years, arrests did increase for gay men who were charged with nonviolent offenses such as consensual sodomy, sexual perversion, and public indecency, as well as for both men and women charged with patronizing a gay bar, touching in public, or wearing the clothing of the other gender. Some of these people, under the new laws, were sent to prison or committed to mental hospitals, then, upon their release, forced to register as sex offenders with their local police departments.[7]

The national trend toward enacting sex psychopath laws was only one indication that the progressive psychiatrists who had been active in reforming military policies during the war were losing ground to their more punitive colleagues in matters of public policy concerning homosexuality. During the postwar decade, a small number of vehemently antihomosexual psychoanalysts, focusing on causes and cures, dominated the psychiatric discussion of homosexuality while the majority of their colleagues either concurred or stood silently on the sidelines.[8] In 1952 the American Psychiatric Association, building on the standardized nomenclature developed by the Army in 1945, developed its first *Diagnostic and Statistical Manual of Mental Disorders* (DSM-I), which firmly established homosexuality as a sociopathic personality disorder. When the next gay generation became politically active in the early 1970s, they considered psychiatrists to be the enemy rather than allies and made the annual meetings of the American Psychiatric Association a target of their militant protests.[9]

But the liberal tradition among researchers on homosexuality, as exemplified during the war by Lewis Loeser, Carl Jonas, Clements Fry, and Edna Rostow, also continued after the war, primarily among those who worked outside the field of psychiatry. In 1948 Alfred Kinsey and his research team published *Sexual Behavior in the Human Male*, which revealed the high incidence of homosexual behavior among white male Americans, criticized the psychiatric profession's notion that homosexuals were psychopathic personalities (while many psychiatrists in turn aggressively and publicly attacked Kinsey's research), and made a case for the tolerance of homosexual behavior as a statistically common occurrence. In 1951 Donald Webster Cory, a gay sociologist writing under a pseudonym, wrote the popular book *The Homosexual in America*, in which he described everyday realities of gay life, attacked antihomosexual prejudice, catalogued injustices against gay Americans, and made a plea for their equal rights as an "unrecognized minority." And in 1954 research psychologist Evelyn Hooker began a series of studies that established the mental health of homosexual men and weakened the mental illness assumptions underlying DSM-I.[10] All these researchers challenged stereotypes, described the lived experience of real people, promoted tolerance, called for the integration of homosexuals into American society, and often placed themselves in opposition to psychiatry. As a result both the liberal and punitive approaches in research on homosexuals grew stronger in the postwar decade, further broadening the public discussion of homosexuality.

While the sex psychopath panic was underway, military officials set out to consolidate the experimental antihomosexual policies they had developed during the war, but now working unconstrained by the wartime pressure to utilize all available personnel. The Navy Department led the other branches in centralizing and refining its homosexual procedures. In September 1947, Secretary of the Navy John L. Sullivan initiated the Navy's first postwar study of the way it managed homosexual personnel, hoping that the Navy would "take the leadership in a medical attack on a problem which appears to be growing." [11] The secretary established a special "Committee for the Review of the Procedures for the Disposition of Naval Personnel Involved in Homosexual Offenses," which proposed several reforms, most of which in July 1949 were incorporated into a directive that superseded all the homosexual policy directives that the Navy had issued during the war.

This more comprehensive directive affirmed most aspects of existing policy while extending the Navy's power over its homosexual personnel. It directed officers to consider both the active and passive partners, whether two men or two women, as equally homosexual and equally responsible for their acts. It attempted to protect heterosexuals from "malicious charges" of homosexuality by requiring a more complete system of investigation and record keeping on each case. And it tried to protect the Navy from gay dischargees' charges of unjust discrimination by requiring homosexuals to sign the following statement of consent before being discharged: ''I understand that I may be deprived of virtually all rights as a veteran under both Federal and State legislation; and that I may expect to encounter substantial prejudice in civilian life.'' A refusal to sign this statement of consent meant that the suspect would instead be tried by court-martial on criminal charges.[12]

These Navy procedures in turn became the model for Department of Defense administrators as they designed a uniform antihomosexual policy for all the military branches. This project was part of the broader postwar reorganization and centralization of the military in which Congress consolidated the separate military branches into the Department of Defense. In August 1949 a subcommittee of the Defense Department Personnel Policy Board completed a study, called Project M-46, recommending standardized policies and procedures for all branches of the services regarding homosexual personnel. Finding the greatest degree of uniformity and centralization in Navy procedures, the committee proposed that the Navy plan be used as the basis for a uniform policy in all other branches.

The Defense Department adopted the committee's recommendations, extending the reach of the military's antihomosexual net even farther. These included adopting a clear policy statement that ''homosexual personnel, irrespective of sex, should not be permitted to serve in any branch of the Armed Forces in any capacity, and prompt separation of known homosexuals from the Armed Forces is mandatory.'' This was broader than wartime policies that had required the rehabilitation of some gay male and lesbian personnel. The committee also recommended that each branch of the armed forces give indoctrination lectures on homosexuality modeled on existing venereal disease lectures. They proposed dividing all homosexual cases into three classes—those who used force, those who were consenting adults, and those with tendencies who had committed no provable acts in the service. The committee also recommended conducting more careful investigations of suspected homosexuals, placing a female officer on boards reviewing lesbian cases, and establishing new lines of communication between all the branches to facilitate the exchange of information about homosexuals. On October 11, 1949, the Department of Defense issued a memorandum giving the Army, Air Force, Navy, Marine Corps, and Coast Guard two months to make their own policies and procedures conform with these guidelines.[13]

At the same time Congress was taking steps to increase civilian control over military disciplinary procedures. In 1950 it enacted the Uniform Code of Military Justice (UCMJ), which was designed to protect the due process rights of individual military personnel and went into effect on May 21, 1951. Congress also established an all-civilian Court of Military Appeals to review court-martial decisions. By 1951 the Uniform Code, together with the Defense Department's uniform guidelines, established the basic policies, discharge procedures, and appeal channels for the disposition of homosexual personnel that remained in effect, with periodic modifications, in all branches of the armed forces for the next four decades.

While these changes were taking place at the policy level, the military's grip on homosexual personnel was tightening in practice as well. From 1947 to early 1950, both the Army and Navy discharged about one thousand men and women as homosexuals per year, half the average annual number it had discharged during the war. But the decrease in numbers discharged masked an increase in discharge rates as the military reduced its troop strength. A rough estimate of the rates of homosexual discharges per one hundred thousand troops shows more clearly how the military clamped down on homosexual personnel after the war. During the peacetime years from 1947 to early 1950, the rate of discharge for homosexuals more than tripled the wartime rate. Except for a sharp drop in the Navy during the Korean War—suggesting that once again the military found it expedient to utilize homosexual personnel during a time of war—the discharge rate remained at postwar levels throughout the 1950s.[14]

Nowhere was this tightening grip after the war more dramatic than in the military's about-face treatment of lesbians. During World War II the personnel shortages had allowed large numbers of American women to enlist in the armed forces. After the war when women were encouraged to return to civilian life and reassume traditional gender roles, those unmarried women who chose to remain in the military or who enlisted during peacetime increasingly stood out as members of a deviant group that was easily stereotyped as lesbian. As the wartime constraints against antilesbian witch hunts were lifted, purges of lesbians increased. Pat Bond, a Wac stationed in Tokyo, and Sarah Davis, a Wave stationed in Florida, were both interrogated during extensive antilesbian witch hunts in the late 1940s, and each narrowly escaped being discharged as an undesirable, Bond because she had wed a gay man in a marriage of convenience and so passed as heterosexual, Davis because she successfully denied knowing her friends. During the Tokyo purge one woman committed suicide.[15] By the mid-1950s, Navy officials secretly acknowledged that the homosexual discharge rate had become "much higher for the female than the male." [16]

Another dramatic shift in postwar policy and practice was the introduction of programs to give all recruits lectures on homosexuality. This was a reversal of wartime policies to protect recruits from any discussion of homosexuality, especially in the women's branches, that might arouse their curiosity. The postwar introduction of lectures expanded the military's antihomosexual apparatus by adding a system of indoctrination to the prewar criminal justice system and the wartime systems for screening, discharge, and appeal.

These lectures reflected the growing preoccupation during the 1950s with stigmatizing not only homosexuals but also any women or men who deviated from a narrow gender norm. Retreating from the psychiatric advances of the war, Navy lecturers in 1952 were instructed that homosexuality "is not to be condoned on the grounds of 'mental illness' any more than other crime such as theft, homicide or criminal assault." Postwar lectures to WAVES recruits specifically rejected the guidance, counseling, and reassignment that had been recommended to WAC officers during the war. They told WAVES recruits that first-timers were as guilty as "confirmed" lesbians, encouraged them to inform on one another and warned that homosexuality threatened their ability to assume their proper roles in life as feminine women, wives, and mothers. While the wartime lectures had minimized the differences between lesbians and other women, the postwar lectures portrayed lesbians as exotic and dangerous perverts ready to seduce any woman who was young and naive.[17]

The postwar lectures to male recruits were even more vehemently antihomosexual. They encouraged revulsion toward homosexuality and "homos" as normal and manly, projected the Cold War image of homosexuals as dangerous sexual psychopaths, and gave explicit advice on how to spot them, reject their advances, and report them to authorities. In order to "emphasize the seriousness of this business and the danger in associating with 'homos' in any way whatsoever," a 1948 Navy lecture linked grisly murders with homosexuality. "You read in the newspapers of fiendish and horrible sex crimes committed against men, women, and ofttimes, small children," the lecture explained. "Sometimes the bodies of these victims are horribly mutilated." In most every case, this kind of sexual perversion "can be related to homosexuality," and "ofttimes the person who commits such an act is found to be a homosexual." The lecture added that the recruit would find many such men hidden in the Navy, a fact that military officials had learned during the war when "many homosexual persons were discovered and discharged from the Armed Forces." [18]

With these and other lectures, the military began to teach millions of young men and women to accept a uniform image of homosexuals, to fear them and report them, and to police their own feelings, friendships, and environment for signs of homosexual attractions. In a word, military officials began systematically to indoctrinate in its young recruits a response that psychiatrists and the gay rights movement later identified as homophobia: the irrational fear of homosexuality and of homosexual people. This fear reinforced a set of Cold War political beliefs regarding homosexuals: To ensure public safety it was necessary to discuss the "homosexual menace" openly and to increase public awareness that unidentified homosexuals could be lurking anywhere; the government had a duty to root out and eliminate them; and all citizens needed to be ever vigilant in order to identify hidden sex perverts and report them to authorities. In this context Kinsey's findings on the high incidence of homosexual behavior among American males were used to indicate the magnitude of the homosexual threat.

While they began to indoctrinate enlisted personnel about the evils and dangers of homosexuality, military officials conducted ever-more-extensive but secret studies of homosexuals in the ranks. The wartime research on homosexual patients and prisoners, the top-level reviews of homosexual policies, and the secret investigative hearings into the extent of homosexual activity at Fort Oglethorpe, Wright Field, and other military installations were forerunners of studies that continued in the armed forces long after the war. In 1956 alone Navy officials studied at least 743 homosexual cases. In a 1955 study of 37 homosexuals, naval intelligence officers extended their investigation beyond the military by traveling to each individual's hometown and questioning family, neighbors, police, and employers about the individual's marital status, work record, reputation, and sexual orientation. The Navy conducted major reviews of its antihomosexual policies in 1948, 1952, and 1957. None of the military reports found evidence in the performance records of homosexual soldiers to justify their exclusion as unsuitable for military service or as security risks. [19]

One of the thorniest administrative problems that military officials confronted as their antihomosexual project expanded after the war was what to do with the growing lists of names that were being generated as by-products of the discharge system. Some officials proposed releasing these names to the FBI and other government agencies to protect the general public by keeping known or suspected homosexuals under government surveillance. In January 1946, during the brief period of tolerance and gratitude following the war, such a proposal from the 12th Naval District in San Francisco was stopped by the strong objections of Navy Surgeon General Ross McIntire. He argued that turning these files over to the FBI and local police would betray "the confidence of the individuals concerned" and "would be a prostitution of the art of medicine and contrary to the ethics of the medical profession." He also argued that it would jeopardize the chances of discharged homosexual men to reestablish themselves as "useful and self-supporting citizens in civil life" and questioned whether these men "constitute any particular danger to the security of the social order as a whole." It was generally known, he explained, "that assaults committed by homosexuals are comparatively rare." The chief of naval personnel, Rear Admiral T. L. Sprague, supported McIntire's position, adding that the Navy's own study preceding its 1943 antihomosexual directive had concluded that these men were "harmless" and "do not constitute any menace to society." The commandant of the Marine Corps concurred. In September the secretary of the Navy rejected the proposal to release the names.[20]

But as the names continued to accumulate, and the social and political climate became increasingly hostile to homosexuals, pressure to release the lists mounted, especially from the offices of Army and Navy intelligence. These had been largely responsible for compiling the lists of names from the confessions, seized letters, and address books of the gay men and lesbians their personnel had interrogated. As a result intelligence officers earned a reputation as being among the most antihomosexual in the armed forces. They eventually found sympathetic ears not among top military administrators but rather among senators who began their own crusade against the employment of homosexuals in the federal government.

The military organization has often served as a testing ground for social policies and programs that later have been adopted by civilian bureaucracies. The military's expansion of its antihomosexual policies during and after the war served as such a model for senators who in 1950 launched the most aggressive attack on homosexual employees that had ever taken place in the federal government. Their crusade was in sharp contrast to the sympathetic concern congressmen had expressed in 1946 for the plight of the blue-discharge veterans.

The 1950 antihomosexual hearings in the Senate began as a by-product of the Cold War anticommunist scare. On February 28 Under Secretary of State John Peurifoy, testifying before a Senate Committee investigating the loyalty of government employees, admitted that most of the ninety-one State Department employees who had been dismissed as security risks were homosexual. Republicans seized the opportunity to attack the Truman administration and turned Peurifoy's revelation into a partisan issue that each month increased in intensity and even gained the support of several Democrats. For the rest of the year, new antihomosexual revelations or actions took place in Washington almost weekly. Republican Senator Kenneth Wherry of Nebraska and Democratic Senator Lister Hill of Alabama immediately formed a subcommittee to make preliminary investigations into the "Infiltration of Subversives and Moral Perverts Into the Executive Branch of the United States Government." In June the full Senate authorized the formation of a subcommittee, headed by Senator Clyde Hoey of North Carolina, to investigate the "Employment of Homosexuals and Other Sex Perverts in Government." The subcommittee submitted its report to the Senate on December 16, describing its "Government-wide" investigation into homosexuality as "unprecedented."

It was through the vehicle of these hearings by Senators Wherry, Hill, and Hoey that the military's policies and procedures for discharging homosexual personnel were extended to every employee of the federal government. Until these hearings, the Hoey committee reported, government administrators had never considered homosexuality to be a "personnel problem" and were grossly negligent in employing homosexuals. Some administrators actually "condoned the employment of homosexuals" based on the "false premise that what a Government employee did outside of the office on his own time . . . was his own business." Others took a "head-in-the-sand attitude toward the problem of sexual perversion," hoping to avoid dealing with an unpleasant issue by ignoring it. Civil Service Commission regulations had not explicitly mentioned homosexuals or "perverts" as candidates for removal from the federal service, making it easier for personnel officers to retain them as employees.

The result of this negligence, the Hoey committee noted, was that few homosexuals had been fired from government jobs. Instructing federal agencies to submit statistics regarding homosexual dismissals, the committee discovered that from January 1, 1947, to the end of 1950, the government had handled 4,954 homosexual cases, the vast majority (4,380) of which were in the military. Two-thirds of the few civilian cases during this four-year period occurred in 1950, mostly after the antihomosexual campaign had received wide publicity in March. The armed services clearly had a head start on other government agencies because they had discharged the most homosexuals and because, a decade earlier, they had been the first branch of the government to define homosexuality as a personnel problem. The committee concluded that the military's policy and procedures should be used as the model for other government agencies.

To strengthen their arguments, members of the Hoey committee invited intelligence officers—whose job it was to interrogate suspected homosexuals—to present the military's rationale for eliminating such people. They testified that male homosexual personnel were dangerous because they preyed on young boys in the service, they were high-strung and neurotic from leading double lives, and they were security risks. "This reasoning by authorities in the Armed Forces," concluded Senator Wherry, "based on years of observation and experience applies with equal force to other departments and agencies of the Government." In the areas of explicit policies, standardized procedures, uniform enforcement, constant vigilance, and coordination with law enforcement agencies regarding homosexuals, the committee regarded the armed services as the standard against which all other government agencies were compared and found lacking.

The hearings addressed the controversial issue of what to do with the steadily growing lists of homosexuals that government agencies were accumulating. Navy intelligence officers testified that since the beginning of World War II they had accumulated "a file of 7,859 known or alleged homosexuals," both within and outside the military, which they had "acquired incidental to the investigation of Naval and Marine Corps personnel." Army intelligence officers testified that since 1946 they had accumulated the names of five thousand persons, both military and civilian, within the Military District of Washington, D.C., alone. Heads of metropolitan vice squads also testified that they had accumulated huge lists of government workers who had been arrested on charges related to homosexuality. The committee recommended that the FBI serve as the conduit through which these names, lists, and records would be transmitted from one agency or department to another and from local police departments to personnel and intelligence officials of federal agencies.

The major purpose and achievement of both the Hoey and Wherry-Hill committees, however, was to construct and promote the belief that homosexuals in the military and the government constituted security risks who, as individuals or working in conspiracy with members of the Communist Party, threatened the safety of the nation. They wanted to apply this reasoning to military as well as federal personnel policies. But the military had its own rationale for excluding homosexual personnel based on the belief that they were unfit for military service and that they disrupted morale and discipline. The Navy Surgeon General's Office in 1941 and the Defense Department's 1949 Project M-46 report had both raised the security risk issue but considered it unimportant; the 1948 Navy lectures, although vehemently antihomosexual, had not mentioned the security risk issue at all. The military establishment had won the greatest war in its history without anyone in its ranks having threatened national security because of their homosexuality. Even under pressure from senators and their own intelligence officers, the initial response of military authorities was to give the security risk argument little credence except as a political issue outside the military domain.[21]

To build their case that homosexuals were security risks, the Senate committees solicited testimony from intelligence officers working in police departments, the FBI, the CIA,' and the armed forces. The senators interpreted the opinions of military intelligence officers as representing those of the armed forces and concluded, without releasing the testimony, that "all of these agencies are in complete agreement that sex perverts in Government constitute security risks." The evidence that these witnesses provided, however, was flimsy at best, consisting of one anecdote about an Austrian intelligence officer, Colonel Alfred Redl, who was blackmailed in 1912. Witnesses also referred to unspecified cases in which "Nazi and Communist agents have attempted to obtain information from employees of our Government by threatening to expose their abnormal sex activities," and reported unsubstantiated rumors that during the war Adolf Hitler had "amassed the names of homosexuals around the world" and that this list had been "acquired by Russia" after Germany's defeat.[22]

Ironically the strongest argument for portraying homosexuals as susceptible to blackmail by communists was the military's own success in emotionally breaking down gay men and lesbians during and after the war. Intelligence officers testified that, in their own experience, "perverts are vulnerable to interrogation by a skilled questioner and they seldom refuse to talk about themselves." Despite the fact that in all of these cases the interrogators and blackmailers were officers of the United States military, not agents of enemy governments, the Hoey report concluded that homosexuals did constitute security risks. They recommended that government officials should "get sex perverts out of Government and keep them out," and that all government agencies should pool their information on homosexuals through the FBI to make this process more efficient.[23]

The immediate impact of the 1950 antihomosexual scare in Congress on the careers of civilian government workers was dramatic. Before the investigations, from 1947 through April 1950, the government had dismissed an average of five homosexuals each month. During the second half of 1950, this rate had grown to more than sixty per month.[24] In July Max Lerner, in a *New York Post* column entitled "Panic on the Potomac," compared these Cold War "witch hunts" to the military's wartime actions against homosexuals. "In the Army it used to be called 'blue discharge,'" Lerner wrote. "The Senators call it the 'purge of the perverts.'"[25]

While the panic generated by the Senate hearings led to an immediate increase in firings, members of Congress, as well as government and military officials, began to translate the Hoey committee's recommendations into new laws and policies. In June, responding to direct pressure from the Senate committees, the Army extended its antihomosexual policies to all its civilian employees. At the same time the secretary of defense and the Civil Service Commission established new internal procedures to prevent the reemployment of "sexual perverts" in any government job. If homosexual employees refused to resign, they would be charged, investigated, and fired, with their names reported to several civilian and military offices.[26] In 1951 and 1952, national registration laws were introduced into Congress that would set up a federal pool of the names of everyone who had been identified by cities, states, and the armed services as sexual psychopaths.[27] In October 1953 the Navy, in a marked change of its own policy, issued a memorandum to all ships and stations warning officers that one of the "primary reasons" for promptly discharging homosexuals was that they were dangerous security risks.[28] But the strongest action was taken by President Dwight Eisenhower shortly after he took office. In April 1953 he signed Executive Order 10450, which tightened loyalty and security regulations and, for the first time in civil service law, explicitly stated that "sexual perversion" was necessary grounds for not hiring and for firing federal workers.

With Eisenhower's executive order the government's antihomosexual policies and procedures, which had originated in the wartime military, expanded to include every agency and department of the federal government and every private company or corporation with a government contract, such as railroad companies and aircraft plants. This affected the job security of more than six million government workers and armed forces personnel. By the mid-1950s, similar policies also had gone into effect in state and local governments, extending the prohibitions on the employment of homosexuals to over twelve million workers, more than 20 percent of the United States labor force, who now had to sign oaths attesting to their moral purity in order to get or keep their jobs.[29] Similar policies were adopted independently by private companies and even by private organizations such as the American Red Cross, which "summarily dismissed" employees involved in homosexual conduct, whether they were "habituals, one-time offenders, or mere tendency cases." [30] Within only a few years antihomosexual policies had spread from the military to nearly all levels of employment in the United States.

The prominent coverage given to this federal antihomosexual campaign, combined with state crusades against sexual psychopaths, contributed to a climate that fostered local panics and crackdowns. The gay and lesbian bars that had proliferated after the war became particular targets. As they emerged in more cities and multiplied in others, the legislatures of California, Michigan, and other states, which were charged with the duty of licensing and regulating liquor establishments, took steps in conjunction with local police to regulate or ban those they identified as "homo hangouts" or "resorts for sexual perverts." [31] Highly publicized antigay crusades swept through Miami, Wichita, Boise, Portland (Oregon), Tacoma, San Francisco, and many other cities, especially where gay bars were expanding or where politicians exploited the antihomosexual climate to further their careers, leading to street sweeps and mass arrests of hundreds of people at a time. As refugees from these local crackdowns and from federal and military purges looked for safer harbors, city after city imagined that an "invasion of homosexuals" was turning it into the homosexual capital of America. In the words of one newspaper's headline, the 1950s had turned into a "war on homosexuals," one that was more widespread and publicized than any antihomosexual campaigns that had occurred during World War II.[32]

Under heavy attack during the postwar decade, most gay male and lesbian citizens refrained from publicly standing up for themselves, fighting for their rights, or even talking about their lives. In 1951, Donald Webster Cory, protected by his pseudonym, tried to explain why he and other gay people didn't fight back. The "worst effect of discrimination," he wrote, "has been to make the homosexuals doubt themselves and share in the general contempt for sexual inverts." When an injustice was done against them, the fear of exposure led many to accept what had happened and then "make an effort to hide their homosexuality even more carefully." When arrested in gay bar raids, most people pleaded guilty, fearful of publicly exposing their homosexuality during a trial that might prove they were innocent of any crime. Legally barred from many forms of private and government employment, from serving their country, from expressing their opinions in newspapers and magazines, from gathering in bars and other public places as homosexuals, and from leading sexual lives, gay men and women were denied the civil liberties and even the channels of protest that were open to many other minorities. To make matters worse, no civil liberties organizations were willing to speak up in their behalf. Caught in what Cory called a "vicious circle," those who were honest about their lives became outcasts and martyrs, while those who lived a lie faced the shame of their own debasement, wondering if the contempt so many people felt toward them was justified. Such conditions led to stifled anger, fear, isolation, and helplessness, not collective protest or political action.[33]

But the postwar years were also a period of new possibilities that helped to strengthen and develop gay culture. Despite and sometimes because of the mounting political war against them, the generation of World War II gay veterans did find ways to break through their isolation. They responded to a hostile environment by expanding their "closet," making it a roomier place to live. Previous generations had invented the closet—a system of lies, denials, disguises, and double entendres— that had enabled them to express some of their homosexuality by pretending it didn't exist and hiding it from view. A later generation would "come out of the closet," learning to live as proud and openly gay men and women and demanding public recognition. But the World War II generation slowly stretched their closet to its limits, not proclaiming or parading their homosexuality in public but not willing to live lonely, isolated lives.[34]

In increasing numbers these men and women went to gay and lesbian bars that proliferated despite new state laws designed to put them out of business. In the late 1940s gay bars opened for the first time in such medium-size cities as Kansas City, Missouri; Richmond, Virginia; Worcester, Massachusetts; and San Jose, California.[35] These meeting places evolved into the primary gay social institution in cities after the war. By providing patrons with public spaces in which to gather, bars helped shape a sense of gay identity that went beyond the individual to the group. When patrons were caught in raids, they knew they were being arrested and harassed for gathering in public as homosexuals. Throughout the 1950s and 1960s, gay and lesbian bars became a major battleground in the fight to create public gathering places for homosexuals that were legal and free from harassment. In June 1969 gay riots in response to a routine police raid of the Stonewall Inn, a gay bar in New York's Greenwich Village, sparked the beginning of the gay liberation movement. Another gay institution, the bathhouse, also proliferated after the war, creating a relatively safe, semipublic space that affirmed gay male eroticism and provided any man an anonymous outlet for his homosexual desires.[36]

Their widespread use of pseudonyms enabled this generation to expand the closet while minimizing the risk of being exposed. Under pen names they wrote honestly about their lives and their sexuality in books, paperbacks, magazines, and pornography. Gay men published male physique magazines, creating a market that evolved into a flourishing gay erotica industry. Lesbians wrote and devoured hundreds of lesbian romance paperbacks, which became so popular that they were sold in five-and-dimes and drugstores across the country, reaching even the loneliest, most isolated lesbian or gay man in Kansas or North Dakota.[37]

While the small gay publishing market began to expand, an increasing number of postwar novels and short stories began to deal with the subject of homosexuality.[38] A great many of these publications, from best-selling novels such as *The Naked and the Dead* to gay male pornography, were set in World War II or used imagery that referred to the war. As the veil of wartime censorship lifted, authors of fiction began to write openly about the homosexual tensions that had surfaced during the war. Many years later, novelist John Steinbeck, who had been a war correspondent, acknowledged that he and his colleagues had known about the wartime "sex deviation" in the armed forces, but this was among the many "things not mentioned" in their reports. They had felt a duty "to protect the armed services from criticism" and to protect the home front "from the whole account of what war was like." Steinbeck believed that such protection had left the civilian public unprepared for the shock of reading fiction by ex-soldiers about the gritty realities of World War II.[39]

In war novels and stories, the American soldier's private experience with homosexuality was confirmed, explored and exploited. Some novels, such as Loren Wahl's *The Invisible Glass* (1950) and James Barr's *Quatrefoil* (1950), had homosexuality as their main theme.[40] Other war novelists introduced into American literature characters who were explicitly portrayed as homosexual officers and enlisted men, usually as villains or victims.[41] By contrast, few gay characters had populated American war fiction after World War I. In 1950 the first lesbian-themed paperback original, *Women's Barracks* by Tereska Torrès, introduced into the genre lesbian characters who had served in the military. The popularity of these books was magnified by the postwar boom in the paperback industry, which published war novels as originals or reprints.[42] The postwar growth and commercialization of gay male erotica in the form of mail-order

8mm films, photographic stills, and physique magazines were developed in part by veterans and drew heavily on World War II uniforms and iconography for erotic imagery.[43] Whenever these daring novels and publications were censored, even more public attention was drawn to their existence.

Some critics interpreted the trend toward discussing homosexuality more openly in literature as a sign that the war had had a corrosive influence on American culture and morality. Others believed that the war had helped emancipate American authors from sexual repression and hypocrisy. The war had fostered a "rebellion against undue restraints," observed one literary critic in 1954, so that "after World War II, homosexuality became the conventional thing. One gay youngster remarked to me, 'Give us another war and the world is ours.' "[44]

It was in this social climate—when antihomosexual campaigns terrorized gay Americans while the expansion of gay culture and the public discussion of homosexuality opened up new possibilities—that the first signs of a continuous gay political movement and press emerged in the United States.[45] In 1950 the Mattachine Society was organized in Los Angeles in response to the antihomosexual campaigns in Washington, police arrests in Los Angeles, the state sexual psychopath panics, the treatment of homosexuals by the military, and the crackdowns on gay and lesbian bars. In 1955 women in San Francisco started the Daughters of Bilitis, the first lesbian rights organization in the United States. The esoteric names of both of these groups hid that they were homosexual, helping to protect them from harassment. Most of their officers used personal pseudonyms as well.

Charles Rowland recalled that he and most of the other founders of the Mattachine Society had been veterans. Rowland's own interest in starting a gay organization grew indirectly out of his military experience. World War II was a war against fascism, he explained. After his discharge he continued his wartime "save the world" idealism first by organizing other veterans in the Midwest as a field representative of the liberal American Veterans Committee, then by joining the Communist Party. When he fled the Midwest to Los Angeles during the anticommunist scare, it was this same idealism that led him to join original founder Harry Hay and others in starting a homosexual rights organization.[46]

From the start the gay male and lesbian organizations published and distributed their own little magazines, which actively took on the cause of homosexual soldiers and veterans. Beginning in 1953 issues of the predominantly gay male magazines *ONE* and *Mattachine Review* and the lesbian magazine the *Ladder,* published by the Daughters of

Bilitis, included pieces on the status of lesbians and gay men in the military. They reprinted congressional testimony and newspaper clippings concerning veterans with undesirable discharges and printed anonymous interviews with lesbian and gay male veterans as well as their poems, letters, stories, and personal statements. They published editorials and advice columns, as well as news of witch hunts, changes in military policy, and accounts of individuals who appealed their bad discharges. They ran special features, including cover stories, with such titles as "Homosexuals in Uniform," "Homosexual Servicemen," and "Undesirable Discharges."

In 1954 *Mattachine Review* published an open letter to Senator Everett Dirksen, who had made an offhand complaint that it had been "no picnic" to purge homosexuals from the government. The letter's anonymous author, writing in memory of the gay soldiers who had died in World War II, captured many veterans' sense of quiet outrage at being persecuted by the government they had fought for. "Thousands of graves in France," the letter read, "many many thousand more graves on South Pacific Islands and beneath the seas, contain the sad remains of men who were brave soldiers, airmen, sailors, and marines *first* and homosexuals second. They were no less brave, they did no less to win the war for democracy, than did their heterosexual compatriots. But the democracy for which they did fight and die, and still fight and still die, and will yet fight and yet die, denies them and us our rights." [47]

The issue of military discrimination remained of vital concern to the growing gay rights movement. In 1966 the first nationwide protest by gay male and lesbian organizations in the United States was one that opposed the military's discrimination against gay personnel and veterans. But by this time such a position appeared old-fashioned to a baby-boom generation of gay activists who, as the Vietnam War heated up, began to question why homosexuals wanted to join the military at all.

While the gay movement expanded its opposition to military policies in its press and in the streets, individuals began to challenge the same antihomosexual procedures by appealing their bad discharges for homosexuality through the courts. One outcome of the 1951 Uniform Code of Military Justice, which had implemented new safeguards for personnel accused of sodomy but none for those eliminated through administrative discharge, was that military officials relied even more heavily on discharging rather than prosecuting homosexual personnel. [48] Throughout the 1950s, as administrative discharges for homosexuality increased in actual numbers and in proportion to court-martial prosecutions, more veterans whose appeals had been rejected by discharge review boards tried to gain access to civil courts. These courts had traditionally remained closed to military personnel because federal judges always had deferred to military courts and appeal boards as the highest authority in military cases.

But in 1953 the Supreme Court ruled for the first time that federal civil courts could in a limited way review convictions in court-martial cases, and in 1957 that these courts had the authority to review military administrative discharges. As they opened their doors to GIs and veterans, civil courts handed down the first decisions in homosexual discharge appeal cases. In a 1979 review of the published cases that followed, legal historian Rhonda Rivera identified two broad periods. The first, from 1960 through 1975, involved appeals on due-process grounds by veterans who did not admit to being homosexual. The second, from 1973 to the 1980s, which roughly corresponded with the emergence of the gay liberation movement in 1969, also involved appeals on substantive constitutional grounds—freedom of speech and association and right to privacy—by soldiers, officers, and veterans who freely declared themselves to be gay men or lesbians. By the 1970s the military was responding to the onslaught of due-process challenges by once again granting honorable discharges to homosexual personnel who had committed no inservice acts, thus preserving its stringent discharge policy. As a result subsequent appeals focused less on the discrimination and stigma resulting from undesirable discharges and more on direct challenges to the military's fundamental rationale for excluding homosexuals.[49] Unaware that they were echoing the conclusions of many secret military studies dating to World War II, plaintiffs argued that the discharge policy was unenforced and unenforcable, was irrational and based on prejudice, and undermined military efficiency by wasting valuable personnel.

Responding to these substantive appeals, the military closed loopholes in regulations and in the process made its antihomosexual policies even more restrictive. In World War II, Army regulations had required the "reclamation," whenever possible, of known homosexuals, establishing that during a national emergency even some "confirmed" homosexuals could be retained for military service. By contrast, the more extreme Department of Defense 1982 regulations stated that homosexuality was never compatible with military service and catalogued all the antihomosexual arguments the military had accumulated since World War II: the presence of homosexuals constituted a serious threat to discipline, good order, morale, mutual trust, privacy, recruitment, security, and public relations. Partly in response to changes brought about the gay movement, military officials extended their antigay prohibitions beyond sexual behavior and self-confession to other forms of speech and to private association and even sexual desires. As churches began openly to perform gay male and lesbian marriages, Department of Defense regulations explicitly prohibited members of the armed forces from marrying or attempting to marry a person they knew to be of the same biological sex. Membership in gay male or lesbian organizations, including churches and synagogues, also became grounds for discharge.[50]

The military's antihomosexual discharge policies, while rarely affecting more than three thousand veterans a year, have had a powerful cumulative effect. In the late 1980s the total number of men and women discharged from the military as homosexuals since 1941 approached a hundred thousand, averaging fifteen hundred to two thousand per year. Witch hunts did not cease, with purges of lesbians occurring especially during periods when the status of women as armed forces personnel was under attack.[51] The slow accumulation of discharges created an expanding population of disenfranchised gay citizens in the United States, including some, like San Francisco Supervisor Harvey Milk, Leonard Matlovich, Miriam Ben Shalom, and Perry Watkins, who subsequently became national leaders in the gay rights movement and brought the cause of the homosexual soldier to the covers of *Time* and other national magazines and newspapers as well as to the Supreme Court.[52]

The military's policy remains staunchly antihomosexual while many other bureaucracies, from federal agencies to private corporations, have abandoned similar stands and have even adopted policies of nondiscrimination. It defines homosexuality as a threat to the very essence of the military organization, and the bureaucracy that puts this ideology into practice both legalizes and reinforces the social hostility toward homosexuals that helps to keep it in place. By taking such an extreme position, policymakers make it difficult for themselves to stop excluding gay personnel without losing face and credibility, and without appearing to condone homosexuality and embrace homosexuals.

Despite the strictness of their policies, military officials can never eliminate homosexuals or homosexuality from the armed forces. During World War II military psychiatrists and other administrators began to identify some of the most common personnel problems regarding homosexuality: Gender-segregated living conditions intensify homosexual fears and tensions; the hostility that some soldiers express toward homosexuals can threaten morale and affect job performance; and sexual relations between officers and enlisted personnel, whether homosexual or heterosexual, can threaten discipline. But the solution that was developed during the war—the punitive elimination of homosexuals—only magnified the military's "homosexual problem." The discharge policy increased fear, reinforced hostility and prejudice, encouraged scapegoating and witch hunting, and helped to solidify gay men and women into a political movement against the military's exclusion of homosexuals. The discharge policy continues to intensify the importance of homosexuality as a military problem rather than make it go away.

Since the antigay policies were introduced during World War II, military officials have spent much time and resources denying that the armed forces have any significant problem with homosexuality. They have done this by erasing the history of the policies, refusing to discuss them in public, and suppressing even the friendliest internal criticism. In the process, military officials have successfully perpetuated three myths: that the armed forces always had an antigay discharge policy, that known homosexuals cannot fit into the military organization and are routinely discharged, and that organized opposition to the policy comes only from outside and not from within. A policy that appears to have existed for all time, to be unanimously supported within the military, and to allow for no exceptions, is not easily abandoned.

But the military's hidden history shows that the discharge policy itself was the product of liberal reform, having been put in place in 1943 by officers who in part wanted to improve the lot of the homosexual soldier out of a sense of fairness and justice. It has always been used flexibly, being modified or completely ignored—although usually in se-cret—to meet the demands of fluctuating personnel needs particularly during times of war. And since its inception the discharge policy has been surrounded by internal debate.

The long tradition of dissent within the military, as old as the discharge policy itself, has continually offered alternatives to the blanket elimination of homosexuals from the military, identifying antihomosexual prejudice rather than homosexuals as the problem. In 1945 Lewis Loeser, Clements Fry, and Edna Rostow all recommended that homosexuals not be treated as a class but be accepted and integrated into the military, assigned to duty based on individual skills and talents, and discharged only if their homosexuality prevented them from doing their jobs. In 1952 a Defense Department committee appointed to review homosexual policy could not reach agreement and issued two reports, with only the dissenting minority maintaining that homosexuals constituted security risks and that no homosexuals should be retained in the service.[53] In 1957 the Navy's Crittenden Board concluded that there was no evidence to support the idea that homosexuals as a class "cannot acceptably serve in the military'' or that they were security risks. The board even suggested that homosexuals might be more reliable in espionage and other top-secret jobs that some heterosexuals.[54]

This long tradition of dissent, however, has been accompanied by a long record of suppression. The reports of Fry and Rostow, the Crittenden Board, and virtually every other team of military researchers have been kept secret or destroyed. In September 1977, after thirty-five years of studying homosexuals and their own antihomosexual policies, Army officials stated that their files revealed ''no evidence of special studies pertaining to homosexuals'' and Navy officials maintained that they could not locate any of their own studies on homosexuality. It was only under orders from a federal judge in 1977 that the Crittenden Report and other Navy studies were released.[55]

Today the same pattern of dissent and suppression continues, although it has become more public. In October 1989 members of Congress released to the press a report by researchers at the Defense Department's Personnel Security Research and Education Center (PERSEREC) in Monterey, California. The report concluded that homosexuals were no more of a security risk and no more susceptible to blackmail than heterosexuals, and that the military should consider accepting homosexuals. It recommended that the military begin research to test the hypothesis that gay men and women ''can function appropriately in military units,'' as the military had done before it integrated blacks into the military immediately after World War II. Members of Congress released another report from the same research center that concluded that personnel discharged as homosexuals were better qualified and had fewer personal problems than the average heterosexual in the service. Defense Department officials rejected and condemned both these reports. They charged that the research was biased and technically flawed and that the researchers had exceeded their authority by criticizing policy. Refusing to participate in a public debate, the Pentagon stated that ''we cannot comment on matters that remain unresolved before the court.''[56]

In 1957, the secret Crittenden Report had made nearly the same conclusions as the 1989 PERSEREC Reports. The Crittenden Report, however, recommended no change in policy because the military ''should not move ahead of civilian society'' in accepting homosexuals, although it advised the Navy to ''keep abreast of any widely accepted changes in the attitude of society.''[57] In the three decades that followed the Crittenden Report, dramatic changes significantly altered social attitudes, leading to the rise of movements for women's rights and gay rights, the repeal of sodomy laws, and the adoption of corporate and government nondiscrimination policies. The PERSEREC Report, addressing the issue of leadership raised by the Crittenden Report, suggested that the military had fallen behind civilian society and the time had come for it to stop excluding homosexuals. Summarizing the broad changes that had taken place during the twentieth century, the report concluded that the earlier categorizations of homosexuality as "sin, crime and sickness" were obsolete and that the military should begin to accept homosexuals as members of a "minority group." With this recommendation, the process by which the military's expanding antigay policy had pressured gay men and women to identify themselves as members of a persecuted minority had come full circle: Military researchers were now using the idea that homosexuals constituted a minority group to call for an end to the antigay policy.[58]

The generation of gay men and women who served in World War II grew into adulthood fighting one war for their country and another to protect themselves from their government's escalating mobilization against them. When they returned to civilian life, some fought for their right to be treated fairly as patients, veterans, and citizens. For others a quiet sense of belonging was victory enough, to have the chance to fit into the country they fought for, leading ordinary but unapologetic lives. As they grow into old age and once again face their own and each others' deaths, most still blend into the world around them, while some have come out either under fire or on their own. Today they witness an expanding public debate over the military's exclusion of homosexuals. If that debate is to be at all serious, it must include a sense of history—not only of how the military established its antigay policy during World War II and then suppressed all internal dissent, but also of how the men and women who were the policy's first targets fought and died for their country with the rest of their generation.

A Note on Sources

"How did you find any sources?" people asked me when I told them I was writing a book on lesbians and gay men in World War II. Histories of World War II rarely mention gay Americans, and histories of gay Americans rarely mention World War II. With few secondary sources available, I had to create as well as uncover documents to tell this story. Armed with a tape recorder, a library card, and the Freedom of Information Act, I traveled the country interviewing veterans about their lives, combed through hundreds of wartime newspapers, magazines, and psychiatric journals, and searched through hundreds of boxes and files of military records at the National Archives.

In their professional journals, psychiatrists left the most public record of their involvement with homosexuality in the military during the war. Particularly in the pages of *Psychiatry, War Medicine,* and the *American Journal of Psychiatry,* they described their role in developing the rationale behind the military's first antihomosexual screening and discharge procedures and discussed their ethical dilemmas when faced with having to diagnose, reject, and discharge actual men and women. Other professional journals that published articles during and shortly after the war regarding homosexuality in the armed forces include *Bulletin of the Menninger Clinic, Journal of the American Medical Association, American Journal of Sociology, Psychiatric Quarterly, Psychosomatic Medicine, Journal of Projective Techniques,* and *Journal of Clinical Psychopathology.* The most informative books that discuss psychiatry's wartime role regarding military policy toward homosexuals are William Menninger, *Psychiatry in a Troubled World* (New York: Macmillan, 1948); Medical Department U.S. Army, *Neuropsychiatry in World War II,* vols. 1 and 2 (Washington, D.C.: USGPO, 1966); and Mattie E. Treadwell, *The Women's Army Corps* (Washington, D.C.: USGPO, 1954).

Government records that document the early history of the military's antihomosexual policies are more difficult to find than the published materials on psychiatry. Few indexes of wartime records include homosexuality as a subject heading. With the help of the National Archives staff and the power of the Freedom of Information Act, I was able to locate and request access to these records. Using as a guide the Army and Navy subject classification systems— which coded each piece of paper generated during the war—we were able to locate thousands of pages of documents on homosexuality. The Army subject heading and its code was "Discipline: Morals and Conduct" (250.1) and the Navy's was "Vice" (P13-7). Many of these records were still sealed under war restrictions and required a declassification process before they were released for scholarly use. The following record groups, located at the National Archives Building in Washington, D.C., and at the Washington National Records Center in Suitland, Maryland, contained the bulk of these documents and are identified by record group number in the notes:

RG 52	Navy Bureau of Medicine and Surgery
RG 80	General Records of Department of the Navy 1798–1947
RG 112	Office of Army Surgeon General
RG 159	Office of Army Inspector General
RG 160	Headquarters, Army Service Forces
RG 165	War Department General and Special Staffs
RG 200	National Archives Gift Collection, American Red Cross
RG 247	Office of the Army Chief of Chaplains
RG 330	Office of Secretary of Defense
RG 407	Army Adjutant General's Office, 1917–
RG 418	Saint Elizabeths Hospital

Major military reports and sets of documents in these record groups and from other sources are identified in the notes as follows:

Fort Oglethorpe Report and Testimony: Report from Lt. Col. Birge Holt and Capt. Ruby Herman, IGD, to the Acting Inspector General, Subject: Investigation of conditions in the 3d WAC Training Center, Fort Oglethorpe, Georgia, 29 July 1944, File 333.9, 3d WAC Training Center, RG 159. Testimony is Exhibit B of Report.

AGO "Sodomists" File: Army Adjutant General's Office compilation of correspondence 1941–44 regarding "sodomists" and homosexuality. File 250.1, Decimal File 1940–44, RG 407.

G-1 "Sodomists" File: Army G-1 Personnel Division compilation of correspondence 1941–44 regarding homosexuality, Box 438, RG 165.

Crittenden Report: Report of the Board Appointed to Prepare and Submit Recommendations to the Secretary of the Navy For the Revision of Policies, Procedures and Directives Dealing with Homosexuals, 21 December 1956 to 15 March 1957, Department of the Navy.

Wright Field Report and Testimony: Report of Investigation of Homosexual Practices Amongst Military Personnel at Wright Field, Dayton, Ohio, Conducted by Lt. Col. Buron Fitts, Office of Air Inspector, during the period 9–22 April, 1945, AG 250.1, Classified Decimal File 1943–45, RG 407.

The following collections are also identified in the notes as the sources for documents regarding either the military's wartime homosexual policies or its use of female impersonation:

Overholser Papers: The papers of Dr. Winfred Overholser, superintendent of Saint Elizabeths Hospital, Washington, D.C., and chair of the National Research Council Committee on Neuropsychiatry. Entry 54, RG 418.

Robert Porter Patterson Papers: Under secretary of war 1940–45, secretary of war 1945–47. Manuscript Room, Library of Congress.

Army Signal Corps Photographs: Photographs of GI female impersonators in soldier shows. Still Picture Branch Research Room, National Archives, Washington, D.C.

Pentagon Reading Room: Case files on microfilm of veterans who have appealed bad discharges from the military. Discharge Review Board Reading Room, located in the Concourse of the Pentagon.

The following abbreviations for military and other government agencies appear in the text and notes:

BuMed	Navy Bureau of Medicine and Surgery
SecNav	Secretary of the Navy
NavPers	Bureau of Naval Personnel
BuNav	Bureau of Navigation
SGO	Surgeon General's Office
JAG	Judge Advocate General
TAG	The Adjutant General
NRC	National Research Council
WD	War Department

In three cases government officials denied me access to important sets of records that document the origins and effects of the military's World War II antihomosexual policies. In September 1981 the copy of the 1957 Crittenden Report that I requested and received from the Navy was missing parts 2 and 3. These contained copies of directives and memoranda regarding homosexual policies, verbatim testimony from Navy officials on the evolution of the wartime antigay policies, and an unidentified "confidential supplement." Despite further communications, the Navy Freedom of Information Act coordinator refused to send me a written explanation for what had happened to the documents, stating only that neither the original of the report nor any related materials could be found—the standard response that both Army and Navy officials have used to avoid the release of their studies on homosexuality that have been proved to exist.[*]

Other important Navy records also disappeared. After I made a series of requests from 1983 to 1987, Navy officials were able to locate the case files of several thousand veterans who appealed their undesirable discharges from 1944 to 1946. These files presumably included letters of appeal from homosexual veterans. At first the Navy legal counsel informed me that the "case files for 1946 were destroyed through inadvertent error in January 1980" but that those for 1944–45 were stored in record archives. After I negotiated procedures for "sanitizing" the names from the records to protect the privacy of the veterans and agreed to pay Navy personnel hourly rates to process the files for release, the legal counsel notified me that he had been informed by the Accession and Disposal Branch of the Washington National Records Center that these files had also been destroyed in January 1980.[†] Their destruction raises questions about what guidelines federal archivists use to determine which records are worth preserving as well as questions about how more than seven thousand case files were "inadvertently" destroyed. These records promised to contain critical documentation not only of how gay veterans of World War II perceived and expressed their sense of injustice at being the first GIs to be discharged as homosexuals but also of how other American soldiers, including many black veterans, used their new rights under the GI Bill to appeal undesirable discharges from the armed forces.

The most arbitrary denial of access to government records on homosexuality has come not from the military but from the Senate. From 1982 to 1989 I tried to gain access to documents generated during the 1950 executive session hearings held by the Senate Permanent Subcommittee on Investigations regarding the "Employment of Homosexuals and Other Sex Perverts in Government." Although the subcommittee issued a public report, its secret correspondence and the testimony it heard from intelligence officers promised to reveal much about the military's actual enforcement of its homosexual policies during and immediately after the war. In 1982 the National Archives and Records Service, upon my request, located "20 linear inches of correspondence, memoranda, exhibits, and other unpublished materials relating to the subcommittee's investigation" of homosexuals in the federal government.[‡] While congressional records are not subject to the Freedom of Information Act, under Senate Resolution 474 (Ninety-sixth Congress, Second Session) the subcommittee was allowed

---

[*] For examples of these responses, see E. Lawrence Gibson, *Get Off My Ship: Ensign Berg vs. the U.S. Navy* (New York: Avon Books, 1978), pp. 366–67.

[†] Correspondence and telephone communication between author and Office of the Director, Naval Council of Personnel Boards, Navy Department, March 1986–October 1987.

[‡] Letter, David R. Kepley, Legislative and Diplomatic Branch, Civil Archives Division, National Archives and Records Service, to author, May 18, 1982.

to release investigative documents that do not pertain to individual personnel after a period of twenty years and had to release them after fifty years.

When I requested access to these records, I emphasized that my sole interest was in documents relating to policy rather than those relating to the names or cases of individuals. Yet successive subcommittee chairs—Republican Senator William Roth, Jr., and Democratic Senator Sam Nunn—adamantly denied my requests. Their bogus rationale was that the privacy of individuals must be protected, yet I had requested no files on individuals. The senators refused to respond to my appeals for an explanation why the secret testimony of public officials about public policy could not be made public for historical purposes nearly forty years after the fact.[*] Historians can never write a thorough history of how the federal government developed and enforced its first antihomosexual policies so long as the Senate, the Navy, the Army, and federal archivists and records managers continue to suppress or destroy thousands of pages of irreplaceable government documents.

Published and archival sources for how lesbian and gay male GIs perceived their military experience during World War II were virtually nonexistent when I began work on this book. The letters between gay GIs that came my way in 1979 (identified as the Taylor Correspondence in the notes) were the first I had seen written by gay GIs. In the same year Donald Vining published his daily diary from the war years which, although he had been a gay civilian, documented many encounters with gay servicemen and his own observations about being gay during the war. In 1981 Jim Kepner showed me dozens of wartime letters between him and several Army pen pals (identified as the Kepner Correspondence in the notes). His letters and those of Jerry Watson, A.B., and Henry Gerber are in the collection of the International Gay and Lesbian Archives in West Hollywood and are excerpted with the kind permission of Jim Kepner. In response to presentations of my slide show "Marching to a Different Drummer" and to appeals in magazine articles and by word of mouth, more than one hundred lesbians and gay men—many of whom had kept letters, diaries, photographs, service records, and memorabilia regarding their lives in the military—offered to be interviewed about their experiences during World War II. Some of these documents are now being preserved by the World War II Project in San Francisco.

Reflecting the demographics of the wartime military population, the majority of gay World War II veterans are white men. Of the fifty-six lesbian and gay veterans I was able to interview, forty-eight were white men, six were white women, and two were black men. Of the fifteen people I interviewed who were gay civilians during the war, nine were white men and six were white women. Members of lesbian and gay Asian, Hispanic, black, and Native-American

---

[*] Correspondence between author and Senate Permanent Subcommittee on Investigations, April 1982–February 1989.

organizations helped me to consider what the experience of minority gay men and women might have been in the military during the war when we couldn't find such veterans to interview. I met some of the lesbian veterans I interviewed at the First West Coast Reunion of Lesbian Wacs on May 16, 1987. Interviews were conducted from 1979 to 1987 in Capitola, San Rafael, Oakland, Palo Alto, Davis, Los Angeles, San Diego, and San Francisco, California; Durham and Greensboro, North Carolina; Honolulu and the Big Island, Hawaii; Providence, Rhode Island; Portland, Oregon; and Seattle, Chicago, New York City, Baltimore, Philadelphia and Washington, D.C. All of the interview tapes, transcripts and related materials are in the collection of the World War II Project in San Francisco.

To supplement my own interviews, I have drawn on published interviews with and first-person accounts by lesbians and gay men about their experiences during World War II, including those published in Nancy Adair and Casey Adair, *Word Is Out: Stories of Some of Our Lives* (1978); Evelyn Torton Beck, ed., *Nice Jewish Girls* (1982); Studs Terkel, *The Good War* (1984); George Stambolian, *Male Fantasies/Gay Realities: Interviews With Ten Men* (1984); Keith Vacha and Cassie Damewood, eds., *Quiet Fire: Memoirs of Older Gay Men* (1985); Marcy Adelman, ed., *Long Time Passing: Lives of Older Lesbians* (1986); Andrea Weiss and Greta Schiller, *Before Stonewall: The Making of a Lesbian and Gay Community* (1988); *Other Countries: Black Gay Voices* (Spring 1988); and the *Gay Community News*. I also have drawn on letters, interviews, biographies, and autobiographies regarding more famous gay and bisexual men that discuss their experiences with the draft and U.S. military service during the war, including those of James Baldwin, John Cheever, Montgomery Clift, Roy Cohn, Robert Duncan, Rock Hudson, Christopher Isherwood, Liberace, Merle Miller, Tyrone Power, Bayard Rustin, Gore Vidal, and Minor White.

I have used oral-history interviews and biographical materials not as a representative sample but to identify what issues, dilemmas, and choices some gay male and lesbian GIs faced as homosexuals in military service, how they perceived their own experiences, and how they described the gay life during the war.

Although some veterans I interviewed chose to use pseudonyms to protect their privacy, it is remarkable that so many interviewees chose to use their real names, considering that gay men and women are still the targets of prejudice, discrimination, and criminal prosecution. I have identified with pseudonyms the authors of the found letters (Taylor Correspondence) as Marty Klausner, Tommy Martz, J. D., D. M., D., C. M., Denny, and Howard Taylor, and the authors of letters to Jim Kepner as Jerry Watson and A. B.

People I interviewed for this book include:

Phillis Abry	Jacqueline Beyer
David Barrett	Pat Bond
Neel Bate ("BLADE")	Edward Burrows [interviewed by
Richard Bernstein (pseudonym)	Allan Troxler]

R.O.B. (pseudonym)
Vince Carelli (pseudonym)
Stan Carlow
Ernest Cole
Ralph Davidson (pseudonym)
Sarah Davis [interviewed by JoAnn
    Castillo]
William DeVeau
Raymond Devine
Haviland Ferris (pseudonym)
Robert Fleischer
Josh Flynn (pseudonym)
Dr. Allan Fredericks (pseudonym)
Elizabeth Freeman
Burt Gerrits
Robert Gervais (pseudonym)
Maxwell Gordon (pseudonym)
Robert Green (pseudonym)
Jack Hansen (pseudonym)
Helen Harder
Frank Jacober
William Johnson (pseudonym)
Jim Kepner
Pete King (pseudonym)
Jim Kuzell
Stuart Loomis
Raymond Mailloux
Vincent Miles
Burt Miller

Oren Myerly
Raymond Myers
George Peterson (pseudonym)
Stanley Phillips
Richard Plant
Ernie Potvin
Tom Reddy
Robert Ricks
Ted Rolfs
Charles Rowland
Bob Ruffing
Norman Sansom
James Shea
Ben Small
Betty Smith (pseudonym)
Donna Smith
Maynard Smith
Betty Somers (pseudonym)
Stew (pseudonym) [interviewed by
    Greg Lamb]
Martin Stow
Chuck Tarrance
Fred Thayer (pseudonym)
Bill Thompson/"Rebecca" (pseu-
    donyms)
Jim Warren (pseudonym)
Jerry Watson (pseudonym)
Woodie Wilson

Notes

Introduction: "Why We Fight"

1. Robert K. Griffith, Jr., "Quality Not Quantity: The Volunteer Army During the Depression," *Military Affairs* 43 (December 1979): 171–77; Geoffrey Perrett, *Days of Sadness, Years of Triumph* (Baltimore: Penguin, 1973), pp. 25–40; Maurice R. Stein, *The Eclipse of Community* (New York: Harper & Row, 1960), pp. 175–98; Samuel A. Stouffer et al., *The American Soldier* (Princeton: Princeton University Press, 1949), vol. 1, pp. 54–81; Allan R. Millett and Peter Maslowski, *For the Common Defense* (New York: Free Press, 1984), pp. 377–414.
2. On the military's wartime rationale for excluding or segregating black men, see Richard Polenberg, *One Nation Divisible* (New York: Penguin, 1980), p. 76.
3. *Selective Service and Victory: The 4th Report of the Director of Selective Service*, (Washington, D.C.: USGPO, 1948), pp. 605, 608–9, 610, 612, 613; D'Ann Campbell, *Women at War with America* (Cambridge: Harvard University Press, 1984), pp. 22–23; Polenberg, *One Nation Divisible*, pp. 54, 72–78; Matt S. Meier and Feliciano Rivera, *The Chicanos: A History of Mexican Americans* (New York: Hill and Wang, 1972), p. 186; "A More Perfect Union: Japanese Americans and the United States Constitution," exhibition at the National Museum of American History, Smithsonian Institution, Washington, D.C., October 1, 1987.
4. Kinsey found 4 percent of the white males he surveyed to be "exclusively homosexual throughout their lives" after the onset of adolescence, and 10 percent to be "more or less exclusively homosexual" for at least three years between the ages of sixteen and fifty-five. Alfred C. Kinsey et al., *Sexual Behavior in the Human Male* (Philadelphia: W. B. Saunders, 1948), pp. 650–51.
5. "Rock Hudson," *Current Biography Yearbook, 1961* (New York:

H. W. Wilson, 1962), pp. 211–13; "Tyrone Power," *Current Biography Yearbook, 1950,* pp. 463–65; Hector Arce, *The Secret Life of Tyrone Power* (New York: William Morrow, 1979); *Minor White: Rites and Passages,* biographical essay by James Baker Hall (Millerton, N.Y.: Aperture Monograph, 1978), pp. 21, 54–55; "Gore Vidal," *Current Biography Yearbook, 1965,* pp. 431–34; Benjamin Cheever, ed., *The Letters of John Cheever* (New York: Simon & Schuster, 1988); Merle Miller, *On Being Different* (New York: Popular Library, 1971); "John Horne Burns," *Dictionary of American Biography: Yearbook 1985* (Detroit: Gale Research Co., 1986), pp. 338–43; Gore Vidal, "John Horne Burns," *Homage to Daniel Shays* (New York: Vintage, 1973), pp. 181–85; John Mitzel, *John Horne Burns* (Dorchester, Mass.: Manifest Destiny Books, 1974).

6. Perrett, *Days of Sadness, Years of Triumph,* p. 325; Lee Kennett, *G.I.* (New York: Scribner's, 1987), p. 235.

7. Gershon Legman, "The Language of Homosexuality," in George Henry, *Sex Variants: A Study of Homosexual Patterns* (1941); reprinted in Jonathan Ned Katz, *Gay/Lesbian Almanac* (New York: Harper & Row, 1983), pp. 571–84.

Chapter 1. Getting In

1. Figure for draft boards is from *Selective Service and Victory: The Fourth Report of the Director of Selective Service* (Washington, D.C.: USGPO, 1948), p. 50. Figure for induction stations is from William Menninger, *Psychiatry in a Troubled World* (New York: Macmillan, 1948), p. 277. His source is Surgeon General's Office. Figure for total number of examinees is from *Historical Statistics of the United States, Colonial Times to 1957* (Washington, D.C.: U.S. Bureau of the Census, 1960), p. 735: Series Y 715–762, Selected Characteristics of the Armed Forces, by War.

2. Helen Swick Perry, *Psychiatrist of America: The Life of Harry Stack Sullivan* (Cambridge: Belknap Press of Harvard University, 1982), pp. 335, 389–93; Patrick Mullahy, *The Beginnings of Modern American Psychiatry: The Ideas of Harry Stack Sullivan* (Boston: Houghton Mifflin, 1973).

3. On the membership of Overholser's committee and the National Research Council's preparation for the military mobilization, see Sanford V. Larkey, "The National Research Council and Medical Preparedness," *War Medicine* 1 (January 1941): 77–94.

4. The account in this chapter of the evolution of the screening policies is drawn in part from the following sources: Menninger, *Psychiatry in a Troubled World,* pp. 266–92; Harry Stack Sullivan, "Psychiatry and the National Defense," *Psychiatry* 4 (May 1941): 201–17; id., "Selective Service Psychiatry," *Psychiatry* 4 (August 1941): 440–64; id., "Psychiatric Selection," *Psychiatry* 5 (February 1942): 102–5; id., "Psychiatry, the

Army, and the War," *Psychiatry* 5 (August 1942): 435–42; Winfred Overholser, "Military Psychiatry," *American Journal of Psychiatry* 98 (January
1942): 581–83; Harry A. Steckel, "Report of the Committee on Military
Mobilization," *American Journal of Psychiatry* 98 (September 1941):
295–98, id., "The Organization of Psychiatry for the Emergency," *American Journal of Psychiatry* 98 (May 1942): 791–94; "Psychiatry and the
Selective Service System," comment in *American Journal of Psychiatry*
98 (January 1942): 615–16; "Selective Service System Program," comment in *American Journal of Psychiatry* 100 (November 1943): 419–20.
See also Rebecca Schwartz Greene, "The Role of the Psychiatrist in
World War II," (Ph.D. dissertation, Columbia University, 1977).

5. Menninger, *Psychiatry in a Troubled World,* p. 267; Martin Cooley, "The
Economic Consequences of Inadequate Psychiatric Examinations," *Psychiatry* 4 (May 1941): 261–63.

6. Perry, *Psychiatrist of America,* pp. 209–11, 334, 335–45; Edouard Roditi,
"American Psychoanalysis and Homosexuality," *Dissent* (Summer 1986):
369–70.

7. Correspondence between Overholser and Dr. J. E. Moore, chairman, National Research Council Subcommittee on Venereal Disease, December
23 and 26, 1942, Folder: "Homosexuality NRA Comm. on Neuropsychiatry 1942," Box 14, Overholser Papers.
   For Overholser's views on homosexuality and the military, see, for
example, letter, Overholser to Dr. Franklin G. Ebaugh, August 11, 1941,
Folder: "NRC Cmte on NP, SubCmte on Psychiatry, Dr. Franklin G.
Ebaugh, Chairman," Box 17; correspondence between Overholser and
Dr. J. E. Moore, NRC Subcommittee on Venereal Diseases, December
23 and 26, 1942, Folder: "Homosexuality NRC Comm. On Neuropsychiatry 1942," Box 14; letter, Overholser to Capt. Forrest M. Harrison, BuMed,
November 3, 1942, Folder: "NRC Committee on Neuropsychiatry & Subcommittees," Box 14; all in Overholser Papers.

8. "The William Alanson White Psychiatric Foundation Bulletin: A Minimum
Psychiatric Inspection of Registrants," October 27, 1940, published in
Psychiatry 3 (November 1940): 625–27.

9. Selective Service System Medical Circular No. 1, November 7, 1940.
See also [Harry Stack Sullivan], "Selective Service Psychiatry," *Psychia-
try* 4 (August 1941): 440–43; Albert Deutsch, "Military Psychiatry: World
War II, 1941–1943," in *One Hundred Years of American Psychiatry*
(New York: Columbia University Press, 1944), pp. 419–22; *Selective
Service in Wartime,* Second Report of the Director of Selective Service
1941–42 (Washington, D.C.: USGPO, 1943), p. 31.

10. Sullivan, "Psychiatry and the National Defense," p. 202.

11. "Neuropsychiatric Examination of Applicants for Voluntary Enlistment
and Selectees for Induction," Circular Letter No. 19, War Department,

March 12, 1941, reprinted in *War Medicine* 1 (May 1941): 418–25; Selective Service Medical Circular No. 1 (revised May 19, 1941).

On the addition of the homosexual sections, see Patrick S. Madigan, "Military Psychiatry," *Psychiatry* 4 (May 1941): 228–29; and *Report of Meeting of the Psychiatric Advisory Committee,* National Headquarters, Selective Service System, February 25, 1941, Folder: "Selective Service System, C. A. Dykstra, Director," Box 23, Overholser Papers.

12. Forrest M. Harrison, "Psychiatry in the Navy," *War Medicine* 3 (February 1943): 122.

13. For a history of early medical terms used for homosexuality, see Jonathan Ned Katz, *Gay/Lesbian Almanac* (New York: Harper & Row, 1983), pp. 137–74. For a sample article in United States medical journals describing techniques for treating homosexuality from 1884–1920, see id., *Gay American History* (New York: Crowell, 1976), pp. 129–58.

14. Army Regulation No. 40–105, 1921.

15. For a discussion of the late-nineteenth-century criminologist C. Lombroso's theory of atavastic anatomical and social stigmata, from which these Army categories were in part derived, see Stephen Jay Gould, *The Mismeasure of Man* (New York: W. W. Norton & Company, 1981), chap. 4: "Measuring Bodies: Two Case Studies on the Apishness of Undesirables," pp. 113–45.

16. "In Uniforms and Their Right Minds," *Time,* June 1, 1942, pp. 36–37; Menninger, *Psychiatry in a Troubled World,* p. 268.

17. Sullivan, "Selective Service Psychiatry," p. 443; Menninger, *Psychiatry in a Troubled World,* p. 269.

18. Lectures from the Menninger Clinic seminars were published in *Bulletin of the Menninger Clinic,* vol. 5, no. 5, September 1941; see also vol. 5, no. 4, pp. 121–22, for program of seminars. Lectures from the Bellevue Hospital seminars were published in *War Medicine,* vol. 1, no. 2, March 1941. Most of the lectures from the Selective Service System seminars were published in *Psychiatry,* the organ of the William Alanson White Foundation, edited by Harry Stack Sullivan, and in *War Medicine,* published by the American Medical Association and edited by members of the National Research Council.

19. Published Selective Service System seminar lectures that included discussions of homosexuality include Douglas A. Thom, "Schizoid and Related Personalities," *War Medicine* 1 (May 1941): 410–17; Dexter Means Bullard, "Selective Service Psychiatry: Schizoid and Related Personalities; Mood Disorders and Psychopathic Personalities," *Psychiatry* 4 (May 1941): 231–39; William C. Porter, "Military Psychiatry and the Selective Service," *War Medicine* 1 (May 1941): 364–71; William H. Dunn, "The Psychopath in the Armed Forces," *Psychiatry* 4 (May 1941): 251–59; William C. Menninger, "A Condensed Neuropsychiatric Examination for

Use by Selective Service Boards," *War Medicine* 1 (November 1941): 843–53; Patrick S. Madigan, "Military Psychiatry," *Psychiatry* 4 (May 1941): 225–29; and Elliot C. Cutler, "What Physicians Expect From Psychiatry," *War Medicine* 1 (May 1941): 352–57.

Menninger Clinic seminar lectures that included discussions of homosexuality were published in the *Bulletin of the Menninger Clinic*, vol. 5, no. 5, September 1941, and included Karl A. Menninger, "Recognizing and Renaming 'Psychopathic Personalities,'" pp. 150–56; Robert P. Knight, "Recognizing the Psychoneurotic Registrant," pp. 161–66; Carl-Gustaf D. Tillman, "Detecting Schizoid and Pre-Schizophrenic Personalities," pp. 167–70.

20. For a history of the development of the sexual psychopath category in the United States and its political and social uses, see Estelle B. Freedman, " 'Uncontrolled Desires': The Response to the Sexual Psychopath, 1920–1960," *Journal of American History* 74 (June 1987): 83–106.

21. Porter, "Military Psychiatry and the Selective Service," pp. 367, 369, 371; Thom, "Schizoid and Related Personalities," p. 416.

22. Leo H. Bartemeier, "Schizoid Personality and Schizophrenia," *War Medicine* 1 (September 1941), p. 677.

23. Menninger, *Psychiatry in a Troubled World*, p. 273.

24. Bullard, "Selective Service Psychiatry," pp. 231–32.

25. Ibid.

26. Thom, "Schizoid and Related Personalities," pp. 415–16.

27. Bullard, "Selective Service Psychiatry," pp. 234–35.

28. Ibid.

29. Sullivan, "Selective Service Psychiatry," pp. 447–49, 452–53.

30. Perry, *Psychiatrist of America*, pp. 392–93; Menninger, *Psychiatry in a Troubled World*, p. 270.

31. *Physical Examination of Selective Service Registrants*, Selective Service System Special Monograph No. 15, vol. 1, 1947, pp. 242–44.

32. Subsection 93(h), "Sexual Perversions," section 20, "Psychoses, Psychoneuroses, Personality Disorders," Mobilization Regulations No. 1–9, Standards of Physical Examination During Mobilization, War Department, Washington, March 15, 1942; and Subsection 98(d)(1), "Psychopathic personalities," section 21, "Psychoses, Psychoneuroses, Personality Disorders," Mobilization Regulations No. 1–9, "Standards of Physical Examination During Mobilization," War Department, Washington, April 19, 1944. Minutes of the third meeting, March 10, 1941, Subcommittee on War Neuroses, National Research Council, Folder: "NRC, Committee on Neuropsychiatry, Revision M.R. 1–9," Box 13, Overholser Papers.

33. Tillman, "Detecting Schizoid and Pre-Schizophrenic Personalities," p. 166.

34. Ibid.; Wilfred Bloomberg, M.D., and Capt. Robert W. Hyde, "A Survey of Neuropsychiatric Work at the Boston Induction Station" [February 1942], Folder: "Overholser, Induction Data," Box 8, Overholser Papers.
    A National Research Council study also concluded that effeminate men who were not homosexual were still unfit. Arthur H. Ruggles and F. Lyman Wells, "The Effective Use of Psychiatric and Psychological Knowledge Applicable in the Selection of Men For Military Service," Supplementary Report to the National Research Council, July 31, 1942, pp. 24–25, Folder: "NRC Committee on Neuropsychiatry Oct. 21, 1940– Feb. 28, 1941 I," Box 15, Overholser Papers.

35. Arthur Weider et al., "The Cornell Selectee Index: A Method for Quick Testing of Selectees for the Armed Forces," *Journal of the American Medical Association* 124 (January 22, 1944): 224–28. For copies of various versions of the Cornell Selectee Index, see Folder: "NRC, Meeting Sub-Committee on Psychiatry, 6/29/44," Box 12, Overholser Papers.

36. Form reprinted in *Physical Examination of Selective Service Registrants, SSS Special Monograph No. 15*, vol. 2, 1947, pp. 69–73.

37. Most of the seventeen men rejected as homosexual by local draft board physicians in New York City through the first eight induction periods to April 22, 1941, had made voluntary statements "that they are sexual perverts when they come up to the physician for examination." Letter, Col. Samuel J. Kopetzky, Medical Division, Selective Service, New York City Headquarters, to Dr. J. Paul De River, April 23, 1941, Subject File S-13, "Sex Crimes," Box 824, Papers of Mayor Fiorello La Guardia, New York City Municipal Archives. I wish to thank George Chauncey, Jr., for bringing this correspondence to my attention.

38. "Homosexuals in Uniform," *Newsweek*, June 9, 1947, p. 54. For use of the term *reverse malingerer*, see, for example, testimony of Dr. Francis Braceland, January 31, 1957, Enclosure 1(k), p. 1, Crittenden Report.

39. Sullivan, "Selective Service Psychiatry," pp. 449–50. On stigma management among homosexuals and members of other stigmatized groups, see Erving Goffman, *Stigma: Notes on the Management of Spoiled Identity* (New York: Simon & Schuster, 1963).

40. Carl Binger, M.D., "How We Screen Out Psychological 4-Fs," *Saturday Evening Post*, January 8, 1944, pp. 19, 75–76; Miriam Ottenberg, "How the Navy's 'Mind Detectives' Seek Men of Sound Nerve for Warfare," *Sunday Star*, Washington, D.C., January 10, 1943, p. B5; "In Uniform and Their Right Minds," *Time*, June 1, 1942, pp. 36, 38.

41. Leonard Lyons, "Lyon's Den," *San Francisco Chronicle*, May 14, 1943, p. 28.

42. Redvers Jeanmarie, "An Interview with Bayard Rustin (March 17, 1912– August 24, 1987)," *Other Countries: Black Gay Voices* 1 (Spring 1988): 3–16; Christopher Isherwood, *My Guru and His Disciple* (New York:

Farrar Straus Giroux, 1980), pp. 93–98; Patricia Bosworth, *Montgomery Clift* (New York: Bantam, 1978), p. 88; Bob Thomas, *Liberace* (New York: St. Martin's, 1987), p. 29; W. J. Weatherby, *James Baldwin: Artist on Fire* (New York: Donald I. Fine, 1989), pp. 33–34; Nicholas von Hoffman, *Citizen Cohn* (New York: Doubleday, 1988), pp. 73–74.

43. Donald Webster Cory, *The Homosexual in America* (New York: Greenberg, 1951), p. 77.

44. Christopher Isherwood, *The World in the Evening* (1952; New York: Ballantine, 1967), pp. 265–66.

45. Correspondence from "D.C.," Los Angeles, to author, January 10, 1982, with enclosed transcript of interview with his friend Lester Ellis (pseudonym).

46. "Warns on 'Mental Ills': Protestant Weekly Sees Exaggeration in Army Psychiatric Cases," *New York Times,* July 25, 1944, p. 21.

47. Donald Vining, *A Gay Diary: 1933–1946* (New York: Pepys Press, 1979), pp. 213–14, 216, 224, 226–27.

48. For a discussion of the ethics of psychiatrists reporting their patients to military authorities, see Report of the Committee of Ethics, Proceedings of Societies, *American Journal of Psychiatry* 99 (September, 1942): 296–97.

49. Letter, Dr. ———, Laguna Beach, California, to Dr. Walter E. Barton, Medical Corps, U.S. Army, September 9, 1943, Folder 250. to 250.1, Box 307, Entry 29 1943–44, General Subject Index, RG 112.

50. Letter, [physician] to Winfred Overholser, December 23, 1942, Folder: "Homosexuality NRC Comm. on Neuropsychiatry 1942," Box 14, Overholser Papers.

51. Memorandum from Otis L. Anderson, U.S. Public Health Service, Division of Venereal Disease, to the U.S. Surgeon General, November 4, 1941, regarding letter from anonymous physician in Chicago, dated October 30, 1941, in Folder 250. to 250.1, Box 108, Entry 29 1941–42, General Subject File, RG 112.

52. D'Ann Campbell, *Women at War with America* (Cambridge: Harvard University Press, 1984), pp. 19–20, 256 n.8; Susan M. Hartmann, "Women in the Military Service," in *Clio Was a Woman,* ed. Mabel E. Deutrich and Virginia C. Purdy (Washington: Howard University Press, 1980), pp. 195–205.

53. Medical Department U.S. Army, *Physical Standards in World War II* (Washington, D.C.: USGPO, 1967), pp. 56–61; Menninger, *Psychiatry in a Troubled World,* p. 111–15.

54. Menninger, *Psychiatry in a Troubled World,* p. 112.

55. Mattie E. Treadwell, *The United States Army in World War II, Special Studies, The Women's Army Corps* (Washington, D.C.: USGPO, 1954), p. 177.

56. For the reports on screening Women Marines at Camp LeJeune, North Carolina, see Philip Solomon, Meyer Brown, and M. R. Jones, "Neuropsychiatry in the United States Marine Corps, Women's Reserve—Criteria for Rejection," *War Medicine* 6 (November 1944): 291–95; and id., "Neuropsychiatry in the U.S. Marine Corps, Women's Reserve: I. Methods and Procedures in the Neuropsychiatric Selection of Recruits," *American Journal of Psychiatry* 101 (March 1945): 643–49. WAC instructors also taught WAC officer candidates that masculine women were not necessarily lesbian and could make good soldiers. See War Department Pamphlet No. 35-1, "Sex Hygiene Course," Officers and Officer Candidates, Women's Army Auxiliary Corps, May 27, 1943, Lecture 5, "Homosexuality," pp. 25–26.

57. Memoranda, Enrollment of Auxiliaries with Physical Defects or of Doubtful Reputation, to Adjutant General, Appointment and Induction Branch, from Director of Personnel, WAAC, November 19, 1942; from Chief, Appointment and Induction Branch, AGO, to Director of WAAC, November 23, 1942; and to Adjutant General, Appointment and Induction Branch, from Director of WAAC, December 5, 1942; all in Box 111, Entry 54, Army G-1 WAC Decimal File 1942–46, RG 165.

58. Memorandum to Captain Edlung, War Department, from Executive Vice President of Ayer Research, reporting on results of research at request of Lt. Col. Vance L. Sailor, December 23, 1942, Box 111, Entry 54, Army G-1 WAC Decimal File 1942–46, RG 165.

59. Memorandum from Joan G. Murray, Third Officer, WAAC Director's Office, to Director of Personnel, re: Recruiting, December 19, 1942, with inclosures, Box 110, Entry 54, Army G-1 WAC Decimal File 1942–46, RG 165.

60. Treadwell, *The Women's Army Corps*, pp. 168–77.

61. Ibid., pp. 602–6; *Physical Standards in World War II*, pp. 56–61.

62. Menninger, *Psychiatry in a Troubled World*, pp. 112, 114; Treadwell, *The Women's Army Corps*, pp. 602–6.

63. Treadwell, *The Women's Army Corps*, pp. 625–26, 632.

64. Fort Oglethorpe Report, pp. 31, 33, 34. Letter from mother making charges is Inclosure 11 to Exhibit A of this report.

65. Fort Oglethorpe Testimony, pp. 285, 286, 310.

66. Ibid., pp. 218–19.

67. Ibid., pp. 290, 291.

68. Fort Oglethorpe Report, pp. 32–34.

69. War Department Technical Bulletin, TB MED 100, WAC Recruiting Station Neuropsychiatric Examination, 4 October 1944, Order of Chief of Staff George C. Marshall, Box 31, RG 112. Margaret D. Craighill, "Psychi-

atric Aspects of Women Serving in the Army,'' *American Journal of Psychiatry* 104 (October 1947): 227. See also Menninger, *Psychiatry in a Troubled World,* p. 114, and Treadwell, *The Women's Army Corps,* pp. 602–6.

70. Nancy Adair and Casey Adair, *Word Is Out* (San Francisco: New Glide, 1978), pp. 57–58.

71. For discussions of stereotypes and sexuality, see Sander L. Gilman, *Difference and Pathology: Stereotypes of Sexuality, Race and Madness* (Ithaca: Cornell University Press, 1985), and Gordon W. Allport, *The Nature of Prejudice* (New York: Addison-Wesley, 1958).

72. Memorandum: Statistics on Army Homosexuals Furnished by the Surgeon General's Office, 22 June 1950, Source: Mr. McDowell, Medical Statistics Division, Army SGO, From Charles O. Perrin, Administrative Assistant, Precedent and History Section, Army AGO; and Memorandum for the Record, Subject: Information on Homosexuality, 23 June 1950, Arthur J. McDowell, Assistant Chief, Medical Statistics Division, Army SGO; both in Folder: "Homosexuals," Case 1438, AGO Precedent File, RG 407.

Chapter 2. Fitting In

1. Winfred Overholser to Alfred A. Gross, January 29, 1942, Folder: "Selective Service System, Brig. Gen. Lewis B. Hershey, Director," Box 24, Overholser Papers.

2. Letter, Lt. Col. Malcolm J. Farrell, Acting Director, Neuropsychiatry Consultants Division, Army SGO, to Cap. Frank R. Barta, Mental Hygiene Unit, Fort Bliss, Texas, September 12, 1944, Folder 250. to 250.1, Box 307, Entry 29 1943–44, General Subject File, RG 112.

3. William Menninger, *Psychiatry in a Troubled World* (New York: Macmillan, 1948), p. 106.

4. Lee Kennett, *G.I.: The American Soldier in World War II* (New York: Charles Scribner's Sons, 1987), p. 42.

5. Joy Bright Hancock, *Lady in the Navy* (Annapolis: Naval Institute Press, 1972), pp. x, 101–9; Mattie E. Treadwell, *The United States Army in World War II, Special Studies, The Women's Army Corps* (Washington, D.C.: USGPO, 1954), pp. 631–36.

6. "The Wacs Sight New Objectives," *New York Times Magazine,* September 2, 1945, p. 12.

7. On the demands of basic training, see Gwynne Dyer, *War* (New York: Crown, 1985), p. 112; Kennett, *G.I.,* pp. 53–54.

8. Kennett, *G.I.,* pp. 46–57; Dyer, *War,* pp. 102–29.

9. Menninger, *Psychiatry in a Troubled World,* p. 185–86.

10. Henry Elkin, "Aggressive and Erotic Tendencies in Army Life," *American Journal of Sociology* 51 (March 1946): 412; Frederick Elkin, "The Soldier's Language," *American Journal of Sociology* 51 (March 1946): 414–22; Donald Vining, *A Gay Diary: 1933–1946* (New York: Pepys Press, 1979), p. 280.

11. James Jones, *WW II* (New York: Ballantine, 1975), pp. 16–17. See also R. Robert Cohen, "Factors in Adjustment to Army Life," *War Medicine* 5 (February 1944): 84.

12. Elkin, "Aggressive and Erotic Tendencies," p. 412.

13. Irving L. Janis, "Psychodynamic Aspects of Adjustment to Army Life," *Psychiatry* 8 (May 1945): 170–71. For a fictional account of how GIs joked about "queers" in the barracks, see Gore Vidal, *The City and the Pillar* (1948; New York: Signet, 1965), pp. 90–91.

14. Howard Brotz and Everett Wilson, "Characteristics of Military Society," *American Journal of Sociology* 51 (March 1946): 371–75.

15. Ibid.; Kennett, *G.I.,* p. 58.

16. Rudy Grillo, "On Record: Homosexuals and Popular Song," *Christopher Street* 11 (October 1988): 40–48.

17. Menninger, *Psychiatry in a Troubled World,* pp. 224–25.

18. Lincoln Kirstein, *Rhymes of a Pfc* (New York: New Directions, 1964), p. 30.

19. Janis, "Psychodynamic Aspects," pp. 170, 171.

20. New York Central Railroad advertisement, *Life,* September 13, 1943, p. 61. This advertisement explained that such pairing up in lower berths was necessary to fit "39 men to a car" on crowded troop trains. A full-page New Haven Railroad advertisement that was published in many magazines and newspapers showed two unclothed young soldiers sleeping in the lower berth facing away from each other; see, for example, *Life,* December 21, 1942, p. 21.

21. Menninger, *Psychiatry in a Troubled World,* p. 179.

22. "Saul" is a pseudonym. This is quoted from case files in the George W. Henry Foundation, established in 1948 in New York City. George W. Henry, *Society and the Sex Variant* (New York: Collier Books, 1965), p. 119.

23. In a parody of this overcrowding, the Statler-Hilton Hotel ran an advertisement cartoon of several men sleeping in a hotel-room bed. *Life,* March 27, 1944, p. 43. For a fictional account of the sexual tensions experienced by GIs sleeping in the same hotel-room beds, see Vidal, *The City and the Pillar,* pp. 91–93.

24. In his wartime diary, Donald Vining describes numerous sexual encounters with servicemen he never saw again and who rarely acknowledged the homosexual nature of their activity. See, for example, pp. 325, 328–29, 330, 333, 334, 344.

25. For a fictional account of how a gay soldier presented himself as heterosexual to seduce another soldier, see Vidal, *The City and the Pillar,* pp. 88–92.

26. Treadwell, *The Women's Army Corps,* p. 625.

27. Fort Oglethorpe Testimony, [embraces] p. 12; [shoulder] p. 34; [bed] p. 55; [couples] p. 113.

28. Fort Oglethorpe Testimony, pp. 15, 264–65.

29. Ibid., pp. 11, 42–44, 119.

30. On butch/femme relationships among lesbians in Buffalo, New York, see Madeline Davis and Elizabeth Lapovsky Kennedy, "Oral History and the Study of Sexuality in the Lesbian Community: Buffalo, New York, 1940–1960," *Feminist Studies* 12 (Spring 1986): 7–26. I wish to thank Liz Kennedy for pointing out that *girlfriend, girl,* and *lady* seem to have been used among lesbians in the 1940s and *femme* was used beginning in the 1950s.

31. Fort Oglethorpe Testimony, pp. 113, 115.

32. Ibid., pp. 13, 86–87, 103.

33. Ibid., pp. 86–87, 92.

34. Ibid., p. 103.

35. Fort Oglethorpe Testimony, [latrines] pp. 159, 171; [hallways] p. 168; [dugouts] p. 253; [barracks] p. 166; [service club] pp. 155, 178; [parking lot] pp. 116, 186; [woods] pp. 110, 113–16, 261; [South Post Service Club] p. 279; [butches during basic training], p. 198; [hotels] p. 158; [USO] p. 137.

36. Letter, F. M. Harrison, BuMed, to Winfred Overholser, NRC, August 5, 1942, P13-7, General Correspondence, RG 52.

37. Cpl. Barret McGurn, "WAACS Drop an 'A'," *Yank,* August 20, 1943, p. 9; William Manchester, *Goodbye, Darkness* (New York: Little, Brown, 1979), pp. 120–21; Nancy Shea, *The Waacs* (New York: Harper & Brothers, 1943), pp. 121–22.

Lectures to trainees on sodomy and oral sex offenses were at least considered if not implemented early in the century. In 1916 the Navy judge advocate general recommended that the "commandants and commanding officers of the naval training stations be instructed to cause lectures or talks to be given to apprentices under training, setting forth the nature of such offenses [sodomy, sexual perversion, etc.], the liability of all parties concerned, and the fact that the [Navy] department insists upon severe punishment being meted out in such cases." File 26251-11479a, JAG, February 18, 1916, cited in *Naval Digest,* prepared by Capt. Edwin N. McClellan, 1916, reprinted 1920 (Washington, D.C.: GPO, 1921), p. 580.

38. See, for example, Menninger, *Psychiatry in a Troubled World,* "Stresses

During Training Period," pp. 56–68; Janis, "Psychodynamic Aspects," pp. 159–76; Elkin, "Aggressive and Erotic Tendencies," pp. 408–13; David M. Schneider, "The Social Dynamics of Physical Disability in Army Basic Training," *Psychiatry* 10 (1947): 323–33; Cohen, "Factors in Adjustment to Army Life," pp. 83–91; Maskin and Altman, "Military Psychodynamics," pp. 263–69.

39. Menninger, *Psychiatry in a Troubled World*, pp. 223–25.

40. Meyer H. Maskin and Leon L. Altman, "Military Psychodynamics: Psychological Factors in the Transition from Civilian to Soldier," *Psychiatry* 6 (August 1943): 264–66.

41. Harry Benjamin, "The Sex Problem in the Armed Forces," *The Urologic and Cutaneous Review* 48, no. 5 (1944): 231–44.

42. The popularization of psychiatry helped spread the belief that homosexuality was an occupational hazard of both military service and prison life. See, for example, William S. Sadler and Lena K. Sadler, *Living a Sane Sex Life* (Chicago: American Publishers, 1938), pp. 95, 101.

43. "Sex Hygiene Course," Officers and Officer Candidates, Women's Army Auxiliary Corps, May 27, 1943 (revised as "Sex Hygiene Course," Women's Army Corps, May 1945), War Department Pamphlet No. 35–1, pp. 24–29; Treadwell, *The Women's Army Corps*, pp. 616–17, 625.

44. For proposals in the Army Chaplain's Corps, see correspondence between Captain Charles O. Dutton, Post Chaplain, Fort Bliss, Texas, and Chief of Chaplains, U.S. Army, August 1943, in Folder: "250.1 Morals and Conduct—Misc. Volume I From 12/10/40 to 12/31/43," Box 195, Entry 1, Office Management Division, Decimal File 1920–45, RG 247.

   One of the most complete lectures on homosexuality was developed in the Women's Auxiliary Army Corps in May 1943 as the fifth of five lectures in the Sex Hygiene Course presented to officers and officer candidates. See also "WAC Recruiting Station Neuropsychiatric Examination," War Department Technical Bulletin, TB MED 100, October 4, 1944, pp. 4–5, Box 31, RG 112.

45. Fort Oglethorpe Testimony, pp. 225, 288.

46. Testimony of Captain Eleanor Furst Roberts, Director of Training, Fort Oglethorpe Testimony, pp. 271–73.

47. Fort Oglethorpe Testimony, pp. 278–79.

48. Ibid., p. 291.

49. Ibid., pp. 271–73, 309.

50. Ibid., pp. 31–32.

51. Correspondence re: Course of Instruction on Homosexuality, September, 1944, between Surgeon General's Office and Army Service Forces, Box 437, G-1 Personnel, RG 165.

52. Lt. Col. Patrick Madigan to J. Paul de River, November 17, 1941, Folder: "250. to 250.1," Box 108, Entry 29, 1941–42, General Subject File, RG 112.

53. "Lecture Outlines For Enlisted Men on Personal Adjustment Problems," War Department Technical Bulletin, TB MED 21, March 15, 1944 and December 29, 1945, Box 31, RG 112; Cohen, "Factors in Adjustment," pp. 83–91

54. "Sex Hygiene Course," pp. 1, 3.

55. Kennett, *G.I.*, p. 62; Park Kendall, *Gone With the Draft* (New York: Grosset & Dunlap, 1941), in unpaged "Army Slang" appendix under entry "See the Chaplain!"

56. Medical Department U.S. Army, *Neuropsychiatry in World War II*, vol. 1 (Washington, D.C.: USGPO, 1966), p. 367; Edward G. Billings et al., "Comparison of One Hundred Army Psychiatric Patients and One Hundred Enlisted Men," *War Medicine* 4 (September 1943): 283–98.

57. *Psychology for the Fighting Man*, Prepared for the Fighting Man Himself by a Committee of the National Research Council with the Collaboration of Science Service as a Contribution to the War Effort, Second Edition (Washington and New York: Infantry Journal and Penguin Books, 1944), pp. 280–82; Menninger, *Psychiatry in a Troubled World*, p. 73.

58. D'Ann Campbell, *Women At War with America* (Cambridge: Harvard University Press, 1984), pp. 25–26.

59. Ibid., p. 29. Women's colleges had a long tradition in which women students formed intimate couplings known as "crushes" or "smashing" and in which professors coupled in what were known as "Boston Marriages." On the tradition of "crushes," "smashing," and lesbian relationships in women's colleges in the United States, see, for example, Nancy Sahli, "Smashing: Women's Relationships Before the Fall," *Chrysalis*, no. 8 (Summer 1979), pp. 17–27; Judith Schwarz, "Yellow Clover: Katharine Lee Bates and Katharine Coman," *Frontiers* 4, no. 1 (1979): 59–67; Anna Mary Wells, *Miss Marks and Miss Woolley* (Boston: Houghton Mifflin, 1978); Lillian Faderman, *Surpassing the Love of Men* (New York: William Morrow, 1981), pp. 190–203, 225–30; Jonathan [Ned] Katz, *Gay American History* (New York: Crowell, 1976), pp. 58–60, and id., *Gay/Lesbian Almanac* (New York: Harper & Row, 1983), pp. 175–79.

60. "Sex Hygiene Course," p. 28.

61. Ibid., pp. 26–28.

62. Ibid., p. 27.

63. Menninger, *Psychiatry in a Troubled World*, p. 223.

64. *Psychology for the Fighting Man*, pp. 280–81.

65. Murray D. Kirkwood, "A Soldier Looks at Conscription," *New York Times Magazine*, March 25, 1945, p. 9. See also "Tolerance," letter

from Pvt. Arthur Feldman, *New York Times Magazine,* December 3, 1944, p. 20.

66. Florence Powdermaker, "Review of Cases at Merchant Marine Rest Centers," *American Journal of Psychiatry* 101 (March 1945): 650–54.

67. Bill Mauldin, *Up Front* (Cleveland and New York: World Publishing Company, 1945), p. 84.

68. Schneider, "Social Dynamics," p. 331.

69. On common types in the barracks, see Menninger, *Psychiatry in a Troubled World,* p. 179; and Kennett, *G.I.,* pp. 60–61.

70. On nicknames see Murray Schumach, "What Happens to a Man in the Barracks," *New York Times Magazine,* February 20, 1944, p. 44; Menninger, *Psychiatry in a Troubled World,* pp. 175–76, 180.

71. Hank Vilas interview in *Before Stonewall,* film by Greta Schiller, John Scagliotti, and Robert Rosenberg (New York: Before Stonewall, Inc., 1986).

72. Letter, Jerry Watson to Jim Kepner, September 8, 1944, Kepner Correspondence.

73. Kendall, *Gone With the Draft,* "Army Slang" appendix.

74. Schumach, "What Happens to a Man in the Barracks," p. 18. *Yank* published cartoon caricatures of and poems about some of these effeminate types; see, for example, August 13, 1943, p. 22; "So You Want to be a 1st. Sergeant," February 26, 1943, p. 9; and "I Want—," October 28, 1942, p. 16.

75. For a discussion of the "sissy" role in early Hollywood films, especially under the antihomosexual restrictions of the Motion Picture Production Code beginning in 1930, see Vito Russo, *The Celluloid Closet: Homosexuality in the Movies* (New York: Harper & Row, 1981), chap. 1, "Who's a Sissy?" pp. 2–59.

76. For a cartoon spoof of soldiers' sewing duties, see "Needle Pointers," *Yank,* February 26, 1943, p. 15.

77. Elkin, "Aggressive and Erotic Tendencies," p. 412.

78. John Horne Burns, *Lucifer with a Book* (1949; New York: Avon, 1977), p. 113.

79. Keith Vacha, *Quiet Fire: Memoirs of Older Gay Men* (Trumansburg, N.Y.: Crossing Press, 1985), pp. 198–99.

80. Letter, Jerry Watson to Jim Kepner, June 12, 1943, Kepner Correspondence.

81. Copy or draft of letter from Howard Taylor to the base psychiatrist, dated February 19, 1944; copy or draft of undated letter by Howard Taylor circa February 1944; unidentified manuscript by Howard Taylor dated August 13, 1944; Taylor Correspondence.

82. See, for example, cartoon caricatures of these cliques in *Yank,* October 14, 1942, p. 16.

83. Fort Oglethorpe Testimony, p. 17.

84. Fort Oglethorpe Report, p. 29.

85. Fort Oglethorpe Testimony, pp. 138, 176, 185.

86. Ibid., p. 184.

87. Fort Oglethorpe Testimony; author's interviews with Pat Bond, May 18, 1981, and Betty Somers, August 14, 1982. On cliques in the WAVES, see Joy Bright Hancock, *Lady in the Navy,* p. 106.

88. Lt. Comdr. Philip Solomon and Capt. Marjorie C. Winfield, "Needs and Problems of Military Women in Readjusting to Civilian Life," *American Journal of Orthopsychiatry* 15 (July 1945): 454–62.

89. [Junior, Brat] author's interview with Pat Bond, May 18, 1981; [Slugger] author's interview with Helen Harder, May 11, 1982; [Butch] Pete Paris, "The Waacs in North Africa," *Yank,* July 9, 1943, pp. 2–4, and Fort Oglethorpe Testimony pp. 154–57; [Detail] Paris, "The Waacs in North Africa," p. 2–4; [Mike, Spike, Tommie] Fort Oglethorpe Report, p. 5, and Fort Oglethorpe Testimony, pp. 15, 256.

90. Hancock, *Lady in the Navy,* pp. 11, 13; Shea, *The Waacs,* p. 79.

91. Hancock, *Lady in the Navy,* pp. 275–76.

92. *Stars and Stripes* [London], August 22, 1942, p. 2.

93. Lt. Herbert Greenspan and Comdr. John D. Campbell, "The Homosexual as a Personality Type," *American Journal of Psychiatry* 101 (March 1945): 685.

94. Lt. Col. Lewis H. Loeser, "The Sexual Psychopath in the Military Service (A Study of 270 Cases)," *American Journal of Psychiatry* 102 (July 1945): 96.

95. Clements C. Fry and Edna G. Rostow, "Some Observations on Homosexuality in Military Service," Interim Report No. 337, 1 April 1945, Committee on Medical Research of the Office of Scientific Research and Development, pp. 22–24, 36–38, Archives of the National Academy of Sciences, Washington, D.C.; and id., "Reflections on Some Aspects of Homosexuality as it Relates to Military Administration," [May 10, 1948], pp. 10–11, Box 65, Entry 356, RG 330.

96. Menninger, *Psychiatry in a Troubled World,* pp. 62–64; Treadwell, *The Women's Army Corps,* pp. 543–44; Campbell, *Women at War with America,* pp. 31–32; Susan Hartmann, *Home Front and Beyond* (Boston: Twayne, 1982) p. 37; Marie Bennett Alsmeyer, *The Way of the Waves* (Conway, Ark.: Hamba Books, 1981), p. 19.

97. Fry and Rostow, "Reflections," p. 5.

98. Bernard C. Nalty, *Strength for the Fight* (New York: Free Press, 1986), pp. 178–79.

99. On the masculine and lesbian reputations of the branches, see Donald Webster Cory, *The Lesbian in America* (1964; New York: MacFadden-Bartell Books, 1965), pp. 170–71; Helen Rogan, *Mixed Company* (New York: G. P. Putnam's Sons, 1981), pp. 151–59; Treadwell, *The Women's Army Corps*, pp. 623, 625; Campbell, *Women at War with America*, pp. 28, 39; "WAACS: First Women Soldiers Join the Army," *Life*, September 7, 1942, p. 75.

    On propaganda, see Maureen Honey, *Creating Rosie the Riveter: Class, Gender, and Propaganda during World War II* (Amherst: University of Massachusetts Press, 1984), p. 117.

    On official taboos against lesbian behavior, see *Handbook for the Women's Army Auxiliary Corps*, Fort Des Moines, Iowa, 1943, pp. 7, 20.

    Articles in *Yank* and the Fort Oglethorpe Testimony described many women soldiers with mannish haircuts or boyish bobs.

100. Philip Solomon, Meyer Brown, M. R. Jones, "Neuropsychiatry in the U.S. Marine Corps, Women's Reserve," *American Journal of Psychiatry* 101 (March 1945): 543–49.

101. Hartmann, *The Home Front and Beyond*, p. 37; Treadwell, *The Women's Army Corps*, pp. 559, 593–97; Campbell, *Women at War with America*, p. 31.

102. Campbell, *Women at War with America*, p. 34.

103. Treadwell, *The Women's Army Corps*, p. 140.

104. Paris, "The Waacs in North Africa," pp. 2–4. See also Treadwell, *The Women's Army Corps*, "Physical Training," pp. 638–40.

105. Marcy Adelman, ed., *Long Time Passing: Lives of Older Lesbians* (Boston: Alyson Publications, 1986), p. 165.

106. Treadwell, *The Women's Army Corps*, p. 643; Shea, *The Waacs, p. 142.*

107. Treadwell, *The Women's Army Corps*, p. 643; Shea, *The Waacs, pp. 142–46.*

108. Albert Preston, Jr., "The Mental-Hygiene Unit in a W.A.C. Training Center," *Mental Hygiene* 30 (July 1946): 368–80.

109. Cpl. E. M. Halliday, "WAACS," *Yank*, June 4, 1943, pp. 6–7; Treadwell, *The Women's Army Corps*, p. 645.

110. "WAACS," *Yank*, June 4, 1943, p. 7.

111. Fort Oglethorpe Testimony, p. 269.

112. Treadwell, *The Women's Army Corps*, p. 645; Paris, "The Waacs in North Africa," p. 2–4; Shea, *The Waacs, pp. 63–64.*

113. Fort Oglethorpe Testimony, pp. 280–81.

114. On how the military branches utilized women during the war, see Campbell, *Women at War with America*, chap. 1, "A Crushing Defeat in This Man's Army," pp. 17–46.

115. See individual entries in Elbridge Colby, *Army Talk: The Language of U.S. Soldiers* (Princeton: Princeton University Press, 1942); and Kendall, *Gone with the Draft*, "Army Slang" appendix.

116. Treadwell, *The Women's Army Corps*, pp. 337–38.

117. "Pharmacist's Mate Receives Letter for 'Other Woman,' " *The Stars and Stripes* [London], October 31, 1942, p. 4; "Queen Penicillin," in John Horne Burns, *The Gallery* (1947; New York: Bantam, 1970), pp. 291–323; Christopher Isherwood, *World in the Evening* (1952; New York: Ballantine, 1967), pp. 265–66.

118. W. P. Briggs, "Men Nurses in the U.S. Navy," *American Journal of Nursing* 43 (January 1943), pp. 39–42.

119. Benjamin Cheever, ed., *The Letters of John Cheever* (New York: Simon & Schuster, 1988), p. 78.

120. Letter from H. Richard Musser, R.N., *American Journal of Nursing* 41 (December 1941): 1449.

121. David M. Schneider, "The Culture of the Army Clerk," *Psychiatry* 9 (May 1946): 123–27.

122. Greenspan and Campbell, "The Homosexual as a Personality Type," pp. 685–86.

123. Eli Ginzberg et al., *Breakdown and Recovery* (New York: Columbia University Press, 1959), pp. 60–62.

124. Letter, Brother Athanasius to Julia Flikke, January 25, 1942, Folder: "(Nurses A to Z) (1941–42)," Box 104 (231 Nurses), Entry 29 1941–42, General Subject File, RG 112.

125. Letter, *Yank*, March 9, 1945, p. 14.

126. Letter, Brig. Gen. Albert G. Love, Acting the Surgeon General, to Mrs. Mary A. Hickey, R.N., Secretary, American Nurses' Association, April 7, 1941, Folder: "(Nurses A to Z) (1941–42)," Box 104 (231 Nurses), Entry 29 1941–42, General Subject File, RG 112; letter, Maj. Gen. George F. Lull, Deputy Surgeon General, to U.S. Senator Joseph F. Guffey, February 3, 1945, Folder: "231. (Nurses A to Z) (1945)," Box 548 (231 Titles & Grades H–Z), Entry 29 1945–46, General Subject File, RG 112.
    For letters of protest, resolutions from professional organizations, and the response of Army officials concerning the treatment of men nurses in the Army, see Folder: "(Nurses A to Z) (1941–42)," Box 104 (231 Nurses), Entry 29 1941–42; Folder: "(Nurses A to Z) (1943–44)," Box 304 (231.-1 Titles and Grades H to Occupational Therapists), Entry 29 1943–44; and Folder: "231. (Nurses A to Z) (1945)," Box 548 (231 Titles & Grades H–Z), Entry 29 1945–46; General Subject File, RG 112. See also articles and letters to the editor in *American Journal of Nursing*, vols. 41–46 (1941–46).

On the status of male nurses in the armed forces during World War II, see Philip A. Kalisch and Beatrice J. Kalisch, "Male Nurses and Military Nursing," in *The Advancement of American Nursing* (Boston: Little, Brown, 1978), pp. 576–83; and "Men Nurses," chap. 31, in Mary M. Roberts, *American Nursing: History and Interpretation* (New York: Macmillan, 1954), pp. 312–27. See also Philip A. Kalisch and Margaret Scobey, "Female Nurses in American Wars: Helplessness Suspended for the Duration," *Armed Forces and Society* 9 (Winter 1983): 215–44.

127. Joel T. Boone, "The Sexual Aspects of Military Personnel," *Journal of Social Hygiene* 27, no. 3 (1941): 119.

Chapter 3. GI Drag: A Gay Refuge

1. In the Navy and Merchant Marine, for example, there is a long tradition, which still continues, of ritualized drag, sexual humiliation, and role reversal called "Crossing the Line," practiced aboard ship to initiate the new sailors as they cross the equator or International Date Line for the first time. Lt. Comdr. Leland P. Lovette, *Navy Customs: Traditions and Usage* (Annapolis: United States Naval Institute, 1939), pp. 42–47; Vice Adm. William P. Mack (Ret.) and Lt. Comdr. Royal W. Connell, *Navy Customs: Traditions and Usage* (Annapolis: Naval Institute Press, 1980), pp. 180–92. For a gay newspaper's coverage of this ritual, see "High Heels On the High Seas," *San Francisco Sentinel,* August 12, 1988, pp. 1, 3.

2. On the USO soldier entertainment campaign, see Richard Fawkes, *Fighting For a Laugh: Entertaining the British and American Armed Forces 1939–1946* (London: Macdonald and Jane's, 1978), chap. 9, pp. 112–22; Julia M. H. Carson, *Home Away From Home: The Story of the USO* (New York: Harper & Brothers, 1946); Joe E. Brown, *Your Kids and Mine* (Garden City and New York: Doubleday, Doran and Co., 1944).

3. H. I. Brock, "Army's Morale Builder," *New York Times Magazine,* September 7, 1941, pp. 12, 19; Louis Simon, "Theatre in the Camps," *Theatre Arts* (July 1942): 423–28; Raymond B. Fosdick, "The Leisure Time of a Democratic Army," *Recreation* (September 1942): 319–25, 364; "Army Probing Hidden Talent in Camps," *Variety,* September 30, 1942, p. 1; Lloyd Shearer, "Brightening the Corners Where They Are," *New York Times Magazine,* November 1, 1942, p. 19; Joint Army and Navy Committee on Welfare and Recreation, *A Report on Army Special Service Activities and Facilities* (Washington, D.C.: USGPO, 1942); "The Theatre and the Armed Forces," *Theatre Arts* (March 1943): 149–68; Bob Stuart McKnight, "Original Army Shows," *Theatre Arts* (July 1943): 426–33; "This Man's Army Makes Its Own Fun Thanks to Special Services Division," *Newsweek,* August 7, 1944, pp. 72, 74.

4. "The Theatre and the Armed Forces," pp. 149–68.

5. "A Plea for Navy Entertainment," *Variety,* October 14, 1942, pp. 3, 52; "Actresses in Uniform," *Theatre Arts* (March 1943): 196; "The Things They Want to Do," *Recreation* (October 1944): 349–50; "Navy Sets Up Talent Program as Answer to Morale Program," *Variety,* March 7, 1945, p. 4.

6. Simon, "Theatre in the Camps," pp. 425–26.

7. Memorandum, from Frederick M. Warburg, Lt. Col., A.G.D., Chief Technical Operation Branch, Special Services Division, to Commanding General, Camp Sibert, Alabama, February 17, 1943, Subject: "Training Plan for Theatrical Section of Course Taught by Special Service Technical Training Center," 353.8, Box 247, Section I, Entry 196A, Director of Administrative Army Exchange Services, General Correspondence 1941–43, RG 160; "Pvt. Pedrick Gets a Paint Job," *The Stars and Stripes,* April 28, 1943, p. 4; "The World and the Theatre," *Theatre Arts* (September 1943): 514; Rosamond Gilder, "Theatre Overseas," *Theatre Arts* (April 1944): 220; "Wac . . . demonstrates to a soldier audience how to create a female for a soldier show" for "a two-day demonstration in London on staging of soldier shows," April 9, 1945, Army Signal Corps photograph No. SC-204637.

8. "About Face," Soldier Shows "Blueprint Special," prepared by Headquarters, Army Service Forces, Special Services Division, Army Service Forces [n.d.]. See also, "Hi Yank!" Soldier Shows Blueprint Special No. 2, Special Services Division, Headquarters, Army Service Forces [n.d.]; and Sgt. Walter Bernstein, "Report on 'Hi, Yank!' " *Theatre Arts* (November 1944): 654–60.

9. Ezra Stone and Weldon Melick, *Coming, Major!* (New York and Philadelphia, Lippincott, 1944), pp. 192–93.

10. On June 12, 1942, Donald Vining wrote in his diary that a gay soldier from the *TITA* cast had asked him out on a date. Vining, *A Gay Diary: 1933–1946* (New York: Pepys Press, 1979), p. 220.

11. Anthony Slide, *The Vaudevillians* (Westport, Conn.: Arlington House, 1981), pp. 50–53.

12. Robert C. Toll, *On with the Show: The First Century of Show Business in America* (New York: Oxford University Press, 1976), chap. 9: "Only Skin Deep: The Impersonators," pp. 239–63.

13. An extensive literature exists on Eltinge. See, for example, "This Is Julian Eltinge—But Who Do You Think This Is?" *American Magazine* 85 (May 1918): 36; *Julian Eltinge Magazine;* Toll, *On with the Show,* pp. 239–63; Slide, *The Vaudevillians,* pp. 46–47; Anthony Slide, *Great Pretenders* (Lombard, Ill.: Wallace-Homestead, 1986), pp. 20–29. Eltinge's obituaries were published in the *New York Times,* March 18, 1941, p. 19; *Time,* March 17, 1941, p. 63; *Variety,* March 12, 1941, p. 49. On the Eltinge Theater, see "Eltinge Theater," *New York Times,* February

26, 1921. On Eltinge in Hollywood films, see Homer Dickens, *What a Drag: Men as Women and Woman as Men in the Movies* (New York: Quill, 1984), pp. 16, 17; Vito Russo, *The Celluloid Closet* (New York: Harper & Row, 1981), p. 15; Daniel Blum, *A Pictorial History of the Silent Screen* (New York: Grosset & Dunlap, 1953), pp. 128, 148, 152, 163, 275; and Toll, *On with the Show*, p. 248.

14. Slide, *Great Pretenders*, pp. 43–44; W. A. S. Douglas, "The Passing of Vaudeville," *American Mercury* (October 1927): 188–94; "Year in Vaudeville," *Variety*, January 4, 1928, p. 17.

15. Joe Laurie, Jr., *Vaudeville: From the Honky-Tonks to the Palace* (New York: Henry Holt, 1953), pp. 92–93.

16. C. J. Bulliet, *Venus Castina* (1928; New York: Bonanza Books, 1956), p. 7.

17. Slide, *Great Pretenders*, pp. 140–41.

18. Antony James, "Remembering the Thirties," *The Yellow Book* [n.d. (1973?)], pp. 6–10; Bruce Rogers, "Degenerates of Greenwich Village," *Current Psychology and Psychoanalysis* (December 1936), excerpted in Martin Bauml Duberman, "About Time," *New York Native*, July 27, 1981, p. 15; Gregory Sprague, "Chicago Past," *The Advocate*, August 18, 1983, pp. 28–31, 58; id., "Gay Balls: An Old Chicago Tradition," *Lesbian/Gay History Researchers Network Newsletter*, No. 4 (March 1981): 4–5; Leah Garchik, "Finocchio's: 45 Years of Guys Dolled Up As Women," *San Francisco Sunday Examiner and Chronicle*, Datebook, July 12, 1981, pp. 19–20; LaForest Potter, *Strange Loves* (New York: Dodsley, 1933), Chapter 11, "The Drag," pp. 182–94; Blair Niles, *Strange Brother* (New York: Horace Liveright, 1931), pp. 207–20; Eric Garber, " 'Tain't Nobody's Business': Homosexuality in 1920s Harlem," in Michael J. Smith, ed., *Black Men/White Men* (San Francisco: Gay Sunshine Press, 1983), pp. 11–14; George Chauncey, Jr., "The Way We Were: Gay Male Society in the Jazz Age," *Village Voice*, July 1, 1986, pp. 29–30, 34.

19. See, for example, "Liquor-Show Permit Action Upheld," *Los Angeles Times*, February 21, 1940; Phil Black, "I Live in Two Worlds," *Our World* (October 1953): 12–15; Brian Lee, "Everybody's Baby Estella," *NewsWest*, February 3, 1977, p. 14.

20. Slide, *Great Pretenders*, p. 29.

21. "Francis Renault, Last of Major Femme Mimics, Dies of Stroke at 62," *Variety*, May 25, 1955, p. 64.

22. William Howard Taft et al., *Service With Fighting Men: An Account of the Work of the American Young Men's Christian Association in the World War* (New York: Association Press, 1922), vol. 1, pp. 334–35. On the CTCA, see Allan Brandt, *No Magic Bullet: A Social History of Venereal Disease in the United States Since 1880* (New York: Oxford University

Press, 1985), chap. 2; Weldon B. Durham, " 'Big Brother and the Seven Sisters': Camp Life Reforms in World War I," *Military Affairs* 42 (April 1978): 57–60. On the moral agenda of soldier shows, see "Show History of Cantonments," *Variety*, December 27, 1918, pp. 10, 56; Montrose J. Moses, "Keeping the Soldier Amused," *Theatre* (January 1918): 16–17; "Smile and the World Smiles With You," *Theatre* (May 1918): 280–81.

23. Vera Bloom, " 'Biff-Bang!' Creates the Stage-Door Jane," *Theatre* (August 1918): 96.

24. Slide, *Great Pretenders,* p. 33; "Irving Berlin's 'Yip, Yip, Yaphank,' " *Variety,* July 1, 1942, pp. 2, 18.

25. For contemporary reviews of "Yip, Yip, Yaphank," see "New York Cheers 'Yip, Yip, Yaphank!' " *Theatre* (August 1918): 222–23; " 'Yip, Yip, Yaphank' Coming," *New York Times,* July 27, 1918, p. 7; "Actors' Houses At Camp Upton," *New York Times,* July 28, 1918, p. 19; " 'Yip! Yip! Yaphank!' Makes Rousing Hit," *New York Times,* August 20, 1918, p. 7; "Berlin's Show in Demand By Producing Managers" and "Yip Yip Yaphank," *Variety,* August 23, 1918, pp. 12, 222–23. See also Alexander Woollcott, *The Story of Irving Berlin* (New York: G. P. Putnam's Sons, 1925), pp. 107–25; Michael Freedland, *Irving Berlin* (New York: Stein and Day, 1974), pp. 52–57. For a synopsis of the plot and songs, see David Ewen, *Complete Book of the American Musical Theater* (New York: Henry Holt, 1958), p. 20.

26. Bloom, " 'Biff-Bang!' " p. 96; " 'Biff-Bang' Has Fine Start," *Variety,* May 31, 1918, p. 12; " 'Biff-Bang'," *Variety,* June 14, 1918, p. 8; "Atta Boy" and "Good Luck Sam," *Variety,* January 3, 1919, p. 8; "Army and Navy Frolic," *Variety,* January 17, 1919, p. 8; Harold Seton, "Female Impersonation," *Theatre* (July 1918): 18–19. For reviews of other stateside soldier and sailor shows with female impersonations, see "In the Service" sections on page 8 of the World War I and immediate postwar issues of *Variety.*

27. "Female Impersonators Very Abundant," *Variety,* March 8, 1923, p. 1.

28. Quotes from Taft, *Service With Fighting Men,* vol. 1, pp. 620, 632. On the soldier show campaign in Europe, see ibid., pp. 619–36; James W. Evans and Capt. Gardner L. Harding, *Entertaining the American Army* (New York: Association Press, 1921); "With the Argonne Players," *Theatre* (April 1919): 215; Charles M. Steele, "Say, Let's Have a Show," *Theatre* (November 1918): 284; Alfred E. Cornebise, "Der Rhein Entlang: The American Forces in Germany, 1918–1923, A Photo Essay," *Military Affairs* 46 (December 1982): 183–89.

29. Evans and Harding, *Entertaining the American Army,* pp. 164–79.

30. Taft, *Service With Fighting Men,* vol. 1, pp. 341, 636.

31. Evans and Harding, *Entertaining the American Army,* pp. 179, 237. General Headquarters, American Expeditionary Forces, General Orders No. 241,

France, December 29, 1918; and Entertainment Bulletin No. 1, France, January 28, 1919; both reprinted in Taft, *Service With Fighting Men,* vol. 2, pp. 566–70. See also ibid., vol. 1, pp. 631–32; and "General Pershing in France Sends Aid for Entertainment," *Variety,* January 31, 1919, p. 7.

32. "Irving Berlin's All Soldier Show 'This Is the Army,' " Souvenir Book, Army Emergency Relief and Army Special Services [n.d.].

33. Reviews of *This Is the Army* include Walter Bernstein, "Inhale! Outhale!" *The New Yorker,* June 20, 1942, pp. 34–39; " 'This Is the Army,' " *New York Times,* July 5, 1942; "Irving Berlin's 'This Is the Army,' " *New York Post,* July 6, 1942; "Hail to 'This Is the Army,' " *New York Daily News,* July 6, 1942; "Historic Event," *New York Herald Tribune,* July 6, 1942; Abel Green, " 'This Is the Army' a 100% Smash As Show and Inspiring Americanism," *Variety,* July 8, 1942, p. 24; " 'This Is the Army,' " *New York Times Magazine,* July 12, 1942, cover and pp. 6–7; "Soldiers' Chorus," *Time,* July 13, 1942, p. 36; " 'This Is the Army,' " *Newsweek,* July 13, 1942, pp. 52, 54; "This Is the Army," *The Commonweal,* July 17, 1942, pp. 303–4; "This Is the Army," *Life,* July 20, 1942, pp. 72–74; Nelson B. Bell, " 'This Is the Army' Scores Hit of Hits at National," *Washington Post,* September 30, 1942, p. 8B; Kyle Crichton, "This Is the Army," *Collier's,* October 17, 1942, pp. 14, 15, 28; "This Is a Show! Berlin and Army Get the Credit," *Chicago Daily Tribune,* January 5, 1943, p. 11; " 'This Is the Army' On the Screen," *New York Times Magazine,* June 27, 1943, pp. 12–13; "Army Units Stage Show on Broadway," *New York Times,* July 29, 1943, p. 11.

34. Sheilah Graham, " 'This Is the Army' Goes to London," *San Francisco Chronicle,* November 7, 1943, This World, p. 18.

35. On the cast's combat-readiness, see the Souvenir Book for the show; " 'This Is the Army,' and Civilian Morale," *Variety,* January 6, 1943, p. 238; Nelson B. Bell, "Screen Goes Realistic: 'This Is the Army' Means It," *Washington Post,* October 4, 1942, section 6, p. 3; and reviews in *Newsweek* (July 13, 1942), *Collier's* (October 17, 1942), *New York Times Magazine* (July 12, 1942), *The New Yorker* (June 20, 1942).

After the United States tour, a detachment of 165 members of the cast was sent on the show's overseas tour until the end of the war. Sergeant Milton Rosenstock, "Reunion With Broadway," *Saturday Review,* January 26, 1946, pp. 7–8, 48–49; Stone and Melick, *Coming, Major!,* pp. 163, 265–67.

36. "President Takes Couple Hours Off to See 'This Is the Army'—He Laughed and Laughed," *Washington Post,* October 9, 1942, pp. 1, 17.

37. Stone and Melick, *Coming, Major!,* p. 193.

38. Stone and Melick, *Coming, Major!,* pp. 192–93, 245, 264–66.

On the show's tours and honors, see Nelson B. Bell, " 'This Is the Army' Scores Hit of Hits at National," *Washington Post,* September 30, 1942, p. 8B; id., "The Army Orders Capital to Have Itself a Time," *Washington Post,* October 6, 1942, section 6, p. 3; "President Greets Entire Cast of 'This Is the Army,' " *Washington Post,* October 11, 1942, p. 10; "Berlin Takes London," *New York Times Magazine,* November 21, 1943, p. 20; Lewis Nichols, "A Show Goes Home," *New York Times,* May 28, 1944, section 2, p. 1; Stone and Melick, *Coming, Major!;* Abel Green, "Irving Berlin Winds Up 3-Year Hitch in 'Army,' Nets AER $10,000,000," *Variety,* April 18, 1945, p. 1; "Honored for 'This Is the Army,' " *New York Times,* October 2, 1945, p. 6; " 'This Is Army' Finale," *New York Times,* October 23, 1945, p. 14; Rosenstock, "Reunion With Broadway;" Freedland, *Irving Berlin,* pp. 149–67.

39. "Sad Sack Makes His Stage Debut," *New York Times Magazine,* September 3, 1944; "All-Soldier Musical at Fort Dix," *New York Times,* October 15, 1943, p. 15; [armored chorus] *Yank,* August 20, 1943, p. 18; [Gypsy's Girls] *Yank,* March 17, 1944, p. 19; "Greenland GIs Have Perfect Nights But No Gals," *Yank,* August 13, 1943, p. 7; " 'Yard Birds' in Algiers," *New York Times,* October 26, 1943, p. 18.

On impersonations of famous stars, see, for example, "New GI Show Opens Sept. 15, 'Colonel Eternal' Features 'Blonde Bomb-Shell,' Soldier Cast," *The Stars and Stripes* [London], August 24, 1943, p. 4; and soldiers impersonating Veronica Lake and Carmen Miranda, Signal Corps photograph No. SC200276.

40. " 'Stars and Gripes' at Fort Hamilton," *New York Times,* July 16, 1943, p. 21; *Yank,* August 13, 1943, p. 19; "The Theatre and the Armed Forces," *Theatre Arts,* March 1943, pp. 149–68.

For photographic coverage of the drag routines in soldier shows in the civilian press, see "This Is the Army," *New York Times Magazine,* July 12, 1942, pp. 6–7; " 'This Is the Army,' " *Newsweek,* July 13, 1942, p. 52; "Soldiers' Chorus," *Time,* July 13, 1942, p. 36; "This Is the Army," *Life,* July 20, 1942, pp. 73–74; photograph of "prima ballerina" from "This Is the Army," *Washington Post,* Sunday, October 4, 1942, Section VI, p. 2; Kyle Crichton, "This Is the Army," *Collier's,* October 17, 1942, pp. 14–15, 28; "Speaking of Pictures," *Life,* December 21, 1942, pp. 14–16; "The Theatre and the Armed Forces," *Theatre Arts* (March 1943): 149–68; "Two Worlds," *Newsweek,* August 7, 1944, p. 33; Sgt. Walter Bernstein, "Report on 'Hi Yank!' and Other Soldier Shows," *Theatre Arts* (November 1944): 654–60.

For photographic coverage in the military press, see *Yank:* "Musical comedy queens in a Pacific base show," December 23, 1942, p. 6; "British Guiana," July 9, 1943, p. 11; "Greenland GIs Have Perfect Nights But No Gals" and "Girdle Trouble," August 13, 1943, pp. 7, 19; "Armored Chorus," August 20, 1943, p. 18; Sgt. Ed Cunningham, " 'Hump

Happy,' " February 11, 1944, p. 10; "Gypsy's 'Girls,' " March 17, 1944, p. 19; "Consequences," July 14, 1944, p. 19; "Showmanship Gives Lift To Orientation," July 21, 1944, p. 18; "Sad Sack Comes to Life in GI Show," September 8, 1944, p. 18; "Alaskaleut Newsreel," July 27, 1945, p. 6. See also *North Islander*, vol. 1, no. 1, October 1942, p. 8; and Harold A. Biller, "Grass-Skirted MP Wows 'Em, Fools 'Em With Strip-Tease," *The Stars and Stripes* [London], October 29, 1943, p. 4.

Special Services souvenir show programs with photographs of GIs in drag, in addition to the program for *This Is the Army*, include *Sad Sacks*, October 15, 1943, Army Air Base, Fort Dix, New Jersey; *On The Beam*, August 1943, Fort Wayne, Indiana; and *'First Hitch' Ball*, September 1943, 39th Coast Artillery Brigade (AA) Headquarters, West Group; all in Box 246, sections 1, 5, and 10, Entry 196A General Correspondence 1941–43 353.8, Director of Administration Army Exchange Service, RG 160.

41. For an all-black show, see " 'QM' Caravan," *Newsweek*, February 14, 1944; " 'Uncle Sambo,' Negro Soldier Show, On Tap," *Variety*, August 5, 1942, p. 1; [Jumping With Jodie] Signal Corps photograph No. SC208040. For blackface soldier drag, see Signal Corps photograph No. SC133015. When the *TITA* cast encountered discrimination while touring the United States, their policy was to refuse invitations that excluded the show's black members; Stone and Melick, *Coming, Major!*, pp. 204–5. Racially integrated shows included one at the 70th Station Hospital in Assam, India, Signal Corps photographs Nos. SC200276 and SC259150.

42. "Actresses in Uniform," *Theatre Arts* (March 1943): 196; "55 in Coast Guard Show, Service Musical 'Tars and Spars' Opens Tour in Miami," *New York Times*, April 7, 1944, p. 23; "WAVES' Musical May Be Hypoed for B'way," *Variety*, September 13, 1944, p. 1.

43. "WAAC Troop Departs," *New York Times*, June 17, 1943, p. 19.

44. Mattie E. Treadwell, *The United States Army in World War II, Special Studies, The Women's Army Corps* (Washington, D.C.: USGPO, 1954), p. 554.

45. Ibid., pp. 553–56.

46. See, for example, "All-Soldier Musical at Fort Dix," *New York Times*, October 15, 1943, p. 15.

47. "Pvt. Pedrick Gets a Paint Job," *The Stars and Stripes* [London], April 28, 1943, p. 4; "Wac . . . demonstrates to a soldier audience how to create a female for a soldier show," Signal Corps photograph No. SC204637.

48. "Army Musical in Algiers Will Have Wacs in Cast," *New York Times*, December 14, 1943, p. 6; "New Show For Algiers: 'Swing, Sister Wac' Is Scheduled to Open With Real Girls Christmas Eve," *New York Times*, December 19, 1943, section 2, p. 3; " 'Sister Wac' May Tour," *New*

York Times, January 17, 1944, p. 14; "WAC Revue Held Recruiting Brake, Show Already Closed Ordered Halted by War Department—Harem Scene Objected To," *New York Times,* February 9, 1944, p. 7.

49. See, for example, Kaier Curtin, *"We Can Always Call Them Bulgarians,"* (Boston: Alyson Publications, 1987); Lew Levenson, *Butterfly Man* (New York: McCauley, 1934); Fitzroy Davis, *Quicksilver* (New York: Harcourt, Brace, 1942).

50. Newsletter from Fort Wayne Service Men's Clubs, vol. 1, no. 16, Sept. 15 to 21, 1943, p. 1, Box 246, section 1, Entry 196A, General Correspondence 1941–43, 353.8, Director of Administration Army Exchange Service, RG 160. For how the cast of *TITA* was fitted for dresses, see Stone and Melick, *Coming, Major!* pp. 160–61.

51. On the Red Cross supplying materials and personnel to outfit soldiers for female impersonation routines, see "An Overseas Worker 'Lets His Hair Down,' " *Recreation* (January 1943): 562, 592–93; "All-Soldier Musical At Fort Dix," *New York Times,* October 15, 1943, p. 15.

52. Instructions for reproducing these makeshift drag outfits were incorporated into the costume list for the 1949 musical *South Pacific. South Pacific,* Music by Richard Rogers, Lyrics by Oscar Hammerstein II, Book by Oscar Hammerstein II and Joshua Logan (Williamson Music, 1949), p. 128.

53. *South Pacific,* pp. 70–75, 128.

54. Slang words from Legman, "The Language of Homosexuality," reprinted in Jonathan Ned Katz, *Gay/Lesbian Almanac* (New York: Harper & Row, 1983), pp. 571–84. See also Bruce Rodgers, *The Queen's Vernacular: A Gay Lexicon* (San Francisco: Straight Arrow Books, 1972). Some of the earliest published discussions of camp in the United States were in John Horne Burns, *The Gallery* (1947; New York: Bantam, 1970), p. 151; and in Christopher Isherwood, *The World in the Evening* (1952; New York: Ballantine, 1967), pp. 98–111.

55. On the complexities of camp, see Esther Newton, *Mother Camp: Female Impersonators in America* (Chicago: University of Chicago Press, 1972, 1979); Philip Core, *Camp: The Lie That Tells the Truth* (New York: Delilah, 1984); Mark Booth, *Camp* (London, Melbourne, New York: Quartet Books, 1983); Michael Bronski, *Culture Clash: The Making of Gay Sensibility* (Boston: South End Press, 1984); Susan Sontag, *Against Interpretation* (1966; New York: Dell, 1969), "Notes on 'Camp,' " pp. 277–93; and M. D. Sterling, "Playing Roles," *Blueboy* 11 (April–May 1977): 10–13.

56. *About Face,* p. 16; *Hi Yank!,* p. 13.

57. Curtin, *"We Can Always Call Them Bulgarians,"* 57–58.

58. *South Pacific,* p. 71.

59. Curtin, *"We Can Always Call Them Bulgarians,"* pp. 57–58; Boze Hadleigh, *Conversations With My Elders* (New York: St. Martin's, 1986), "George Cukor," pp. 132–74.

60. " 'Women' To Be Enacted By Soldiers," *Variety,* November 18, 1942, p. 4; "All-Soldier Cast Nets 100G Bond Sale in Va. Prod. of 'The Women,' " *Variety,* December 2, 1942, p. 4; "Speaking of Pictures . . . Guess What Goes On Here," *Life,* December 21, 1942, pp. 14–16. In the 1980s an annual showing of "The Women" at the Castro Theatre in San Francisco had become a citywide gay event. Mick LaSalle, "The Roar of the Crowd," *San Francisco Chronicle,* December 18, 1985, p. 66.

61. "Guadalcanal Interlude," film by S/Sgt. Bob Woodside and Cpl. Neil Carrier, 13th AAF Combat Camera Unit, Prepared by First Army Air Forces Combat Film Service, Army Air Forces Combat Film Report C-430, 1944, National Archives Building, Washington, D.C.; Moss Hart, *Winged Victory: The Air Force Play* (New York: Random House, 1943), pp. 177–78; Wilella Waldorf, "Moss Hart and the Army Airmen Score a Hit With 'Winged Victory,' " *New York Post,* November 22, 1943; Dickens, *What a Drag,* p. 183.

62. Gilder, "Theatre Overseas," p. 219.

63. Hart, *Winged Victory,* p. 177; Sgt. Ed Cunningham, "Hump Happy: The GI Musical Comedy Covers the India Circuit By Air," *Yank,* February 11, 1944, p. 10; Cpl. Arnold B. Horwitt, "Formula For 'Egg in Your Beer,' " *New York Times,* May 13, 1945, section 2, p. 1; C. L. Sulzberger, *American Heritage Picture Book of World War II* (New York: Crown, 1966), p. 413; Dickens, *What a Drag,* p. 180.

   A memorandum from Robert R. Johnston, 1st Lieut., AUS, Special Service Officer, U.S. Army Reception Center, New Cumberland, Penna., to Lt. Col. Rankin R. Boone, Asst. Executive Officer, Special Service Div., War Department, Washington, D.C., July 26, 1943, Subject: Stage production, "Pennsylvania On Parade," lists one of the acts as " 'The Andrews Sisters' as interpreted by three soldiers using a phonograph recording of the singing trio;" Box 246, section 4, Entry 196A, Director of Administrative Army Exchange Service, General Correspondence 1941–43, 353.8, RG 160.

64. "Three Little Sisters," by Irving Taylor and Vic Mizzy (1942), copyright Unison Music Company (ASCAP), reprinted with permission.

65. "Air Base Show Draws Big Crowd," *Savannah Morning News,* June 2, 1943.

66. A wartime Munsingwear advertisement portrayed a GI in his underwear standing in front of the barracks mirror with his hand on his hip, his other hand in the air, saying to his buddy, "No wonder I'm the pin-up boy of Act III." *Life,* October 30, 1944, p. 6.

67. Biller, "Grass-Skirted MP."

68. These joking propositions were included in the musical *South Pacific*, when, according to the stage directions, Billis, as "Honey-Bun," "has his backside pinched by one of the men in the G.I. audience." *South Pacific*, p. 73.

69. Rosamond Gilder, " 'You Bet Your Life,' " *Theatre Arts* (September 1944): 521–27.

   On camoufleurs, see William McK. Spierer, "The Fine Art of Camouflage," *New York Times Magazine*, January 24, 1942, pp. 7–9; Merrill De Longe, "How To Baffle a Bombardier," *Saturday Evening Post*, July 11, 1942, pp. 18–19; Sgt. Merle Miller, "Capt. Evans's New Hit, It's 'Hey, Mac' and the Soldiers of the Pacific Are Eating It Up," *New York Times*, April 11, 1943, section II, p. 1; "The Camoufleurs," *Time*, August 6, 1943, p. 27; Leonard S. Marcus, *The American Store Window* (New York: Whitney Library of Design, 1978), pp. 39–40, 62–64.

70. "Navy Sets Up Talent Program As Answer To Morale Problem," *Variety*, March 7, 1945, pp. 4, 58; "Navy Installs 25-Man Staff in N.Y. To Prep at Sea, Hosp Entertainment," *Variety*, May 2, 1945, pp. 31, 34; "Sailor-Made Show Unit Peps Up Plans," *Variety*, July 25, 1945, p. 10; "Navy Dept. Huddles On Entertainment," *Variety*, August 29, 1945, p. 10; "Navy Show Units Off Today," *New York Times*, October 5, 1945, p. 26.

71. "Where Are the USO Shows Asks Ex-B'way P.A., Now GI," *Variety*, July 4, 1945, p. 4.

72. "3,000,000 Troops Post-VE Day Will Need Shows: Army and USO Rally Producers," *Variety*, April 25, 1945, pp. 1, 24; "Todd to Run Troop Shows," *New York Times*, May 10, 1945, p. 19; "Pacific Now Show Wise, Says Kazan; GI Program Gets MacArthur Nod," and "Maj. Melvyn Douglas' EPU Unit in CBI Zone Builds 10-Show Circuit," *Variety*, May 16, 1945, p. 4; "Mike Todd in London, Takes Job Seriously In Sizing Up GI Program," *Variety*, June 6, 1945, pp. 1, 4; "Melvyn Douglas in N.Y. In Talent Quest for India-Burma EPU Unit" and "Army's Long Range Show Program Rolls Under Way in ETO," *Variety*, July 18, 1945, p. 29; Sgt. Daniel L. Schorr, "Army Battles Boredom," *New York Times*, July 22, 1945, section 2, p. 4; "AEF Sets Up Pacific Program; Nabs Talent For GI Variety Show," *Variety*, July 25, 1945, p. 10; "Somervell Views Camps In France," *New York Times*, July 30, 1945, p. 10; "GI Drama School In Biarritz With Name Pix–B'way Directors," *Variety*, August 1, 1945, pp. 1, 20; "Army Crashes Into Show Biz in ETO; Forms Special Battalion to Aid GIs," *Variety*, August 1, 1945, p. 8; "Audience Tomorrow," Elia Kazan, *Theatre Arts* (October 1945): 568–77; Stanley Wood, "Soldier Show Company," *Theatre Arts* (July 1946): 397–8.

73. Treadwell, *The Women's Army Corps*, pp. 553–56; "New Soldier Musical," *New York Times*, January 10, 1945, p. 28; "Wounded Men See Show," *New York Times*, February 19, 1945, p. 5. In 1944, a few male Army shows integrated Wacs into their casts. See, for example, "Camp Shanks Army Show Big Click In Debut As Blueprint For Other GIs," *Variety*, May 31, 1944, p. 13; and " 'Hi Yank' A Success," *New York Times*, August 8, 1944, p. 14. Helen Harder, a lesbian who served in the Women's Army Air Corps, in the summer of 1945 performed in a mixed male and female Fourth Air Force soldier show entitled "How About It?" that went on air tour across the country. Author's interview with Helen Harder, May 11, 1982, and her clippings, Army papers, and photographs regarding the show at the Lesbian Herstory Archives, New York City.

74. "Actresses Sought For Army," *New York Times*, July 2, 1945, p. 12; "Army Recruiting 100 Femmes to Act In GI Shows in Europe for a Year," *Variety*, July 4, 1945, p. 2; "GIs Lonely Femmes a Tactical Problem for Army Overseas Show Auditioners," *Variety*, July 11, 1945, p. 1; "100 Femmes Set For Europe Jaunt," *Variety*, July 18, 1945, p. 29; "To Take Part In GI Shows," *New York Times*, August 7, 1945, p. 17; "Army Seeks Actresses," *New York Times*, October 25, 1945, p. 19; "Women Who Are C.A.T.S.," *Independent Woman* (September 1946): 270–71; "They're the CATS," by Clayton Going, *New York Times Magazine*, May 15, 1949, pp. 58–59.

On civilian women who volunteered to play female roles in soldier shows, see "Tributary Theatre at War," *Theatre Arts* (November 1943): 691; Gilder, "Theatre Overseas," pp. 215–26.

75. See, for example, Alfred Towne, "The New Taste in Humor," *American Mercury* 74 (September 1951): 22–27; "I Live in Two Worlds," by Phil Black, *Our World* (October 1953): 12–15; Eric Garber, "Gladys Bentley: The Bulldagger Who Sang the Blues," *Out/Look* 1 (Spring 1988): 52–61.

76. " 'Yard Birds' in Algiers," *New York Times*, October 16, 1943, p. 18; "Eisenhower Commends Army Show in Algiers," *New York Times*, October 29, 1943, p. 4.

Chapter 4. "The Gang's All Here": Gay Life and Vice Control

1. John Horne Burns, *The Gallery* (1947; New York: Bantam, 1970), pp. 58–59.

2. Letters, Marty Klausner to Howard Taylor, January 30 and 31, 1945, Taylor Correspondence.

3. Fort Benning, Georgia, reached a population of 95,000 in 1945, and Camp Shelby, Mississippi, a population of 86,000. Lee Kennett, *G.I.* (New York: Scribner's, 1987), pp. 44–45, 57–58.

4. In his letters Jerry Watson described glances thrown for erotic purposes as "a jam-session of the eyes," and referred to eye contact as a way "to exercise the unlawful freedom of the eyes" or to give someone "the works with his eyes." Letters, Jerry Watson to Jim Kepner, April 17 and June 12, 1943, Kepner Correspondence. "They had an acuteness in their eyes," wrote John Horne Burns of the patrons in a wartime gay bar. "When Momma's bar was full it was like a peacock's tail because she could see nothing but eyes through the cigarette smoke. Restless and unsocketed eyes that wheeled all around, wholly taken up in the business of looking and calculating. Eyes of every color. Momma's bar when crowded was a goldfish bowl swimming with retinas and irises in motion." *The Gallery*, pp. 139, 158–59. Poet Walt Whitman, who was homosexual, wrote about the "frequent and swift flash of eyes offering me love" on the streets of Manhattan. Robert K. Martin, *The Homosexual Tradition in American Poetry* (Austin: University of Texas Press, 1979), p. 74.

5. In 1944 Private Howard Taylor's clique of gay soldiers also met each night in the service club at Camp Crowder, Missouri. Letter, Howard Taylor to C. M., December 12, 1944, Camp Crowder, Missouri, Taylor Correspondence.

6. Letters from Tommy Martz to Howard Taylor, March 13, April 26, April 30, 1945, Camp Beale, California, Taylor Correspondence. See also letter from Howard Taylor to "miss dix," December 8, [1944], from Camp Crowder, Missouri.

7. Fort Oglethorpe Testimony, pp. 130–37, 154–56, 158–61, 165–67, 171, 173–74, 177–82, 186–87.

8. Fort Oglethorpe Testimony, p. 155.

9. Keith Siddons Beggs, "Some Legal, Social and Psychiatric Aspects of Homosexual Behavior—A Guide For the Social Worker in the Sex Clinic " (Master of Science (Social Work) thesis, University of Wisconsin, Madison, 1950), p. 162.

10. Fort Oglethorpe Testimony, pp. 275–6, 279.

11. Letters, Jerry Watson to Jim Kepner, March 19, March 26, and May 14, 1943, Kepner Correspondence.

12. Fort Oglethorpe Testimony, p. 263.

13. Author's interview with Woodie Wilson, December 21, 1983; Taylor Correspondence. In John Horne Burns's novel *The Gallery*, the gay technical sergeant complains that he is "fed up" and "bored with sitting around in cliques and drinking and talking poetry and scandal" with "the arty boys" among the medical corpsmen in the hospital. Burns, *The Gallery*, pp. 57, 317.

14. Rusty Brown, "Always Me," in Marcy Adelman, ed., *Long Time Passing: Lives of Older Lesbians* (Boston: Alyson Publications, 1986), pp. 144–

51; Madeline Davis and Elizabeth Lapovsky Kennedy, "Oral History and the Study of Sexuality in the Lesbian Community: Buffalo, New York, 1940–1960," *Feminist Studies* 12 (Spring 1986): 7–26.

15. Fort Oglethorpe Testimony, p. 178.

16. Fort Oglethorpe Testimony, pp. 204–6, 263, 284.

17. Letters, Howard Taylor to ——, November 13, 1944; Tommy Martz to Howard Taylor, January 23, 1945; in Taylor Correspondence.

18. Letter, Jerry Watson to Jim Kepner, May 31, 1943, Kepner Correspondence.

19. In addition to *Yank: The Army Weekly*, which enlisted men published with Army approval for other enlisted men and women, GIs published newsletters on their local bases. See, for example, "GI News in the Pacific," *New York Times Magazine*, January 14, 1945, p. 41; "They Call It the *Virgin Squeal;* It's the Navy's Treat Once a Week," *Yank,* April 16, 1943, p. 6. The State Historical Society of Wisconsin in Madison has a large collection of military newspapers and periodicals published during the Second World War.

20. For a more detailed account of the *Myrtle Beach Bitch,* see Allan Berube, "Rediscovering Our Forgotten Past," *The Front Page* (Durham, North Carolina), June 26, 1984, pp. 1, 9–11; condensed and reprinted as "The Myrtle Beach Bitch," *Southern Exposure* 16 (Fall 1988): 20–23.

21. Fort Oglethorpe Testimony, pp. 189–95, 231–41.

22. Letters, Jerry Watson to Jim Kepner, March 21, April 6 and 17, 1943, Kepner Correspondence.

23. Robert O'Brien, "San Francisco," *San Francisco Chronicle,* November 2, 1943, p. 11.

24. Donald Vining, *A Gay Diary: 1933–1946* (New York: Pepys Press, 1979), p. 219.

25. The plot of one war novel centered on a gay civilian who was murdered by the soldiers he picked up on the route from Fort Belvoir to Washington D.C. Richard Brooks, *The Brick Foxhole* (Garden City, N.Y.: Sun Dial Press, 1945).

26. Letter, "Comfort For Soldiers," *Washington Post,* October 1, 1942, p. 10; editors of *Look, Movie Lot to Beachhead* (Garden City, N.Y.: Doubleday, Doran, 1945), p. 238. Some gay or bisexual civilian men volunteered to work at the canteens and YMCAs where they could enjoy the company of servicemen and pursue romance and sex. See Vining, *A Gay Diary,* pp. 257–58, 282, 304, 312; Bruce Kellner, ed., *Letters of Carl Van Vechten* (New Haven: Yale University Press, 1897), pp. 186, 188, 191, 202, 211, 213, 217, 218; George W. Henry, *Society and the Sex Variant* (New York: Collier Books, 1955, 1965), pp. 245–47.

For an example of the events and accommodations available to servicemen on passes, many of which were identified by race, ethnic groups, rank, or gender, see the "U.S.O. Events" column in the *San Francisco Call-Bulletin*, May 7, 1943, p. 12.

27. John Morton Blum, *V Was For Victory* (New York: Harcourt Brace Jovanovich, 1976), p. 210.

28. Author's interview with Betty Somers, August 14, 1982.

29. Donald Vining, "The Art and Artifice of Cruising," *The Advocate*, March 31, 1983, pp. 16–17, 22; id., "Gay Ghosts Dispossessed," *New York Native*, October 28, 1985, p. 34; id., "Back to the Gay Future: Master Classes in Subtle Passes?" *New York Native*, July 7, 1986, pp. 26–27; id., *A Gay Diary*, pp. 245, 257, 261, 276, 286–87, 374, 376. Vining identifies the "theaters of the gay cruising circuit" in wartime Manhattan as the Beverly, the New Yorker, the Selwyn, the Lyric, and the Apollo.

30. John Nichols, "The Way It Was: Gay Life in World War II America," *QQ Magazine* 7 (August 1975): 51.

31. Oral histories with Jim Warren, April 25, 1985, and Ben Small, July 22, 1980; Nichols, "The Way It Was," pp. 9–11, 51, 54; Vining, *A Gay Diary*, pp. 233–34, 238, 270, 274, 276, 278–79, 369, 370, 372, 376; id., "Back to the Future," pp. 26–27.

32. For a gay civilian's wartime account of picking up sailors, see Paul Goodman, "Sailors," in Taylor Stoehr, ed., *Paul Goodman, The Facts of Life: Stories 1940–49* (Santa Barbara, Calif.: Black Sparrow Press, 1979), pp. 65–73.

33. Vining, *A Gay Diary*, pp. 286–87, 324–25, 328, 330, 332–33, 341, 344, 347.

34. Ibid., pp. 324–25.

35. In an interview with the author, Jim Warren described cruising other GIs on the blacked-out beaches of Waikiki. "Coney Biz 50% Off, But Dimout Booms Necking," *Variety*, August 5, 1942, p. 1. On public-beach cruising during the war, see Armistead Maupin, "Isherwood's Last Interview," program, San Francisco Lesbian and Gay Pride Parade, 1987, pp. 28–30.

36. Sailors' anxieties about the boyishness, tightness, and effeminacy of their uniforms surfaced during the war when thousands of sailors wrote letters to *Yank* about changing the Navy enlisted men's uniforms. *Yank*, letters columns, October 20, 1944, p. 14, and December 8, 1944, p. 14; "Navy Notes: 'Blues in the Navy,' " July 20, 1945, p. 21; and "Navy Notes: 'Farewell to Bell Bottoms,' " October 26, 1945, p. 21.

37. Vining, *A Gay Diary*, p. 328–30; Nichols, "The Way It Was," p. 11.
    For James Baldwin's account of being taunted and beaten up as a "faggot" in wartime Greenwich Village, see "Here Be Dragons" in James Baldwin, *The Price of the Ticket* (New York: St. Martin's, 1985),

pp. 681–88. For fictional accounts of violence against gay men during the war, see Donald Vining, "Show Me the Way to Go Home," in Edwin Seaver, ed., *Cross Section 1945* (New York: Book Find Club, 1945), pp. 272–81; and Brooks, *The Brick Foxhole.*

38. Letter, Jim Kepner to Jerry Watson, May 31, 1943, Kepner Correspondence. See also the description of a gay male party in rural Tennessee in letter from "Elsa Clavel Baganna Leslee Tanya de Hayworthe-Baledotte" to "Ma plus chère soeur Juliette," April 7, 1943, Crossville, Tennessee, Folder: "AG250.1 (9–1–43 to 9–30–43)," Classified Decimal File 1943–45, RG 407.

39. Eric Garber, " 'Tain't Nobody's Business': Homosexuality in 1920s Harlem," in Michael J. Smith, ed., *Black Men/White Men* (San Francisco: Gay Sunshine Press, 1983), pp. 11–14.

40. In their interviews with the author, Stuart Loomis (March 25, 1980), Bob Ruffing (May 14, 1980), Haviland Ferris (May 20, 1983), and Ted Rolfs (June 5, 1980) described the gay social circles of the 1930s in Omaha, Manhattan, and Washington, D.C. See also Garber, "T'ain't Nobody's Business," and George Chauncey, Jr., "The Way We Were," *Village Voice,* July 1, 1986, pp. 29–30, 34. American fiction from the 1930s included vivid descriptions of gay parties and social circles. See, for example, James T. Farrell, "Just Boys," in Seymour Kleinberg, ed., *The Other Persuasion: Short Fiction About Gay Men and Women* (New York: Vintage Books, 1977), pp. 87–97; Blair Niles, *Strange Brother* (New York: Liveright, 1931); Robert Scully, *A Scarlet Pansy* ([no city]: Nesor Publishing, 1937); Charles Henri Ford and Parker Tyler, *The Young and Evil* (1933; New York: Gay Presses of New York, 1988).

41. Author's interview with Haviland Ferris, May 20, 1983.

42. "Barmaids Come Back," *New York Times Magazine,* March 18, 1945, p. 27; Geoffrey Perrett, *Days of Sadness, Years of Triumph* (Baltimore: Penguin, 1973), p. 348; Susan Hartmann, *The Home Front and Beyond* (Boston: Twayne, 1982), pp. 180–81; John D'Emilio and Estelle Freedman, *Intimate Matters* (New York: Harper & Row, 1988), pp. 260–61; Allan Brandt, *No Magic Bullet* (New York: Oxford University Press, 1985), pp. 165–70.

43. Evelyn Torton Beck, ed., *Nice Jewish Girls: A Lesbian Anthology* (Trumansburg, N.Y.: Crossing Press, 1982), p. 231.

44. Leland Moss, "An Interview with Lisa Ben," *Gaysweek,* January 23, 1978, pp. 14–16; author's interview with Donna Smith, October 21, 1981.

45. Nichols, "The Way It Was," p. 51.

46. Others included the St. Francis Hotel's Oak Room in San Francisco; the Olympic Hotel in Seattle; the Dome at the Sherman House, and the Town and Country at the Palmer House in Chicago; the Statler Hotel in Boston; the Shubert Hotel in Philadelphia; the Roosevelt Hotel's Sazerac Room

in New Orleans; the Royal Hawaiian, Alexander Young and Mauna hotels in Honolulu; the Sealback Hotel in Louisville; the Buena Vista Hotel in Biloxi; the Westward Ho Hotel in Phoenix; the Gibson Hotel in Cincinnati; the Statler Hotel in Cleveland; the Deshler-Walleck Hotel in Columbus; the Continental Bar at the William Penn Hotel in Pittsburgh; the Saint Anthony Hotel in San Antonio. Nichols, "The Way It Was," pp. 11, 51, 54; author's interviews with Burt Gerrits (February 9, 1980), Stuart Loomis (March 25, 1980), Haviland Ferris (May 20, 1983), Jim Warren (April 25, 1985), Burt Miller (January 19, 1982), Bob Ruffing (May 14, 1980), and Jim Kepner (June 2, 1981).

47. Nichols, "The Way It Was," p. 51; Paul Forbes, "mrs. astor's bar," *Drum,* No. 20 (1966): 11–12.

48. "Look me up in New York. And stay out of the Astor Bar, hear?" says one officer to another in Burns, *The Gallery,* p. 57.

49. Forbes, "mrs. astor's bar," pp. 11–12.

50. "Bea Lillie Previews OK Nitery Act as Charity," *Variety,* April 4, 1945, p. 49; "Dwight Fiske," promotional advertisement, *Variety,* January 5, 1944, p. 213; S. J. Woolf, "Beatrice Lillie's Recipe for Laughter," *New York Times Magazine,* November 26, 1944, p. 13; "Oval Room, Boston," *Variety,* June 27, 1945, p. 49; Nichols, "The Way It Was," p. 54; "Never Looking Back: The Incomparable Hildegarde," *New York Native,* February 3, 1986, p. 22; "Beatrice Lillie, 94—A Master of Comedy" [obituary], *San Francisco Chronicle,* January 21, 1989, p. C11; Boyd McDonald, "When Hope Emerson Eats a Stack of Wheats," *Christopher Street* 8, (May 1984): 13–15; "Hope Springs Eternal," letter, *Christopher Street* 8, (July 1984): p. 7.

51. See, for example, Theodore C. Mason, *Battleship Sailor* (Annapolis: Naval Institute Press, 1982), pp. 38–41.

    Gay bathhouses during the war included the Everard Baths, the Penn-Post Baths, the Murray Hill Baths, the Times Square Baths, and the Mark Morris Baths in New York City; the Howard Baths in Newark, New Jersey; Jack's Baths and the Palace Baths in San Francisco; the Lincoln, Terminal, Wacker, and Wabash Baths in Chicago; the Carver Baths in Boston; the Bellevue Baths in Philadelphia; the Crystal Baths in Los Angeles; the Liberty Baths in Pittsburgh; and Keith's Baths in Washington, D.C. Nichols, "The Way It Was," p. 11; Loren Wahl, *The Invisible Glass* (1950; Washington: Guild Press, 1965), p. 211.

    Tom Driberg described a 1942 visit to a gay male brothel in San Francisco in *Ruling Passions* (New York: Stein and Day, 1978), p. 123. For accounts of a wartime gay brothel near the Brooklyn Navy Yard, see Jonathan Ned Katz, *Gay/Lesbian Almanac* (New York: Harper & Row, 1983), pp. 584–85.

52. Nichols, "The Way It Was," pp. 51–54.

53. James Baldwin described the hostility he felt from white people when he left Harlem and entered the gay life in Greenwich Village as a young black man. Baldwin, *The Price of the Ticket*, pp. 683–88.

54. Garber, "T'ain't Nobody's Business," pp. 11–14.

55. "Harlem's Strangest Night Club," *Ebony* (December 1953): 80–85.

56. Personal communication with George Chauncey, Jr., April 10, 1989.

57. "Female Impersonators Hold Costume Balls," *Ebony* (March 1952): 62–67; "Female Impersonators," *Ebony* (March 1953): 64–68.

58. Author's interview with Vincent Miles, March 14, 1984.

59. Nichols, "The Way It Was," p. 9.

60. Donald Webster Cory, *The Homosexual in America* (New York: Greenberg, 1951), pp. 107–8.

61. For fictional portrayals of the camaraderie, eroticism, diversity, and conflicts in wartime gay and lesbian bars, see "Momma" in *The Gallery*, John Horne Burns, pp. 133–64; Wahl, *The Invisible Glass*, pp. 202–13; Lonnie Coleman, *Ship's Company* (1955; New York: Dell, 1957), "Bird of Paradise," pp. 115–34.

62. Letter, A. B. to Jim Kepner, May 26, 1943, Kepner Correspondence.

63. Wahl, *The Invisible Glass*, p. 210.

64. Rusty Brown, "Always Me," in Adelman, *Long Time Passing*, pp. 144–51; Davis and Kennedy, "Oral History and the Study of Sexuality in the Lesbian Community: Buffalo, New York, 1940–1960," pp. 7–26.

65. Wahl, *The Invisible Glass*, p. 212.

66. Vining, *A Gay Diary*, p. 344.

67. Letters, D. M. to Howard Taylor, June 26, [1945], Taylor Correspondence.

68. Will Irwin and Thomas M. Johnson, "The All-Seeing 'I,' " in Lt. Col. Karl Detzer, ed., *The Army Reader* (Indianapolis and New York: Bobbs-Merrill, 1943), p. 70.

69. Letter, Jerry Watson to Jim Kepner, July 14, 1943, Kepner Correspondence.

70. Brandt, *No Magic Bullet*, pp. 165–70.

71. Ibid., pp. 161–70.

   A few military doctors were aware that venereal disease could be transmitted between men. The military's largest wartime study of hospitalized gay soldiers and officers concluded that their rate of venereal disease was "not high in contrast to figures of the Army as a whole." Lt. Col. Lewis H. Loeser, "The Sexual Psychopath in the Military Service," *American Journal of Psychiatry* 102 (July 1945): 92–101. On venereal disease in male prisons, see Joseph F. Fishman, *Sex in Prison* (1934; [no city]: Padell, 1951), pp. 140–41.

72. Brandt, *No Magic Bullet*, pp. 162, 166.

73. Ibid., p. 167.

74. Don Wharton, "The New MP," in Detzer, *The Army Reader*, pp. 302–8.

75. Burns, *The Gallery*, pp. 141–42.

76. Memorandum, from Lt. Col. Sidney T. Telford, 750th Tank Batallion, to Provost Marshal General, Washington, D.C., December 26, 1943, Subject: Investigation of Enlisted Man, Folder: "250.1 Morals and Conduct 11-1-43 to 12-31-43," Decimal File 1940–45, RG 407.

77. A wartime photograph of the interior of the Black Cat in San Francisco shows no people in uniform present, except for MPs standing in the back of the room, whose job it was to keep out military personnel. Lawrence Ferlinghetti and Nancy J. Peters, *Literary San Francisco* (San Francisco: City Lights and Harper & Row, 1980), pp. 148–49.

78. William Manchester, *Goodbye, Darkness* (New York: Little, Brown, 1979), p. 122.

79. "Army, Navy Clamp Down on Chi to Prevent Gyp on Servicemen; 4 Cafes Shut for Liquor Violation," *Variety*, August 5, 1942, pp. 53, 57; "Women Tabu at Bars Via New Chi Edict," *Variety*, August 12, 1942, p. 51. Without female patrons, night clubs lost customers including servicemen with female dates who could not find seats at the crowded tables where women were allowed. In December 1942, the city council passed an ordinance allowing women with male escorts to drink at bars; "Chi Awaits OK by Mayor on Gals at Bars," *Variety*, December 9, 1942, p. 43.

80. "Philly Drive," *Variety*, August 5, 1942, p. 57.

81. "Army, Navy Issue 'Toughest' Curbs to Miami Night Clubs; New Curfews," *Variety*, July 8, 1942, p. 45.

82. "Strict Curbs Seen for D.C. Burlesk," *Variety*, August 12, 1942, p. 52.

83. "3 More Hotels Taken Over by Army in A.C.," *Variety*, July 8, 1942, p. 45; "4 More Hotels to Army in A.C.," *Variety*, July 15, 1942, p. 46; "A.C. Niteries Get Further Orders to Tone Down; More Hotels to Army," *Variety*, July 29, 1942, p. 44; "20 More Hotels in A.C. Taken by Army," *Variety*, August 12, 1942, p. 51; "Atlantic City Flounders at Mid-Season, Usually Its Peak," *Variety*, August 12, 1942, p. 52; "3 More A.C. Hotels Taken by the Army," *Variety*, September 2, 1942, p. 51; "Atlantic City Mayor Blames Enemies for Resort's Vice Influx," *Variety*, September 30, 1942, pp. 1, 52; "Vice Expert Would Purge Atlantic City," *Variety*, October 7, 1942, p. 73; "Atlantic City Granted Judicial Reprieve on Military Clamp-Down," *Variety*, October 21, 1942, pp. 2, 29.

84. "Board Sees Ban on 'Loose' Tavern," *New York Times*, November 4, 1944, p. 17.

85. "A.C. Niteries Get Further Orders to Tone Down," *Variety,* July 29, 1942, p. 44; "Det. Raid Jails Acts, Cafe Show 'Postponed,'" *Variety,* October 7, 1942, p. 74; "13 More Niteries Cited in Frisco," *Variety,* September 2, 1942, p. 52.

86. On the impact of the war mobilization on nightlife in war boom towns, see, for example, "Greenwich Village Nitery Upbeat Another Wartime Boom Result," *Variety,* October 14, 1942, p. 46; "San Diego Rated With the Klondike as Boom Town," *Variety,* December 30, 1942, pp. 1, 45; "New Orleans, La.," *Yank,* May 5, 1944, p. 11; "Hollywood, Calif.," *Yank,* May 27, 1945, p. 10; "Boston, Mass.," *Yank,* March 10, 1944, p. 10; "Chicago, Ill.," *Yank,* July 14, 1944, p. 8.

87. Author's interview with Haviland Ferris, May 20, 1983; Haviland Ferris, "An Extract From Washington Gay History," *Washington Blade,* September 11, 1980, p. A5.

88. Thomas Jacob Noel, "Gay Bars and the Emergence of the Denver Homosexual Community," *The Social Science Journal* 15 (April 1978): 59–74.

89. "Barbary Coast Days Recalled by Frisco Boom," *Variety,* November 4, 1942, pp. 1, 52.

90. "Liquor Code: Taverns Sign Pledge for Army, Navy," *San Francisco Chronicle,* January 1, 1943, p. 9.

91. "Reilly, Rebuked on Liquor Rule, Blames Samish," *San Francisco Call-Bulletin,* May 7, 1943, p. 11; "Venereal Disease: City and Federal Officials Blame the Navy for Its Own High Rate," *San Francisco Chronicle,* May 3, 1943, p. 13; "Army, Navy Vice Control," *San Francisco Chronicle,* May 7, 1943, p. 6; "S.F. Vice Cleanup Slated to Protect Servicemen," *San Francisco News,* May 6, 1943, p. 1; "Strub Pledges Action on S. F. Soldier Housing," *San Francisco Chronicle,* May 4, 1943, p. 12; "Progress in Vice Control," *San Francisco Chronicle,* May 29, 1943, p. 9. See also, "Payoff Probe Stirs Memories of S.F.'s Wide-Open Days," *San Francisco Chronicle,* August 8, 1986, p. 8.

92. Letters, Jim Kepner to Jerry Watson, April 21, May 3, 1943, Kepner Correspondence.

93. Letter, Jim Kepner to Jerry Watson, May 9, 1943, Kepner Correspondence.

94. Letter, Kepner, to Jerry Watson, May 17, 1943, Kepner Correspondence.

95. Letter, Tommy Martz to Howard Taylor, April 2, 1945, Taylor Correspondence.

96. Oral-history interview with Bill Thompson, March 15, 1984 [on San Diego bars]; Noel, "Gay Bars and the Emergence of the Denver Homosexual Community," pp. 59–74.

97. Burns, *The Gallery,* p. 57.

98. Letters, Jim Kepner to Jerry Watson, April 21, May 3, 1943, Kepner Correspondence.

99. Letter, Jerry Watson to Jim Kepner, May 21, 1989, Kepner Correspondence.

Chapter 5. The Fight for Reform

1. Memorandum from Lt. Col. Ernest H. Burt to General Gullion, Subject: Sodomists, May 14, 1941, AGO "Sodomists" File.
2. Case File 28727, Court Martial Cases, RG 80.
3. Crittenden Report, p. 22.
4. Joseph F. Fishman, *Sex in Prison* (1934; [no city]: Padell, 1951), pp. 68–69.
5. Ibid., pp. 99–100.
6. Correspondence September 25, 1918, to March 12, 1920, in Case File 26288-951, and correspondence July 26, 1921, to November 24, 1922, in Case File 28639, RG 80.

    Memorandum, JAG to Chief, BuNav, Subject: Memorandum re: prisoners, March 18, 1927; U.S. Naval Message, JAG, June 1929; both in Folder: "P13-10/A to A9-9," Box No. 1224, Office of the Secretary, General Correspondence 1926–1940, RG 80.

    Navy prison census reports from 1933 to 1939 are in Folder: "P13-10/A9-10," Box 1224, Office of the Secretary, General Correspondence 1926–1940, RG 80.
7. Memorandum, P. S. Madigan, Army SGO, to Assistant Chief of Staff, G-1, June 7, 1941; Memorandum, Allen W. Gullion, Army JAG, to Assistant Chief of Staff, G-1, Subject: Sodomists, July 9, 1941; Memorandum, from TAG to The Commanding Generals, Subject: Sodomists, July 15, 1941; all in AGO "Sodomists" File.
8. For protests from the U.S. Army Department in Puerto Rico and from the 8th Service Command Headquarters in Texas, see letter and inclosures, from Maj. Gen. James L. Collins, Commanding General, Puerto Rican Department, to TAG, Washington, D.C., December 15, 1941; and letter and attachments, from Maj. Gen. Richard Donovan, Headquarters, 8th Service Command, Fort Sam Houston, Texas, to TAG, September 12, 1942; both in AGO "Sodomists" File.
9. Fishman, *Sex in Prison*, pp. 142–43; Estelle B. Freedman, " 'Uncontrolled Desires': The Response to the Sexual Psychopath, 1920–1960," *Journal of American History* 74 (June 1987): 88–91.
10. Memorandum from JAG to TAG, October 16, 1931, pp. 4–6, in AGO "Sodomists" File.
11. Ibid. On the military's handling of sodomy cases in the early twentieth century, see Capt. Edwin N. McClellan, *Naval Digest* (1916; Washington, D.C.: GPO, 1921), p. 580; *A Manual For Courts-Martial, U.S. Army*, Revised in the Office of the Judge Advocate General of the Army and

published by the direction of The President (Washington, D.C.: USGPO, 1936), pp. 177; and *Digest of Opinions of the Judge Advocate General of the Army 1912–1940* (Washington, D.C.: USGPO, 1942), pp. 203, 207, 217, 333–34.

For a rare early defense of the harsh punishment of sodomists, see Josephus Daniels, Secretary of the Navy, to William E. Egan, Esq., July 7, 1913, General Correspondence 1897–1915, RG 80.

12. William Menninger, *Psychiatry in a Troubled World* (New York: Macmillan, 1948), pp. 241–42; Medical Department U.S. Army, *Neuropsychiatry in World War II*, vol. 1 (Washington, D.C.: USGPO, 1966), pp. 124–25.

13. Correspondence, January 2 to 16, 1942, in Box 14, Folder: "Homosexuality NRC Comm. on Neuropsychiatry 1942"; and Minutes of the Seventh Meeting, January 12, 1942, Committee on Neuropsychiatry, Box 14, Folder: "NRC Committee on Neuropsychiatry and Subcommittees"; both in Overholser Papers.

14. Memorandum, from Chief of BuMed to Chief of NavPers, September 21, 1942, File P13-7, RG 52.

15. Letter, from F. M. Harrison, BuMed, to Winfred Overholser, NRC, August 5, 1942, File P13-7, General Correspondence, RG 52; Letter, from John C. Whitehorn and Winfred Overholser, NRC, to Harrison, November 3, 1942, AGO "Sodomist" File. On the NRC Committee on Neuropsychiatry discussion regarding their reply, see correspondence between Whitehorn and Overholser, October 30 to November 6, 1942, in Box 14, Folder: "Homosexuality NRC Comm. on Neuropsychiatry 1942"; and Minutes of the Tenth Meeting, October 1, 1942, and Minutes of the Eleventh Meeting, November 30, 1942, in Box 14, Folder: "NRC Committee on Neuropsychiatry and Subcommittees"; all in Overholser Papers.

16. On the Newport Scandal, and its detrimental effects on Roosevelt's early political career, see Ted Morgan, *F.D.R.: A Biography* (New York: Simon & Schuster, 1985), Chapter 9, "The Newport Scandal," pp. 234–45; Lawrence R. Murphy, *Perverts by Official Order* (New York: Haworth, 1988); George Chauncey, Jr., "Christian Brotherhood or Sexual Perversion? Homosexual Identities and the Construction of Sexual Boundaries in the World War One Era," *Journal of Social History* 9 (Winter 1985): 189–211.

17. In response to Roosevelt's request for a study of such men, the judge advocate general reported that two men convicted of sodomy and forty-one men convicted of scandalous conduct had been restored to duty in 1918. He justified the restorations of some convicted men to duty during wartime if they had been young and had committed their crimes thoughtlessly and "without viciousness." Correspondence, September 25, 1918, to March 12, 1920, in File 26288-951, RG 80.

18. On the Sumner Welles controversy, see Morgan, *F.D.R.*, pp. 677–86; on the David Walsh scandal, see Morgan, p. 684; Lawrence R. Murphy, ''The House on Pacific Street: Homosexuality, Intrigue, and Politics During World War II,'' *Journal of Homosexuality* 12 (Fall 1985): 27–49.

19. On Roosevelt's support for military psychiatry, see Menninger, *Psychiatry in a Troubled World*, pp. 296–99.

20. Memorandum, Chief of Staff to Commanding Generals, November 10, 1942, Subject: Discipline and Courts-Martial, File 250-4, Decimal Classification File, RG 407.

21. Memorandum, from Col. John M. Weir, Executive, JAG, to The Assistant Chief of Staff, G-1, December 6, 1942, in AGO ''Sodomists'' File.

22. Memorandum, from Chief of BuMed to Chief of NavPers, Subject: Proposed procedure for the disposition of cases of homosexuality among personnel of the U.S. Naval Service, September 21, 1942, File P13-7, RG 52.

23. Letter, Overholser and John C. Whitehorn to Capt. Forrest W. Harrison, BuMed, November 3, 1942, in AGO ''Sodomists'' File.

24. Wrapper indorsement, from SGO to JAG, November 14, 1942, AGO ''Sodomists'' File.

25. Memorandum, from neuropsychiatric staff of Brooke General Hospital, Fort Sam Houston, Texas, to JAG, 8th Service Command, September 9, 1942; and indorsement, from SGO to JAG, November 17, 1942; both in AGO ''Sodomists'' File; Memorandum, from Chief of BuMed to Chief of NavPers, File P13-7, General Correspondence, RG 52.

26. Memorandum, from Col. John M. Weir, Executive, JAG, to Director of Military Personnel, Headquarters Services of Supply, December 17, 1942, in AGO ''Sodomists'' File.

27. Memorandum, Weir to Assistant Chief of Staff, December 6, 1942, in AGO ''Sodomists'' File.

28. Letter, McIntire to W. W. Bauer, M. D., June 2, 1945, File P13-7, General Correspondence, RG 52.

29. On efforts in the Navy and Army to promote the discharge of homosexuals as undesirables, see ''Neuropsychiatric Procedure,'' Ross T. McIntire, January 2, 1941, Folder: ''P3-1/P11 to P3-1/S38,'' Box 148, General Correspondence 1926–1941, RG 52; joint letter, from Chiefs of BuNav and BuMed, to Commanding Officers, All Naval Training Stations, Subject: Plan and procedure for elimination of recruits unfit for service by reason of psychiatric or neurologic handicaps, April 3, 1942; correspondence among Commandant 11th Naval District, Chief of BuMed, and Chief of BuNav, Subject: Medical Survey of Recruits, April/May 1942; Memorandum for the Surgeon General from Howard H. Montgomery, Subject: Discharges of Recruits for physical and neuropsychiatric disabilities after

arrival at Naval Training Stations, April 8, 1943; letter, McIntire to Bauer, June 2, 1945; all in File P3-1/P19-1, General Correspondence, RG 52. Bureau of Naval Personnel Manual, 1942, sections D-9110 to D-9112. Circular Letter No. 12, Subject: Classification of psychoses with constitutional psychopathic state or constitutional inferiority, February 19, 1941, SGO, War Department, Box 11, RG 112.

In a March 1945 revision, the sexual psychopath category was formally written into Army regulations governing undesirable discharges. AR 615-368 provided that individuals having "a psychopathic personality manifested by antisocial or amoral trends, criminalism, chronic alcoholism, drug addiction, pathological lying, or sexual misconduct in the service," a category that explicitly included "homosexual offenses," would be removed with undesirable discharges. Army Regulations No. 615-368, "Enlisted Men, Discharge, Undesirable Habits or Traits of Character," March 7, 1945.

30. For these 1942 discussions regarding reform of Army and Navy policies, see letter, Capt. Forrest M. Harrison, BuMed, to Winfred Overholser, NRC, August 5, 1942; letter, Ross T. McIntire, Surgeon General, to Overholser, November 26, 1942; and memorandum, Chief of BuMed to Chief of NavPers, September 21, 1942; all in File P13-7, General Correspondence, RG 52. See also letter, Overholser and John C. Whitehorn to Harrison, November 3, 1942; letters, Col. John M. Weir, Executive, JAG, to Assistant Chief of Staff, G-1, December 6, 1942, and to Director of Military Personnel, Headquarters Services of Supply, December 17, 1942; memorandum, Col. Russel B. Reynolds, Director of Military Personnel, Services of Supply, to Assistant Chief of Staff, G-1, Subject: Sodomists, December 11, 1942; memorandum from neuropsychiatric staff of Brooke General Hospital, Fort Sam Houston, Texas, to JAG, 8th Service Command, September 9, 1942; and indorsement, from SGO to JAG, November 17, 1942; all in AGO "Sodomists" File.

31. Menninger, *Psychiatry in a Troubled World,* pp. 296–98, 535.

32. "Sodomists," Memorandum No. W615-4-43, January 10, 1943, TAGO, WD, Washington, D.C.

33. "Chronological Development of Policy and Practice on Disposition of Naval Personnel Involved in Homosexual Activity," compiled by Naval Personnel, February 25, 1957, Crittenden Report.

34. Confidential letter, from the Secretary of the Navy to All ships and stations, Subject: Procedure for the DISPOSITION OF HOMOSEXUALS Among Personnel of the U.S. Naval Service, January 1, 1943, in Crittenden Report [pp. 373–75].

35. Roy D. Halloran and Malcolm J. Farrell, "The Function of Neuropsychiatry in the Army," *American Journal of Psychiatry* 100 (July 1943): 14–20.

See also "Disposition of Overt Cases of Homosexuality," *The Army Medical Bulletin,* no. 66 (April 1943): 83–85.

36. Editorial, "Neuropsychiatry in the Army," *Journal of the American Medical Association* 121 (April 3, 1943): 1154–55.

37. For objections from hard-line officers, see memoranda from Maj. Gen. Myron C. Cramer, JAG, to The Chief of Staff, Subject: Disposition of Sodomists, October 25 and December 4, 1943, G-1 "Sodomists" File.

38. On policies toward women, see memorandum and attached summary of review, from Maj. Gen. M. C. White, Assistant Chief of Staff, G-1, Personnel Division, to Chief of Staff, November 4, 1943, and memorandum from Maj. B. W. Davenport, Asst. Secretary, General Staff, to Lt. Col. Murray C. Bernays, December 15, 1943, both in G-1 "Sodomists" File. D'Ann Campbell, *Women at War with America* (Cambridge: Harvard University Press, 1984), p. 29.

39. "Homosexuals," War Department Circular No. 3, January 3, 1943; Circular Letter No. C-44-12, from BuPers to All Ships and Stations, Subject: Procedure for the Disposition of Homosexuals Among Personnel of the United States Naval Service, January 28, 1944. Copy in Crittenden Report (p. 372).

40. Memorandum and attached summary of review, from Maj. Gen. M. C. White, Assistant Chief of Staff, G-1, Personnel Division, to Chief of Staff, November 4, 1943, in G-1 "Sodomists" File.

41. House Report No. 1510, "Blue Discharges," January 30, 1946, Investigations of the National War Effort, Committee on Military Affairs, House of Representatives, Seventy-ninth Congress, Second Session, p. 5.

42. Transcript of hearing and reports of psychiatric examinations, February 9 and 20, 1943, Folder: "250.1 Morals and Conduct, 2-7-43 to 2-28-43," Decimal File 1940–45, RG 407.

43. Affidavits, psychiatric examination reports, and proceedings of disposition board, Folder: "250.1 Morals and Conduct 4-1-44 to 4-30-44," Decimal File 1940–45, RG 407.

44. The Army conducted its own study of what to do with the latent homosexual, and in 1945 issued the first of its many directives on the matter. Menninger, *Psychiatry in a Troubled World,* pp. 230–31.

45. Correspondence between Bauer and McIntire, May/June 1945, File P13-7, RG 52.

46. Memorandum from Army Service Forces JAG, to Assistant Chief of Staff, G-1, WD General Staff, August 1, 1944, Subject: Homosexuals, Box 437, G-1 Personnel, RG 165.

47. From fiscal year 1904 to 1939, the Navy conducted a total of 224 court-martial trials for sodomy. Frederick S. Harrod, *Manning the New Navy:*

The Development of a Modern Naval Enlisted Force 1899–1940 (Westport, Conn.: Greenwood, 1978), pp. 196–97. Convictions for sodomy and related offenses in the Army from July 1938 to May 1941 totaled 34. "Sodomy Cases Review, July 1938 to May 1941," in AGO "Sodomists" File.

48. Medical Department U.S. Army, *Neuropsychiatry in World War II, Volume 1: Zone of Interior* (Washington, D.C.: USGPO, 1966) p. 459; Ruth Chenery Streeter, "History of the Marine Corps Women's Reserve: A Critical Analysis of Its Development and Operation, 1943–45," December 5, 1945, pp. 360–61, Schlesinger Library, Radcliffe College, Cambridge.

49. Memorandum for record, from Arthur J. McDowell, Assistant Chief, Medical Statistics Division, Army SGO, Subject: Information on Homosexuality, June 23, 1950, Folder: "Homosexuals," Case 1438, Box 101, AGO Precedent File, RG 407; memorandum from Capt. A. A. Marsteller (MC) and Vice Adm. Ross T. McIntire, Surgeon General, to SecNav, re: review of cases of personnel discharged for homosexual reasons, September 24, 1946, File P13-7, RG 52. The estimate of less than one thousand homosexual soldiers returned to duty is from *Neuropsychiatry in World War II*, vol. 1, p. 237.

50. Menninger, *Psychiatry in a Troubled World*, p. 231.

Chapter 6. Pioneer Experts: Psychiatrists Discover the Gay GI

1. Author's interview with Burt Gerrits, February 9, 1980. "Dr. Wynn" is a pseudonym.

2. William Menninger, *Psychiatry in a Troubled World* (New York: Macmillan, 1948), pp. 26, 237–38; Francis J. Braceland, "Psychiatric Lessons From World War II," *American Journal of Psychiatry* 103 (May 1946): 588.

3. School of Military Neuropsychiatry, Detailed Schedule, January 1943, and SMNP Nos. 56 and 57, Sept. 9, 1943, in Folder: "Atlanta School of Military NP, (Colonel William C. Porter) 1943," Box 2, Entry 54, Overholser Papers.

4. On the training of military psychiatrists, see Menninger, *Psychiatry in a Troubled World*, pp. 27–29; and Medical Department, U.S. Army, *Medical Training in World War II* (Washington: USGPO, 1974), pp. 65–66.

5. Carl H. Jonas, "Psychiatry Has Growing Pains," *American Journal of Psychiatry* 102 (May 1946): 820.

6. William C. Menninger, "The Military Psychiatrist," *Bulletin of the Menninger Clinic* 7 (July 1943): 132. Navy Surgeon General Ross McIntire hoped that by "proven research with the tremendous amount of clinical material on hand," there was the possibility of scientific breakthroughs that could contribute much to "future psychiatric information." Ross McIntire, "Psychiatry and the U.S. Navy," *American Journal of Psychiatry* 101 (May 1945): 718.

7. Lt. Herbert Greenspan and Comdr. John D. Campbell, "The Homosexual as a Personality Type," *American Journal of Psychiatry* 104 (March 1945): 682.

8. Among the male homosexual soldiers and sailors studied during the war were 100 soldiers in the Army's 6th Service Command (Wisconsin, Michigan, and Illinois); 20 homosexual airmen at Truax Field in Madison, Wisconsin; 20 soldiers at Camp Wheeler, Georgia; 60 soldiers at Camp Haan in Riverside County, California; 270 soldiers and officers at the Army's 36th Station Hospital in England; 200 sailors at an unidentified Navy base; 42 sailors on another unidentified Navy base; and 183 soldiers and officers in the Army, Navy and Air Force who had been students at Yale and Harvard universities before the War. Some 1404 soldier patients at unidentified Army hospitals and clinics were studied for their history of fellatio. Other reports did not specify the number of homosexual subjects studied.

Letter, P. V. Wegley, Medical Superintendent, Pontiac State Hospital, January 1950, Records of the Michigan Governor's Study Commission on the Deviated Criminal Sex Offender, 62-41-A, Records of the Dept. of Mental Health, Michigan State Archives (I wish to thank George Chauncey, Jr., for bringing this document to my attention); E. L. Sevringhaus and Maj. John Chornyak, "A Study of Homosexual Adult Males," *Psychosomatic Medicine* 7 (Sept. 1945): 302–5; M. S. Bergmann, "Homosexuality on the Rorschach Test," *Bulletin of the Menninger Clinic* 9 (1945): 78–83; Maj. Carl H. Jonas, "An Objective Approach to the Personality and Environment in Homosexuality," *Psychiatric Quarterly* 18 (1944): 626–41; Lt. Col. Lewis H. Loeser, "The Sexual Psychopath in the Military Service," *American Journal of Psychiatry* 102 (July 1945): 92–101; Comdr. A. C. Cornsweet and Lt. Comdr. M. F. Hayes, "Conditioned Response to Fellatio," *American Journal of Psychiatry* 103 (July 1945): 76–78; Lt. Comdr. Floyd O. Due and Lt. (jg) M. E. Wright, "The Use of Content Analysis in Rorschach Interpretation: 1. Differential Characteristics of Male Homosexuals," *Journal of Projective Techniques* (formerly *Rorschach Research Exchange*) 9, No. 1 (1945): 169–77; Clements C. Fry and Edna G. Rostow, "Some Observations on Homosexuality in Military Service," Interim Report No. 337, 1 April 1945, Committee on Medical Research of the Office of Scientific Research and Development, Archives of the National Academy of Sciences, Washington, D.C.; id., "Reflections on Some Aspects of Homosexuality as it Relates to Military Administration," [May 10, 1948], Box 65, Entry 356, RG 330; Nicolai Gioscia, "The Gag Reflex and Fellatio," *American Journal of Psychiatry* 107 (Nov. 1950): 380.

9. A 1954 compendium of the international psychiatric literature that grew out of World War II includes ten psychiatric studies of American homosexual soldiers, while only four were in any way related to the sexuality of

other soldier populations (neurotics and venereal disease patients). A socio-logical study that was listed examined the "aggressive and erotic tendencies in army life" and included a discussion of homosexuality. Nolan D. C. Lewis and Bernice Engle, eds., *Wartime Psychiatry* (New York: Oxford University Press, 1954).

10. William Needles, "The Regression of Psychiatry in the Army," *Psychiatry* 9 (August 1946): 167–85.

11. Gioscia, "Gag Reflex," p. 380.

12. Cornsweet and Hayes, "Conditioned Response to Fellatio," pp. 76–78.

13. Bergmann, "Homosexuality on the Rorschach Test," p. 78–83.

14. Due and Wright, "Rorschach Interpretation," pp. 169, 177. For a brief history of the use of the Rorschach test for diagnosing homosexuality beginning in World War II, see Stephen J. Hendlin, "Homosexuality in the Rorschach: A New Look at the Old Signs," *Journal of Homosexuality* 1, no. 3 (1976): 303–12.

15. For Rorschach, Thematic Apperception, and Bender Gestalt tests on homo-sexuals, see Capt. David M. Wayne, Lt. M. Adams, and T/4 Lillian A. Rowe, "A Study of Military Prisoners at a Disciplinary Barracks Suspected of Homosexual Activities," *Military Surgeon* 101 (December 1947): 499–504. For Goodenough Drawing a Man Tests and their possible applicability to lesbians, see George A. Geil, "The Use of the Goodenough Test For Revealing Male Homosexuality," *Journal of Clinical Psychopathology* 6 (October 1944), pp. 307–22.

16. Maj. Isidore I. Weiss, "Homosexuality," *Psychiatric Quarterly* 20, No. 3 (1946): 503–4.

17. "Homosexuals in Uniform," *Newsweek,* June 9, 1947, p. 54. For hormonal research on homosexual Army Air Corpsmen, see Sevringhaus and Chorn-yak, "Homosexual Adult Males," pp. 302–5.

18. "Homosexuals in Uniform," p. 54.

19. On the trend in psychoanalysis during the 1930s and 1940s toward describ-ing "the homosexual," see Kenneth Lewes, *The Psychoanalytic Theory of Male Homosexuality* (New York: Simon & Schuster, 1988), pp. 113–21. Wartime psychiatric research also studied other populations of soldiers in an effort to determine personality profiles of neurotics, psychotics, psychopaths, disciplinary cases, criminal offenders and venereal disease patients. See, for example, John P. Brady and Harold M. Hildreth, "Char-acteristics of a Disciplinary Group in an Naval Hospital," *U.S. Naval Medical Bulletin* 45 (Sept. 1945): 500–5; and Keith D. Heuser, "The Psychopathic Personality," *American Journal of Psychiatry* 103 (July 1946): 105–12.

20. Greenspan and Campbell, "Personality Type," pp. 685–86.

21. Jonas, "Objective Approach," p. 630.

22. Greenspan and Campbell, "Personality Type," p. 683.

23. Findings of Psychiatric Section in the case of Cpl.————, April 8, 1944, 298th Station Hospital, Miami, Florida, Folder: "250.1 Morals and Conduct 4–1–44 to 4–30–44," Decimal File 1940–45, RG 407.

24. Cornsweet and Hayes, "Conditioned Response," p. 77.

25. Greenspan and Campbell, "Personality Type," p. 683.

26. Ibid., p. 685.

27. Cornsweet and Hayes, "Conditioned Response," pp. 77–78.

28. Greenspan and Campbell, "Personality Type," p. 685.

29. "The esthetic interest which absorbs so many of these men is an additional bond that ties them to their own kind." Cornsweet and Hayes, "Conditioned Response," p. 76.

30. Due and Wright, "Rorschach Interpretation," p. 172.

31. Greenspan and Campbell, "Personality Type," p. 685.

32. Due and Wright, "Rorschach Interpretation," p. 172.

33. Greenspan and Campbell, "Personality Type," p. 685.

34. The Army also designated the 96th General Hospital (NP) in England as an observation and recommendation center for homosexuals. *Neuropsychiatry in World War II,* vol. 2, p. 237.

35. Loeser, "The Sexual Psychopath," pp. 92–101.

36. Cornsweet and Hayes, "Conditioned Response," pp. 77–78.

37. Special Examination Report in the case of Michael O'Connor (pseudonym), February 18, 1944, U.S. Navy Unit, U.S. Public Health Service, Fort Worth, Texas [copy in possession of author]. Hereafter referred to as "O'Connor Report."

38. O'Connor Report.

39. Due and Wright, "Rorschach Interpretation," p. 172.

40. O'Connor Report.

41. Weiss, "Homosexuality," pp. 505–6

42. Greenspan and Campbell, "Personality Type," p. 687.

43. O'Connor Report.

44. See, for example, Report of Psychiatric Examination of Enlisted WAC Sergeant, June 9, 1944, by Capt. Alice E. Rost, Exhibit D, Fort Oglethorpe Report.

45. Clinical abstract of case of Pfc. Leo M. Koski (pseudonym), May 3, 1944, 36th Station Hospital (NP), File AG 250.1, Subj.: Records of Hospitalization, Classified Decimal File 1943–45, RG 407.

46. Menninger, *Psychiatry in a Troubled World,* pp. 18–19, 22, 318.

47. Maj. Gen. William R. Arnold to Chaplain William P. Byrnes, January 11, 1945, Folder: "250.1 Morals and Conduct—Misc. Vol. II from 1/1/

44 to 12/45,'' Decimal File 1920–45, Box 195, Entry 1, Office Management Division, RG 247.

48. Menninger, *Psychiatry in a Troubled World,* p. 230.

49. Loeser, "Sexual Psychopaths," p. 92.

50. Menninger, *Psychiatry in a Troubled World,* p. 227. See also "The Military Problem of Malingering," Abstract of Round Tables Discussion, Proceedings of Societies, *American Journal of Psychiatry* 101 (January 1945): 553–54.

51. John H. Young III, "Courier Launches Probe of Blue Discharges," *Pittsburgh Courier,* October 20, 1945, p. 1; Rutherford B. Stevens, "Racial Aspects of Emotional Problems of Negro Soldiers," *American Journal of Psychiatry* 103 (January 1947): 497.

52. Menninger, *Psychiatry in a Troubled World,* p. 15. Roy D. Halloran and Malcolm J. Farrell, "The Function of Neuropsychiatry in the Army," *American Journal of Psychiatry* 100 (July 1943): 17–18. On treatment priorities in the military, see Menninger, *Psychiatry in a Troubled World,* pp. 35–36; Lauren H. Smith, "Treatment Activities in War Psychiatry," *American Journal of Psychiatry* (November 1944): pp. 303–9.

53. For examples of the various treatments used experimentally to cure homosexuality, see Jonathan [Ned] Katz, *Gay American History* (New York: Crowell, 1976), pp. 129–207. On testicle irradiation, see Weiss, "Homosexuality," p. 522.

54. See, for example, "Case 3" in Weiss, "Homosexuality," pp. 506–7. In 1947 a gay Navy veteran wrote a novel, based on his own experience, about a Navy psychiatric ward that included a episode in which a despondent gay patient is treated with Metrazol shock therapy. Robert Plant Armstrong, "The Sky Room " (Master's thesis, Department of English, State University of Iowa, February 1947), pp. 295–303; correspondence from Armstrong to author, February 7 and March 8, 1983.

55. Letter, from Committee on Neuropsychiatry, NRC, to Chief of BuMed, January 13, 1942, Folder: "Homosexuality NRC Comm. on Neuropsychiatry 1942," Box 14, Overholser Papers.

56. Menninger, *Psychiatry in a Troubled World,* p. 230.

57. Menninger, *Psychiatry in a Troubled World,* p. 229.

58. Francis Braceland testimony, January 31, 1957, Enclosure 1(k), p. 2, in Crittenden Report.

59. Letter, Capt. Charles O. Dutton, Post Chaplain, Fort Bliss, Texas, to Chief of Chaplains, Washington, D.C., August 9, 1943, Folder: "250.1 Morals and Conduct-Misc. Volume I from 12/10/40 to 12/31/43," Box 195, Entry 1, Office Management Division, Decimal File 1920–45, RG 247.

60. W. Edgar Gregory, "The Chaplain and Mental Hygiene," *American Journal of Sociology* 52 (March 1947): 420–23.

61. The chaplain referred him to the medical officer. He was hospitalized and discharged without honor. Eli Ginzberg et al., *Breakdown and Recovery* (New York: Columbia University Press, 1959), vol. 2, *The Ineffective Soldier*, p. 247.

62. On homosexual trainees who voluntarily went to training center consultation services "desperately appealing for help," see Manfred S. Guttmacher, "Army Consultation Services (Mental Hygiene Clinics)," *American Journal of Psychiatry* 102 (May 1946): 744, and *Neuropsychiatry in World War II*, vol. 1, p. 367.

63. On "latent" homosexuals who went AWOL or "dr[a]nk themselves into a stupor" to flee the homosexual tensions of military life, see Weiss, "Homosexuality," pp. 509–11.

64. One wartime study concluded that "suspected homosexuals became suspicious of the intent of the examiner" and were "extremely guarded in their responses," undermining the clinical value of diagnostic tests. Wayne, Adams and Rowe, "Military Prisoners," pp. 501–2.

65. Case AD78-00827, Pentagon Reading Room Case Files.

66. On the history of lies and deceptions that took place during interviews between social workers and their clients in Boston, see Linda Gordon, *Heroes of their Own Lives* (New York: Viking, 1988), especially pp. 12–20.

67. Braceland testimony, p. 2, Crittenden Report.

68. Menninger, *Psychiatry in a Troubled World*, p. 229. On the various forms of deliberate misdiagnoses to protect homosexual soldiers, see W. A. Hunt and C. L. Wittson, "Some Sources of Error in the Neuropsychiatric Statistics of World War II," *Journal of Clinical Psychology* 5 (October 1949): 354. Kinsey described the effects of such misdiagnoses on the collection of accurate information about the number of homosexuals who were discharged during the war. Alfred C. Kinsey et al., *Sexual Behavior in the Human Male* (Philadelphia: W. B. Saunders, 1948), p. 622.

69. Hunt and Wittson, "Some Sources of Error," p. 354.

70. Menninger, *Psychiatry in a Troubled World*, pp. 35, 230.

71. Letter, Dutton to Chief of Chaplains, August 9, 1943, RG, 247.

72. Menninger, *Psychiatry in a Troubled World*, pp. 121–33, 257–65; *Neuropsychiatry in World War II*, vol. 2, pp. 522–23.

73. Menninger, *Psychiatry in a Troubled World*, p. 230.

74. Fry and Rostow, "Reflections," p. 33.

75. "Observations in a Regional Hospital Neuropsychiatric Section," p. 404. For another psychiatrist's wartime protest against the injustices of the homosexual discharge system, see Guttmacher, "Army Consultation Services," p. 744.

76. Braceland testimony, p. 2, Crittenden Report.

77. Menninger, *Psychiatry in a Troubled World,* pp. 229–31.

78. Ibid., pp. 228–29. Braceland concurred that in the Navy there was to his knowledge "no satisfactory solution" to the problem of managing homosexual personnel. Braceland, "Psychiatric Lessons," p. 592.

79. Lewes, *The Psychoanalytic Theory of Male Homosexuality,* pp. 24–47.

80. William C. Porter, "What Has Psychiatry Learned During the Present War?" *American Journal of Psychiatry* 99 (May 1943): 853.

81. Testimony of Captain Alice E. Rost, June 26, 1944, pp. 103, 106, 107, and Report of Psychiatric Examination of Enlisted WAC Sergeant by Captain Alice E. Rost, June 9, 1944, Exhibit D, both in Fort Oglethorpe Testimony.

82. Jonas, "An Objective Approach," p. 634.

83. Fry and Rostow, "Reflections," pp. 21–22, 41.

84. One hundred of the 270 "sexual psychopath" patients at the 36th Station Hospital had declared their homosexuality to their officers, 113 had been reported by others, and most of the rest had been caught in the act. In civilian life, 100 of these gay GIs had been service workers, 46 clerical workers, 38 technicians, 21 managers or salesmen, 20 professionals, 18 students, 15 farmers, 6 unskilled workers and 3 executives. Two-thirds had entered the service from urban areas. Their "average mental age" was "well above the average for the Army," they held a higher Army rating than the average soldier, and there were "no illiterates in the entire group." Fifty-four were married. Only 2 had been addicted to drugs, but 95 admitted excessive use of alcohol. Most had "impressive" health records, with a rate of venereal disease no higher than the army average. Loeser's staff decided that slightly over half of these men were masculine in appearance. Because only 19 were black—proportionately less than in the hospital's general population—Loeser concluded that there was "less reported homosexuality among colored troops than white." Loeser, "The Sexual Psychopath," pp. 92–101.

85. Menninger, *Psychiatry in a Troubled World,* p. 227.

86. Greenspan and Campbell, "Personality Type," pp. 686–88.

87. Fry and Rostow, "Observations," p. 65; "Reflections," pp. 4–6.

88. Fry and Rostow, "Reflections," p. 25.

89. Loeser, "The Sexual Psychopath," pp. 92–101.

90. Fry and Rostow, "Reflections," p. 17.

91. Fry and Rostow, "Observations," p. 65.

92. Fry and Rostow, "Reflections," pp. 41–42.

93. Lewes, *The Psychoanalytic Theory of Male Homosexuality,* pp. 96–172.

Chapter 7. Comrades in Arms

1. Citation, Award of the Bronze Star Medal to Robert G. Fleischer, January 28, 1946, Major General Harry J. Collins, Commanding General, Head-quarters 42nd (Rainbow) Infantry Division. Copy in collection of the World War II Project.

2. On combat as a proving ground for manhood and masculinity, see Samuel A. Stouffer et al., *The American Soldier*, vol. 2 (Princeton: Princeton University Press, 1949) pp. 131–35.

3. Clements C. Fry and Edna G. Rostow, "Reflections on Some Aspects of Homosexuality as it Relates to Military Administration," [May 10, 1948], pp. 4, 5, Box 65, Entry 356, RG 330.

4. Stouffer, *The American Soldier*, vol. 1, pp. 312–13.

5. By June 1944, 76 percent of all Army enlisted men were twenty-nine years old or younger. William Menninger, *Psychiatry in a Troubled World* (New York: Macmillan, 1948), pp. 605–6.

6. Roger W. Little, "Buddy Relations and Combat Performance," in *The New Military: Changing Patterns of Organization*, ed. Morris Janowitz (New York: Russell Sage Foundation, 1964), pp. 202–4.

7. S. L. A. Marshall, *Men Against Fire* (New York: William Morrow, 1947), pp. 50–63, 78–79. Combat soldiers also chose not to fire their weapons in order to conserve ammunition and out of concern for the men who would have to be sent under fire for more. Little, "Buddy Relations," pp. 222–23.

8. Stouffer et al., *The American Soldier*, vol. 2, pp. 8, 41–44.

9. Menninger, *Psychiatry in a Troubled World*, pp. 50–55.

10. On the myths and realities of the American combat soldier, see Richard H. Kohn, "The Social History of the American Soldier: A Review and Prospectus for Research," *American Historical Review* 86 (June 1981): 553–67.

11. World War II veterans interviewed for this book and Clements C. Fry and Edna G. Rostow, "Some Observations on Homosexuality in Military Service," Interim Report No. 337, 1 April 1945, Committee on Medical Research of the Office of Scientific Research and Development. pp. 22–24, 36–38, Archives of the National Academy of Sciences, Washington, D.C.; id., "Reflections," pp. 10–11.

12. "From my own personal experience," wrote a veteran in his master's thesis after the war, "I know of several men who saw combat with my platoon and who handled themselves with great personal heroism and calmness who had homosexual relations before entering combat and after leaving combat." Keith Siddons Beggs, "Some Legal, Social and Psychiat-

ric Aspects of Homosexual Behavior'' (Master's thesis, University of Wisconsin, Madison, 1950), p. 170.

13. Studs Terkel, *"The Good War"* (New York: Pantheon, 1984), p. 179.

14. For histories of the Nazi campaign against homosexuals, see Richard Plant, *The Pink Triangle* (New York: Henry Holt, 1986); Heinz Heger, *The Men With the Pink Triangle* (Boston: Alyson Publications, 1980); Frank Rector, *The Nazi Extermination of Homosexuals* (New York: Stein and Day, 1981); and James Steakley, *The Homosexual Emancipation Movement in Germany* (New York: Arno, 1975).

For excerpts from 1933 *New York Times* articles about the Nazi raids on the Berlin headquarters of homosexual emancipationist Magnus Hirschfeld and the 1934 articles on the execution of Ernst Roehm on the "night of the long knives," see Jonathan Ned Katz, *Gay/Lesbian Almanac* (New York: Harper & Row, 1983), pp. 480–1, 501–3.

15. Author's interview with Richard Plant, May 25, 1983; Hans Mayer, *Outsiders: A Study in Life and Letters* (Cambridge: MIT Press, 1984), pp. 243–52; Anthony Heilbut, *Exiled in Paradise* (New York: Viking, 1983), pp. 51–53, 266–73.

16. Allan Brandt, *No Magic Bullet* (New York: Oxford University Press, 1983), pp. 169–70.

17. *Selective Service As the Tide of War Turns,* the third report of the Director of Selective Service 1943–44 (Washington, D.C.: USGPO, 1945), pp. 164–70. Roger Daniels, *Concentration Camps USA: Japanese Americans and World War II* (New York: Holt, Rinehart and Winston, 1970), p. 123. Geoffrey Perrett, *Days of Sadness, Years of Triumph* (Baltimore: Penguin, 1973), pp. 317–18.

18. Correspondence between Commanding General, Moffett Field, and the Adjutant General, Washington, February 28 to March 24, 1942, Folder: "1-1-40 to 12-31-41, 250.1 Sodomy, practice of in the Army," RG 407.

19. Circular Letter No. 77, July 29, 1942, Office of the Surgeon General, Box 12, RG 112.

20. Army Regulations No. 615-360, War Department, November 26, 1942, Enlisted Men: Discharge; Release From Active Duty, Section 8, Inaptness or Undesirable Habits or Traits of Character, pp. 23–24.

21. Memorandum, from Brigadier General James B. Crawford, President, Secretary of War's Discharge Review Board, to Assistant Chief of Staff G-1, March 13, 1945, and memorandum, from Assistant Chief of Staff G-1 to TAG, March 24, 1945, in Folder: "10-16-44, 220.8 Discharge, other separations," RG 407.

22. The psychiatric consultants in the Surgeon General's Office, although recommending that the Army consider convicted murderers for duty in such units, warned against using homosexuals, who they believed "should be excluded as a class," because, as sexual psychopaths, "they will remain

such and if the opportunity presents itself chances favor their again getting into trouble." Memorandum, Major Ivan C. Berlien, SGO, to Director, Corrections Division, AGO, March 1, 1945, in Box 130, Folder: "Disciplinary Barracks (and Rehabilitation Centers)," Robert Porter Patterson Papers, Library of Congress.

23. WD Memorandum No. W615-4-43, "Sodomists," January 10, 1943; Fort Oglethorpe Report, p. 25.

24. Andrea Weiss and Greta Schiller, *Before Stonewall* ([no city]: Naiad, 1988), p. 34.

25. Terkel, *"The Good War,"* p. 183.

26. Medical Department U.S. Army, *Neuropsychiatry in World War II,* vol. 2, (Washington, D.C.: USGPO, 1966), pp. 701–3. Dana L. Farnsworth and Robert S. Wigton, "Psychiatric Practice Aboard a Hospital Ship in a Combat Area," *American Journal of Psychiatry* 101 (January 1945): 506; Keith D. Heuser, "The Psychopathic Personality," *American Journal of Psychiatry* 103 (July 1946): 106–7; Ivan F. Duff and C. W. Shilling, "Psychiatric Casualties in Submarine Warfare," *American Journal of Psychiatry* 103 (March 1947): 610–11.

27. *Neuropsychiatry in World War II,* vol. 2, p. 637.

28. Maj. George Creswell Burns, "Neuropsychiatric Problems at an Aleutian Post," *American Journal of Psychiatry* 102 (September 1945): 205.

29. Maurice M. Witherspoon, "The Cowan Hut," *Recreation* (January 1944): 537.

30. F. Gelbman, "Retrospection on Part of the Aleutian Campaign," *American Journal of Psychiatry* 106 (August 1949): 136–39.
    Such local practices were reinforced by orders from higher up the chain of command. Orders from the commanding general of the Alaskan Department during the critical manpower shortage of 1944 directed "all commanders to make the best use of personnel available." Any company commander "who permitted the discharge of an enlisted man in preference to making the necessary effort to place him properly and train him failed to meet command responsibilities." Charles H. Jones, "Neuropsychiatry in the Aleutian Islands," *Diseases of the Nervous System* 12 (June 1951): 172–77.

31. *Neuropsychiatry in World War II,* vol. 2, p. 702. For other accounts of the conditions on the Aleutian Islands, see ibid., pp. 681–737; "Alaska Sweats It Out," March 30, 1945, p. 11, and "Yanks in Alaska," June 8, 1945, p. 6, July 6, 1945, p. 6, July 13, 1945, p. 6, and July 27, 1945, p. 7, all in *Yank;* "Cold, Fog, Mud—Life in the Aleutians," *New York Times Magazine,* August 22, 1943, pp. 4–5; "Airmen in the Aleutians," *Life,* May 22, 1944, pp. 56–62; and "The Aleutians: They Are Barren Links Between Two Worlds," *Life,* March 13, 1944, pp. 71–86.

32. Keith Vacha, *Quiet Fire: Memoirs of Older Gay Men* (Trumansburg, N.Y.: Crossing Press, 1985), p. 172.

   Another gay infantryman recalled that when he and "others with me in the infantry 'confessed' to being gay," the "policy then was to keep gays in service; the army didn't know at that time whether we would lose the war or win it. . . . They were desperate." Letter to the editor from "A Gay Veteran," *Gay Community News,* July 12, 1975, p. 5.

33. DeWitt MacKenzie, *Men Without Guns* (Philadelphia: Blakiston, 1945), p. 1.

34. George Dohmann, "A Medic in Normandy: 'Suddenly I Knew I Was Hit,' " *American History Illustrated* (June 1969): 8–17; letter, Dohmann to author, November 11, 1981.

35. Fry and Rostow, "Observations," p. 35.

36. Letter, Robert Gervais to author, September 27, 1981.

37. Gelbman, "Retrospection on Part of the Aleutian Campaign," pp. 136–39.

38. Marshall, *Men Against Fire,* pp. 42–43, 149–55.

   One of the emotional underpinnings that might explain the vehemence with which military officials pursued their antihomosexual policies was a fear that gay soldiers threatened to disrupt this often-life-saving camaraderie. This fear permeates military arguments that gay and "normal" men could not identify with each other and therefore could not be each other's "buddies"; that gay men were misfits who could not be accepted into groups of "normal" men; that gay men could not cope with the sexual tension of an all-male environment; and that gay men endangered other men with sexually aggressive behavior. The military's antigay policies promised to protect the comradely love among combat soldiers from being "tainted" by homosexual desire. Fry and Rostow, "Observations," pp. 1–2; William P. Snyder and Kenneth L. Nyberg, "Policy Paper: Gays and the Military: An Emerging Policy Issue," *Journal of Political and Military Sociology* 8 (Spring 1980): 72–73.

39. Charles G. Bolte, *The New Veteran* (New York: Reynal and Hitchcock, 1945), p. 5. On the tendency among white soldiers to ignore race prejudice as black soldiers left service duties and became more deeply involved in combat, see Sgt. August Loeb, "Negroes in Combat," *Yank,* February 23, 1945, p. 7; John Morton Blum, *V Was For Victory* (New York: Harcourt Brace Jovanovich, 1976), p. 210.

40. Quoted in Gwynne Dyer, *War* (New York: Crown, 1985), p. 127.

41. Jack Belden, *Still Time to Die* (New York: Harper & Bros., 1944), p. 27; quoted in John Ellis, *The Sharp End: The Fighting Man in World War II* (New York: Charles Scribner's Sons, 1980), p. 314.

42. Letter from George Dohmann to author, November 11, 1981.

43. Vacha, *Quiet Fire,* p. 172.

44. For the homosexual soldier, noted Fry and Rostow, "the life of tension at least in conditions of combat may lead to relations of friendship, comradeship (the 'buddy' relation) which may be a satisfactory kind of sublimation, even of fulfillment." Fry and Rostow, "Observations," p. 35.

45. Stern drew on his experiences in World War II to create the intense male camaraderie among the gang members in the 1955 film *Rebel Without a Cause*. Vito Russo, *The Celluloid Closet* (New York: Harper & Row, 1981), p. 109.

46. This photograph is in *Life*, September 13, 1943, p. 130. Author's conversation with Samuel Steward.

   For other images of physical affection among buddies, see, for example, "Don't Travel," *Life*, December 21, 1942, p. 43; Pullman advertisement, *Life*, February 8, 1943, p. 45; cover, *Life*, July 3, 1944; Kodak advertisement, *Life*, October 30, 1944, p. 3; Christopher Phillips, *Steichen At War* (New York: Harry N. Abrams, 1981), pp. 100, 154.

47. On "emergency" homosexuality, see John Costello, *Virtue Under Fire* (Boston: Little, Brown, 1985), p. 102.

48. A veteran who served with the 3rd and 70th Infantry Divisions in Europe reported that in his platoon during one month in 1945, "a decided majority of the men had sex relations with frauleins and at least a few had homosexual relations. . . . Two or more men having relations with fräuleins in the same room at the same time was not uncommon." Beggs, "Some Legal, Social and Psychiatric Aspects of Homosexual Behavior," p. 171.

49. Quentin Crisp describes cruising American soldiers in London in *The Naked Civil Servant* (1968; New York: Signet, 1977), pp. 151–58. One of Howard Taylor's GI buddies described an evening at the Pink Elephant in Manila. Letter, Denny to Taylor, September 12, 1945, Taylor Correspondence. Gay bars catering to American servicemen in Italy during the war are described in fictional accounts in John Horne Burns, *The Gallery* (1947; New York: Bantam, 1970), "Momma," pp. 133–64; and in Loren Wahl, *The Invisible Glass* (1950; Washington, D.C.: Guild Press, 1965), pp. 202–19. For an account of the Shepheard's Hotel in Cairo and gay spots in Algiers and Naples, see Costello, *Virtue Under Fire*, pp. 115–16.

50. Two studies of homosexual GIs during the war, one of discharge patients and one of prisoners, concluded that their homosexual samples had the same or lower rate of venereal disease than their control groups. Lt. Col. Lewis H. Loeser, "The Sexual Psychopath in the Military Service," *American Journal of Psychiatry* 102 (July 1945): 95, 100; David M. Wayne, M. Adams, and L. A. Rowe, "A Study of Military Prisoners at a Disciplinary Barracks Suspected of Homosexual Activities," *The Military Surgeon* 101 (December 1946): 500–1.

   A popular belief that sex between men would not lead to venereal disease persisted at least until the 1960s. See, for example, memorandum,

Chief of Naval Personnel to All Ships and Stations, October 6, 1953, Subject: Information Concerning Homosexuality, in Crittenden Report; "Venereal Disease–Public Health," *The Ladder* 5 (September 1961): 4–5.

51. Vacha, *Quiet Fire,* p. 172.

52. Memorandum to Commandant U.S. Marine Corps from Captain Howard H. Montgomery (MC), BuMed, 18 November 1943, Subject: Undesirable discharge of Marine Corps Personnel, File, P13-7, General Correspondence, RG 52.

   In the 24th Infantry Division "an unusual amount of homosexual practice" took place among the men when they were stationed at Goodenough Island (Guadalcanal) in the South Pacific prior to their first combat mission. *Neuropsychiatry in World War II,* vol. 2, pp. 636–37.

53. Herbert S. Ripley and Stewart Wolf, "Mental Illness Among Negro Troops Overseas," *American Journal of Psychiatry* 103 (January 1947): 510.

54. Author's interview with Robert Gervais, March 18, 1984.

55. Vacha, *Quiet Fire,* p. 172.

56. Costello, *Virtue Under Fire,* pp. 116–17.

57. Dick Hasbany, "Marching to a Different Drummer," *San Francisco Sentinel,* May 15, 1981, p. 1.

58. F. M. Richardson, *Fighting Spirit: A Study of the Psychological Factors in War* (London: Leo Cooper, 1978), p. 8; Costello, *Virtue Under Fire,* pp. 105–6.

   Much of the literature on homosexuals in the military refers to the bravery of homosexual military men throughout history in order to defend the abilities of the gay soldier in the United States. See, for example, James Barr, *Quatrefoil* (1950; reprint ed., Boston: Alyson, 1982), pp. 309–10; Donald Webster Cory, *The Homosexual in America* (New York: Greenwood, 1951), p. 160; Robert Gregory, "The Homosexual Draftee," *ONE: The Homosexual Viewpoint* 8 (August 1960): 12; Katherine Bourdonnay et al., *Fighting Back: Lesbian and Gay Draft, Military and Veterans Issues* (Chicago: Midwest Committee for Military Counseling, 1985), p. 2.

59. In one survey of a division of infantrymen who had seen combat in two Mediterranean campaigns, only 2 percent mentioned anger or revenge as their motives, while 39 percent named "ending the task" and 14 percent named "solidarity with group" as their combat incentives. Stouffer, *The American Soldier,* vol. 2, pp. 108–11.

60. *Minor White: Rites & Passages,* biographical essay by James Baker Hall (Millerton, N.Y.: Aperture Monograph, 1978), p. 43.

61. Terkel, *The Good War,* p. 182.

62. A soldier "may maim his own personality permanently," explained one doctor during the war, "If he is fool enough to roll over his enemy's corpse with his boot to study the face of the enemy he had to kill, or if he personally had to bury his slain enemy." Harold S. Hulbert, "Questions and Answers," *Journal of Criminal Law and Criminology* 35 (1944–45): 184–5.

Christopher Isherwood became a conscientious objector because he did not want to face this same situation only to discover that he had killed his drafted German lover. "Heinz is in the Nazi army," Isherwood wrote in his diary in June 1942. "I would refuse to kill Heinz. Therefore, I have no right to kill anybody." Isherwood, *My Guru and His Disciple* (New York: Farrar Straus Giroux, 1980), pp. 94–95.

63. Letter to the editor from "A Gay Veteran," *Gay Community News*, July 12, 1975, p. 5.

64. Terkel, *"The Good War,"* pp. 181–82.

65. Studies of American soldiers in Japanese prisoner-of-war camps found little homosexual behavior or any interest in sex when the men were severely malnourished. When food was available, both overt and covert homosexual behavior was common, as were makeshift variety shows that included much female impersonation. For literature on homosexuality and female impersonation among American soldiers in German and Japanese prisoner-of-war camps, see Menninger, *Psychiatry in a Troubled World*, p. 226; Noel Barber, "Recreation Behind Barbed Wire," *Recreation* (December 1943): pp. 504–5; "Theatre Adventures, Sea and Prison," *Theatre Arts* (April 1944): 253–54; J. E. Nardini, "Survival Factors in American Prisoners of War of the Japanese," *American Journal of Psychiatry* 109 (October 1952): 241–48; C. Hall Thompson, "The Prisoners," in Edwin Seaver, ed., *Cross Sections 1945* (New York: Book Find Club, 1945), pp. 253–71; *Neuropsychiatry in World War II*, vol. 2, p. 953.

Chapter 8. Fighting Another War

1. For a lesbian veteran's account of declaring herself to get out of the WAC, see Rita Laporte, "Living Propaganda," *The Ladder* (June 1965): 21–22.

2. William Menninger, *Psychiatry in a Troubled World* (New York: Macmillan, 1948), p. 16.

3. Letters, Marty Klausner to Howard Taylor, January 23, 1945; and Tommy Martz to Taylor, March 12 and 16, 1945, Taylor Correspondence.

4. Letter, Marty Klausner to Howard Taylor, January 31, 1945, Taylor Correspondence.

5. Comdr. A. C. Cornsweet and Lt. Comdr. M. F. Hayes, "Conditioned

Response to Fellatio," *American Journal of Psychiatry* 102 (July 1945): 76–78.

6. E. L. Sevringhaus and Maj. John Chornyak, "A Study of Homosexual Adult Males," *Psychosomatic Medicine* 7 (Sept. 1945): 302–5.

7. Lt. Col. Lewis H. Loeser, "The Sexual Psychopath in the Military Service," *American Journal of Psychiatry* 102 (July 1945): 99. See also Lt. Herbert Greenspan and Comdr. John D. Campbell, "The Homosexual as a Personality Type," *American Journal of Psychiatry* 104 (March 1945): 684.

8. Letters, J. D. to Taylor, December 16, [1944], and May 4, 1945, Taylor Correspondence.

9. Author's interview with David Barrett, February 22, 1983. Author's interviews with Stan Carlow, August 24, 1981; Woodie Wilson, December 21, 1983; Norman Sansom, August 7, 1981; and "Stew" (interviewed by Gregory Lamb, November 2, 1982) confirm that military interrogators used similar techniques on suspected homosexuals in Australia, Mississippi, South Carolina, and Chicago during the war.

10. Fort Oglethorpe Testimony, pp. 30–46. "Lieutenant Foster" is a pseudonym.

11. Ibid., pp. 41–46.

12. Letter, Comdr. J. Lloyd Abbott, District Intelligence Officer, 6th Naval District, to Col. Stacy Knopf, Assistant Chief of Staff, G-2, 4th Service Command, August 31, 1943, Folder: "250.1 (9/1/43 to 9/30/43)," Classified Decimal File 1943–45, RG 407. (All names are ethnically appropriate pseudonyms.)

13. See, for example, the transcript of a Section Eight board hearing at Wendover Field, Utah, February 16, 1943, Folder: "2–1–43 to 2–28–43, 250.1 Morals and Conduct," Decimal File 1940–45, RG 407.

14. Author's interview with Robert Green, March 10, 1982.

15. Author's interview with Dr. Allan Fredericks, March 13, 1986.

16. See, for example, Wright Field Testimony, pp. 38, 43, 87.

17. Fort Oglethorpe Report: "real perverts" are women "who engage in oral practices with other women," p. 14; "these women effect mannish appearance by haircut, by the manner of wearing the clothing, by posture, by stride, by seeking 'to date' other girls such as a man would, and when with other girls pay all the bills and be solicitous and otherwise conduct themselves as normally a man would with a woman. . . . these addicts have certain signals by which they recognize each other and . . . they use certain terms indicative of their practices," pp. 29–30. See also Fort Oglethorpe Testimony, p. 136.

18. Wright Field Testimony, p. 50.

19. Ibid., pp. 43, 26.

20. Fort Oglethorpe Testimony, pp. 337–45.

21. Ibid., pp. 317–21.

22. Keith Vacha, *Quiet Fire: Memoirs of Older Gay Men* (Trumansburg, N.Y.: Crossing Press, 1985), p. 159.

23. During the Fort Oglethorpe investigation, three women were hospitalized while the psychiatrist tested and interviewed them to diagnose their homosexuality. Fort Oglethorpe Testimony, pp. 60, 64, 69, 80, 98–108.

24. Menninger, *Psychiatry in a Troubled World*, pp. 19, 38; Medical Department U.S. Army, *Neuropsychiatry in World War II* (Washington, D.C.: USGPO, 1966), vol. 1, p. 257.

25. Letter, Howard Taylor to ———, November 13, 1944, Taylor Correspondence.

26. Letter, Tommy Martz to Howard Taylor, January 23, 1945, Taylor Correspondence.

27. Letters, J. D. to Howard Taylor, December 4, [1944], and May 4, 1945, Taylor Correspondence.

28. Letter, Marty Klausner to Howard Taylor, January 31, 1945, Taylor Correspondence.

29. Letter, Howard Taylor to Tony, undated, Taylor Correspondence.

30. Letter, Tommy Martz to Howard Taylor, January 23, 1945, Taylor Correspondence.

31. Letter, Marty Klausner to Howard Taylor, January 23, 1945, Taylor Correspondence.

32. Letter, from F. M. Harrison, Commander (MC), BuMed, to Dr. Winfred Overholser, Chairman, NRC Committee on Neuropsychiatry, August 5, 1942, File P13-7, General Correspondence 1941–46, RG 52.

33. Memorandum, from Rear Admiral Ross McIntire, Surgeon General, to Dr. Overholser, November 26, 1942, File P13-7, General Correspondence, RG 52.

34. Correspondence between Headquarters 8th Naval District and SecNav, July–August 1944, Subject: Procedure for the disposition of homosexuals among personnel of the U.S. naval service, File P11-2, Box 1362, Confidential Files of SecNav, RG 80. I wish to thank John Costello for bringing these records to my attention.

35. Rumors of these wartime purges stayed alive after the war and even reached members of Congress. In October 1949 Congressman Foster Furcolo of Springfield, Massachusetts, a member of the House Committee on Appropriations, asked the Pentagon to investigate a rumor that "thousands of men between the ages of fifty and fifty-five, in the 98th Division, were given blue discharges, mostly for homosexuality." Furcolo had been informed, he wrote to a Pentagon official, that "as many as five or ten thousand were discharged as homosexuals between 1941 and 1946, with

the bulk of them occurring between 1942 and 1945." Despite a "careful and thorough search of the records" by the Surgeon General's and the Adjutant General's Offices, the Pentagon could provide Congressman Furcolo with neither the total number of men who had served in the 98th Infantry Division nor the number of men in the division discharged as homosexuals. But the Pentagon reassured Furcolo that annual medical reports disclosed "no mention whatsoever of homosexuality or sexual perversion" in the 98th Infantry Division. Correspondence between Furcolo and Army AGO, October–November 1949, Folder: "9–1–49 to 12–31–49," 056 Army Statistics, RG 407.

36. Memoranda, between Joseph H. McDowell, Commandant, U.S. Marine Corps, and BuMed, November 10 and 18, 1943, Subject: Undesirable discharge of Marine Corps personnel, File P13-7, General Correspondence 1941–46, RG 52.

37. Memorandum, from A. C. Bennett, Commandant, Headquarters Eighth Naval District, to SecNav, July 20, 1944, Subject: Procedure for the disposition of homosexuals among personnel of the U.S. naval service, General Correspondence of SecNav, RG 80. I wish to thank John Costello for bringing these records to my attention.

38. John Hammond Moore, *Over-Sexed, Over-Paid and Over Here: Americans in Australia 1941–1945* (St. Lucia, London, New York: University of Queensland Press, 1981), p. 213. I wish to thank Gary Wotherspoon for bringing this passage to my attention.

   Antihomosexual witch hunts were not new in the United States nor limited to the military organization. See, for example, Lawrence R. Murphy, *Perverts by Official Order* (New York: Harrington Park Press, 1988); and George Henry, *Sex Variants* (1941; New York: Paul B. Hoeber, 1948), pp. xv–xvii.

39. Fort Oglethorpe Testimony, p. 286.

40. Because of the stereotype of psychiatric patients as "wild and dangerous, even homicidal," some psychiatric wards already were surrounded with high fences topped with barbed wire. Menninger, *Psychiatry in a Troubled World*, p. 19.

41. Alfred Hitchcock's *Rebecca*, starring Laurence Olivier and Joan Fontaine, won the Academy Award for best picture in 1940.

42. Memorandum, from Maj. Norman Q. Brill, Medical Corps, Assistant Surgeon General, to Maj. Rene H. Juchli, Medical Corps, Prisoner of War Division, Provost Marshal's Office, 12 April 1944, Subject: Segregation of Homosexuals, Folder: "250. to 250.1," Box 307, Entry 29 1943–44, General Subject File, RG 112.

43. In 1967 the practice of segregating gay naval prisoners into a queer brig

at Treasure Island, known as the Lavender Barracks, was discontinued. T. Parker, ''R.I.P. Demise of the 'Lavender Barracks,' '' *Vector* (December 1967): 6, 41.

44. In an interview with the author (March 13, 1984), former Army chaplain Charles Tarrance described being raped by a sadistic sergeant who was in charge of the psychiatric ward of an Army hospital in Texas to which Tarrance had been admitted as a self-declared homosexual.

45. Vacha, *Quiet Fire,* p. 198.

46. James A. Michener, *Tales of the South Pacific* (1947; New York: Fawcett Crest, 1983), p. 177.

47. Memorandum, TAG, Washington, to Commanding General, Moffett Field, California, February 28, 1942, Folder: ''1–1–40 to 12–31–41, 250.11 Sodomy, Practice of in the Army,'' RG 407. The judge advocate general used this memo to prevent the discharge of other men who were charged with sodomy. Memorandum, John M. Weir, JAG, to Assistant Chief of Staff G-1, June 4, 1942, G-1 ''Sodomists'' File.

48. ''Sex Hygiene Course,'' May 27, 1943, and May 1945, War Department Pamphlet No. 35-1, Lecture 5, ''Homosexuality.''

49. Menninger, *Psychiatry in a Troubled World,* p. 106; Mattie E. Treadwell, *The United States Army in World War II, Special Studies, The Women's Army Corps* (Washington, D.C.: USGPO, 1954), p. 625; Margaret D. Craighill, ''Psychiatric Aspects of Women Serving in the Army,'' *American Journal of Psychiatry* 104 (October 1947): 228.

Chapter 9. Rights, Justice, and a New Minority

1. Testimony of Dr. Francis Braceland, January 31, 1957, enclosure 1(k), p. 4, Crittenden Report.

2. On the statistical profile of veterans and the extent of their benefits, see Geoffrey Perrett, *Days of Sadness, Years of Triumph* (Baltimore: Penguin, 1973), pp. 338–42; John Morton Blum, *V Was For Victory* (New York: Harcourt Brace Jovanovich, 1976), pp. 333–40; and Charles G. Bolte, *The New Veteran* (New York: Reynal & Hitchcock, 1945), Appendix C, p. 205.

3. On VA discrimination against black veterans, see Blum, *V Was For Victory,* p. 336. On VA discrimination against homosexual blue-discharge veterans, see House Report, No. 1510 , ''Blue Discharges,'' U.S. House of Representatives, Seventy-ninth Congress, Second Session, January 30, 1946, pp. 8–9; and Donald Webster Cory, *The Homosexual in America* (New York: Greenberg, 1951), pp. 44–45 and 278–79 (excerpts from VA Instructions 1945, 1946, and 1949).

4. Letter, Marty Klausner to Howard Taylor, June 30, 1945, Taylor Correspondence.

5. Letter, Marty Klausner to Howard Taylor, October 9, 1945, Taylor Correspondence.

6. Letter, Marty Klausner to Howard Taylor, April 25, 1946, Taylor Correspondence. For an account of the discrimination faced by "L. B. F.," a black member of an Army engineer regiment who was given an undesirable discharge for homosexuality, see Eli Ginzberg et al., *Breakdown and Recovery* (New York: Columbia University Press, 1959), pp. 246–48.

7. Letters, Marty Klausner to Howard Taylor, June 30 and September 30, 1945, and January 8, 1946, Taylor Correspondence.

8. John H. Young III, "Blue Discharges Reach Senate," *Pittsburgh Courier,* November 17, 1945, pp. 1, 5.

9. Estimate of 68,000 Army discharges that were other than honorable or dishonorable, of which 42,000 were "not honorable" or "blue" discharges, is based on Surgeon General's Office figures from 1942–1946 in John M. Caldwell, Jr., "The Problem Soldier and the Army," *American Journal of Psychiatry* 105 (July 1948): 46; estimate of 48,603 Army blue discharges, of which 10,806 were issued to black soldiers, is based on War Department figures from December 1, 1941, to June 30, 1945, from "Senate, Legion, to Scan Discharges," *Pittsburgh Courier,* November 10, 1945, pp. 1, 5; estimate of 51,936 Army blue discharges from December 7, 1941, to June 30, 1945, is from House Report "Blue Discharges," p. 3; estimate of 57,000 Army blue discharges from December 1941 to June 30, 1945, is from memorandum from Neuropsychiatry Consultants Division, SGO, to General W. C. Menninger (Record), 27 June 1946, Folder: "220.811 Discharge for Disability 1945–46," Box 545: 220.811 Discharge and Other Separations, Entry 29 1945–1946, General Subject File, RG 112; estimate of 5,000 homosexuals discharged from the Army is from memorandum from Arthur J. McDowell, Subject: Information on Homosexuality, June 23, 1950, File: "Homosexuals," Case 1438, Box 101, AGO Precedent File, RG 407; estimate of 4,000 homosexuals discharged from the Navy is from memorandum from Capt. A. A. Marsteller and Vice Adm. Ross T. McIntire, Surgeon General, to Sec.Nav. Re: Review of cases of personnel discharged for homosexual reasons, September 24, 1946, File P13-7, RG 52.

10. John H. Young III, "Army's Blue Discharges," *Pittsburgh Courier,* October 30, 1945, pp. 1, 4; House Report, "Blue Discharges," pp. 2–5.

11. House Report, "Blue Discharges," pp. 5–6.

12. Blum, *V Was For Victory,* p. 208.

13. "*Courier* Launches Probe of Army's Blue Discharge," October 20, 1945, pp. 1, 4; "*Courier* Asks Secretary of War to Limit Army Blue Discharges," October 27, 1945, pp. 1, 3; "Blue Discharges Reach Senate," November 17, 1945, p. 1; all in *Pittsburgh Courier.*

14. "*Courier* Launches Probe," pp. 1, 4; "*Courier* Asks Secretary of War,"

pp. 1, 3; *Appendix to the Congressional Record,* vol. 91, part 13, Seventy-ninth Congress, First Session, p. A4778.

15. "Courier Asks Secretary of War," pp. 1, 3; "Attorney General Clark Studies Blue Discharges," November 3, 1945, pp. 1, 3; "Senate, Legion to Scan Blue Discharges," pp. 1, 5; "House Committee Studies Discharges," December 1, 1945, pp. 1, 4; all in *Pittsburgh Courier;* and *Appendix to the Congressional Record,* vol. 91, part 13, Seventy-ninth Congress, First Session, p. A4778.

16. "Blue Discharges," Extension of Remarks of Hon. Edwin C. Johnson of Colorado in the Senate of the United States, November 8 (legislative day of Monday, October 29), 1945, *Appendix to the Congressional Record,* vol. 91, part 13, Seventy-ninth Congress, First Session, p. A4778.

17. The other members of the Special Committee were Robert L. F. Sikes (Florida), Arthur Winstead (Mississippi), Melvin Price (Illinois), Thomas E. Martin (Iowa), Ivor D. Fenton (Pennsylvania), and J. Leroy Johnson (California). House Report, "Blue Discharges."

18. House Report, "Blue Discharges," p. 1.

19. Ibid., pp. 8–9.

20. Ibid., pp. 11, 13.

21. Letter, Marty Klausner to Howard Taylor, January 8, 1946, Taylor Correspondence.

22. Ted Morgan, *F. D. R.* (New York: Simon & Schuster, 1985), p. 676.

23. Letter quoted in George W. Henry, *Society and the Sex Variant* (New York: Collier Books, 1955, 1965), pp. 121–22.

24. Letter, from "(Name Withheld) Columbus, Ohio," *Yank: The Army Weekly,* November 16, 1945, p. 18. See also other letters on same page regarding "Forms of Discharge," and letters on the same subject in issues of *Yank:* February 2, 1945, p. 16; October 5, 1945, p. 14; and October 19, 1945, pp. 18–19.

25. William Menninger, *Psychiatry in a Troubled World* (New York: Macmillan, 1948), p. 231.

26. Correspondence between Senator C. Wayland Brooks and officials in BuMed, June 11, June 17, and June 19, 1947; and correspondence between Council on Veterans' Affairs, Kent County [Michigan] Veterans' Counseling Center, and BuMed, November 13 and 20, 1946; both in File P13-7, General Correspondence, RG 52.

27. Memorandum, Capt. C. R. Ball to Capt. McDaniel and Adm. Willcutts, Subject: Correspondence . . . regarding disposition of homosexual service personnel, February 18, 1948, File P13-7, General Correspondence, RG 52.

28. Letter, Rear Admiral C. A. Swanson, Surgeon General, U.S. Navy, to R.P.O., M.D., March 9, 1948, File P13-7, General Correspondence, RG 52.

29. Application for Review of Discharge or Separation From the Armed Forces of the United States, DD Form 293, October 1949.

30. Letter from Director, Kent County Council on Veterans' Affairs, Grand Rapids, Michigan, to BuPers, November 13, 1946, File P13-7, RG 52.

31. Minutes of Meeting of Policy Committee on Service to Veterans, October 3, 1944; Review of Discharge—American Red Cross Service to Applicants, December 26, 1944; memorandum from Earl J. Stout to Anne T. West, November 8, 1949, re: Reviews of Discharge and Correction of Military Records; all in Folder: "617.2 Discharge and Retirement Review," Correction of Military and Naval Records (July 18, 1944 to July 1, 1963), RG 200. By the late 1970s, the American Red Cross was actively assisting gay veterans in appealing their bad discharges. "Guidelines for Staff: Discharge Review Application and Representation," American Red Cross, 1978, especially pp. 15–17 and appendix 1.

32. "Psychopathic Ills Are Emotional, Not Due to a Lack of Intelligence," *New York Times,* April 3, 1944, p. 24.

33. Letter, Jerry Watson to Jim Kepner, September 8, 1944, Kepner Correspondence.

34. Letter, mother to Howard Taylor, November 20, [1944], Taylor Correspondence.

35. Letter, Tommy Martz to Howard Taylor, May 26, 1945, Taylor Correspondence.

36. Keith Vacha, *Quiet Fire: Memoirs of Older Gay Men* (Trumansburg, N.Y.: Crossing Press, 1985), p. 159.

37. Postcard, Tommy Martz to Howard Taylor, April 14, 1945, Taylor Correspondence.

38. Letter, Marty Klausner and Tommy Martz to Howard Taylor, March 21, 1945, Taylor Correspondence; "*Courier* Launches Probe," October 20, 1945, p. 1.

39. Braceland testimony, p. 2.

40. Menninger, *Psychiatry in a Troubled World,* pp. 230–31; Medical Department U.S. Army, *Neuropsychiatry in World War II* (Washington, D.C.: USGPO, 1966), vol. 1, pp. 238–39. Correspondence re: Discharge of Homosexuals, July–October 1945, File 250.1, Classified Decimal File 1943–45, RG 407; correspondence re: Discharge of Homosexuals, October 1945 to March 1946, File 250.1, Box 437, RG 165.

41. Memoranda and correspondence between Secretary of War's Discharge Review Board and Assistant Chief of Staff G-1, March 13, 1945 to June 13, 1945, Box 426, RG 165.

    Neither the Army nor the Navy has been able to locate administrative records from the 1940s for their Discharge Review Boards. The Army has not been able to locate its review board's case files from the same period, and the legal counsel to the Naval Council of Personnel Boards has informed the author that the Navy case files from 1944 through 1946 were "destroyed through inadvertant error in January 1980." The Navy board did not tabulate how many of its cases were related to discharges for homosexuality, but it did keep records of the total number of appeals that it reviewed:

1944 and 1945 combined	1,886 cases
1946	5,833
1947	7,784
1948	6,834
1949, 1950, 1951 combined	17,023

Correspondence from Legal Counsels of Naval Council of Personnel Boards, Office of the Director, Department of the Navy, to author, March 26, 1986, and October 14, 1987.

By 1948 the Army Discharge Review Board had "taken favorable action" in 4,038 (17 percent) of the 23,189 total cases it had heard. It had also "screened the records of World War II soldiers" with blue discharges and "changed on its own volition a total of 1,509 cases to either honorable discharges or discharges under honorable conditions." *Annual Report of the Secretary of the Army, 1948* (Washington, D.C.: USGPO, 1949), p. 94.

42. "New Discharge Plan Is Adopted By Army," *New York Times,* May 21, 1947, p. 4.

43. Army Regulation No. 615-368, May 14, 1947, "Enlisted Men, Discharge, Unfitness (Undesirable Habits or Traits of Character);" *Neuropsychiatry in World War II,* vol. 1, p. 239.

44. Fred Brown, "What American Men Want To Know About Sex," *Journal of Social Psychology* 27 (1948): 119–25; Fred Brown and Rudolf T. Kempton, *Sex Questions and Answers* (New York: Whittlesey House, 1950), pp. 226–44.

45. Letter, D. to Howard Taylor, December 17, 1945, Taylor Correspondence.

46. Letter to Howard Taylor, March 25, [1945?], Taylor Correspondence.

47. Vacha, *Quiet Fire,* pp. 23–28. On the particular experiences of lesbians and gay men of color in their own communities, see, for example, Juanita Ramos, ed., *Compañeras: Latina Lesbians* (New York: Latina Lesbian History Project, 1987); Cherrie Moraga and Gloria Anzaldua, eds., *This Bridge Called My Back* (Watertown, Mass.: Persephone, 1981); *Gay Sunshine,* Latin American Issue (Winter 1975–76); Joseph Beam, ed., *In The Life: A Black Gay Anthology* (Boston: Alyson Publications, 1986); *Black Men/White Men: A Gay Anthology* (San Francisco: Gay Sunshine Press, 1983); Will Roscoe, ed., compiled by Gay American Indians, *Living the Spirit* (New York: St. Martin's, 1988).

48. Erika O. Fromm and Anna S. Elonen, "Case Study: The Use of Projective

Techniques in the Study of a Case of Female Homosexuality," *Journal of Projective Techniques* 15 (1951): 185–230.

49. J. S. Kasanin, Emanuel Windholz, and Charl Rhode, "Criteria of Therapy of War Neuroses," *American Journal of Psychiatry* 104 (October 1947): 259–66; George N. Thompson, "Electroshock and Other Therapeutic Considerations in Sexual Psychopathy," *Journal of Nervous and Mental Disease* 109 (1949), "Case 6," pp. 537–38.

50. Chris Guilfoy, "Coming Out in the '40s and '50s," *Gay Community News*, November 15, 1980, pp. 8–9, 13.

51. Letter, D. to Howard Taylor, December 17, 1945, Taylor Correspondence.

52. Bolte, *The New Veteran*, pp. 80–81.

53. The four original members filed incorporation papers with the State of New York in 1948. E[dward] Sagarin, *Structure and Ideology in an Association of Deviants* (dissertation, Department of Sociology and Anthropology, New York University, 1966), pp. 64–66 [in 1951 Sagarin had written *The Homosexual in America* under the pseudonym "Donald Webster Cory"]; Jonathan [Ned] Katz, *Gay American History* (New York: Crowell, 1976), p. 635, n. 116.

54. Lester Strong, "Gays and Aging: Bill and Roy: 32 Years Together," *Gay Community News*, June 25, 1983, pp. 10–11.

55. John H~ ne Burns, *The Gallery* (1947; New York: Bantam, 1970), p. 161.

56. Veterans of all kinds felt emboldened by their combat experience. "Having known the fear of sudden and painful death, we are returning afraid of none of the usual bogeys of civilian life. . . . 'He can't kill me, anyway,' will be the final answer and dismissal of the new 12 million." Bolte, *The New Veteran*, p. 5.

57. Robert Duncan, "The Homosexual in Society," *Politics* (August 1944): 209–11; Ekbert Faas, *Young Robert Duncan* (Santa Barbara: Black Sparrow Press, 1983), pp. 114, 147–54; Jonathan Ned Katz, *Lesbian/Gay Almanac* (New York: Harper & Row, 1983), pp. 591–95.

58. Jo Sinclair, *The Wasteland* (New York: Harper and Brothers, 1946), p. 189; Katz, *Lesbian/Gay Almanac*, pp. 598–604; Burns, *The Gallery*, p. 142.

59. "Homosexual Minority," letters in *Saturday Review of Literature*, 1949: June 4 (p. 25), June 18 (p. 21), July 9 (pp. 25–26), July 16 (p. 24), July 30 (p. 24), October 8 (pp. 28–29); "The Unmentionable Minority," *Cosmopolitan* (May 1949): 50–51, 116–18. See also "The Skeptic's Corner," Bergen Evans, *The American Mercury* (May 1947): 598, and letters in response (July 1947): 123–25 and (October 1947): 505–7.

On the increasing sense among homosexuals during the late 1940s and 1950s of being members of a minority, see Katz, *Lesbian/Gay Almanac*, pp. 144, 627, 628, 646.

60. "Homosexuals in Uniform," *Newsweek,* June 9, 1947, p. 54.

61. Bernard C. Nalty, *Strength for the Fight* (New York: Free Press, 1986), p. 206; Lee Kennett, *G.I.* (New York: Scribner's, 1987), p. 237; Blum, *V Is for Victory,* p. 210–11.

62. Henry Gerber to Dr. Leopold Wexburg, July 18, 1946, Kepner Correspondence. For more on Gerber's life and early efforts at starting a gay movement, see Katz, *Gay/Lesbian Almanac,* pp. 553–66.

63. Letter, Jerry Watson to Jim Kepner, June 12, 1943, Kepner Correspondence.

64. Letter from "(Name Withheld) Columbus, Ohio," *Yank,* November 16, 1945, p. 18.

Chapter 10. The Legacy of the War

1. On the power relations between homosexuals and government, see Bob Gallagher and Alexander Wilson, "Michel Foucault: An Interview: Sex, Power and the Politics of Identity," *Advocate,* August 7, 1984, pp. 26–30, 58.

2. On such attitudes among second-generation Japanese Americans (Nisei), see Roger Daniels, *Concentration Camps USA: Japanese Americans and World War II* (New York: Holt, Rinehart and Winston, 1971), pp. 24–25.

3. Ibid., pp. 80–81.

4. On the overlap in the use of these terms, see Estelle B. Freedman, " 'Uncontrolled Desires': The Response to the Sexual Psychopath, 1920–1960," *The Journal of American History* 74 (June 1987): 103.

5. Ibid., pp. 83–106; John D'Emilio, *Sexual Politics, Sexual Communities: The Making of a Homosexual Minority in the United States, 1940–1970* (Chicago: University of Chicago Press, 1983), pp. 17–18, 50; Letter, Marty Klausner to Howard Taylor, January 8, 1946, Taylor Correspondence.

6. On the Cold War stereotype of the violent homosexual, see Freedman, " 'Uncontrolled Desires,' " pp. 100–4. Headlines are from *ONE* (April 1954): 16–17.

7. On the arrest rates for violent sexual crimes, see Freedman, " 'Uncontrolled Desires,' " pp. 84, 97. On the arrests for sex offenses and police harassment of gay men and women who gathered in public during the 1950s, see D'Emilio, *Sexual Politics, Sexual Communities,* pp. 49–51.

8. Kenneth Lewes, *The Psychoanalytic Theory of Male Homosexuality* (New York: Simon & Schuster, 1988), pp. 140–72.

9. William Menninger, *Psychiatry in a Troubled World* (New York: Macmil-

lan, 1948), pp. 256–65, 557–71. Ronald Bayer, *Homosexuality and American Psychiatry: The Politics of Diagnosis* (New York: Basic Books, 1981).

10. Evelyn Hooker, "The Adjustment of the Male Overt Homosexual," *Journal of Projective Techniques* 21 (1957): 18–31; "Male Homosexuality in the Rorschach," *Journal of Projective Techniques* 22 (1958): 33–54; "A Preliminary Analysis of Group Behavior of Homosexuals," *Journal of Psychology* 42 (1956): 217–25. For a discussion of Hooker's research and involvement with the early homosexual rights movement, see D'Emilio, *Sexual Politics, Sexual Communities,* pp. 73–74, 84, 112–113, 117, 141, 217.

11. Memorandum, Secretary of the Navy to Admiral [C. A.] Swanson, September 22, 1947, Folder: "P11-4/A21 to P14-2/OM," Headquarters General Correspondence 1947–1951, RG 52.

12. Memoranda, September 22, 1947, to July 2, 1948, Subject: Committee for the Review of the Procedures for the Disposition of Naval Personnel Involved in Homosexual Offenses, Folder: "P11-4/A21 to P14-2/OM," Headquarters General Correspondence 1947–51, RG 52. Memorandum, from SecNav to the Chief of Naval Personnel et al., October 18, 1948; Letter, from the Secretary of the Navy to All Ships and Stations, July 14, 1949, Subject: Homosexuality—procedure for the disposition of cases involving naval personnel; both in Crittenden Report.

13. "Study to Revise Regulations for the Handling of Homosexuals in the Armed Services, Project No. M-46," August 24, 1949; Memorandum, Hubert E. Howard, Chairman, Personnel Policy Board, to Secretaries of the Army, Navy, and Air Force, October 11, 1949; Memorandum, Anna M. Rosenberg, Office of Assistant Secretary of Defense, to Secretaries of the Army, Navy, and Air Force, July 28, 1952, Subj: Committee to Review Policy on Discharge of Homosexuals; all in Crittenden Report.

14. Data for the total number of discharges and corresponding troop strengths are incomplete and cover different periods of time. To arrive at a rough estimate of the rate per hundred thousand troops, I used the maximum troop strength in each period as a base, so that the bias would be toward a lower rate. Source for annual discharges is Colin J. Williams and Martin S. Weinberg, *Homosexuals and the Military* (New York: Harper and Row, 1971), pp. 45–53. Source for annual troop strengths is *Historical Statistics of the United States, Colonial Times to 1957* (Washington, D.C.: U.S. Bureau of the Census, 1960), p. 1141.

15. Pat Bond in Nancy Adair and Casey Adair, *Word Is Out* (San Francisco: New Glide Publications, 1978), pp. 60–61. On the postwar antilesbian witch hunts and the response of lesbians in the Air Force who tried to fight them, see Allan Berube and John D'Emilio, "The Military and Lesbians During the McCarthy Era," *Signs* 9 (Summer 1984): 759–75.

16. Crittenden Report, pp. 40–42.

17. Crittenden Report, vol. A, appendix 23, "Samples of Standard Indoctrination Lectures." For a discussion of and excerpts from these lectures, see Berube and D'Emilio, "The Military and Lesbians During the McCarthy Era," pp. 759–75.

18. Memorandum, Chief of NavPers to Chief of BuMed, January 12, 1948, Subject: Proposed Talk to be Utilized in the Indoctrination of Recruits, Folder: "P11-4/A21 to P14-2/OM," General Correspondence 1947–1951, Headquarters, RG 52.

19. E. Lawrence Gibson, *Get Off My Ship* (New York: Avon, 1978), pp. 356–67.

20. Correspondence regarding "Additional Reports and Files to be Required in the Procedure for the Disposition of Homosexuals Among Personnel of the United States Naval Service—Recommendations for," January 8, January 11, March 1, March 19, April 5, April 11, and September 6, 1946, File P13-7, RG 80.

21. The 1957 Crittenden Board traced the origin of the government's concern with homosexuals as security risks to the 1950 Hoey Committee hearings and report. Crittenden Report, p. 6.

22. In 1957 the Crittenden Board noted that intelligence officers who testified at these hearings had provided no factual evidence to support the notion that homosexuals were security risks. Ibid.

23. Report of the Investigations of the Junior Senator of Nebraska, A Member of the Subcommittee Appointed by the Subcommittee on Appropriations for the District of Columbia, on the Infiltration of Subversives and Moral Perverts Into the Executive Branch of the United States Government, May 1950, Eighty-first Congress, Second Session; Report of Subcommittee on Appropriations For the District of Columbia Made by the Chairman, the Senior Senator From the State of Alabama, Mr. Hill, with Reference to Testimony on Subversive Activity and Homosexuals in the Government Service, May 1950, Eighty-first Congress, Second Session; Employment of Homosexuals and Other Sex Perverts in Government, Interim Report, Submitted to the Committee on Expenditures in the Executive Departments, by Its Subcommittee on Investigations, Document No. 241, December 15, 1950, Eighty-first Congress, Second Session.

    For a discussion of these reports and their political context, see D'Emilio, *Sexual Politics, Sexual Communities,* pp. 41–49.

24. D'Emilio, *Sexual Politics, Sexual Communities,* p. 44.

25. Max Lerner, "The Washington Sex Story: #1—Panic on the Potomac," *New York Post,* July 10, 1950, p. 4.

26. "Report of Homosexual Cases—Civilian Employees," June 14 to December 4, 1950, Folder: "230.741 (1948–1949–1950)," Box 3593, Classified Decimal File 1948–50, RG 407.

27. "Are You Now Or Have You Ever Been a Homosexual?" *ONE* (April 1953): 5–13.

28. Memorandum, Chief of Naval Personnel to All Ships and Stations, October 1953, Subject: Information concerning homosexuality, Crittenden Report.

29. Executive Order 10450, Security Requirements for Government Employees, Dwight D. Eisenhower, April 27, 1953; "The Administration: Tightened Security," *Time,* May 4, 1953, p. 23; *Historical Statistics of the United States, Colonial Times to 1957,* pp. 710, 736; D'Emilio, *Sexual Politics, Sexual Communities,* p. 46.

30. "Are You Now or Have You Ever Been a Homosexual?" pp. 5–13. The Security Division of the American Red Cross described its antihomosexual policy before the Crittenden Board in 1957. "Red Cross Policy," Crittenden Report, p. 54.

31. In 1948 the Michigan Liquor Control Commission issued Administrative Rule 436-3, which prohibited bars, taverns, and cocktail lounges from serving liquor to homosexuals or their licenses would be revoked. "Prohibition Repealed," *Gay Community News,* April 11, 1981, p. 2.

    In 1949 the California Board of Equalization, in an attempt to use existing laws to shut down gay bars, charged the Black Cat Cafe in San Francisco with being a disorderly house because "persons of known homosexual tendencies" used it as a "meeting place." The bar owner appealed the charges to the State Supreme Court, beginning several rounds of charges and appeals that led the California legislature in 1955 to pass a law prohibiting the licensing of gay bars because they were "resorts for sexual perverts." Allan Berube, "Resort For Sex Perverts," slide lecture, 1984.

    Some cities tried to enact their own ordinances against gay bars. See, for example, "City May Have to Write Law to Halt Perverts," *Miami Herald,* August 28, 1954, p. 18B, and "Ordinance Would Kill Pervert Bars' Permits," *Miami Herald,* September 10, 1954.

32. D'Emilio, *Sexual Politics, Sexual Communities,* pp. 49–53; Berube, "Resorts for Sex Perverts."

33. Donald Webster Cory, *The Homosexual in America* (New York: Greenberg, 1951), pp. 3–14, 38–48.

34. For an historical discussion of the "closet," see Robert Dawidoff, "In My Father's House Are Many Closets," *Christopher Street* 12 (April 1989): 28–41.

35. D'Emilio, *Sexual Politics, Sexual Communities,* p. 32; Bob Swisher, "One Big Community: Gay Life in Richmond After 1944," *Southern Exposure* 14 (Fall 1988): 29.

36. Allan Berube, "The History of Gay Bathhouses," declaration submitted to Superior Court of California, November 5, 1985, excerpted in *Coming Up!* 6 (December 1984): 15–19.

37. Gene Damon, "The Lesbian Paperback," *Tangents* 1 (June 1966):

4–15; Roberta Yusba, "Twilight Tales: Lesbian Pulps," *On Our Backs* 2 (Summer 1985): 30–31, 43.

38. On postwar gay and lesbian fiction, see Roger Austen, *Playing the Game: The Homosexual Novel in America* (Indianapolis/New York: Bobbs-Merrill, 1977), and Jeannette Foster, *Sex Variant Women in Literature,* 2d ed. (Baltimore: Diana Press, 1975).

39. John Steinbeck, *Once There Was a War* (1958; New York: Bantam, 1960) pp. vii–xii.

40. Such novels also include Richard Brooks's *The Brick Foxhole* (Garden City, N.Y.: Sun Dial, 1945), Lonnie Coleman's *Ship's Company* (1955; New York: Dell, 1957), Ensan Case's *Wingmen* (New York: Avon, 1979), and Christopher Bram's *Hold Tight* (New York: Donald T. Fine, 1988).
   For similar themes in short stories, see "The Prisoners," by C. Hall Thompson and "Show Me the Way to Go Home," by Donald Vining, both in *Cross Section 1945* (New York: Book Find Club, 1945), pp. 253–71, 272–81; "Queer Island," by Jock Ember, in *American Aphrodite* 4, no. 14 (1954): 119–123; and "The Theban Warriors" and "Bird of Paradise," by Lonnie Coleman, in *Ship's Company,* pp. 93–114, 115–34. Lincoln Kirstein's *Rhymes of a Pfc* (New York: New Directions, 1964) includes several narrative poems about gay American soldiers in World War II.

41. These included James Michener's *Tales of the South Pacific* (New York: Macmillan, 1947), John Horne Burns's *The Gallery* (New York: Harper & Row, 1947), Norman Mailer's *The Naked and the Dead* (New York: Rinehart, 1948), Ward Thomas's *Stranger in the Land* (Boston: Houghton Mifflin, 1949), James Jones's *From Here to Eternity* (New York: Scribner's 1951), Russell Thacher's *The Captain* (New York: Macmillan, 1951), and Martin Dibner's *The Deep Six* (New York: Doubleday, 1953).
   Characters who had gay experiences during World War II were portrayed in such novels as Charles Jackson's *The Fall of Valor* (New York: Rinehart, 1946), Gore Vidal's *The City and the Pillar* (New York: Dutton, 1948), Christopher Isherwood's *The World in the Evening* (New York: Random House, 1952), and Allen Drury's *Advise and Consent* (New York: Doubleday, 1959).

42. Geoffrey O'Brien, *Hardboiled America* (Van Nostrand Reinhold, 1981); Thomas L. Bonn, *Under Cover: An Illustrated History of American Mass Market Paperbacks* (New York: Penguin, 1982); Kenneth C. Davis, *Two-Bit Culture: The Paperbacking of America* (Boston: Houghton Mifflin, 1984).

43. BLADE, *The Barn 1948 and More Dirty Pictures* (New York: Stompers, 1980); Clark P. Polak, "The Story Behind Physique Photography," *Drum* 5 (October 1965): 8–15; Jim Dolin, "Odes on a G-String," *Christopher Street* 9 (September 1986): 27–35; Tom Waugh, "A Heritage of Pornogra-

phy," *The Body Politic* (January/February 1983): 29–33, and id., "Photography, Passion and Power," *The Body Politic* (March 1984): 29–33; William Doan and Craig Dietz, *Photoflexion: A History of Bodybuilding Photography* (New York: St. Martin's, 1984); *Athletic Model Guild* (Amsterdam: Intermale, 1987).

44. George Sylvester Viereck, "The Erotic Note in Recent American Fiction," *American Aphrodite* 4, no. 15 (1954): 166–75. See also *Mattachine Review* (November/December 1955): 31; Alfred Towne, "Homosexuality in American Culture," *The American Mercury* 73 (August 1951): 3–9; John W. Aldridge, *After the Lost Generation* (1951; New York: Arbor House Edition, 1985), pp. 99–102.

45. For a history of the emergence of a gay male and lesbian movement in the United States, see D'Emilio, *Sexual Politics, Sexual Communities.*

46. Author's interview with Charles Rowland, March 19, 1984; D'Emilio, *Sexual Politics, Sexual Communities,* pp. 60–63.

47. Anonymous, "Open Letter to Senator Dirksen," *Mattachine Review* (January/February 1955): 14.

48. In 1964, two legal commentators who had been military officers observed that by 1958, according to the judge advocate general of the Air Force, "there had been a remarkable increase in administrative discharges, with a corresponding decrease in courts-martial, since the enactment of the Uniform Code. In its 1960 report," they added, "the Court of Military Appeals commented that it suspected the military services of resorting to the administrative discharge as a means of circumventing the requirements of the Uniform Code." Clifford A. Dougherty and Norman B. Lynch, "The Administrative Discharge: Military Justice?" *George Washington Law Review* 33 (1964): 500.

49. Rhonda R. Rivera, "Our Straight-Laced Judges: The Legal Position of Homosexual Persons in the United States," *Hastings Law Journal* 30 (March 1979): 837–55.

50. Section H, "Homosexuality," Enlisted Administrative Separations, Directive 1332.14 (encl. 3), January 28, 1982, Department of Defense, pp. 1–9 to 1–13.

51. See, for example, accounts of antilesbian purges in 1980 on the U.S.S. Norton Sound in Randy Shilts, "The Ship That Dare Not Speak Its Name," *Village Voice,* September 24, 1980, pp. 13–14, 16, 63; and accounts of 1988–89 purges of lesbians at Parris Island Marine Corps Recruit Depot in Christina Smith, "The Military's Plan to Straighten Up," *Coming Up!* 10 (December 1988): 12.

52. Randy Shilts, *The Mayor of Castro Street: The Life and Times of Harvey Milk* (New York: St. Martin's, 1982); Mike Hippler, *Matlovich: The Good Soldier* (Boston: Alyson Publications, 1989); Dave Walter, "After 11-

Year Battle, Ben-Shalom Set To Return to Army," *Advocate,* September 29, 1987, pp. 16–17; "Homosexual Ban in Army Rejected by Appeals Court" [Perry Watkins case], *New York Times,* February 11, 1988, p. 1.

53. Report of Committee to Review Policy on Discharge of Homosexuals, October 24, 1952, and Dissenting Report, November 28, 1952, Department of Defense, in Crittenden Report.

54. Crittenden Report, pp. 5–7.

55. For a summary of some of these suppressed reports, and a description of how in 1977 a federal judge ordered their release, see Gibson, *Get Off My Ship,* pp. 356–67. For denial of access to this author of military and congressional studies and reports regarding policies toward homosexuals, see A Note on Sources in this book. In 1950 when, in response to pressure from the Surgeon General's Office to release the 1948 Fry and Rostow report, the Chief of the Army's Public Information Division decided to suppress it instead, he argued that its release might create "serious distortions" in the "public mind" that could lead to "possible reactions" against the Army. Correspondence among officials from the Army SGO, Army Office of the Chief of Information, and Department of Defense Office of Medical Services, June 23 to August 11, 1950, Folder: "Homosexuality as It Relates to Military Administration," Box 65, RG 330.

56. Elaine Sciolino, "Report Urging That Military End Ban on Homosexuals Is Rejected," *New York Times,* October 22, 1989, pp. 1, 18; John Diamond, "Gays in the Military Found Better Suited Than Average," *San Francisco Examiner,* October 29, 1989, p. A6.

57. Crittenden Report, p. 69.

58. On the notion of the gay "minority" as an American phenomenon, see D'Emilio, *Sexual Politics, Sexual Communities;* Dennis Altman, *The Homosexualization of America, the Americanization of the Homosexual* (New York: St. Martin's, 1982); Katz, *Gay/Lesbian Almanac,* pp. 161–62; and Steven Epstein, "Gay Politics, Ethnic Identity: The Limits of Social Construction," *Socialist Review* 93/94 (May–August 1987): 9–54.

Illustration Credits

Harry Stack Sullivan: Courtesy of the Washington School of Psychiatry
Winfred Overholser: Photograph courtesy of the Commission on Mental Health Services, Washington, D.C.
Physical exam: By J. Baylor Roberts © 1941 National Geographic Society
Abry: Courtesy of Phillis Abry
Bond: Courtesy of Pat Bond
Davis: Courtesy of Sarah Davis
Freeman: Courtesy of Elizabeth Freeman
Harder: Courtesy of Lesbian Herstory Archives (gift of estate of Helen Harder, Rhio Hiersch executor)
Miles: Courtesy of Vincent Miles
Loomis: Courtesy of Stuart Loomis
Gerrits: Courtesy of Burt Gerrits, in collection of World War II Project
DeVeau: Courtesy of William DeVeau
Cole: Courtesy of Ernest Cole
". . . no time to be FRAIL": Illustration from Fleischman's Yeast magazine advertisement, December 1942
Abry: Courtesy of Phillis Abry
Davis: Courtesy of Sarah Davis, in collection of World War II Project
Male GI chained to typewriter: WAC recruiting poster, Army photograph, in Mattie E. Treadwell, *United States Army in World War II, Special Studies, The Women's Army Corps* (Washington, D.C.: USGPO, 1954), p. 185
Smith: Courtesy of Maynard Smith
DeVeau at piano: Courtesy of William DeVeau
This Is the Army, Jumping with Jodie, and *Wac applying makeup to GI:* Army Signal Corps photographs, SC-140522, SC-208040, and SC-204637, courtesy of National Archives
Wilson: Courtesy of Woodie Wilson and Norman Sansom, in collection of World War II Project

Reddy: Courtesy of Thomas Reddy

"Kid in Upper 4": New Haven Railroad magazine advertisement, December 1942

"Training is Mack's life work now!": From "The Story of Mack and Mike," cartoon booklet by Training Aids Section at Army Service Forces Training Center, Aberdeen Proving Ground, Maryland, reproduced in Lt. Col. R. Robert Cohen, "Visual Aids in Preventive Psychiatry," *War Medicine* 6 (July 1944): 22–23

"Lost, Sweetheart?": Drawing by Garrett Price; © 1941, 1969 The New Yorker Magazine, Inc.

Black Cat: By Samuel A. Cherry

Fleischer: Courtesy of Robert Fleischer

Myerly: Courtesy of Oren Myerly

Ricks: Courtesy of Robert Ricks, in collection of World War II Project

Harder: Courtesy of Lesbian Herstory Archives (gift of estate of Helen Harder, Rhio Hiersch executor)

Beyer: Courtesy of Jacquelyn Beyer

Article 93: Panel of "Articles of War Part VII," *GI Joe* cartoon by Lt. Dave Breger, *Stars and Stripes* [London], October 21, 1943, Special Feature Supplement, p. 4

William C. Menninger: Army photograph, in Medical Department U.S. Army, *Neuropsychiatry in World War II,* vol. 1 (Washington, D.C.: USGPO, 1966), p. 32

Psychiatric ward, Loeser, and *stockade:* Army photographs, in *Neuropsychiatry in World War II,* vol. 2, pp. 223, 230, 528

Sansom, and *blue discharge:* Courtesy of Norman Sansom, in collection of World War II Project

Robert Plant Armstrong: From *San Diego Union,* August 22, 1941, courtesy of San Diego Historical Society, *Union-Tribune* Collection

Pittsburgh Courier *headline:* From *Pittsburgh Courier,* October 20, 1945, p. 1, courtesy *Pittsburgh Courier* and The Library, University of California at Berkeley

ONE *magazine:* Cover, August 1960, courtesy of ONE, Inc., and San Francisco Bay Area Gay and Lesbian Historical Society

Rally flyer: Obtained by William Hartman in 1979 through the Freedom of Information Act from the Federal Bureau of Investigation, which sent a secret agent to the rally and kept the sponsoring organizations under surveillance.

Gay veterans marching: By Scott Martin, courtesy of Alexander Hamilton Post 448 of the American Legion

Index

Printed in the United States
134719LV00011B/1/A

9 780743 210713